Questioning Romanticism

Questioning Romanticism

edited by John Beer

The Johns Hopkins University Press
Baltimore and London

Printed in the United States of America on acid-free paper
04 03 02 01 00 99 98 97 96 95 5 4 3 2 1

The Johns Hopkins University Press
2715 North Charles Street
Baltimore, Maryland 21218-4319
The Johns Hopkins Press Ltd., London

Library of Congress Cataloging-in-Publication Data will be found at the end of this book.
A catalog record for this book is available from the British Library.

ISBN 0-8018-5052-5
ISBN 0-8018-5053-3 (pbk.)

Contents

II
Romanticism in Criticism

Abbreviations

Abrams ML
M. H. Abrams, *The Mirror and the Lamp: Romantic Theory and the Critical Tradition* (London: Oxford University Press, 1953; New York: W. W. Norton, 1958).

APrW
Matthew Arnold, *Complete Prose Works,* ed. R. H. Super, 11 vols. (Ann Arbor: University of Michigan Press, 1960–77).

BE
The Poetry and Prose of William Blake, ed. D. V. Erdman and H. Bloom (New York: Doubleday, 1965).

BK
Blake, *Complete Writings, with Variant Readings,* ed. G. Keynes, 1957; reprinted with additions and corrections in the Oxford Standard Authors series (Oxford: Oxford University Press, 1966).

BLJ
Byron, *Letters and Journals,* ed. Leslie A. Marchand, 11 vols. (London: John Murray, 1973–82).

CAR
Coleridge, *Aids to Reflection* (1825, 1831), ed. John Beer, CC 9 (1993).

CBL
Coleridge, *Biographia Literaria* (1817), ed. James Engell and Walter Jackson Bate, CC 7 (2 vols., 1983).

CC
The Collected Works of Samuel Taylor Coleridge, general ed. Kathleen Coburn, associate ed. Bart Winer (Princeton, N.J.: Princeton University Press; London: Routledge & Kegan Paul, 1969–)

C Friend
Coleridge, *The Friend* (1809–1818), ed. Barbara E. Rooke, *CC* 4 (2 vols., 1969).

CL
Coleridge, *Collected Letters,* ed. E. L. Griggs, 6 vols. (Oxford: Clarendon Press, 1956–71).

C Lects 1808–19
Coleridge, *Lectures 1808–1819: On Literature, CC* 5 (2 vols., 1987).

CLS
Coleridge, *Lay Sermons* (1816–1817), *CC* 6 (1972).

CM
Coleridge, *Marginalia,* ed. George Whalley, *CC* 12 (5 vols. in progress, 1980–)

CN
The Notebooks of Samuel Taylor Coleridge, ed. Kathleen Coburn, 4 vols. to date (Princeton: Princeton University Press; London: Routledge & Kegan Paul, 1959–).

CPL
Coleridge, *The Philosophical Lectures, Hitherto Unpublished,* ed. Kathleen Coburn (London: Pilot Press, 1949; Routledge & Kegan Paul, 1950).

CPW
Coleridge, *Poetical Works,* ed. E. H. Coleridge, 2 vols. (Oxford: Clarendon Press, 1912).

C Sh C
Coleridge's Shakespearean Criticism, ed. T. M. Raysor, 2 vols. (London: Constable, 1936); quoted here from 2d edition, in Everyman series, 2 vols. (London: Dent; New York: Dutton, 1960).

CTT
Coleridge, *Table Talk,* ed. Carl Woodring, CC 14 (2 vols., 1990).

DQL
Thomas De Quincey, *Confessions of an English Opium-Eater and Other Writings* ("On the Knocking at the Gate in Macbeth," "Suspiria De Profundis," and "The English Mail Coach"), ed. Grevel Lindop, The World's Classics (Oxford: Oxford University Press, 1985).

DQW
The Collected Writings of Thomas De Quincey, ed. D. Masson, 14 vols. (Edinburgh: A. & C. Black, 1889–90).

HA
G. W. F. Hegel, *Aesthetics: Lectures on Fine Art,* trans. T. M. Knox, 2 vols. (Oxford: Clarendon Press, 1975).

HW
The Complete Works of William Hazlitt, ed. P. P. Howe, 21 vols. (London: Dent, 1930–34).

KL
Letters of John Keats, 1814–1821, ed. H. E. Rollins, 2 vols. (Cambridge, Mass.: Harvard University Press, 1958).

ScP
F. W. J. Schelling, *The Philosophy of Art,* ed. and trans. Douglas W. Stott (Minneapolis: University of Minnesota Press, 1989).

SW
The Complete Works of Percy Bysshe Shelley, ed. R. Ingpen and W. E. Peck, 10 vols. (London: Benn, 1926–30).

WL 1787–1805
The Letters of William and Dorothy Wordsworth: The Early Years, 1787–1805, ed. E. de Selincourt, 2d ed., rev. ed. C. L. Shaver (Oxford: Clarendon Press, 1967). (Dated similarly for other volumes.)

W Prel
Wordsworth, *The Prelude,* ed. E. de Selincourt, 1926; rev. ed. Helen Darbishire (Oxford: Clarendon Press, 1959); quoted from 1805 version.

WPrW
Wordsworth, *Prose Works,* ed W. J. B. Owen and J. W. Smyser, 3 vols. (Oxford: Clarendon Press, 1974).

WPW
Wordsworth, *Poetical Works,* ed. Ernest de Selincourt and Helen Darbishire, 5 vols. (Oxford: Clarendon Press, 1940–49).

Introduction

The questions of Romantic criticism inevitably involve the question of Romanticism itself, a term that has proved notoriously difficult of definition. There are, indeed, those who believe that a concept that has by now been projected through so many perspectives has become so miasmic in the process that the very term should be dropped from the critical vocabulary.[1]

Attempts by critics and theorists of criticism to find a set of terms that will catch and hold the ideas involved have been going on since the early nineteenth century. Some years ago, A. O. Lovejoy argued that we should learn to think not of Romanticism but of Romanticisms, and he proceeded to distinguish three such.[2] The first, associated initially with England in the 1740s, he saw as a Romanticism of nature; the second, coming into favor at the end of the eighteenth century and associated primarily with German critics, was a Romanticism of human consciousness, involving an assumption of its superiority to nature; his third, a French strain as expressed by Chateaubriand in 1801, had strong links back to the neoclassicism rejected by the other two.

Lovejoy did not pretend that the number of possible Romanticisms was in any way exhausted by his three categories. In the course of making manifest the difficulties involved in such discrimination, nevertheless, his essay contrived to demonstrate the importance of one distinction in particular: between a mid–eighteenth-century English tradition of Romanticism, rather loosely conceived, and a movement from the 1790s onward which, although detectable also in England, reached more immediate and open expression in Germany.

René Wellek, who has given more thought to the matter than most people, resisted Lovejoy's tolerance of proliferation, arguing for the possibility of characterizing Romanticism more closely. At the beginning of his most extended discussion he offered two ways of doing so. His first, more general definition was "a view of poetry centered on the expression and communication of emotion." This corresponds, of course, to the most commonly accepted view of what Romanticism is, preserved even now in the term *romance,* for a certain kind of popular commercial fiction, and retaining roots which, like those of Lovejoy's Romanticism of nature, go back to the eighteenth century.

Wellek's more sophisticated version of the concept was then outlined as follows: "In a more narrow sense we can speak of romantic criticism as the establishment of a dialectical and symbolist view of poetry. It grows out of the organic analogy, developed by Herder and Goethe, but proceeds beyond it to a view of poetry as a union of opposites, a system of symbols."[3] Wellek also stressed that early Romantic critics in Germany had guarded such a view against the dangers of emotionalism, naturalism, and mysticism.

Wellek's formulation as stated here is recognizably one that has not only been widely accepted by exponents of Romanticism but has provided a basis for recent attacks on it as an "ideology." Yet the difficulty of pinning down the concept so firmly had already been tacitly acknowledged in an earlier discussion, where he characterized it rather by way of its dominant modes. These he specified as imagination for the view of poetry, nature for the view of the world, and symbol and myth for poetic style.[4]

Such a view of Romanticism immediately extends the historical perspective to cover the fuller range suggested by Lovejoy, since not only was nature already a central concern in mid–eighteenth-century England but the idea of "imagination" was then acquiring prestige and the study of mythology was being pursued as a source of original significances. Both critics, in addition, were inclined to overlook the political dimension to Romanticism—a shortcoming that has been amply remedied in recent years. They did not mention, for example, a point which is so obvious as to be easily overlooked, that from the 1740s the idea of liberty was a crucial factor in European thinking. Once looked to as an element in Romanticism, it reveals its presence everywhere.

Much can be achieved by way of such processes of categorization and organization, yet they must always be open to further scrutiny. In her piece below, for instance, Anne Mellor argues that many of the qualities identified by Wellek could be regarded as characterizing a "male" Romanticism, and that when one looks at the writing of the period as a whole it is equally possible to locate a "female" Romanticism which has in the event been more lastingly influential.

It may also be observed that the urge to define Romanticism is itself one of the products of a movement that, through the nineteenth century and after, was, in its more active modes at least, fostering a desire for the clear-cut and the graspable. In its more passive mode, on the other hand, the theorizing involved has proved equally friendly to modes of thinking that mingle and dissolve categories; and here it is closer to twentieth-century developments. Having pursued the aspiration to unity that was characteristic of much thinking in the Romantic period itself, therefore, it may be time to learn from that side of it which is sensitive to disparities and displacements in the culture—and in the human mind itself. Instead of searching for and hunting down the great unifying concepts to contain and account for Romanticism, it may be more profitable to consider it as a site of fragmentation. Important changes in artistic taste and practice do not, after all, take place in a sealed continuum but are made by human beings reacting to their culture as a whole. Yet it must still be borne in mind that the fragmentation involved may be occurring either in the social context of the culture or in the human beings that compose it.

These considerations have affected the conception of the present volume, which came out of a suggestion for the compilation of a history of literary criticism in the Romantic period, and my subsequent conviction, as I considered the project, that other ways of approaching the issues involved might be more appropriate to the present age. Accordingly, the scholars and critics who have contributed to this volume were each asked to deal with some major question connected with Romanticism and its history. There has been no attempt at exhaustive coverage; on the contrary, it is hoped that the discussions will help to raise further issues and open up other avenues of inquiry, producing a kind of comprehensiveness not commonly seen in more orthodox histories of criticism. In view of the wide range, however, it has proved profitable to divide the essays into two sections: one containing discussions undertaken primarily from a historical point of view and focused more specifically on the Romantic period itself, and another devoted more to questions of theory. It will soon become evident that the difference is mainly one of emphasis. The essays concerned with the context of Romantic writing also contain questions about the underlying principles and theories of the time, while those devoted more to theory tend to anchor their discussions in the writings of the period. The question of Romanticism itself is addressed directly at one point, in Drummond Bone's piece, but for the most part that issue is left in solution, to be returned to in the concluding piece.

One effect of the essays is to shed light on a crucial matter, that of the difference between English and German criticism. The history of literary criticism all too easily becomes the history of German literary criticism, since that exhibits the kind of unfolding that we like to discover when looking for historical development. But to set that process against the more haphazard line of thinking that characterized English Romanticism is to bring out one of the most important issues: that of the part played in Romantic thinking by the relationship between systematic and unsystematic thinking. It is in that ultimate interplay (the importance of which was recognized by some of the most intelligent writers in both countries) that the richer possibilities of Romanticism can be found. To that point, also, we return at the end of the volume.

I

Romantic Criticism in Its Time

A. C. Goodson

Romantic Theory and the Critique of Language

The cultural work of Romanticism has always been associated with the values of the French Revolution, in ways argued openly by *William Wordsworth and the Age of English Romanticism* (1989). The bicentennial exhibition and its critical accompaniment traced the fault lines of late Georgian English society and culture in the palimpsest of Wordsworth's lived experience. Public and private, politics and poetry are the four points of his compass. These supplied key words for a range of critical voice-overs which took his transitions as signs of the times. His leveling muse pointed the way to poetry in the democratic public sphere, while his retreat to Grasmere reckoned the cost of public commitment. In this landmark transatlantic production Romanticism was less a settled kind of thinking than a searching way of life.

Yet from Mill to modern ideology, something more has been at stake here than a lifestyle. In England, as in Germany and America, the cultural work of Romanticism usually has been thought to involve a trial of the new empire of reason. Under terrific historical pressures, the writers concerned aspired to new kinds of holistic understanding. Romantic anthropology, as we might think of their experimental modeling of the human situation, is a child of Rousseau's vision of man in nature and society, which Lévi-Strauss has recognized at the ideological foundations of modern social science. It represents an essential link between the new science of Bacon and the emergent sciences of man. Its legacy is not merely an ideological one, a matter of history reflected in the rearview mirror of the postmodern breakup. The Romantic intervention bears significantly on *was heisst Aufklärung*—on what we call the Enlightenment. It tells us something distinctive about the formation of modern rationality in the crucible of experience.

The Romantic critique of language, my point of entry into the scene of the literary mind at its cultural work, joins the social and poetic concerns of the Romantic company in a foundational dialogue which has never been adequately theorized. This line of Romantic reflection contributes materially to modern ways of thinking about the condition of language and to the utilitarian defense of poetry. Romantic theory is identified with the critique of language from the start, or what we usually take to be such, in the momentous claims of the *Lyrical Ballads* Preface on behalf of the poetic power of "the real language of men." This ringing formula flies in the face of informed critical opinion in the period, and it has come to define the Romantic challenge to tradition. The defense of the ordinary in modern poetics depends on Wordsworth's early energies even where it takes its modern bearings from Wittgenstein or Bakhtin. With the extraordinary authority of his claims in mind, I want to provide extended context for Wordsworth's attack on conventional language, backgrounding it with the propositions of Bacon and Locke, and situating it within a range of Romantic mediations. The aim is to construct the intelligibility of Romantic criticism around the Enlightenment critique of language inaugurated by Bacon. In this setting, I will consider Romantic theory as a stage of reflection on the condition of language, the essential means not only of poetry but also of politics. At the crossroads of polity, linguistic practice links poetry with social attitude, the aesthetic with the moral and political. Wordsworth's provocation is taken for granted; his is not a speaking role until the end.

Trying the Tartars' Bow

wordes are grown so false
I am loath to prove reason with them
—Twelfth Night *III.i.23*

To the clown of Shakespeare's skeptical romance, wondering about words is a mug's game. In the nearly contemporary voice of Francis Bacon, complaining about the tongue represents a way forward for common understanding. Bacon's exasperation with "wordes grown false" proved provocative and influential, a source of inspiration for the empiricists who followed him, and later among the English Romantic company. Burke and Blake, Peacock and Shelley, Coleridge and Wordsworth are all significantly involved in the Baconian enterprise of reconstructing common understanding from within the recalcitrant idiom of ordinary language. Their accommodations of Bacon's new science are distinctive, and full of implication for their reformations of literary value.[1] Romantic criticism is typically concerned with the idea and the socially situated practice of language—not with rhetoric, nor with the kind of judgments to which it gave rise.[2] In emerging arguments about signs and signification, words and things, the Romantic intervention reflects Enlightenment concerns about the state of the language, and about the cognitive value of the vernacular tongues that were replacing Latin as the idiom of knowledge. The incitements of Romantic critics to a modern idea of language represent for later literary and cultural theory something like what Bacon represented for them.

The critique of language, as I propose to call this long conversation about words, is an engine of Enlightenment thinking, an essential means of social and epistemological observation that reaches from Bacon and Locke through to logical positivism and the language revolution of literary modernism.[3] Bacon's feeling for the subversive working of words *against* understanding looks forward to a long struggle for steady linguistic ground. He writes of "the cheating slights and charms of words, which many waies abuse us, and offer violence to the understanding; and after the manner of the Tartars Bow, do shoot back upon the judgment from where they came. . . . Wherefore this disease must have a remedy, and of more efficacy."[4] The "Tartars' Bow," associated by Shakespeare with swift shooting, here bears a contrary sense. Geoffrey Hill has recently shown how Bacon wrestled with this image trying to get it into

Latin.[5] The passage exemplifies "the cheating slights and charms of words, which many waies abuse us," even as it points to problems that language poses for human understanding. Bacon is far from philosophical about it, in the modern way of an Empson, for whom ambiguity is interesting. His tone is exasperated, his diagnosis urgent. Like J. L. Austin, whose provocatively titled *How to Do Things with Words* (Oxford, 1962) is said to have been inspired by his experience at war, Bacon is concerned to get language straight, to make it do the work of understanding.

Bacon's conviction of words grown false, diseased beyond using, is quite distinct from his strictures on rhetoric. Such wondering about words has something in common with the bantering of Shakespeare's Clown—his aspiration to a new science with a ludic recognition of the collapse of common understanding. False words point to twisted conventions, and to the need for something "of more efficacy." Bacon's crotchets are incentives to fresh thinking. They do not constitute a reformed understanding, much less a new language, but they recognize the need.[6] Trying the Tartars' bow, for Bacon and in those who would follow him this way, involves turning the tongue back on itself, making words do the work of undoing corrupt understanding. For in spite of "the cheating slights and charms of words" it is only within the tongue that such an inquisition can be conducted at all.

Common language figures in Bacon's discussion of *idola fori,* the idols of the marketplace, "most troublesome of all" of the chronic sources of mental idolatry and confusion: "Words commonly are imposed according to the capacity of the People; and distinguish things by such differences, as the Vulgar are capable off; and when a more precise conception, and a more diligent observation would discern, and separate things better; the noise of popular words confounds and interrupts them" (251). Vilifying the vernacular represents an assertion of authority in this primitive stage of the quest for reformed understanding. But whose "more precise conception"—whose authority—was to be recognized as a standard? The heirs of the old science were embroiled in terminological quarrels; they would remain so right into Kant's translation of scholastic concepts into German cognates in his philosophical critiques—a displacement which suppresses the problem of terminology (and in fact the larger problem of language) by starting over in a new tongue. At the end of the line, in Wittgenstein's radical skepticism, the issue of authoritative language remains vivid and unavoidable. "How can we show *any language* at all (public, private, or what-have-you) to be *possible?*" Such is Kripke's formula for the critique of language at Enlightenment endgame.[7]

At this late stage of the game, Bacon's note of urgency sounds all too theoretic, his hope of remedy utopian.

It had not always seemed so. In Locke's epochal effort to reform human understanding, the trouble was traced to the abuse of words, from the start of the 1671 draft of the *Essay* contained in the author's philosophical notebook.[8] The problem was not yet ontological, in the way of Wittgenstein's conundrums, but practical: "men speakeing the proper language of their country ie according to the grammer or rules of that language doe yet speake gibberish to one another" (14). Secure understanding demanded highly conventional signs, since "words necessarily come to have a very uncertaine signification & tis merely about the signification of Words that most of the disputes in the world are" (8). The reform of language involved settling on the meaning of words. As it turned out in book 3 of Locke's *Essay* (1690), this was not a simple matter. Some words, such as particles—prepositions, conjunctions, and the like—eluded immediate reference, clear and distinct sense. Their meanings are largely determined by context, in fact, not by one-to-one lexical correspondences. Locke's reductively empirical idea of words as names led him to mistake language for nomenclature: just the lexicon.

On the other side of the linguistic equation, the ideas that words referenced turned out to be unstable for their users, "the notions their words which are but signes stand for not being agreed & determined amongst them." As Locke plaintively adds, "& Soe they fall into endlesse and often senselesse dispute" (14). The difficulty of signification recognized by Leibnitz, Peirce, and Wittgenstein is already apparent in the unstable sign evoked informally in these jottings, which witness the unraveling of a secure understanding. Locke's promotion of the arbitrary, binary linguistic sign makes him the significant forerunner of Saussure, even of the vertigo of deconstructive reading. To conceive of the sign in this way is to admit, in the end, that words are a negotiation—creatures of flux, hostages to time.

But in the beginning, the reform of language promoted by Locke's *Essay* was meant to alleviate obstacles to community, opening doors to an expanded rationality and to the general human progress it would enable. Language as "the great Instrument and common Tye of Society" (*Essay* III.i.1) was a fulcrum of social integration.[9] Against a background of civil war, the case for a rationalized language was associated with prospects for a new social contract. If words grown false signified collective failure, improving the means of common understanding seemed to point the way to social concord. The course of the critique of language confirms the commitment of ordinary language—the idols of the marketplace—to the uncertainty of the historical condition. Words have not proved a refuge from anything, yet the aspiration to a common vocabulary does represent a commitment to social infrastructure and to the general progress, which depends on a reliable general medium of understanding. It is a condition of the emergence of a genuine public sphere, as Jürgen Habermas acknowledges in his late appeal to the critique of language.[10]

Locke's recognition of semiotics, "the doctrine of signs" (*Essay* IV.xxi.4), as a foundational science remains a vital legacy of his effort to reform the language. It would be continued for more limited purposes by hard-boiled empiricists (David Hartley, Horne Tooke) and by positivists determined to conjure a cognitive empire of signs. Related ideas of language would find a home in the modern culture of letters. The high modernist appeal to the critique of language, as represented by a celebrated jeu d'esprit from the hand of Eugène Jolas, can be read as an ironic rehearsal of three centuries of argument:

> The word presents the metaphysical problem today. When the beginnings of the twentieth century are seen in perspective, it will be found that the disintegration of words and their subsequent reconstruction on other planes constitute some of the most important phenomena of our age. The traditional meaning of words is being subverted, and a panic seizes the upholders of the norm as they contemplate the process of destruction that opens up heretofore undreamed-of possibilities of expression.[11]

The disintegration of words as conventional signs that was noticed by Bacon, deplored by Locke, and apparently feared by the authorities became a premise of the expressive reconstruction of the tongue and the common understanding it represented. The air of political insurgency is unmistakable. It testifies to the deep motives involved in reforming ways of speaking and writing, and the ways that we think about them.

Inspired by the modernist ethic of making it new from the ground up, institutional literary criticism has drawn inspiration from the line of reflection on language that I have been describing, usually in derivative forms. From Richards's dismissal of Saussure's new science of language to Empson's vision of Shakespeare's structure of complex words, language is the obscure object of Cambridge English. In the work of Raymond Williams, literary criticism gives rise to a vigorous critique of the vocabulary of modern culture and society. These remain the vital sources of literary criticism in English; in various ways, all extend the question of language into current academic practice.[12] Known to current readers mainly in the form of the deconstructive turn against structuralist terminology, the critique of language found high disciplinary expression in the critical idiom of Paul de Man. The sublation of the language question in extended quarrels about linguistic reference and literary meaning represents an important chapter in the cultural history of the Enlightenment, as overtly political attacks on literary criticism in the academy confirm.[13]

Romantic criticism is a halfway house. Blake, Peacock and Shelley, Coleridge and Wordsworth are all implicated in the problem of language, in ways that associate literary concerns with social attitudes and with the reformation of human understanding in general. The interventions of English writers of the period link rationalist and early empirical thinking with later reflections on language, and on writing in society. They are instrumental in the formation of modes of critical discourse, at once literary and philosophical, which we recognize under the title of critical theory. The man of letters, as the role came to be recognized, is a fixture of Enlightenment understanding and its institutions largely through his mediation of the question of language.[14] Literary criticism exceeds its limited occasion when it recurs to the critique of language, broaching problems of large social significance, as it has repeatedly done since the Romantic arbitration of the issues under momentous historical pressure. The appeal to language—to its constitution and purpose, its condition and even its possibility—is practically an instinct of modern critical understanding. Its sources and usages remain largely unexamined despite the advanced semiotic awarenesses of postmodern critique.

Blake's Innocence and Burke's Experience

The fall of language is an article of faith for the Romantic company and an obsessive figure of Romantic critique. It provides a striking instance of that humanistic displacement of Christian topoi that the new historicism has taught us to regard as the cultural work of Romanticism. In Blake and Coleridge, the conviction that "words 'were from the beginning'" (*CC* 13:15), coeval with creation, remains a point of reference. Even so, their critique of language is motivated by the new science and its assumptions. In Burke and Wordsworth, resorting to vulgar idiom points to the fall of language against this background, and in the wake of events in France. Burke's *Reflections* represents a deliberate engagement with the voices of experience, in a cunningly pitched intervention inflected by recognition of how time had changed the tongue. If Blake tries to tell us what happened to language, Burke tries to take historical advantage of its drift, translating the fall into political opportunity. Their contrary employments of the language problem underline the historical urgency of the Romantic critique that would follow.

Blake's revolt against the new science of Bacon and Locke is well known; it is the point of departure for Frye's treatment of his poetics.[15] An illuminating recent study by Robert Essick considers paralinguistic implications of Blake's practice against this background, drawing him into early lines of the modern reflection on language.[16] Blake's visionary forms sublime are complex iconic constructions incorporating, but also sublating, natural language. His poetic critique of language is distinctive and interesting for this reason, among others. It confirms the scope of the Romantic quest for an idiom adequate to the conditions of modern understanding, especially its materialism. In Shelley, this quest would try the limits of natural language to contain living experience. Blake's radical skepticism and Shelley's wondering about words throw the more affirmative emphases of Coleridge and Wordsworth into relief, restoring the originality of their commitment to ordinary language.

Blake's critical activity is integral to his larger imaginative projections, not a rationalized by-product of them. His position is characterized by resistance to the encroachment of reason on the energy of poetic vision. Bacon, Newton, and Locke make up the unholy trinity of the demonic new science which would shackle the enthusiasm of inspiration with principles and rules. "Meer Enthusiasm is the All in All!" he objects in his marginalia on Reynolds's *Discourses*.[17] "Bacon's Philosophy has Ruin'd England. Bacon is only Epicurus over again"—by which Blake means to indict the atomistic mentality that would murder to dissect, turning life into museum work. In this context Bacon is hardly more than a cypher. Elsewhere, as in *Jerusalem,* he figures as a name in the rationalizing crowd. Yet it is clear from Blake's letters that he had read Bacon with some attention, and in one place at least he makes Bacon speak for the higher truth of imagination:

> What is it sets Homer, Virgil & Milton in so high a rank of Art? Why is the Bible more Entertaining & Instructive than any other book? Is it not because they are addressed to the Imagination, which is Spiritual Sensation, & but mediately to the Understanding or Reason? Such is True Painting, and such was alone valued by the Greeks & the best

modern Artists. Consider what Lord Bacon says: "Sense sends over to Imagination before Reason have judged, & Reason sends over to Imagination before the Decree can be acted."[18]

Thus is the voice of reason made to limit the claims of reason.

As a statement of literary value, this is practically definitive of Blake's line. He dispenses as much as possible with the machinery of language, associated as it is with the fallen understanding, informed by the judgments of reason. And not only in theory, in what he says about writing. His habitual negligence of syntax, spelling, and punctuation; the gnomic turn; and the intensely figurative cast of his voice would all confirm his evasion of propositional argument. Imagination is immediate vision, reason and understanding intruders on the poetic moment. The Bible, Homer, Virgil, and Milton are exemplary for having circumvented reason, for speaking directly to imagination *around* linguistic understanding, not through it. Disarming conventional understanding is an essential means of his radical poetics of vision: "Allegory address'd to the Intellectual powers, while it is altogether hidden from the Corporeal understanding, is My Definition of the Most Sublime Poetry" (*BK* 825). Angus Fletcher has recently made this observation bear weight for his argument against rationalizing reductions of allegorical discourse.[19] Allegory's address to higher "Intellectual powers" means accepting mystery, forgoing merely "Corporeal understanding." Recognizing the mystery is the genius of allegory.

Blake's blast at Bacon, Newton, and Locke represents an effort to preserve an essential mystery against encroachment.[20] Yet his conviction of the fallen state of the language reflects on the modern situation rather as Bacon's *idola fori* do. The convergence is surprising only if we have accepted, as Whitney argues we should not, wholly secular constructions of Bacon's *idola* (38–39). In fact, as he proposes, scriptural authority underwrites the Platonic source of the word for Bacon. His usage of it is actually turned against Plato to discredit the original Greek εἴδωλον. This counter-Platonic twist is recognized obliquely in Blake's passing notice of Bacon's emphasis on the primary value of imagination in *The Advancement of Learning.* "A certain antipathy to language," as another commentator has put it (138), characterizes Bacon's attitude, and certainly that of Locke and his followers as well. The troubles of the tongue tell on the imperfection of human understanding. Whether the trouble is taken to be congenital (Blake) or situational (the new science), the fall of language is an article of faith for Enlightenment thinking and its Romantic and modern affiliates.

The convergence of prophetic and scientific attitudes in the critique of language is confirmed by Blake's construction of the language of Adam. Essick notices "a shift in orientation from the Ossianic and natural to the Biblical and divine" in Blake's early poetic figures of voice, adding that "the implicit change . . . from a sensibilist to a theological sense of sign origins is most important" (105). The sensibilist position involves speech with natural signs such as thunder, identifying voice with phenomenon. Whatever the poetic conventions underwriting Blake's practice, the association is a revealing one. For it discloses his early participation in that scientific "naturalization of the human" which he later came to resist. The difficulty of his position is plainly indicated in his change of figurative orientation. The very turn of his voice points to a fallen understanding. Like Bacon, he can only criticize the condition of language from within, taking its scientific liabilities with its prophetic possibilities. They are obverse sides of the common coin.

The language of innocence in Blake is a language of names, as Essick proposes in discussing the icon known as "Adam Naming the Beasts" and again in his reading of *Tiriel* (6 f., 115 f.). The cursing and prophetic voices of the poem both reflect the fall of the language of Adam. The vocation of the poet lies in and among these contrary states of the tongue. Committed circumstantially to a naturalized vocabulary and the fallen understanding it expresses, the enlightened poet satirizes the condition of language as he prophesies its resurrection. Blake's pursuit of the implications in his visionary verse affirms his commitment to a critique of language that would not reform the tongue in the manner of Locke, but expose its original state of harmonious transparency to divine creation. Poetic language realizes that state, circumventing fallen understanding as the masters of the art from the Bible and Homer to Virgil and Milton had done.

The strange brew of exaltation and vulgarity in Blake's voice—of prophecy and cursing, sublimity and mockery—modulates the contrary states of the language, dramatizing the struggle for meaning in a debased medium. A similar mix characterizes Burke's *Reflections on the Revolution in France* (1790), as Olivia Smith shows in her study of the politics of language in the period.[21] Early commentators were disturbed by a manner at once "sublime and grovelling, gross and refined" (37). Against the background of the decorous dialect authorized by Johnson's *Dictionary,* Burke's Cassandra-like rattling excited admiration from radicals who disliked the argument but appreciated the deliberate vulgarity of the style, which became a model for Paine and others. Coleridge's private response is indicative: "What repugnant feelings did it [Burke's book] excite? I shuddered while I praised it—a web wrought with admirable beauty from a black bag of Poison!" (*CN* 1:24). Burke's prophetic oratory is a sort of suasive poetry, his famous broadside a handbook of popular rhetoric for the writing of the 1790s.[22] Its influence, usually misconstrued by ideological readers, makes it a critical text by example if not by overt argument.

Burke's participation in the political reformation of public expression elaborated by Smith is not incidental. This epochal struggle for command of the tongue, and for the authority that it was now presumed to contain, constitutes an important episode in the conversation about language that I have been describing. It touches base with Horne Tooke, Locke's radical follower, whose obsessive quest for proof of the empirical value of English has something in common with his political commitments. Burke's vatic exercise of *vox populi* makes a powerful statement about the vernacular, especially about its worthiness to embody truth. His book amounts to a rebuke to Bacon's idols of the marketplace, and it challenges Locke's doubts about the capacity of the tongue to sustain civilized dispute. Against the grain of a neoclassical heritage of fine diction and good manners, Burke actually provided a discursive model for the popular invective his book unleashed. The voice mattered as much as the argument.

His exercise of vulgar idiom for public purpose looks forward to some of the aspirations of the *Lyrical Ballads* Preface (1800), whose radical propositions about language are a familiar landmark. The new-historical effort to tar Burke with the old conservative brush has missed—symptomatically—this inside connection.[23] Burke's example is paramount for Coleridge, though not as Jeffrey and Hazlitt construed things in their hostile review of the *Biographia Literaria* in 1817: not as a model of political ideology.[24] Rather, his vatic vernacular, modulating prophetic and vituperative voices in a manner strangely akin to Blake's, spoke vividly to Coleridge's sense of possibility from the beginning of his career in letters.

A recent commentator has showed how a Burkean-Coleridgean line was institutionalized in John Scott's *London Magazine*, with a restored emphasis on good manners.[25] Periodical criticism represents the public face of the contention over appropriate idiom in this transitional moment. Typically, as in Jeffrey's attack on Wordsworth's *Poems* (1807) in the *Edinburgh*, the poets' effort of expressive reform was criticized on behalf of "poetic diction," or of distinctive discourse. Jeffrey's dismissal of the literary propriety of language "which is coarse, inelegant, or infantine" might as well have been directed at the Burke of the *Reflections* or at the Blake of the contemporaneously engraved books.[26] His broadside confirms how fundamentally linguistic the issues surrounding the reformation of literary value were, and how broadly they applied to new writing. The English critique of language, a cutting edge of Enlightenment discourse, was not translated by such conventional readers into a reformed understanding of writing and its modern vocation. This limitation would, perhaps, make their attitudes more representative of critical value in the period than are the proclamations of the poets, as Marilyn Butler has argued.[27] It does nothing to explain how Romantic writing made its way in a climate of critical conformism and intolerance. The critique of language, skeptical of the tongue and of the polity it represented, spoke to the condition of the poets. Their engagement with it is distinctive, a sign of searching relation to the Enlightenment roots of modern critical discourse.

Defending Poetry

The critique of language served Romantic writers as a vehicle for critical thinking about the culture of letters in a time of transition. Their reputation owes little to their Baconian cultural work. Yet it is not unrelated. Butler has called attention to the extended interest of the Peacock-Shelley exchange, "a philosophical dialogue, the significance of which for the literature of the period has never been recognized" (293). Its significance has something to do with its engagement in the critique of language as I have described it. For it is by appeal to the nature of language that the terms of discussion are established. Butler shows that both arguments were constructed "on classic utilitarian grounds" (292) without observing the way the language question is brought to bear on the utilitarian case. This dialogic context is as suggestive in its way as the contention between Coleridge and Wordsworth over poetic and broadly linguistic value, and for some of the same reasons. Working from assumptions about the nature of language, Peacock and Shelley raise large questions of polity in their accounts of poetry. Their exchange shows how the critique of language promoted utilitarian constructions of literary value.

In Shelley's *Defence of Poetry* an openly Baconian line of reflection leads to extravagant claims for the social value of poetry. Shelley's case for poetry as "the expression of imagination" in general[28] leads him into a consideration of the mimetic origins of expression, in the child as in the savage. His appeal to eighteenth-century ideas of language as expression is qualified in passing by a Lockean recognition of the social constitution and conventional character of language—"for language is arbitrarily produced by the imagination, and has relation to thoughts alone" (113). Yet the emphasis falls on the poet's individual imaginative expression within the repertory of social conventions. Poetic language

> is vitally metaphorical; that is, it marks the before unapprehended relations of things and perpetuates their apprehension, until the words which represent them, become, through time, signs for portions or classes of thought, instead of pictures of integral thoughts; and then, if no new poets should arise to create afresh the associations which have been thus disorganised, language will be dead to all the nobler purposes of human intercourse. These similitudes or relations are finely said by Lord Bacon to be "the same footsteps of nature impressed upon the various subjects of the world"—and he considers the faculty which perceives them as the storehouse of axioms common to all knowledge. In the infancy of society every author is necessarily a poet, because language itself is poetry. (111)

The association of poetry with "the nobler purposes of human intercourse" is basic to Shelley's case. Metaphor as he conceives it here is not a peculiar and private expression; it constitutes a recognition, a form of knowledge of general value. Representative of a discoverable natural order, poetic expression yields the words of the tongue, signs of a common understanding. Language represents the trace of a process of poetic creation and re-creation which is essential to the maintenance of polity. For poets "are not only the authors of language," "they are the institutors of laws and the founders of civil society" (112). It is an extravagant claim, and a deeply Romantic one, both in its exaltation of poetic vocation and in its attention to language as the bond of the body politic.

On the basis of this line of argument, Shelley concludes that "Lord Bacon was a poet" (114), in the more limited sense of the term. Poets are demiurges of language; poetry represents an expansion of its expressive power, of its representational range. For "the nature itself of language" lies in "a more direct representation of the actions and passions of our internal being" (113). As language exceeds other expressive means, so the art of poetry excels sculpture, painting, music, and even legislation and religion in representative value. In the end, Shelley can write of "the words which express what they understand not" (140) as a sign of the poet's visionary condition. He is close to both Blake and Burke here in the conviction of a power which exceeds conventional expression and common understanding. Language is its medium, metaphor its signature, truth its vocation.

The sense of unlimited poetic possibility in this famous paean to imagination is bound to a view of language associated with Bacon and Locke, both of them at odds with the condition of language. Something of their disillusion sounds through Shelley's evocation of a language "dead to all the nobler purposes" because bereft of poetry. But language as he envisions it in the *Defence* provides no resistance to poetic vision. Its social constitution, its conventional habit, are recognized without being recognized as problematic for creative purposes. Language is pure means, undefiled by history, unpolluted by human usages. The idealization so characteristic of Shelley's imaginative frenzy burns at a fever pitch in his concluding vision of poets as "the hierophants of an unapprehended inspiration." The phrase contains a depth charge directed at the Philistine public, and at judgments of taste founded on conventional ideas of what makes sense. Such an observation evokes the fallen understanding characterized by Blake, the dismissiveness of reason about imagination.

Much of the energy of Shelley's demonstration is in fact negative, directed at Peacock's provocative characterization of poetry as a cabinet curiosity, a relic of the childhood of the race surviving into the age of reason. Peacock's "Four Ages of Poetry" is conventionally attentive to points of style in the development of poetic types, and to the state of the language. In the beginning, in the bardic age of iron, "from the exceeding flexibility of the yet unformed language, the poet does no violence to his ideas in subjecting them to the fetters of number" (4), which serve a mnemonic function. As the language grows more civilized and society wise to the world, so does poetic idiom: "The poetry of civilized life . . . is characterized by an exquisite and fastidious selection of words, and a laboured and somewhat monotonous harmony of expression: but its monotony consists in this, that experience having exhausted all the varieties of modulation, the civilized poetry selects the most beautiful, and prefers the repetition of these to ranging through the variety of all" (8–9). Peacock relates the highly conventional character of the poetry of the silver age to "the inflexibility of civilized language." In modern verse, the reaction against such constraints set in with the Lake poets, whose escape from convention is considered simply escapist, a form of nostalgia, a revolt against reason and the known world. "A poet in our times is a semi-barbarian in a civilized community," Peacock famously concludes (16).

It is against this idea of language and this view of poetry that Shelley fulminates in his contrary *Defence.* For Peacock they are of a piece: the civilization of language is the condition of the decline of verse. Modern language represents an improvement on its "unformed" original for reasons undeveloped, yet clear enough against the background of empirical ideas. The progress of language serves reason and understanding, which are in the ascendant. These are enemies of poetry:

> Feeling and passion are best painted in, and roused by, ornamental and figurative language; but the reason and understanding are best addressed in the simplest and most unvarnished phrase. Pure reason and dispassionate truth would be perfectly ridiculous in verse, as we may judge by versifying one of Euclid's demonstrations . . . and as the sciences of morals and of mind advance towards perfection, as reason gains the ascendency in them over imagination and feeling, poetry can no longer accompany them in their progress, but drops into the back ground, and leaves them to advance alone. (9)

Such is the world of Burke and Blake formulated in utilitarian terms. In an obscure exercise indited in a kindred spirit, the young Coleridge contrived a Euclidean demonstration in Pindarics. He did not see fit to include it in *Sybilline Leaves.*[29] The antipathy of reason and imagination was a commonplace to be tried out, as Peacock does satirically, or tested in practice, as Coleridge does rather theoretically in his geometrical verses.

Shelley's reply to Peacock's satire responds in advance to the limited utilitarian position popularized by Mill in his autobiographical account of the therapeutic effect of reading Wordsworth. As Butler points out, "Though Shelley may appear to be advancing the claims of Imagination, and Poetry, over those of Reason, and Philosophy, he is trying to restore an equilibrium disturbed by Peacock; Shelley is careful, in fact, not to be exclusive" (291). The critique of language is the lever of this rebuke to narrow-minded utilitarianism. Like Peacock, Shelley associates poetry with the condition of language in general, but by making poets demiurges of language he retains the imaginative vitality of the tongue which Peacock writes off as a victim of the civilization of language. Where the poetic function fails, as Shelley intimates that it has in modern language, there is a general loss of vitality, not just a loss of poetry. The progress of civilization is at stake when the tongue is "dead to all the nobler purposes of human intercourse." When the life of imagination is blocked, reason suffers. It is the function of language that links them in theory and in social practice.

Bacon's *philosophia prima* has been described as a prototype of this view of "the creative word as an active force in social change" (Whitney, 74). Does Shelley occlude Bacon's "basic interpretive problem . . . of the eloquent text directed against eloquence" (127) in the process? Even in the *Defence,* there is, as I have suggested, an intimation that the vitality of language is waning, that poets are now "hierophants of an unapprehended inspiration." Elsewhere, the failure of language is a specter that haunts Shelley's eloquent verse. A related sense of futility is notoriously at work in *The Triumph of Life,* where a skeptical view of the uses of rhetoric is associated with Rousseau's voice. Deconstructive readings of the poem confirm the unweaving that shadows its figurative construction of meaning.[30] Eloquence comes to the end of aspiration here, with the loose ends of the unfinished text witnessing a bottomless problem formulated as a question: "'Then what is Life?' I cried."

The dramatic irony of Shelley's drowning has made this a kind of testimonial. It recalls the desperation of his turn on the condition of language at the end of "Epipsychidion":

> Woe is me!
> The winged words on which my soul would pierce
> Into the height of Love's rare universe
> Are chains of lead around its flight of fire—
> I pant, I sink, I tremble, I expire!

Even in so histrionic a passage, the poetry witnesses the work of the Baconian Tartars' bow. Here it is not understanding but creative imagination that is undermined by the "cheating slights and charms of words, which many waies abuse us." Whitney's conclusion that "Bacon's use of rhetoric must exclude vision" (148) is matched by Shelley's growing recognition of the expressive limitations of ordinary language. In the end, the "winged words" of vatic poetry, reverting to Homer's formula and example, are bonds—forms of constraint, not of transcendence.[31] There is no remedy, of the sort Bacon enjoins, for "wingless words"; no remedy in language. To begin with words as the poet does means ending with, and within, them.

Shelley's despair is nearly theological, cast like Hölderlin's in the vocabulary of Greek epic, as if to affirm the power of the older language—a power that has passed away in the modern tongues. Naming, in Hölderlin's great elegy, is a sign of loss, of absence.[32] The sacramental world of immediate presence is already past when we resort to words. These stand for absences that they represent, witnessing an irreparable loss. Signification signifies the abstraction of the modern condition—its self-absorption and forgetfulness of what is real. Natural language is a form of alienation, chronically at a loss. Hölderlin compares words with flowers—a figurative construction that would gloss "natural language" as the idiom of "natural man," perhaps, reverting to Blake's parlance. Words, like flowers, pay tribute to the dead, to what is missing in the world of empirical experience—the blinkered world of "single vision and Newton's sleep," the arid Enlightenment of Peacock's progress. The sense of something lost or left behind in modern language is a signature of the vatic Romanticism of the period.

Real Language And Its Discontents

Wordsworth's Baconian affiliations have been developed at length, and polemically redeveloped in a very recent study by Don Bialostosky, who would "link Wordsworth's poetic project to Baconian commitments [in order to] provide us with a proximate source in Bacon's doctrine of the idols for Wordsworth's participation in Gorgian skepticism and permit us to acknowledge the critical and scientific motives of Wordsworth's poetic project along with the artistic and aesthetic motives."[33] On this foundation, Wordsworth becomes for Bialostosky the presiding genius of "progressive institutionalized intellectual enterprise" (44), a modern Bacon who authorizes the pragmatic literary theory of English departments committed to public work. Wordsworth has long been cast as Enlightenment Man, with Arnold in the middle distance, and Bialostosky's case joins Butler and others in taking us back to the future, to a Wordsworth who stands for the modern condition. Deconstructive reading is one scapegoat of the institutionally correct Wordsworth he conjures. Coleridge is another. In the manner of Leavis, though more intelligently, Coleridge's achievement is discredited, along with modes of reading usually associated with his name. It is a familiar move, nearly canonical by now, and one that modern Coleridgeans have encouraged, as Bialostosky implies, by dwelling on his "exaltation of the poet over ordinary people and his celebration of the 'magical' aesthetic faculty that idealizes and unifies an otherwise fallen world" (23). Yet this is an egregious caricature, drawn in quick strokes by critics who would avoid Coleridge's questions about Wordsworth's poetics, and who will not recognize his crucially enabling role in Wordsworth's achievement, nor in the making of his reputation.

For as I have argued elsewhere in a context that concerns Bialostosky in his polemic, Coleridge's idealism is not the whole story. His Baconian affiliations run deeper than his German connection, and reach deeper than Wordsworth's in the same vein. The odd couple of Romantic criticism is joined by an allegiance to the Enlightenment project of remaking the language, and of rethinking polity through it. Coleridge's current relevance lies in this line of his criticism, which turns up in his occasional observations on language and literature in the notebooks, letters, and marginalia, and which found a home in *The Friend,* in the critique of Wordsworth in the *Biographia Literaria,* and in some of the lectures on literature, which have been only partially accessible. This Coleridge does not matter to Bialostosky because he is not "public" enough in such contexts, and because the whole achievement is not a matter of common understanding and assent. So limiting an idea of the public sphere would exclude much of Wordsworth's Baconian musing as well, but there is no reason for scholars working now to ignore materials that were private or obscure in their time, or in our own.

Displacing Coleridge in order to replace him with the more agreeable Wordsworth means sacrificing the force of their collaboration, which enabled Wordsworth's poetic project in ways recognized by Stephen Gill's iconoclastic biography[34] and by several recent commentators on their profoundly symbiotic work. What Bialostosky would theorize as dialogic in their writing, taking a Platonic turn on Bakhtin, has been conceived in other terms by recent Romantic theorists concerned to recover the terms of the collaboration, rather than with declaring a winner.[35] In practice, as they have shown, it is impossible to understand Wordsworth without the Coleridge who contributed so much to his understanding, and to his sense of poetic and social possibility. Bialostosky adopts Wordsworth's position, approving of his "part in shaping Coleridge's vocation and agenda as a critic" (28), without appreciating how deeply implicated in Coleridge's vocation and agenda was the vatic Wordsworth who gave us *The Prelude*—the "poem to Coleridge," as he always called it. Nothing in Bialostosky's occasional evocations of the poem recognizes the central value of *this* dialogue, which runs to the origins of the text. His dialogism is partial, even univocal in its identification with Wordsworth's voice alone.

Bialostosky's account is sensitive to the complexity and contradiction involved in its hero's position, and in his pronouncements about poetry.

Something is lost in Coleridge's absence, all the same; something like the inside interlocutor who was there from the beginning, who contributed materially to the *Lyrical Ballads* and its Preface and whose idea of language is subversively at work there. I want to restore Coleridge's voice to a dialogue from which he is usually excluded now on grounds that have become all too programmatic. If Bacon provides the vehicle of this effort of restoration, it is because he informs Coleridge's thinking in ways that would mediate his difference from Wordsworth, as it is presumed by readers dedicated to Wordsworth's special commitments.

Like Wordsworth's, Coleridge's contribution to the Romantic reflection on language represents a deeply Baconian effort of social application. Under the early influence of Hartley, Coleridge developed an empirical idea of linguistic function and of signification in general. This is qualified and contradicted by other emphases in his thinking—theological and hermeneutic, neoplatonic and rationalist[36]—but it remains basic to his approach, which is essentially modern. Coleridge tries the Tartars' bow in an ambitious effort to reform understanding from within, very much in the manner of Bacon, who was perhaps his most significant intellectual source. His wondering about words is not a lament for the language of Adam nor for the idiom of Homer, though he recognizes both.[37] It is critical, a challenge to an existing vocabulary, ordinary as well as philosophical, and to ways of thinking involved in modern language:

> What is it, that I employ my Metaphysics on? . . . To expose the Folly & the Legerdemain of those, who have thus abused the blessed Organ of Language, to support all old & venerable Truths, to support, to kindle, to project, to make the Reason spread Light over our Feelings.[38]

Pragmatic in temper if metaphysical in aspiration, Coleridge's critique of language reflects on a changing historical scene. It is committed to politics and progress as well as to poetry and theology. Philosophical in approach though not always in method, Coleridge points the way to new dispensations.

Propositions about language haunt the opening passages of the *Lyrical Ballads* Preface (1800) to which, by his telling, he contributed materially. If the shape of the argument belongs to Wordsworth, some of the detail is certainly Coleridgean, as the initial attention to linguistic premises would confirm. These reflect Coleridge's contemporary investigation of Enlightenment thinking about language. Writing years later in the *Biogra-*

phia Literaria (1817), Coleridge took exception to parts of "Wordsworth's theory" (42) with which, he said, he had never concurred; not as a way of dismissing it out of hand in the manner of the magazine critics, Jeffrey and Mrs. Barbauld foremost, but in the positive spirit of critique. Salvaging the deep truth of Wordsworth's best thinking about poetry in the climate of the new science meant limiting claims that appeared to be at odds with his best poetic practice. The second volume of the *Biographia* has often been read defensively, as an act of spleen directed at the friend who turned on him. In fact, it promotes Wordsworth as the preeminent modern poet, worthy despite the problems to stand with Shakespeare and Milton. Coleridge is careful to balance the strengths and the weaknesses, admitting Wordsworth's liability to "matter-of-factness" in order to save his more thoughtful work. A defense of the philosophical value of ordinary language underwrites the case, and characterizes their commonality.

Coleridge's divergence begins at the beginning of the Preface, with Wordsworth's deliberately experimental emphasis on the poetic possibilities of "the real language of men in a state of vivid sensation."[39] A provocative formula, it provided a point of entry for a different construction of linguistic value. What was the "real language of men?"

> Every man's language varies, according to the extent of his knowledge, the activity of his faculties, and the depth or quickness of his feelings. Every man's language has, first, its *individualities;* second, the common properties of the class to which he belongs; and thirdly, words and phrases of *universal* use. (*CBL* 2:55)

Language was not more or less "real," with the implication of a standard of authenticity. It was inflected by intelligence, education, social class. The individual constructed what modern linguistics knows as an idiolect, a language of its own. The real language of men was plural, not singular. It could not be appealed to in Wordsworth's way because it included too much that was merely personal, without extended interest or value. "For 'real' therefore, we must substitute *ordinary,* or *lingua communis,*" Coleridge concludes. "Omit the peculiarites of each, and the result of course must be common to all" (56). Such an idea relies on the social and conventional constitution of the tongue, against the uncritical idealization of "the real language of men." Poetry would have to make sense in the *lingua communis* if it were to enter the public sphere at all. For this was the currency of public exchange, the sign of recognition and of response to known discursive practice. Such an intervention recognizes the conventional condition of verse, with all of its limitations, while trying to leave the door open for something new. Its responsiveness to discursive conditions might even be called dialogic, in Bialostosky's Platonic sense of the word.

Coleridge's pragmatic rejoinder mediates neoclassical and expressive claims on literary value. While the Preface recognizes formulaically "that sort of pleasure and that quantity of pleasure" (69) associated with poetry, "Wordsworth's theory" is driven by other concerns. It proceeds from bald propositions about the superiority of rustic life, informed by a strangely assertive pastoralism. Language is central to the agenda, and Coleridge made this a fulcrum of his case against some of the claims of the Preface, resuming an argument he appears to have inaugurated there himself. In order to treat reasonably of the large issues of poetic value that they had broached, "it would be necessary to give a full account of the present state of the public taste in this country, and to determine how far this taste is healthy or depraved; which, again, could not be determined, without pointing out, in what manner language and the human mind act and re-act on each other, and without retracing the revolutions, not of literature alone, but likewise of society itself" (70). This Baconian appeal is surveyed in so many words at the outset of the Preface. It is left behind in favor of Wordsworth's pastoral idealism, on the calculation that "reasoning" the reader "into an approbation of these particular Poems" (69) would be unworthy. The direction of the Baconian high road not taken is largely Coleridgean, from the critical analysis of public taste to the inquiry into language and mind. The final condition, linking literature and society, would confirm the social vocation of the *Lyrical Ballads* project.

The line of argument indicated here can be reconstructed from Coleridge's later criticism of the Preface and the poems. The public setting of poetry in "the revolutions . . . of society" meant understanding how language, the social code par excellence, functioned in the individual, the reader of poetry. The focus on language and mind should be understood against the social background: "This is the progress of language. As society introduces new relations it introduces new distinctions, and either new words are introduced or different pronunciations" (*CPL,* 369). Social distinctions determine linguistic distinctions and value in a continuing historical progress. The language touches in turn on the condition of "public taste," on what the market will bear. These relations are not rigidly deterministic, but they are all involved in the question of poetry's future in this moment of general crisis. Having put all that behind him, Wordsworth had proceeded in the Preface to idealize the language of "low and rustic life," "because such men hourly communicate with the best objects from which the best part of language is originally derived; and because, from their rank in society and the sameness and narrow circle of their intercourse, being less under the influence of social vanity they convey their feelings and notions in simple and unelaborated expressions" (71). The abrupt transition from the high ground of the opening to such special pleading drew Coleridge's objection: "As little can I agree with the assertion, that from the objects with which the rustic hourly communicates, the best part of language is formed. For first, if to communicate with an object implies such an acquaintance with it, as renders it capable of being discriminately reflected on; the distinct knowledge of an uneducated rustic would furnish a very scanty vocabulary" (*CBL* 2:53). Coleridge's rationalist turn is evident here, in the defense of reflective intelligence and in the emphasis on "distinct knowledge," a Cartesian echo. He proceeds to the contrary assertion that "the best part of human language, properly so called, is derived from reflection on the acts of the mind itself" (54). Coleridge defends modern language, constantly informed by the working of reason, against Wordsworth's pastoral regression and on behalf of modern poetry.

Such a defense of modern language differs fundamentally from neoclassical attacks on Wordsworth which revert to conventional poetic diction as the standard of poetic value. In Jeffrey's famous demolition job of 1807 in the *Edinburgh,* the pleasures of poetry are largely pleasures of recognition: propriety is the operative formula, "the finest passages in Virgil and Pope" (216) the standard of taste for poetry's audience. In this critical setting, the question of language does not arise. Ringing changes on an established poetic diction, and on the conventional "beauties of sweet sound and pleasant associations" (217), involves no effort of critical resistance, only improvisation within a familiar repertory. Wordsworth's "real language of men" reacts openly against desiccated reductions of the tongue current in verse of the sort endorsed by Jeffrey's neoclassical criteria. Coleridge is involved in reforming Wordsworth's revolt, not in disavowing it. His topical adoption of Aristotle's principle "that poetry as poetry is essentially *ideal*" (*CBL* 2:45) does not represent a sort of covert neoclassicism, only an insistence on the primary *representational* values of the art of poetry. Representing Wordsworth means defending his cause; not, as critical commentators have often assumed, attacking him on conventional grounds. Coleridge's critique of the Preface amounts to a critique of language, or rather of an idea of language that exposed Wordsworth to ridicule by neoclassical apologists like Jeffrey.

Earlier reviewers of Wordsworth had tried the theory by the practice and found the theory problematic, sometimes on grounds that look forward to Coleridge's terms. An anonymous reviewer for the *Eclectic,* responding like Jeffrey to the *Poems* (1807), put it that "this is no more the language, than these are the thoughts of men in general in a state of excitement: language more exquisitely elaborate, and thoughts more patiently worked out of the marble of the mind, we rarely meet with."[40] Such an observation would save the real strength of Wordsworth's emergent voice from the implications of his propositions about language. His poetic strength reflects *not* the native dignity of the "real language of men in a state of vivid sensation" but the force of poetic intelligence. The "exquisitely elaborate" language of a poem such as "Tintern Abbey" cannot be a product of "the best objects from which the best part of language is originally derived"—a formula that evokes Blake's language of Adam and the pristine names of prelapsarian Eden. The anonymous critic's point is that poetic language in the modern setting is not a way of naming things in the dawn of the first day of creation. It participates in the laborious rationality of modern experience.

Coleridge too would wonder about Wordsworth's enthusiasm for "vivid sensation" as a criterion of linguistic value—"in a state of excitement," as he translated it (*CBL* 2:56). Yet "vivid sensation" would perhaps relate Wordsworth's idea to Blake's in a more than passing way. If so, Coleridge misses the point here. Reverting to the pristine vision of the unlettered rustic may be a pastoral idealization, but it might also be considered as a mythification of a kind familiar from Blake's *Songs.* The rustic situation is edenic, the topos of man in the state of nature, before the fall into the artifices of society, including all sorts of fraudulent expression—the Preface refers to newspapers, "frantic novels, sickly and stupid German Tragedies, and deluges of idle and extravagant stories in verse" (*WPW* 1:128). The mythic opposition that Wordsworth practices in the Preface between the old and the new ways of life, natural on the one hand, urban and inauthentic on the other, disarms the reality test in advance, perhaps.

The sense of contrast is what matters here, as in Blake's contrary states of innocence and experience. Criticizing his village green for not resembling the real thing is beside the point. The same may be said of Wordsworth's effort to evoke a way of speaking authentically. Against the background of the Romantic reflection on the condition of language,

Wordsworth appears to be defending an ideal of truth in language which is as instinctively antirational as Blake's. The voices of his early lyrics are as deeply ironic in their exposure of the artifices of ordinary language as those of Blake's children, certainly.

Here is the crux of Coleridge's difference. Starting as he does from an empirical idea of language, with its public vocation in mind, he is committed with Bacon and Locke to a general reform, an *instauration* involving the progress of language toward increasing responsiveness to reason as well as to human feeling. Coleridge's allegiance to a socially active rationality would associate him with Burke, and with the Shelley of the *Prometheus Unbound* and perhaps the *Defence:* political visionaries sacred and profane, joined by a conviction of the force and use of words. This is the party of eloquence.[41] Coleridge's defense of the philosophical value of *lingua communis* represents an extension of his commitment to an instrumental reason:

> For active philosophical language differs from common language in this only, or mainly at least, that philosophical language does that more accurately, and by an express compact, which is unconsciously, and as it were by a tacit compact, aimed at and in part accomplished by the common language, though with less precision and consistency. Thus in the philosophic world, each contributing consistently to the finishing of that work, the rudiments of which each man in society at large is unconsciously aiding to furnish, the mighty machinery goes on, at once the consequence and the mark of the symptoms of the mind, the mind of the nation which speaks it. (*CPL* 369)

The organic social idea informing this vision of the work of reason is invested in "the mighty machinery" of language. Its function is realized in representing the collective understanding of the speech community, here identified with the nation. Common language shadows the conscious articulations of "the philosophic world," whose own language is distinct but not different in kind.

Coleridge's investment in *lingua communis* as an agent of the general will and understanding represents an act of faith in a supervening reason. Such a faith appears openly at odds with Locke's doubts about words, and with Bacon's idols of the marketplace, despite the common interest in reforming the tongue. Coleridge recurred to Bacon's *idola* for his own purposes, but especially to gain leverage on Locke's promotion of ideas as the units of human understanding. Critical of the idolatry of the image-idea enshrined by Locke, which was foundational to the empirical understanding that he had come to resist, Coleridge construed Bacon's *idola* anachronistically, as though they responded to a later stage of the quest for stable linguistic currency. He endorsed Bacon's scientific attitude without taking responsibility for its aftermath. "Pity that as we adopted Idea we had not likewise adopted Idola," as he put it, indicatively, some time after seeking refuge from Locke's quandaries.[42] Locke's construction of ideas, even the very word *idea* as it had come to be used, was an idol of the modern marketplace: a problem child requiring treatment. Turning against it meant taking Bacon's querulous tone, making the words bear the burden of a general reformation of understanding. This way of trying the Tartars' bow became the stock in trade of Coleridge's critique of the modern mentality.

A reformation of the reformation, an essay against the empirical essay concerning human understanding: such was the larger purpose of Coleridge's critique of language, pursued in a volume of moral and political discourse, most of it long since forgotten, in which he provided the prototype of the critique of language practiced by Carlyle and Emerson, Richards and Leavis, Empson and Williams. All participate in a critique of the terms of modern understanding, beginning from the categories of culture and civilization as distinguished by Coleridge himself. Skeptical like Bacon of what things are called, of the names by which we recognize the world, modern practitioners of his *idola* follow Coleridge in the conviction of the force of reason and rhetoric, against Locke's corrosive attack on the latter in particular. Blaming the tongue means avoiding the politics involved in the employments of words, deflecting criticism from human intentions to its instruments.

Some of this sticks to Bacon, especially where he would make the *idola* indict vulgar understanding, as if science represented an authoritative alternative. The case of Locke shows how hypothetical such claims could become, and how assertive. With Coleridge, Romantic theory arrives at a defense of ordinary language, *lingua communis,* which is neither nostalgic about better tongues (and better times) nor satisfied with current terms and practices—with modern understanding as it descends from Bacon and Locke. Trying the Tartars' bow involves him in turning back on their informing example, limiting their authority while recognizing its lasting value for thinking about modern conditions.[43] Coleridge's critical attitude is expressed most effectively and influentially in this line of his work, which owes nothing to Kant's critical philosophy. The real authority of his situation is associated with his practice of this socially sensitive line of reflection on language, literature, and culture. Trying the Tartars' bow is the hallmark of the vocation of letters as it has come to be recognized since Coleridge's time. Wondering about words is the sign of criticism's concern not only for language in its literary usages, but for *lingua communis* and ordinary experience.

Anne K. Mellor

A Criticism of Their Own: Romantic Women Literary Critics

❦

When Anna Laetitia Barbauld told Coleridge that his *Rime of the Ancient Mariner* "was improbable and had no moral," she not only articulated her shrewd critical insight into the poem's unresolved romantic-ironic juxtaposition of a chaotic, amoral universe with a Christian theology,[1] she also laid claim to a literary aesthetic that stood in sharp contrast to the myriad forms of what the other authors in this volume are discussing under the rubric "Romantic literary criticism." In this chapter I wish to suggest that the leading women literary critics of the Romantic era—Joanna Baillie, Anna Barbauld, Elizabeth Inchbald, Clara Reeve, Anna Seward, and Mary Wollstonecraft—upheld an aesthetic theory different from but as coherent as those developed by Coleridge, William Wordsworth, Hazlitt, Keats, Percy Shelley, and their male peers.

Other chapters in this volume examine the nuances, complexities, and contradictions within and among those masculine Romantic poetic theories that René Wellek forty years ago simplistically categorized as "the rise of an emotional concept of poetry, the establishment of the historical point of view, and the implied rejection of the imitation theory of the rules and genres" of a neoclassical aesthetic. Wellek further identified the Romantic aesthetic with a conception of poetry as a self-constituting system of symbols grounded on polarity, "multeity-in-unity" or the union of opposites.[2] A feminine Romantic aesthetic existed in dialogue both with the competing versions of this "expressive" or organic Romantic poetics, whose constitutive trope Meyer Abrams identified as the lamp, and with the mimetic theory it displaced—the conception of literature as holding a mirror up to nature, recording what oft was thought but ne'er so well expressed.[3] In place of the mirror and the lamp, we might think of Romantic women literary critics as sustaining an earlier Enlightenment image of literature popularized by Addison and Cowper, the image of literature as a balance or scale that weighs equally the demands of the head and the heart. As they appropriate this aesthetic trope, however, these women literary critics redefine it in an all-important way. In their writings this balance or scale is always held—and here they rely on traditional iconic representations of a female Justice/Justizia—by a woman. It is a woman, both Sybil and mother, who can most wisely judge the competing claims of thought and emotion: what she seeks, in literature as in life, is "right feeling."

Romantic women critics, all practicing poets, playwrights, or novelists as well as critics, thus lay claim to a cultural authority which they used to promote a specific ideology, one endorsed by the majority of the women writers of the period. In my recent *Romanticism and Gender* (1993) I called this ideology "feminine Romanticism" (in order to retain its historical specificity but to differentiate it from the cultural movement, hitherto called "Romanticism," produced predominantly by male writers in England between 1780 and 1830). Feminine Romanticism is a "spirit of the age," a set of personal, political, and literary investments, collectively shared by the leading women writers of the period—by Jane Austen, Mary Brunton, Frances Burney, Maria Edgeworth, Susan Ferrier, Mary Hays, Felicia Hemans, Letitia Elizabeth Landon, Hannah More, Amelia Opie, Sydney Owenson (Lady Morgan), Jane and Anna Maria Porter, Ann Radcliffe, Mary Robinson, Mary Shelley, Charlotte Smith, Jane Taylor, Helen Maria Williams, and Dorothy Wordsworth. These women were, moreover, together with that male "feminine Romantic," Walter Scott, among the most popular writers of the day[4] (only Byron, of the canonized Romantic writers, could outsell them, and Hemans came a close second to Byron, as did Edgeworth).

These women writers focused on issues very different from those that engaged the attention of the canonical male Romantic poets and critics. For the most part Romantic women writers forswore their male peers' concern with the capacities and value of the creative imagination, with the limitations of language, with the relation of the perceiving subject to the perceived object, with the possibility of transcendence or apocalyptic vision, with the development of an autonomous self and the nature of self-consciousness, with political (as opposed to social) revolution, with the role of the creative artist as a political leader or religious savior. Although they read the canonical male Romantic poets with interest and some approval, they often dismissed them as amoral, self-indulgent, or incomprehensible: Felicia Hemans, for instance, enjoyed Percy Shelley's "Ode to the West Wind" but thought Byron's *Don Juan* too "disgusting" to read, while Anna Seward praised Southey's *Joan of Arc* and *Madoc* effusively but found that William Wordsworth, while he had "genius," wrote a poetry that was "harsh, turgid, and obscure."[5]

Instead, Romantic women writers, whether conservative or radical, celebrated not the achievements of genius nor the spontaneous overflow of powerful feelings but rather the workings of the rational mind, a mind relocated—in a gesture of revolutionary social implications—in the female as well as the male body. Following Mary Wollstonecraft's call in *A Vindication of the Rights of Woman* in 1792 for "a REVOLUTION in female manners," they insisted that women should be educated in the same ways and toward the same goals as men and that women were as capable as men of thinking rationally and acting virtuously. They endorsed Wollstonecraft's argument that the ideal marriage is one based not on sexual passion but on mutual respect, self-esteem, affection, and compatibility. Their novels, plays, and poetry repeatedly celebrate the domestic affections and marriages of equality based on such rational love.

Moreover, feminine Romanticism constructed a subjectivity very different from the transcendental ego standing alone, the *spectator ab extra* projected by Kant and so anxiously embodied and interrogated by William Wordsworth. Romantic women writers represent a subjectivity constructed in relation to other subjectivities, hence a self that is fluid, absorptive, responsive, with permeable ego boundaries, the self that Dorothy Wordsworth imaged as a floating, disappearing/reappearing island in her poem "Floating Island at Hawkeshead: An Incident in the Schemes of Nature."[6] In their writings, this self typically locates its identity in its connections with a larger human group, whether the family or a social community.

Taking the family as the grounding trope of social organization, feminine Romanticism opposed violent military revolutions, especially the French Revolution, in favor of gradual or evolutionary reform under the guidance of benevolent parental instruction, a model derived from Erasmus Darwin's theory of natural evolution in *The Botanic Garden* (1789–91) and *Zoonomia, or The Laws of Organic Life* (1794). Although they endorsed Edmund Burke's image in *Reflections on the Revolution in France* (1790) of the state as "a little platoon," a family, they strenuously resisted Burke's assertion that only men "of permanent property" loyal to their "canonized forefathers" could lead such a platoon, and insisted that the mother played as important a role as the father in the governance of the family politic. Here these Romantic women writers and literary critics emphatically broke ranks with both their male and their female eighteenth-century forebears: while they shared an Enlightenment commitment to rationality, they added to it the revolutionary claim that the female mind was not only as rational as the male but perhaps even *more* rational. This claim was based on the argument that an ethic of care, an ethic that takes as its highest value the insuring that, in any conflict, no one should be hurt,[7] is a more rational distribution of social goods and services than those derived from an ethic of justice, an ethic that demands that all persons, regardless of their physical and psychological needs, should be treated the same under the law.

For these writers, Nature is not so much the source of divine creative power, that "mighty mind" that Wordsworth perceived from the top of Mount Snowdon and transgendered into a "Brother" of the (male) poet (*W Prel* [1805] XIII. 69, 89), as a female friend or sister with needs and capacities, one who both provides support and requires cultivation, with whose life-giving powers one eagerly cooperates. In this feminine Romantic ideology, moral reform both of the individual and of the family politic is achieved, then, not by utopian imaginative vision but by the communal exercise of reason, moderation, tolerance, and the domestic affections that can embrace even the alien other, even Frankenstein's monster. Above all, feminine Romanticism insisted on gender equality, on the value and rational capacities of women. And finally, this ideology found certain literary genres more congenial than others: the novel, which enabled the author to represent in the vernacular a human community whose multiple relationships extend over time; the domestic drama, which enables the audience to participate in a mediated resolution of human conflict; and those poetic genres (occasional verse, the sonnet, the shorter lyric, the ballad) which celebrate the value of the quotidian, of daily domestic and social involvements.

I have continued to use the term *Romanticism* in relation to the ideology espoused by these women writers for reasons both pragmatic and theoretical. Current academic curricula in both the United Kingdom and the United States assign to the historical period between the eighteenth century and Victorian England a literature called "Romanticism": if we define these women as "not Romantic," we once again exclude them from both the canon and the curriculum. More important than this practical pedagogical consideration, however, are the theoretical issues at stake in the term *Romanticism*. Philologically derived from *romaunt* ("romance," "roman," i.e., the novel), *Romanticism* has long connoted an association with the imagination, the fictive, the marvelous and strange, the ideal, the utopian, the revolutionary, especially in matters of love and politics. The ultimate social consequences of the ideology collectively produced by many of the women writers in England between 1780 and 1830 were both revolutionary and utopian. At the level of theory, this ideology demanded nothing less than the liberation of women from the physical and psychological oppressions of the historical, specifically patriarchal, construction of gender. Their demand for an education identical to that received by men, for egalitarian marriages grounded in rational love and mutual respect, and for the equal political and civil rights of women applied the principles of the French Revolution for the first time directly to the situation of women. But rather than subscribing to what we now call liberal or equality feminism, the principle that women should be treated in the same way as men, they went one step further, to suggest that those cultural values historically associated with women were superior to those associated with men. They argued that the values of domesticity—the private virtues of sympathy, tolerance, generosity, affection, and a commitment to an ethic of care—should become the guiding program for all *public* or civic action. Insofar as this would require a radical transformation of early-nineteenth-century British society, it is, I submit, a truly "romantic" or revolutionary and utopian ideology.

Committed to this ideology of feminine Romanticism, the women literary critics of the period constructed a coherent program for the production and consumption of literature, clearly defining the proper goals of literature and the nature of the aesthetic response. They were writing at a time when the advent of the circulating or lending library, which spread rapidly throughout England after the 1780s, meant that books, especially novels, poems, and plays, were widely available to women readers of both the middle and the aristocratic classes. It is important to recognize that the bulk of the subscribers to these lending libraries were women who by the late eighteenth century had acquired the literacy, desire, and opportunity to read, and preferred to read literature, especially novels, written by women. This new audience meant that women could, and for the first time did, dominate the production of literature. Ten of the twelve most popular novelists of the period were women. As poets Felicia Hemans and Letitia Landon rivaled Byron and Wordsworth in popularity and sales; Joanna Baillie was everywhere hailed as the period's best playwright.[8] And the publishers of two of the most prestigious reissue series, Longman's *The British Theatre* and Rivington's *The British Novelists,* chose women as their editors (Elizabeth Inchbald and Anna Barbauld, respectively).

Since women were denied access to the institutions of academic learning in England and were typically taught only the "accomplishments" of a well-bred young lady (dancing, singing, sketching, needle-work, a smattering of French and Italian, a little arithmetic and—most important—how to read and write), the women critics of the Romantic period recognized that literature—the reading of a good book—was essential to the rational education of young girls. As literary critics, they repeatedly insisted that contemporary and classical literature must assume the responsibility of educating young people, but especially young women, to be sensible, well-informed, and prudent adults. Promoting the values of the professional middle classes to which they belonged, these women critics endorsed a literature that was necessarily didactic, that demonstrated the rewards of virtue, thrift, and self-control, while punishing the vices of willful impulse, irrationality, lack of foresight, excessive sensibility, and uncontrolled sexual desire (which left girls, as opposed to boys in the days of the sexual double standard, seduced, abandoned, pregnant, and finally condemned to the only career open to them, prostitution).

Insisting that the cultural role of literature is to instruct, these women critics assumed the stance of the mother-teacher, selecting the appropriate books for young people to read at different stages of their growth (Clara Reeve concludes her *Progress of Romance* with a list of recommended novels for girls, based on their age), warning against licentious literature, and correcting the aesthetic taste of their charges. Anna Barbauld's introduction and critical prefaces to *The British Novelists* relentlessly emphasized the moral and pedagogical value of the novels she included. Her comments on Burney and Edgeworth are typical:

> The more severe and homely virtues of prudence and economy have been enforced in the writings of a Burney and an Edgeworth. . . .

> Where can be found a more striking lesson against unfeeling dissipation than the story of the *Harrels* [in *Cecilia*]? Where have order, neatness, industry, sobriety, been recommended with more strength than in the agreeable tales of Miss Edgeworth? If a parent wishes his child to avoid caprice, irregularities of temper, procrastination, coquetry, affectation,—all those faults and blemishes which undermine family happiness, and destroy the every-day comforts of common life,—whence can he derive more impressive morality than from the same source? When works of fancy are thus made subservient to the improvement of the rising generation, they certainly stand on a higher ground than mere entertainment, and we revere while we admire.[9]

At the same time Barbauld roundly criticized those overly sentimental novels that "awaken and increase sensibilities, which it is the office of wise restraint to calm and moderate" (52) and that give young female readers a false notion of the importance of romantic love, which in fact "acts a very subordinate part on the great theatre of the world" (53).

Similarly, Mary Wollstonecraft, reviewing Charlotte Smith's *Emmeline* for the *Analytical Review* in July 1788, condemned Delamere's passion, which "will catch the attention of many romantic girls, and carry their imaginations still further from nature and reason." She further denounced all novels "whose preposterous sentiments our young females imbibe with such avidity" but that foster "vanity and affectation"; they "throw an insipid kind of uniformity over the moderate and rational prospects of life, consequently *adventures* are sought for and created, when duties are neglected, and content despised" (331, 333). Throughout her reviews for the *Analytical,* Wollstonecraft insisted that novels should promote for both sexes, but especially among young women, the virtues of moderation, reason, contentment, and the domestic affections. As Mitzi Myers has documented, Wollstonecraft assumed a "maternal stance" in her reviews, using them as a forum from which to attack excessive feminine sensibility and to redefine the ideal woman as one who balances passion with reason, thus promoting the pedagogical and gender-role reforms she urged more directly in her *Vindication of the Rights of Woman.*[10]

The critic is a mother, educating her children; the mother thus becomes, necessarily, a literary critic. As Mary Hays urged the mothers of England, your daughters should read whatever they like so long as you

> converse with them on the merits of the various authors and accustom them to critical, and literary discussions. They will soon be emulous of

gaining your approbation by entering into your ideas, and will be ashamed of being pleased with what you ridicule as absurd, and out of nature, or disapprove, as having an improper and immoral tendency. You have only to persuade them that you have a confidence in their principles, and good sense, and they will be eager to justify your favourable opinion.[11]

Endorsing Samuel Johnson's view that you become what you read,[12] these female Romantic critics were anxious to instill in young people a taste for virtue and an abhorrence of vice that would govern their behavior throughout their lives. Elizabeth Inchbald defined the goal of good comic writing thus:

> to exhibit the weak side of wisdom, the occasional foibles which impede the full exertion of good sense; the chance awkwardness of the elegant, and mistakes of the correct; to bestow wit on beauty, and to depict the passions visible in the young as well as in the aged;—these are efforts of intellect required in the production of a good comedy, and can alone confer the title of a good comic author. (Preface to Richard Cumberland's *The Brothers*)[13]

They revised the neoclassical dictum that literature must "delight and instruct" in an extremely important way. What you should read and therefore become, all these women critics agree, is a committed advocate of the domestic affections. As Anna Barbauld concluded, the best British novels endorse "our national taste and habits" which "are still turned towards domestic life and matrimonial happiness" (58). Literary instruction must therefore promote more egalitarian gender roles. Romantic women literary critics used their writings to challenge the existing gender ideology promoted by Pope, Johnson, Addison, and a host of male writers and critics, which assumed that men were rational and should dominate the public sphere while women were emotional and should be confined to the private sphere. Instead they developed a new image of the ideal female as one who is rational and socially responsible, one who takes the lead in governing both herself and her children.

As a rational woman, the ideal female prudently chooses only a marriage of equality, founded on enduring compatibility or rational love, and forswears the temptations both of premarital sexuality and of adultery. As Elizabeth Inchbald repeatedly insisted in her 125 prefaces to *The British Theatre,* "conjugal love" produces the highest human happiness and "has a deeper interest in the bosom of every auditor than any other affection" (Thomas Otway's *Venice Preserved*). She spelled out the way to such conjugal love in her preface to Hannah Cowley's *The Belle's Stratagem:* "The love of Sir George [Touchwood] and his wife is fervent, yet reasonable; they are fond, but not foolish; and with all their extreme delicacy of opinions, never once express their thoughts, either in ranting, affected, or insipid sentences." In contrast, the passion of Shakespeare's Romeo and Juliet is too sudden, "childish," and short-lived truly to touch the heart, since to Inchbald it seemed a "matter of doubt whether they would not as quickly have fallen in love a second time, or as soon have become languid through satiety, if all obstacles to their bliss had been removed" (Preface to *Romeo and Juliet*). Similarly, Inchbald found the marriage of Alphonso and Almeria in William Congreve's *The Mourning Bride* to be "merely bridal; neither cemented by long friendship, offspring, or any of those positive ties of affection, which would infallibly win the audience to sympathize in their mutual fondness." Defying her culture's patriarchal assumption that all women must marry to be happy, Inchbald comments sardonically that "to get married, is not to obtain the summit of [the maiden auditor's] wishes, unless in wedlock she gains a friend, a companion, a counsellor, and protector" (Preface to Thomas Morton's *The Way to Get Married*).

As Inchbald's last comment suggests, Romantic women literary critics used their writings not only to advocate new roles and more egalitarian marriages for women but also to condemn the abuses of patriarchy and the traditional construction of masculinity. Inchbald went out of her way to attack her society's tolerance for that "disease," male gambling. As Katherine Rogers points out, Inchbald "was consistently hard headed about money" and was not duped by the amorality of Edward Moore's *The Gamester,* a popular tearjerker that portrays as essentially virtuous and lovable a man who ruins his family through gambling.[14] As Inchbald comments sardonically, "An audience mostly supposes, that [Beverly's wife] performs an heroic action as a wife" when she gives up her last possession, her jewels, to her husband, "but readers call to mind she is a mother; and that she breaks through the dearest tie of nature by thus yielding up the sole support of her infant child, to gratify the ideal honour of its duped and frantic father." As Inchbald concludes, in her effort to reform both genders, "a man without sense, and a woman without prudence, degrade both the masculine and the feminine character."

Anna Barbauld similarly used her prefatory remarks on the novels she included in *The British Novelists* to condemn male folly. She praised

Frances Burney in particular for "her satire upon the affected apathy, studied negligence, coarse slang, avowed selfishness, or mischievous frolic by which [young men who aspire to lead the fashion] often distinguish themselves, and through which they contrive to be vulgar with the advantages of rank, mean with those of fortune, and disagreeable with those of youth" (38:viii–ix). And Mary Wollstonecraft, reviewing Thomas Holcroft's jacobin novel *Anna St. Ives* in May 1792, took this occasion to denounce the patriarchal privileges of aristocratic rank and primogeniture, claiming that "the *moral*" of this novel is "assuredly a good one. It is calculated to strengthen despairing virtue, to give fresh energy to the cause of humanity, to repress the pride and insolence of birth, and to shew that true nobility which can alone proceed from the head and the heart, that claims genius and virtue for all its armorial bearings, and possessed of these, despises all the foppery of either ancient or modern heraldry."[15]

In order to fulfill these didactic and pedagogical purposes, literature must above all be *probable,* the key term in the criticism of these women. Only a work that is realistic, that represents convincing characters in quotidian settings undergoing plausible experiences, can function effectively to educate both old and young people. Here they explicitly defend a mimetic theory of art against the inclinations of the male Romantic poets to invoke visionary experiences or supernatural events in medieval or exotic settings. Elizabeth Inchbald roundly condemns Hannah Cowley's *A Bold Stroke for a Wife* because "however fertile her imagination has been in forming a multiplicity of occurrences, and diversifying the whole exhibition by variety of character, probability is so often violated, that the effect, though powerful, is that of farce, and not a genuine comedy." The passions of the audience, whether at a comedy or a tragedy, are best moved, Inchbald insisted, by a "judicious adherence to nature and simplicity" (Preface to Dryden's *All for Love*). This is an adherence that Inchbald herself did not always achieve, as Mary Wollstonecraft pointed out in her review of Inchbald's novel *Nature and Art,* which she condemned for its "improbability."[16]

To be probable, literature must show how real characters change and grow *over time,* how human beings develop in relation to other people, how uncontrolled passions fester and destroy otherwise admirable people. Joanna Baillie was the first to devote her entire creative effort to representing the origin and the *growth* of the human passions. Her *Series of Plays: in which it is attempted to Delineate the Stronger Passions of the Mind, each Passion being the Subject of a Tragedy and a Comedy,* begun in 1798, initiated the focus on the growth of the human mind later defined by Wordsworth and Coleridge as the essence of masculine Romanticism. Baillie, however, emphasized that human identity is *relational*—that subjectivity is organic, develops over time, responds to external influences, and is shaped by its connections to other selves. Focusing on the growth of the passions, she used her plays to portray both the successful control of the passions by rational thought (significantly, in her plays such prudent self-control is located in her *female* characters) and the damage wrought when a single passion (whether hate, anger, love, jealousy, greed, etc.) takes dominance over all others. Baillie's *male* protagonists, like Basil, De Montfort, and Mr. Charleville, are the ones who cannot control their emotions and wreak havoc on themselves and their families by their obsessive passions. Joanna Baillie believed that the theater could and should function as a school, to teach her audiences—by arousing their curiosity and appealing both to their altruism and to their self-interest—that the passions must be controlled by good sense if the individual and the family are to survive and achieve happiness.

To be probable, literature must balance the mind and the heart. Romantic women critics fully acknowledged the role played by the feelings as well as by reason in human experience. They knew that the female sex had historically been identified with passion, with "sensibility," with the emotions. They embraced the capacity of women readers to feel intensely, and argued that literature should stimulate the reader's ability to feel sympathy and disgust, pity and revulsion. They praised literary texts that used fresh plots, vivid images, scenes of pathos, all able to arouse the reader from lethargy into an alert response, to appeal to what Wollstonecraft called "the *feeling mind*."[17] As Wollstonecraft explained in her essay "On Poetry and Our Relish for the Beauties of Nature," great art is produced by that "genius" (defined by her as "only another word for exquisite sensibility") which is able to both "rouse the passions" and at the same time exercise the "understanding . . . to discriminate things" and thus to "amend the heart."[18] Wollstonecraft particularly praised Helen Maria Williams's *Letters from France,* for instance, because they so vividly displayed "the misery of [France's] prison-houses, and the tyrannic power exercised by parents . . . in a pathetic tale that did not require the aid of fiction to heighten the real distress."[19]

These women critics consistently argued that sensibility must be joined with correct perception, that literature must record not flights of fancy or escapist desire but empirical truth. Even as Wollstonecraft argued that the good or "natural" writer must respond to the world immediately and powerfully, speaking "the language of truth and nature with resistless energy," she warned against a sensibility that produces libertinism, by leading one "to prefer the sensual tumult of love a little refined by sentiment, to the calm pleasures of affectional friendship, in whose sober satisfactions, reason, mixing her tranquillizing convictions, whispers that content, not happiness, is the reward of virtue in this world."[20] Not any feeling, but the *right feeling* must be aroused by good literature.

Probability is also a matter of craft. Both Barbauld and Inchbald were keenly aware that realistic portrayals, whether in the novel or on the stage, required specific literary techniques, techniques that could be identified, analyzed, and evaluated. As Catherine E. Moore has noted, Barbauld understood clearly the various kinds of narrative and their respective limitations.[21] In her preface to Samuel Richardson's *Correspondence* (1804), Barbauld defined three possible narrative strategies or points of view, at the same time recognizing the problems inherent in each: (1) the omniscient narrator—but such narration, she observed, "will not be lively, except [the author] frequently drops himself, and runs into dialogue"; (2) first-person narration, which "confines the author's stile, which should be suited, though it is not always, to the supposed talents and capacity of the imaginary narrator"; and (3) "epistolary correspondence," which "unites, in a good measure, the advantages of the other two" but "is incompatible with a rapid stile" and "highly fictitious: it is the most natural and the least probable way of telling a story."[22] Such well-informed discussions of narrative techniques, as Catherine Moore points out, were rare in the Romantic period; Anna Barbauld here initiated the study of what we now call narratology.

Inchbald, as a successful dramatist, was keenly aware of what worked on the stage and what succeeded only on the printed page. She recognized the role of good acting, acknowledging that a superb actor like Sarah Siddons or Mr. Lewis could rescue an inferior play, such as Thomas Morton's *A Cure for the Heart Ache*. As Katherine Rogers has noted,[23] she understood the necessity of a clear exposition of the plot, as well as the need to sustain dramatic probability even when the plot becomes unbelievable by "the happy art of alluring the attention of the audience, from the observation of every defect, and of fixing it solely upon every beauty which the drama displays," as when Hannah Cowley introduces a masquerade to distract the audience from condemning her hero for falling in love with her heroine after only a few hours of conversation (Preface to *The Belle's Stratagem*). And she condemned Joanna Baillie's *De Montfort* for failing to represent the causes of De Montfort's obsessive hatred, thus rendering her protagonist unconvincing, even, in the eyes of the audience, a "lunatic." Inchbald concluded that "this drama, of original and very peculiar formation, plainly denotes that the authoress has studied theatrical productions as a reader more than as a spectator" (Preface to *De Montfort*).

Anna Seward, focusing her attention as a critic exclusively on poetry, laid down what she considered the technical criteria for good poetry: "Criticism must proceed upon a large scale . . . the only requisites on which she should strongly insist are general consistence of metaphor, and happiness of allusion, appropriation as to character, vigour of idea, perspicuity of expression, accuracy and general grace of style, and picturesque power in the epithets."[24] Using these criteria, her letters abound in detailed and judicious appraisals of the superiority of Shakespeare in drama, of Milton in the epic, of Spenser in allegory, of Dryden, Pope, and Johnson in what she called the poetic sciences of "the ethic, heroic and satiric," of Thomson in the descriptive, of Prior in the narrative and epigrammatic, of Gray in the lyric and elegiac, and of Shenstone in the pastoral mode.

Since probability and morality were their chief literary values, these Romantic women critics initiated a revolutionary reordering of the arts. In the earlier eighteenth century, the epic poem had been ranked first among the literary genres, followed by the tragic drama, the Horatian and Pindaric odes, comic dramas and satires, and the lesser poetic forms (the sonnet, the ballad); at the lowest level of the literary arts were the various forms of prose fiction: stories, legends, romances, novels. The Romantic women critics vigorously contested this hierarchy. They argued that the novel, which they traced back to the Greek romances, was the highest literary form because it was both the most moral and the most realistic.

In order to elevate the novel to the status they thought it deserved, without blindly endorsing Fielding's prefatory claim in *Joseph Andrews* that "a comic romance is a comic epic poem in prose," Romantic women critics first had to deal with their culture's tendency to conflate the novel with the romance. Clara Reeve, in *The Progress of Romance* (1785), insisted both on the literary value of the romance and on the ways in which the novel had developed out of, but gone beyond, the romance. First elevating the genre of the romance, Reeve's spokeswoman Euphrasia claimed that "Epic Poetry is the parent of Romance."[25] She then opposed the conventional definitions of the romance as "a wild, extravagant, fabulous story" or "stories that are built upon fiction, and have no foundation in truth" (1:6), arguing instead that the romance is "an *Heroic fable*—a fabulous Story of such actions as are commonly ascribed to heroes, or men of extraordinary courage and abilities.—Or . . . an Epic in prose" (1:13). Surveying the history of the romance from the medieval period through the seventeenth-century French productions of Calprenède and Scudéry, Reeve emphasized their morality and civilizing influence, claiming that they all helped to inspire their readers with a love of virtue and honor, and especially that they taught young men "to look upon themselves as the champions and protectors of the weaker sex;—to treat the object of their passion with the utmost respect" (1:68).

Yet Reeve, unlike such contemporary German Romantic proponents of the romance as A. W. Schlegel, finally condemned the romance for its failure to distinguish historical truth from fiction, and argued that the novel is a superior genre. Even though the novel originated in the plots of the romance, it has transcended this parentage by providing "a picture of real life and manners, and of the times in which it is written" (1:111). As Reeve concluded,

> The Novel gives a familiar relation of such things, as pass every day before our eyes, such as may happen to our friend, or to ourselves; and the perfection of it, is to represent every scene, in so easy and natural a manner, and to make them appear so probable, as to deceive us into a persuasion (at least while we are reading) that all is real, until we are affected by the joys or distresses, of the persons in the story, as if they were our own. (1:111)

Introducing the Rivington reprint series of *The British Novelists* in 1810, Anna Barbauld endorsed Reeve's claim that the novel is the highest genre of all, superior to the epic poem:

> The invention of a story, the choice of proper incidents, the ordinance of the plan, occasional beauties of description, and above all, the power exercised over the reader's heart by filling it with the successive emotions of love, pity, joy, anguish, transport, or indignation, together with the grave impressive moral resulting from the whole, imply talents of the highest order, and ought to be appreciated accordingly. A good novel is an epic in prose, with more of character and less (indeed in modern novels nothing) of the supernatural machinery. (2–3)

Like Clara Reeve, Anna Barbauld traces the origin of the novel to the romance, and argues that the cultural function of the novel is to promote the growth of morality. Both agree that the novel surpasses all other genres in its ability to describe in detail the ways that human beings interact with one another and how morally correct decisions are made and tested by experience.

Even Elizabeth Inchbald, a committed dramatist, affirmed the superiority of the genre of the novel. She ranked drama over poetry, calling the stage "the best vehicle by which wit, poetry, and morality, could be conveyed to the good and the bad, the wise and the ignorant, of the community" (Preface to John Tobin's *The Honey Moon*), whereas "Poetry, with all its charms, will not constitute a good play" (Preface to George Colman, the Younger, *The Mountaineers*). Worse, whereas on stage it is very difficult to make an evil character sympathetic, "the beautiful and the base" do "combine . . . in the fiction of poetry" (Preface to Nicholas Rowe's *The Fair Penitent*). Yet she acknowledged the moral and psychological superiority of fiction over both poetry and the drama. In her preface to *The Iron Chest,* George Colman the Younger's dramatic adaptation of William Godwin's novel *Caleb Williams,* she commented,

> The finer details in "Caleb Williams" allow of no representation in action: the dramatist was here compelled merely to give the features of the murderer's face; while the novelist portrayed every shade of his countenance, every fibre that played in forgetful smiles, or was convulsed by the pangs of remembrance.
>
> The two arts of dramatic and of novel-writing are thus beheld at such variance, that the reader of the novel shall enter, with Falkland, into all his nice, his romantic notions of honour and posthumous fame; though the auditor, or reader, of "The Iron Chest" shall feel no concern, unless to despise it, about Sir Edward Mortimer's equal enthusiasm for the glory of reputation.
>
> The reason of this difference in consequences, from the self-same story, does not, however, betray the want of skill in the author of the play, but simply argues his want of space. Narrative, on the stage, must never be diffuse: the play must be comprised in a certain number of pages; and when the foundation of a fable is of the magnitude of murder, any abridgement of circumstances, requisite to make description both clear and probable, must be of fatal import to all the scenes so founded. (Preface to *The Iron Chest*)

Not only was the novel capable of depicting a world that was both more probable and more psychologically acute than that found in epic poetry or the earlier romances, it was also more *democratic.* The novel could be read and understood by everyone, regardless of whether one had had an education in Greek and Latin. As Anna Barbauld pointed out,

> Reading is the cheapest of pleasures: it is a domestic pleasure. Dramatic exhibitions give a more poignant delight, but they are seldom enjoyed in perfection, and never without expense and trouble. Poetry requires in the reader a certain elevation of mind and a practised ear. It is seldom relished unless a taste be formed for it pretty early. But the humble novel is always ready to enliven the gloom of solitude, to soothe the languor of debility and disease, to win the attention from pain or vexatious occurrences, to take man from himself (at many seasons the worst company he can be in) and, while the moving picture of life passes before him, to make him forget the subject of his own complaints. (47)

Morality, probability, right feeling—this is what the good work of literature must aim to provide its reader. Turning from the text itself to the reader, Romantic women critics developed what we would now call a "reader-response" theory. They argued that the reader approached the literary text not with Coleridge's "willing suspension of disbelief" but with something very different. Joanna Baillie provided the fullest account of an alternative concept of reader response. She argued that the "great master-propensity" of human nature is our "sympathetic curiosity," our interest in and our ability to empathize with the feelings and experiences of other human beings.[26] Baillie here draws on Shaftesbury's concept of "disinterestedness" as the basis of all moral behavior and anticipates Keats's and Hazlitt's later application of this concept to the aesthetic response, what Hazlitt called "gusto" and Keats called "negative capability." She argues that the best art is that which most directly engages the sympathy of the audience by "faithfully delineating" human nature (6). Focusing specifically on drama, she claims that both tragedy and comedy have historically failed to represent adequately the development and the myriad effects of specific passions, passions which are felt by and exert their control over both sexes equally. Her own dramatic project, carried out in her series of *Plays on the Passions,* was to "trace [the passions] in their rise and progress in the heart" in minute and subtle detail (10), since she was confident that tragedy written on this plan "is fitted to produce stronger moral effect than upon any other" (11). As the audience empathetically participates in such subtle revelations of the workings of the emotions, they will be psychologically and ethically instructed, coming to recognize the ways that reason can protect one against an obsessive passion if not entirely prevent it.

Baillie's reader-response concept of sympathetic curiosity rests on what we might now call a "feminist epistemology," on "women's ways of knowing." This epistemology assumes that every act of knowing requires an active emotional engagement of the knower with the known, that "objectivity" is a psychological and perceptual impossibility. As Mary Hawkesworth has recently summarized this position, every act of cognition is "a human practice" that includes the full "complexity of the interaction between traditional assumptions, social norms, theoretical conceptions, disciplinary strictures, linguistic possibilities, emotional dispositions, and creative impositions."[27] One cannot perceive anything without experiencing some sort of *connection* to it, without bringing to that act of perception the full range of one's ideologically biased experiences, without locating the perceived object within a preexisting framework of coherent meaning. Watching a play, as Joanna Baillie understood, involves an active "enlargement of our ideas in regard to human nature" (10). The role of the literary critic, then, is to reenact this sympathetic curiosity, to fuse empathic involvement with rational understanding.

Writing a criticism of their own, poised midway between a neoclassical mimetic aesthetic, on the one hand, limited by its commitment to abstract universals, to the unities as the definition of "realism," and to an outdated hierarchy of the arts, and, on the other hand, a masculine Romantic aesthetic devoted to celebrating the originality and passionate feeling of the poet, Romantic women literary critics offered a third aesthetic. They insisted that the cultural role of literature is to educate even more than to delight, to educate by teaching readers to take delight in the triumph of moral benevolence, sexual self-control, and rational intelligence. To inculcate such values and practices, literature must be both vivid and realistic, depicting events and characters rendered in sufficiently accurate and telling detail to be convincing. Generically, the novel provides the largest scope and most finely woven texture for such realistic portrayals, followed by the drama—which enables its viewers to participate sympathetically in the resolution of human conflict—and lastly by poetry that is devoted to the quotidian, that "occasional verse" which records individual responses to daily domestic events. Inspired by Wollstonecraft's *Vindication of the Rights of Woman,* these literary critics assumed that the most important social revolutions occur not on the battlefield but in the home. As Elizabeth Inchbald commented,

> Whatever reasons may be urged against the more elevated instruction of the sex at present, than in former days, one good consequence at least accrues from it—they are better qualified than heretofore to choose their lovers and husbands. It was in the age of female ignorance that the Lotharios, and the ye[t] viler Lovelaces, flourished. . . . Now, enlightened by a degree of masculine study, woman's taste and judgment being improved—this best consequence of all ensues—men must improve to win them. (Preface to Nicholas Rowe's *The Fair Penitent*)

Their criticism was profoundly political, insofar as it actively encouraged women as well as men to read, to learn from their reading, and then to teach by writing, thus joining the ranks of the highest cultural authorities in the land.

We must recognize the significance of the fact that all these women critics set themselves up as *judges,* judges not just of aesthetic taste and literary excellence but also of cultural morality. As Anna Seward announced,

> Many excel me in the power of writing verse; perhaps scarcely one in the vivid and strong sensibility of its excellence, or in the ability to estimate its claims—ability arising from a fifty years sedulous and discriminating study of the best English poets, and of the best translations from the Greek, Roman, and Italian. A masculine education cannot spare from professional study, and the necessary acquisition of languages, the time and attention which I have bestowed on the compositions of my countrymen.[28]

And when Henry Colman the Younger attacked Elizabeth Inchbald for daring to criticize the plays of a *man* in public, and especially those of his father, who had briefly been her employer and patron (Colman compared Inchbald to a Deidamia wielding "a battle-axe to slay and maim the gentlemen"), she graciously apologized. At the same time she insisted on the prerogatives of her critical craft, shrewdly observing that her very admiration for the work of both Colmans "warned me against unqualified praise, as the mere substitute for ridicule; and to beware, lest suspicions of a hired panegyrist should bring disgrace upon that production, which required no such nefarious help for its support" (Preface to *The Heir at Law* and letter to George Colman the Younger). She firmly denied his charge of ingratitude, pointing out that her obligations to George Colman the Elder "amounted to no more than those usual attentions which every manager of a theatre is supposed to confer, when he first selects a novice in dramatic writing, as worthy of being introduced, on his stage, to the public." Insisting on their right *as women* both to write literature and to judge it before the public eye, these women critics claimed the highest cultural authority. They claimed the right to control the social sphere, that arena that mediates between the public and the private realms.[29] As Anna Barbauld concluded her essay on the novel, after identifying the majority of her finest contemporary novelists as women:

> [S]urely it will not be said that either taste or morals have been losers by their taking pen in hand. The names of D'Arblay, Edgeworth, Inchbald, Radcliffe, and a number more will vindicate this assertion. . . . It was said by Fletcher of Saltoun, "Let me make the ballads of a nation, and I care not who makes the laws." Might it not be said with as much propriety, Let me make the novels of a country, and let who will make the systems? (59–60)

Not the poet but the novelist, and a female novelist at that, here becomes the unacknowledged legislator of the world.

In raising the novel to the highest rank of the literary arts, these women critics were above all engaging in a gender-politics. The novel was historically a "woman's genre"—one dependent, as Terry Eagleton has noted, on a "feminization of discourse";[30] as the novel gained (or lost) cultural authority, so did women. Significantly, in the Victorian and modern periods, the novel increasingly pushed both poetry and the essay into the literary background, even as a Victorian backlash against female claims to literary authority tried to establish an unbridgeable divide between "high-brow" novels written by and for men and "low-brow" novels written by and for women.[31] This arbitrary division could not be sustained, however, and by the mid twentieth century female novelists finally began to achieve the same recognition and rewards as men, even as gender-equality has gradually increased in most Western societies in recent years. However marginal and defensive the positions taken up by the female Romantic literary critics may seem to those invested in the academic canonization of masculine Romantic literary criticism, we should not forget that these women critics were highly respected by their own peers, both male and female. Nor should we forget that theirs were the critical positions that historically triumphed: the novel (inextricably bound up with the formal conventions of realism) is now indisputably the leading literary genre in all of Western culture, while poetry has become so marginalized that it is almost impossible for a contemporary poet to make a living solely from publishing poetry. In claiming the novel as their own, Romantic women critics also laid claim to a revolution in both female manners and cultural authority.

Martin Aske

Critical Disfigurings: The "Jealous Leer Malign" in Romantic Criticism

Criticism is a noble art when exercised by a noble mind, but it is a deadly and poisoned weapon, when dealt forth by a malicious spirit, with a shrouded head and a muffled hand.

—Blackwood's Edinburgh Magazine, *1836*

Genuine polemics approach a book as lovingly as a cannibal spices a baby.

—*Walter Benjamin,* One-Way Street

I

In his *Autobiography* of 1850 Leigh Hunt has a chapter entitled "Literary Warfare." Its purpose is to explain the critic's "disfavor" with the Tory press and thereby to set the scene for the most notorious episode in his literary life: the publication in 1812 of the libelous *Examiner* article on the Prince Regent, and the subsequent prosecution and imprisonment of both Hunt and his brother John. Although skirmishes had already begun with a number of antigovernment pieces in the *Examiner,* it was, according to Hunt, the publication in 1811 of the satirical *Feast of the Poets,* in his new journal, the *Reflector,* which detonated in the Tory press "convulsions of criticism and contention."[1] The plot of Hunt's poem, based on Suckling's *Session of the Poets,* had been simple enough: "Apollo gives the poets a dinner; and many verse-makers, who have no claim to the title, present themselves, and are rejected."[2] Among the "verse-makers" lampooned by Hunt—and rejected by Apollo—was William Gifford, editor of the *Quarterly Review;* and it is this "sour little gentleman" who comes to figure as Hunt's chief antagonist in his recollections of "literary warfare."[3] The specific object of Hunt's satire in *Feast of the Poets* had been Gifford's own pathetic attempt to write satire, exemplified in the *Baviad* (1791) and *Maeviad* (1795). The former—"a Paraphrastic Imitation of the First Satire of Persius"—was designed "to correct the growing depravity of the public taste," an "infection" spread, so Gifford thought, by the fashionable Della Cruscan poets. A few years later the *Maeviad* was published, to continue the satirical project begun by the *Baviad;* this time Gifford's target was the swarm of "blockheads" aspiring to write for the theater.[4] Hunt is keenly aware of the ironically self-reflexive nature of the situation, since he had formerly had occasion to praise Gifford as "the first satirist of his time": "Strange must have been Gifford's feelings, when, in the *Feast of the Poets,* he found his eulogizer falling as trenchantly on the author of the *Baviad and Maeviad* as the *Baviad and Maeviad* had fallen on the dramatists."[5]

What incensed Hunt in particular was Gifford's treatment of Mary Robinson, a former mistress of the Prince of Wales who, suffering from rheumatism, had "solaced her pains . . . by writing verses." Her verses elicited the following nasty couplet from Gifford:

> See Robinson forget her state, and move
> On crutches tow'rds the grave, to "Light o' Love."[6]

Hazlitt agreed, considering this attack "unmanly": the hand capable of penning such hostility "ought to have been withered in the attempt by the lightning of public indignation and universal scorn" (*HW* 11:125; 9:26n). Such is Hunt's scornful indignation that he singles out Gifford as "the only man I ever attacked, respecting whom I have felt no regret." He goes on to imply that Gifford's general attitude to the Della Cruscans was indeed "unmanly," insofar as the target of his satire scarcely warranted such brutal ridicule: "It was impossible that such absurdities could have had any lasting effect on the public taste. They would have died of inanition." Thus the logic of literary warfare dictates that the satirist must be satirized in turn; Hunt quotes a few lines from the *Baviad* to prove that "the scourge of poetasters was himself a poetaster," a trader in "commonplaces and old phrases" who yet "undertook to despise Charles Lamb, and to trample on Keats and Shelley!"[7]

At this point Hunt recalls a scene that provides a telling coda to the account of his quarrel with Gifford. I must quote the passage in full, since it foregrounds precisely the theme this essay intends to explore:

> I have mentioned the Roxburgh sale of books. I was standing among the bidders with my friend the late Mr. Barron Field, when he jogged my elbow, and said, "There is Gifford over the way, looking at you with *such* a face!" I met the eyes of my beholder, and saw a little man, with a warped frame and a countenance between the querulous and the angry, gazing at me with all his might. It was, truly enough, the satirist who could not bear to be satirized—the denouncer of incompetencies, who could not bear to be told of his own. He had now learnt, as I was myself to learn, what it was to taste of his own bitter medicaments; and he never profited by it, for his *Review* spared neither age nor sex as long as he lived. What he did at first out of a self-satisfied incompetence, he did at last out of an envious and angry one; and he was, all the while, the humble servant of power, and never expressed one word of regret for his inhumanity. The mixture of implacability and servility is the sole reason, as I have said before, why I still speak of him as I do.[8]

It is, of course, a literary occasion primarily—though, on account of its being an auction, not without its internal rivalries. But the scene has a further dimension: it dramatizes an encounter between two figures from virtually opposite ends of the political spectrum. Although Hunt attributes the hostile stare specifically to Gifford's resentment at having his "incompetencies" as a satirist denounced, the passage exposes the underlying dynamic shaping the relationship between these two political rivals. The "humble servant of power," Gifford is represented here as a critic *disfigured by envy.* The focus is on his envious gaze—"looking at you with *such* a face!"—the evil eye whose most famous literary manifestation, of course, is Satan's "jealous leer malign" in *Paradise Lost* (IV.503). Milton's phrase is frequently invoked by Hazlitt in his many aphorisms on envy, for example when he says that "from the moment . . . the eye fixes on another as the object of envy, we cannot take it off. . . . Hence the 'jealous leer malign' of envy, which, not daring to look that which provokes it in the face, cannot yet keep its eyes from it, and gloats over and becomes as it were enamoured of the very object of its loathing and deadly hate" (*HW* 20:312). Perhaps a trace of Satan is still there in Gifford's "warped frame," the twisted body which signifies the necessarily distorting effects of envy (the trope reappears in the "snaky twistings" of that grotesque Victorian monster of envy and resentment, Uriah Heep).[9] The "sour little gentleman" is diminished morally as well as physically ("envy is a littleness of soul," runs one of the maxims in Hazlitt's *Characteristics* [*HW* 9:169]), and in his countenance the tension between the "querulous" and the "angry" expresses the essential impotence of his hatred: the more intense the gaze, the greater the feeling of powerlessness which immobilizes the hatred *in* the gaze. Hence the envy and anger that Hunt ascribes to Gifford.

What the Tory editor specifically resents in Hunt is not only the latter's critical but also his political independence, a position outside the narrow limits of political orthodoxy which allows Hunt to brand Gifford the "humble servant of power," an exponent of what Nietzsche will call the "slave morality" of the "man of *ressentiment*"—a morality that "from the outset says No to what is 'outside,' what is 'different,' what is 'not itself.'"[10] This would also explain Gifford's aversion to the quaint Della Cruscans, which Hazlitt analyzes brilliantly as symptomatic of a deeper anxiety: "Flashes of thought, flights of fancy, idiomatic expressions, he sets down among the signs of the times—the extraordinary occurrences of the age we live in. They are marks of a restless and revolutionary spirit: they disturb his composure of mind, and threaten (by implication) the safety of the state" (*HW* 11:116). Nietzschean *ressentiment* is essentially negative, a form of stultifying "reaction" where impotent "feeling" (the "sentiment" in *ressentiment*) prevails over genuine "action."[11] In Hazlitt's view, then, Gifford's reactionary stance exemplifies a whole state's nervous response to the possible actions of a "restless and revolutionary spirit" in contemporary Britain. The episode recounted by Hunt turns into a "primal scene" which lays bare the mechanism of political struggle in terms of *ressentiment.* Literary warfare becomes political warfare, as their mutual gaze locks the two protagonists into a prolonged moment of silent, hostile combat.

Blake constructs a similar scene in *The Four Zoas:*

> Sullen sat Los plotting Revenge, Silent he eyed the Prince
> Of Light. Silent the Prince of Light view'd Los . . . (*BK* 273)

In a sense these lines reveal a further aspect of the confrontation between Hunt and Gifford. Blake represents Los as the man of *ressentiment,* "plotting Revenge"; but Urizen, "the Prince of Light," repeats Los's silent look, having been described, just two lines earlier, as "Indignant, muttering low thunders." In their gaze the two figures reflect each other's mutual resentment. And the same psychic structure lies concealed in the scene from Hunt's *Autobiography:* the ultimate cause of Gifford's resentment is Hunt's resentment of Gifford, the protesting "No" of the disaffected intellectual who takes it upon himself to criticize those in power.

A sale of books, which provides the occasion for a display of the politics of envy: I take this scene to be emblematic, an allegorical moment that makes visible important tensions in the "public sphere" of Romantic criticism.[12] The space in which criticism finds its voice is indeed a site of contest and "warfare," as Marilyn Butler points out: "Because writers represent groups and attitudes within the community, they come dynamically into contention with one another. They accordingly lose much of their vitality, their strongest, most urgent meanings, when read without the antagonists with whom they contend—the writers found formidable in their own generation, even if excised in ours."[13] One of my assumptions, then, is that we can begin to restore this context of antagonism, and map its precise contours, by tracing a very specific language of envy and resentment within the discursive field of Romantic criticism—a language which is crystallized in Hunt's description of his encounter with Gifford. Why do terms like *envy* and *malignant* appear so regularly in the writings of the period? Why are the so-called "creative" artists—poets, or painters—always ready to construe critical reaction to their work in terms of envy and resentment? If, as Hazlitt believed, the "prevailing spirit of modern literature" was "to defame men of letters" (*HW* 17:211), is the discourse of envy merely a symptom of "the special atmosphere of conflict and opposition" in which, according to Kelvin Everest, "the world of publishing is enveloped throughout the period"?[14] Or could this discourse have its roots elsewhere, implying a larger political and historical context within which Romantic criticism acquires its peculiar temper? Might the language of *ressentiment* tell us something not only about the literary culture of the period but also about the underlying "psychic economy" that helps to define that culture?[15] These are some of the questions providing the impulse behind what is intended to be, in the following pages, nothing more than a preliminary excursion into a very dense field.

II

Pope had warned against the carping critic's "malignant dull delight" in tracking down a writer's "slight faults" (*An Essay on Criticism,* 235–36);

by the time Goethe was complaining of the "criticizing and fragmentizing journals" prevalent in England in 1824, the idea of the critic's "malignancy" had become a commonplace.[16] Sending *Epipsychidion* to Charles Ollier for publication, Shelley desired to "make its author a secret, to avoid the malignity of those who turn sweet food into poison; transforming all they touch into the corruption of their own natures."[17] Wordsworth was likewise resigned to "the envy and malevolence, and all the bad passions which always stand in the way of a work of any merit from a living Poet" (*WL 1806–11* 145)—a feeling tactfully acknowledged by Charles Lamb, who, anxious to placate Wordsworth after his *Quarterly* review of *The Excursion* had been heavily edited by Gifford, maintained that "every *pretty* expression, (I know there were many) every warm expression, there was nothing else, is vulgarized & frozen."[18] And Blake, equal to Milton in his "profound awareness of the nature of envy,"[19] denounced the "pests of the Press" as "Rebellious Spirits of Envy & Malignity." Defending Fuseli's picture of Count Ugolino in a letter to the *Monthly Magazine,* Blake voices his "indignation" against "the widely diffused malice" of "those wretches who, under pretence of criticism, use the dagger and the poison." Writing to William Hayley, he complains that "in London every calumny and falsehood utter'd against another of the same trade is thought fair play. Engravers, Painters, Statuaries, Printers, Poets, we are not in a field of battle, but in a City of Assassinations. This makes your lot truly enviable, and the country is not only more beautiful on account of its expanded meadows, but also on account of its benevolent minds" (*BK* 841–42, 863–64, 847). Hayley's "lot" is "truly enviable" to Blake because it is, ironically, a world that does not know envy—a world inhabited solely by "benevolent minds" and thus purified of the "rancour of malevolence."[20]

It would be wrong, I think, to take these examples merely as anecdotal evidence of Horace's famous maxim on the irritability of poets. Nor is it simply a matter of personal "spleen." Patrick Parrinder quotes a remark from Coleridge's *Table Talk* which could serve as a cogent epigraph to the scene narrated by Hunt: "All men in power are jealous of the preeminence of men of letters; they feel, as towards them, conscious of inferior power, and a sort of misgiving that they are, indirectly, and against their own will, mere instruments and agents of higher intellects."[21] To say that Coleridge here "sounds slightly peevish as he manipulates the concept of power" is perhaps too facile; if his statement is a form of "manipulation," it is also a cunning revaluation of power relations in terms of *ressentiment.* And this new perspective cannot be reduced to personal psychology (Coleridge's "peevishness"); it should be seen, rather, as belonging to a larger cultural debate about the status of "men of letters" and the function of criticism within the public sphere—a debate which assumes unmediated conflict between "men in power" and "men of letters" and which consequently announces itself in the language of envy and resentment.

Nowhere is Coleridge's sense of this debate more sharp than in chapters 2 and 3 of *Biographia Literaria.* These are dismissed by Parrinder as "a tedious parade of self-defence against real and imagined enemies,"[22] but I should want to argue, rather, that Coleridge is demonstrating here a remarkable awareness of the way in which his "literary life" is indissolubly joined to—indeed, constituted by—the public sphere of contemporary periodical criticism. Here is the beginning of chapter 3:

> To anonymous critics in reviews, magazines, and news-journals of various name and rank, and to satirists with or without a name in verse or prose, or in verse-text aided by prose-comment, I do seriously believe and profess, that I owe full two thirds of whatever reputation and publicity I happen to possess. For when the name of an individual has occurred so frequently, in so many works, for so great a length of time, the readers of these works . . . cannot but be familiar with the name, without distinctly remembering whether it was introduced for an eulogy or for censure. (*CBL* 1:48–49)

Perhaps we need to read these sentences less as evidence of the poet's paranoia, and rather as a sober acknowledgment of the position of the English "man of letters" in 1817. Coleridge's "name" is constructed within the discursive realm of "reviews, magazines, and news-journals"; it is out of this textual space that his "literary life" is born and takes shape, all the time sustained by a dialectic of "eulogy" and "censure." Given this sense of himself being "authored" in the public sphere of criticism, it would seem logical for Coleridge to have devoted the previous chapter to a searching analysis of the "complex feeling, with which readers in general take part against the author, in favour of the critic." Why is the reading public so eager to apply "to *all* poets the old sarcasm of Horace upon the scribblers of his time" (*CBL* 1:30)? In fact it is not clear from the way in which he sets about answering this question whether Coleridge is alluding to the irritability of writers or the irritability of readers. The temporary confusion is, I think, deliberate, insofar as Coleridge will later conclude that it is a certain kind of disappointed *author* who turns into the typically captious *critic* (thereby confirming Byron's observation that "Our Bards and Censors are so much alike").[23]

In an uncanny premonition of Nietzsche, Coleridge identifies a certain "class" of "minds" who, suffering from "a debility and dimness of the imaginative power" and possessing "a deficient portion of internal and proper warmth," compensate for their weakness by seeking "a warmth in common, which they do not possess singly. Cold and phlegmatic in their own nature, like damp hay, they heat and inflame by co-acervation; or like bees they become restless and irritable through the increased temperature of collected multitudes." Like Nietzsche's "sick herd," which has banded together in order to make a virtue out of its weakness by embracing a "slave morality" based on resentment and envy,[24] these minds are necessarily prone to anger, since they are only too well aware of their own impotence: "The absence of all foundation within their own minds for that, which they yet believe both true and indispensable for their safety and happiness, cannot but produce an uneasy state of feeling, an involuntary sense of fear from which nature has no means of rescuing herself but by anger. Experience informs us that the first defence of weak minds is to recriminate" (*CBL* 1:31). Coleridge proceeds to categorize such men, "who possess more than mere talent, yet still want something of the creative, and self-sufficing power of absolute *Genius*" as "men of *commanding* genius," ever anxious to "impress their preconceptions on the world without, in order to present them back to their own view with the satisfying degree of clearness, distinctness, and individuality." Their rage for fame manifests itself "in tranquil times" in "palace, or temple, or landscape-garden"; but "in times of tumult" they "come forth as the shaping spirit of Ruin, to destroy the wisdom of ages in order to substitute the fancies of a day, and to change kings and kingdoms, as the wind shifts and shapes the clouds" (*CBL* 1:31, 32, 33). Thus they foreshadow Nietzsche's men of *ressentiment,* who betray their weakness through "an insatiable instinct and power-will that wants to become master not over something in life but over life itself, over its most profound, powerful, and basic conditions."[25] By contrast, "men of the greatest genius" display a Nietzschean strength, a "calm and tranquil temper," an "inward assurance of permanent fame," which leaves them "either indifferent or resigned, with regard to immediate reputation." Coleridge cites Chaucer, Shakespeare, Spenser, and Milton as examples of such men: they all embody "chearfulness," "evenness and sweetness of temper," "calmness," and "self-possession," without the "least trace of irritability" (*CBL* 1:33, 36).

At this point Coleridge's argument acquires a familiar look. These poets "of the greatest genius" belong to a golden age, a time, in Hazlitt's phrase, of "masculine boldness and creative vigour" (*HW* 16:213)—in comparison with which the present marks a falling away, a decline.[26] And this decline shows itself, through a paradox which is apparent rather than real, in "the multitude of books and the general diffusion of literature." One of the "lamentable effects" of "advanced stages of literature, when there exist many and excellent models" is that "a high degree of talent, combined with taste and judgement, and employed in works of imagination, will acquire for a man the *name* of a great genius." A man may now win a fleeting reputation as a writer because the "world of letters" has grown immeasurably since the time of Chaucer and Shakespeare, Spenser and Milton: "In whatever country literature is widely diffused, there will be many who mistake an intense desire to possess the reputation of poetic genius, for the actual powers, and original tendencies which constitute it" (*CBL* 1:37, 38). But the "diffusion of taste," as Hazlitt also argues, is "not the same thing as the improvement of taste"; the "world of letters" in 1817, transformed virtually beyond recognition from the public sphere consolidated a century earlier, is now a site of competition rather than collaboration, a market where "candidates for fame" and "pretenders to criticism" jostle with one another in an atmosphere of intense rivalry—where "the still-life of letters" is riven by "the tug and onset of contending factions" (*HW* 4:163; 17:39).

What Coleridge grasps with unerring perceptiveness is the "psychic economy" that underpins this state of affairs. In a "world of letters" which is now forced to obey "the laws of commodity production,"[27] disappointment and failure lie in wait for the aspiring poet, seduced as he is by a vision of immediate fame: "Men, whose dearest wishes are fixed on objects wholly out of their own power, become in all cases more or less impatient and prone to anger." In an aggressive world where the creation of poetry has given way to the "manufacturing of poems," what could be more natural than that failure should result in "suspicious and jealous irritability" (*CBL* 1:38, 39, 38)? And this, for Coleridge, precipitates the birth of the malignant critic: the logic of the literary marketplace dictates that "men, who being first scribblers from idleness and ignorance, next become libellers from envy and malevolence" (*CBL* 1:41). Quoting in the form of a footnote an observation from *The Friend* that "the sting of personal malignity" is spreading like an "epidemic distemper" through "almost every publication" in "this AGE OF PERSONALITY, this age of literary and political GOSSIPING," Coleridge asserts that these "libellers" acquire their "name" through an "appeal to the bad and malignant passions of mankind," and he offers a remarkably concise etiology of critical *ressentiment:*

> But as it is the nature of scorn, envy, and all malignant propensities to require a quick change of objects, such writers are sure, sooner or later, to awake from their dream of vanity to disappointment and neglect with embittered and envenomed feelings. Even during their short-lived success, sensible in spite of themselves on what a shifting foundation it rests, they resent the mere refusal of praise, as a robbery, and at the justest censures kindle at once into violent and undisciplined abuse; till the acute disease changing into chronical, the more deadly as the less violent, they become the fit instruments of literary detraction, and moral slander. (*CBL* 1:41–42)

Concerned ostensibly with the peculiar circumstances of his own literary life, Coleridge nevertheless demonstrates in his analysis of irritability an acute sensitiveness to the cultural temper of his moment. At this point it might be useful, then, to compare his account of the origins of critical *ressentiment* with similar arguments in the even more volatile realm of art criticism. In 1823 Hazlitt could suggest that "it is folly to talk of the divisions and backbitings of authors and poets while there are such people as painters in the world." "Devoured and consumed by envy," painters are their own worst critics. Their envy, "ludicrous if it were not lamentable," disqualifies them from the delicate task of judging pictures, a point that Hazlitt emphasizes by contrasting the sister arts: "Authors—even poets, the *genus irritabile*—do taste and acknowledge the beauties of the productions of their competitors; but painters either cannot see them through the green spectacles of envy, or seeing, they hate and deny them the more" (*HW* 18:181).

A few years earlier the Reverend R. A. Bromley had wondered whether there might be "any thing in the peculiar circumstances of fine art that should feed an envious and jealous disposition"[28]—a question that was to exercise writers on painting throughout the Romantic period but one that, as chapters 2 and 3 of *Biographia Literaria* testify, was not confined to a single artistic practice. The *Library of the Fine Arts* noted the "ill-blood" circulating "in secret and in private" among painters: "Each seems to envy the success of the other and to think that the reputation of one is raised on the ruins of that of another. This is human nature: and if from this littleness of mind even Titian was not exempt, need we wonder that less exalted artists should share this feeling of envy—this morbid horror of rivalry?"[29] But it is human nature mediated through very specific historical circumstances. Envy might be considered "the most universal passion" (*HW* 9:69), but Hazlitt recognized with Stendhal that it was also a peculiarly modern emotion: "As selfishness is the vice of unlettered periods and nations, envy is the bane of more refined and intellectual ones" (*HW* 12:87).[30] The contrast of "unlettered" and "intellectual" tacitly endorses Coleridge's theory that envy originates in the "diffusion of literature."

In the case of painting it is its specific *institutional* context that fans the flames of envy, particularly at a time when individual patronage is yielding to the more impersonal mechanisms of "corporate bodies" such as the Royal Academy. Hazlitt's typical "corporate body" manifests the same symptoms of intemperate *Schwärmerei* as the "collected multitudes" of Coleridge's weak minds: it is a place where "the principle of private or natural conscience is extinguished in each individual," where "the refinements of private judgment are referred to and negatived in a committee of the whole body," where "the torpedo-touch of so much inert matter operates to deaden the best feelings and harden the heart" (*HW* 8:264, 266).[31] Institutions, then, have the same deleterious consequences as criticism itself, insofar as they create a space in which envy can fester and breed. The occasion of the Royal Academy's fiftieth anniversary, in 1819, prompted the following observations from the *Literary Gazette:*

> It is true that in a large and open field of competition there is more hope of merit starting up than in one darkling and confined. But the result of an overstocked profession, like an overstocked trade, is to depreciate the material and debase its maker. At all events it augments the struggle for precedence, and it is, we fancy, owing to this, in a great measure, that party spirit runs so indecorously high among our artists, and that the complaints against the Academy, and especially against that portion of it vested with authority to regulate the Exhibitions, are so loudly and we must say so generally urged. The *Disappointed* naturally clamour about the neglect they have experienced or supposed; and the *Appointed* as naturally assert their right of judgment and privilege of place. Hence cabals have arisen, and the patrons of the arts, and the public, have been pestered about private grievances and squabbles, in which probably all sides are wrong, and the perfect knowledge of which *either way* would not advance the interests of the arts one iota.[32]

The situation is akin to that described by Coleridge: the diffusion of painting has the same "lamentable effects" as the diffusion of literature, producing, in Coleridge's terms, "an increase of sciolists" and all their "petulance and presumption." This "retrograde movement," with "the critic still rising as the author [sinks]" (*CBL* 1:57, 58, 59), is brilliantly captured in a Rowlandsonesque paragraph from the *Annals of the Fine Arts:*

> Surrounding the temple of Fame runs a deep and muddy ditch, into which all tumble who have neither strength, capacity, or head to cross the narrow plank that leads to the immortal doorway. Endless attempts, made during a series of ages, have filled this ditch with a set who are condemned for their presumption to howl and snarl and bite each other. Indeed, their only consolation is hooting at those who appear upon the narrow bridge which they have vainly endeavoured to get over, and their only happiness, if they can render his head so dizzy, and his heart so failing, that he ultimately tumbles into the dank mud with themselves. The moment a man of genius appears on the horizon, and long before they can see him, they feel his influence, as a sheep-dog does a thunder storm, and begin groaning and howling, to arrest his determined advance.[33]

The disastrous consequence of a general diffusion of taste is that the proper exercise of what Coleridge calls "argumentative criticism" or "permitted and legitimate censure" (*CBL* 2:108, 110) has no currency in the "marts of garrulity or detraction" that now constitute the public sphere of letters. In this modern Babel of competing voices "arbitrary dictation and petulant sneers" make it impossible for "fixed canons of criticism" to be established (*CBL* 1:54, 62). And it is at this point that Coleridge's analysis seems to reach its limit, an impasse beyond which it cannot move. To imagine, as Coleridge does in chapter 21 of *Biographia Literaria,* a domain of criticism founded on the "communication . . . between any number of learned men in the various branches of science and literature," who "administer judgement . . . on the two-fold basis of universal morals and philosophic reason" (*CBL* 2:110) is to project an impossibility, given the "profoundly oppositional spirit" of British criticism in 1817.[34] A belief in "fixed canons of criticism," then, suffers from the same kind of contradiction that Nigel Leask identifies in Coleridge's theory of Imagination.[35] Confronted by the unhappy reality that nothing is less "fixed" than the critical practice of contemporary journals, Coleridge's dedication to "canons of criticism" might be seen as a profoundly defensive measure, the mark of a desire for stability and order in a discursive world of ferment and flux.

Jon Klancher has argued that the early nineteenth century witnessed "social and textual interpretation on an unprecedented scale, a complex contention over a burgeoning culture's texts." It was "an unusually intense time of expounding and castigating texts," where emerging audiences were not only "exercising vastly different 'tastes'" but were also "taking shape as diverging collective interpreters whose 'readings' of the social and intellectual world opened unbridgeable cultural conflicts."[36] If this is indeed the case (and what more eloquent image of such "cultural conflict" than the confrontation between the editors of the *Examiner* and the *Quarterly Review* at a book auction?), then the notion of "fixed canons of criticism" begins to look nothing less than utopian: it assumes a space outside or beyond a contemporary public sphere whose critical practice is by its very nature unfixed, volatile, uncertain. Complaining that it has become "a deplorable [and] almost a universal fault of self-elected critics, and the writers in periodical works, to review the private character of authors with no less critical acumen than the public character of their books," the *European Magazine* concluded that "the present style of criticism" manifests an "utter ignorance of what criticism really is—it is the opinion of *Blackwood,* or of *Jeffrey,* the decision of the *Quarterly,* or the fiat of the *Westminster*—for these writers will all differ so essentially, and so loudly, that truth has little chance of being heard above them."[37]

In an important way this diagnosis repeats Coleridge's problematic belief in "fixed canons of criticism": while recognizing the actuality of contemporary journalistic practice, it stops short of the crucial perception that there is no "truth" that can be located beyond or outside the "essential differences" articulated through the opinions of rival journals. Criticism is constituted by these differences; that is its defining mark, what it "really is." Goethe's phrase—"criticizing and fragmentizing journals"—captures the point well: in their very mode of criticizing the journals are always already fragmenting stable notions of "truth" and "fixed canons." If truth is heard at all, it is heard only in fragmentary form, as it emerges fitfully in the "tug and onset of contending factions" within the reviews. Criticism "really is," then, nothing other than this fissure and fragmentation, this clamorous voicing of essential differences.

III

It is within this sphere of dissension and difference that we can situate Hazlitt's disquieting aphorism, "taste is often envy in disguise" (*HW* 20:331). For all his professed philosophical belief in the "natural disinterestedness of the human mind," Hazlitt recognizes that aesthetic judgment is never innocent; the look the critical eye casts on its object is always "motivated" in some way, always ready to modulate into a "jealous leer malign." The theory of an essential link between taste and envy is articulated most incisively in the *Plain Speaker* essay "On Envy." Constructed as a dialogue between Hazlitt and the painter James Northcote, the essay's drama resembles that of the psychoanalytic moment, where unsavory truths are disclosed, negated, reasserted. Herschel Baker notes that the presence of two voices lends "thrust and tension" to the argument, with Northcote appearing as "an alter ego for the writer, a persona who expresses Hazlitt's own doubts and self-contradictions."[38] Yet once again we should beware of reading the text solely as a piece of self-analysis. "On Envy" is also an essay on criticism, and it is no coincidence that Hazlitt's interlocutor is a professional painter. Throughout the dialogue Northcote's function is to question Hazlitt's apparently specious attempts to redefine envy in other, more acceptable terms. Thus Sir Walter Scott is cited by Hazlitt as an example of "the incongruities in human nature" that make unqualified praise difficult: "Who is there that admires the Author of Waverley more than I do? Who is there that despises Sir W***** S**** more? . . . The only thing that renders this *misalliance* between first-rate intellect and want of principle endurable is that such an extreme instance of it teaches us that great moral lesson of moderating our expectations of human perfection, and enlarging our indulgence for human infirmity." To which Northcote replies:

> You start off with an idea as usual, and torture the plain state of the case into a paradox. There may be some truth in what you suppose; but malice or selfishness is at the bottom of the severity of your criticism, not the love of truth or justice, though you may make it the pretext. You are more angry at Sir W***** S*****'s success than at his servility. You would give yourself no trouble about his poverty of spirit, if he had not made a hundred thousand pounds by his writings. The sting lies there, though you may try to conceal it from yourself.[39]

A similar rebuttal occurs when Hazlitt seeks to explain Wordsworth's antipathy to eighteenth-century verse as the result of mere "narrowness of taste": "I am satisfied that the fine turn of thought in Pope, the gliding verse of Goldsmith, the brilliant diction of Gray have no charms for the Author of the Lyrical Ballads: he has no faculty in his mind to which these qualities of poetry address themselves. It is not an oppressive, galling sense of them, and a burning envy to rival them, and shame that he cannot—he would not, if he could. He has no more ambition to write couplets like Pope, than to turn a barrel-organ." Northcote's intervention is again disconcerting, not least because of the way it anticipates Harold Bloom's theory of the anxiety of influence:

> You mistake the matter altogether. The acting principle in their minds is an inveterate selfishness or desire of distinction. They see that a particular kind of excellence has been carried to its height—a height that they have no hope of arriving at—the road is stopped up; they must therefore strike into a different path; and in order to divert the public mind and draw attention to themselves, they affect to decry the old models, and overturn what they cannot rival. They know they cannot write like Pope or Dryden, or would be only imitators if they did; and they consequently strive to gain an original and equal celebrity by singularity and affectation. Their simplicity is not natural to them: it is the *forlorn-hope* of impotent and disappointed vanity. (*HW* 12:102)

A key term here is "distinction." In the immediate context, of course, it is intended to express the modern poet's basic desire for recognition: artistic "distinction" is achieved (and belatedness overcome) by being "distinct" and different. But the word has social and political resonances as well: as Klancher points out, the "complex contention over a burgeoning culture's texts" was bound up with "the problem of social hierarchy, class structure, and the refashioning of a status-conscious society of 'ranks' typical of the eighteenth century into the more modern, lateral solidarities and conflicts of social class in the nineteenth."[40] And such social and political conflicts are repeated in the realm of taste, where any possibility of "fixed canons of criticism" is swept away by what Hazlitt calls "our modern polemics." "The love of distinction is the ruling passion of mankind," affirms Northcote; there is no contradiction between this and Hazlitt's belief that "envy is the most universal passion" because "love of distinction" is founded on envy—to assert our difference is "to grudge whatever draws attention from ourselves to others" (*HW* 12:100). Behind every positive assertion lurks a negative—so that, for example, "half the cant of criticism . . . is envy of the moderns, rather than admiration of the ancients" (*HW* 16:218). This is exactly the point made by Max Scheler in his description of *ressentiment* criticism:

> All the seemingly positive valuations and judgments of *ressentiment* are hidden devaluations and negations. Whenever convictions are not arrived at by direct contact with the world and the objects themselves, but indirectly through a critique of the opinions of others, the processes of thinking are impregnated with *ressentiment.* The establishment of "criteria" for testing the correctness of opinions then becomes the most important task. Genuine and fruitful criticism judges all opinions with reference to the *object itself. Ressentiment* criticism, on the contrary, accepts no "object" that has not stood the test of criticism. . . .
>
> The formal structure of *ressentiment* expression is always the same: *A* is affirmed, valued, and praised not for its own intrinsic quality, but with the unverbalized intention of denying, devaluating, and denigrating *B. A* is "played off" against *B.*[41]

Coleridge's wish for "a positive, not a comparative, appreciation" of the "*characteristic* excellencies, deficiencies, and defects" (*CBL* 2:107) of Wordsworth's poetry (a "genuine and fruitful criticism," in Scheler's terms) is consistent with his belief in "fixed canons of criticism"—and equally unattainable, because the reality of contemporary criticism is such that it depends and indeed thrives upon the "playing off" of differences. Northcote's diagnosis is brutal:

> Envy is like a viper coiled up at the bottom of the heart, ready to spring upon and poison whatever approaches it. We live upon the vices, the imperfections, the misfortunes, and disappointments of others, as our natural food. We cannot bear a superior or an equal. Even our pretended cordial admiration is only a subterfuge of our vanity. By raising one, we proportionally lower and mortify others. . . . We have one succession of authors, of painters, of favourites, after another, whom we hail in their turns, because they operate as a diversion to one another, and relieve us of the galling sense of the superiority of any one individual for any length of time. By changing the object of our admiration, we secretly persuade ourselves that there is no such thing as excellence. (*HW* 12:105–6)[42]

In his "social critique" of taste, aptly titled *Distinction,* Pierre Bourdieu maintains that "tastes (i.e., manifested preferences) are the practical affirmation of an inevitable difference. It is no accident that, when they have to be justified, they are asserted purely negatively, by the refusal of other tastes. In matters of taste, more than anywhere else, all determination is negation."[43] It is precisely this principle of negation, this play of inevitable differences, which is at the heart of Romantic periodical criticism, and which expresses itself in the language of *ressentiment.* Thus it is not merely spiteful gossip when a journal article alleges that Sir Thomas Lawrence "liked to see bad portraits beside his own, [because] they acted as foils";[44] informing this statement is the same logic that leads Northcote to admit, at the end of "On Envy," "I don't know that I do not admire Sir Joshua [Reynolds] merely as a screen against the reputation of bad pictures" (*HW* 12:107). And Blake would have concurred with the essay's final surmise that Reynolds's professed admiration of Michelangelo was intended "to get rid of the superiority of Titian, Rubens, and Rembrandt, which pressed closer on him, and 'galled his kibe more'" (*HW* 12:107).[45] "Aesthetic intolerance," says Bourdieu, "can be terribly violent." It would scarcely be an exaggeration, I think, to conclude that it is primarily in the language of envy that the violence of critical debate is expressed in Romantic writing.[46]

IV

In the textual evidence that has been marshaled so far, envy is generally assumed to be a malignant force. It guides those "weak minds" identified by Coleridge in their systematic attempt to thwart and block the expansive powers of "genius." Envy is always the enemy of true taste. When Thomas Love Peacock took the *Edinburgh Review* to task for its "wilful and fraudulent misrepresentation" of Coleridge's account of the versification of "Christabel," he wondered whether "any man [would] have ventured to do it if he had not felt conscious that in his capacity of critical purveyor he was catering not for liberality and taste but for envy and malignity."[47] The clear implication is that Coleridge's critic is nothing more than a "purveyor" of malicious untruths, deliberately "catering" to what another writer called "the vitiated palate of a sickly public."[48] And Peacock's choice of terms, where "liberality and taste" are opposed to "envy and malignity," sums up concisely Romanticism's essentially ambivalent view of the nature of criticism—its treacherous duality, already registered in Samuel Johnson's twofold definition of the critic as, first, "a man skilled in the art of judging literature," and, second, "a censurer, a man apt to find fault."[49] Judgment is "liberal" when it is receptive, open-minded, generous, and "genial"—when, presumably, it approaches the "positive" rather than "comparative" principles demanded by Coleridge. *Ressentiment* criticism, on the other hand, is profoundly "illiberal." In Hazlitt's opinion, it is none other than William Gifford who embodies illiberal criticism. As the editor of a journal that is "a receptacle for the scum and sediment of all the prejudice, bigotry, ill-will, ignorance, and rancour, afloat in the kingdom" (*HW* 9:14), Gifford represents "the spirit of the age" as the incarnation of *ressentiment.* Rancour, resentment, and envy dominate his writings and define the illiberal temper of the *Quarterly Review:*

> Its object is as mischievous as the means by which it is pursued are odious. The intention is to poison the sources of public opinion and of individual fame—to pervert literature, from being the natural ally of freedom and humanity, into an engine of priestcraft and despotism, and to undermine the spirit of the English constitution and the independence of the English character. The Editor and his friends systematically explode every principle of liberty, laugh patriotism and public spirit to scorn, resent every pretence to integrity as a piece of singularity or insolence, and strike at the root of all free inquiry or discussion, by running down every writer as a vile scribbler and a bad member of society, who is not a hireling and a slave. (*HW* 11:124)[50]

The imagery of "priestcraft and despotism" anticipates Nietzsche's figure of the "ascetic priest" who, like the Tory editor, is supremely adept at mobilizing the forces of *ressentiment* and putting them to effective use.[51] Thus the *Quarterly Review* is *ressentiment* institutionalized, its primary function "systematically [to] explode every principle of liberty," whether political or intellectual. Gifford is hostile to "free inquiry or discussion" because he is imprisoned by his own "narrowness of feeling" (*HW* 11:125). Like Nietzsche's man of *ressentiment,* whose "soul squints,"[52] Gifford takes a "microscopic view" of things, pernickety and mean: "There is nothing liberal, nothing humane in his style of judging: it is altogether petty, captious, and literal" (*HW* 11:116, 115). Envy of this kind paralyzes progress. In "The Periodical Press" (1823), Hazlitt salutes the modern enfranchisement of letters: "The *Monarchism* of literature is at an end; the cells of learning are thrown open, and let in the light of universal day. We can no longer be churls of knowledge, ascetics in pretension. We must yield to the spirit of change" (*HW* 16:220).[53] The use of the archaic "churls" is evidently intended to signify the oppressive regime of "priestcraft and despotism" from which modern criticism has apparently emancipated itself. But Gifford, the type of new ascetic obdurately resistant to "the spirit of change," sulks like one of Nietzsche's "cellar rodents full of vengefulness and hatred,"[54] who conspires to keep the "cells of learning" locked shut, and whose "narrow, hood-winked perceptions" serve only "to destroy, to 'crib and cabin,' all enjoyments and opinions but [his] own" (*HW* 11:116; 8:224). The gaze of *ressentiment* criticism is a baleful one: like the "juggling eyes" of Apollonius in Keats's *Lamia,* it has the power to blight and ruin whatever it looks upon.

However, I want to propose, by way of conclusion, that Hazlitt admits a contrary view of envy; there are signs in his text of a desire to retrieve from this "astringent and unpopular word" a more constructive and enabling significance.[55] Although he takes it to be "one of the most tormenting and odious of the passions," Hazlitt also concedes that envy is among the "natural secretions of the human heart," and that, as "the most universal passion," envy may have an unsuspected privilege in shaping "the movements and irregularities of passion and opinion which take place in human nature" (*HW* 20:311–12, 322; 17:310). While Lamb could thank God for having "the ingenuousness to be ashamed" of envy and jealousy—"bad passions" to which he admitted he was "not insusceptible"[56]—Hazlitt is rather more unmisgiving and pragmatic. He is prepared to concede that envy, "odious" though it is, is an emotion necessary to life—and particularly necessary, perhaps, to the life of modern criticism. If "literature in our day" has indeed taken a "decided turn into a critical channel" (*HW* 16:212), and if envy is a peculiarly modern condition ("the bane of more refined and intellectual [periods and nations]"), then—by the same logic that reveals envy to be the disguised "other" of taste—it would seem that the conjunction of criticism and envy is historically inevitable, and indeed necessary. The more positive function of envy can only begin to be discerned once the necessity of a strategic alliance between criticism and envy has been acknowledged. When Hazlitt announces that "the *Monarchism* of literature is at an end," he evidently wants us to think of the emancipation of letters in terms of the great political revolution of 1789, whereby the paralyzing *ressentiment* of the old regime (represented in the British establishment by the *Quarterly Review* and its editor) is shattered by a "spirit of change." Yet this spirit of change is itself the product of envy—not the "reactive" envy of a Gifford, which seeks to thwart all possibility of progress in the name of a servile adherence to the status quo, but rather the active envy that has, in Hazlitt's words, "a mixture of the love of justice in it" (*HW* 9:169). In this sense envy is comparable in its moral potential to hating:

without it, "we should lose the very spring of thought and action." Just as "life would turn to a stagnant pool, were it not ruffled by the jarring interests, the unruly passions of men" (*HW* 12:128), so history itself would stagnate, were it not ruffled by the jarring, unruly, and unsettling intervention of envy. It is this kind of envy that Gifford discovers in Hunt (and that makes him "querulous" and "angry")—the resentful and therefore threatening discontent of the radical at odds with the political establishment. Pressed into the service of political critique, envy now contributes to the historical process of intellectual and political emancipation.[57]

Criticism, remarks Northcote in his biography of Reynolds, has "the fatal tendency to paralyze those laudable and energetic efforts to produce works, without which criticism could not exist: criticism is the child that devours its own parent!"[58] And Northcote's colleague at the Royal Academy, Martin Archer Shee, complained endlessly about the current "bigotry of criticism," which was impeding the progress of art by stimulating an "intellectual climate that in a general frost of feeling, nips the tender growth of Taste."[59] From the point of view of the creative artist, then, the new "critical channel" would seem to be systematically narrowing and contracting what Wordsworth calls "the mind's *excursive* power" (*The Excursion* IV.1263). But in an age when the French Revolution continued to be the "master theme,"[60] the image of the child devouring its parent acquires a particular resonance. The envy of the young in collision with the envy of the old, each position constituting the other within the "autoreferential" structure of *ressentiment:* this is one way of representing the spirit of change in an age of revolution.[61] Indeed, it is a trope that infiltrates Hazlitt's text at various important junctures. For example, in his *Table-Talk* essay on "certain inconsistencies" in Reynolds's *Discourses,* Hazlitt concludes that "there is something fastidious and sickly in Sir Joshua's system. His code of taste consists too much of negations, and not enough of positive, prominent qualities. . . . It is, I fear, more calculated to baffle and perplex the student in his progress, than to give him clear lights as to the object he should have in view, or to furnish him with strong motives of emulation to attain it." Consisting "too much of negations," Reynolds's system of imitation "limits nature and paralyses art" (*HW* 8:144, 145); the student's "progress" will be baffled and perplexed by the constraining "no" of what is ultimately an aesthetics of *ressentiment.*

The same criticism is leveled at another great father-figure with whom Hazlitt had to contend. Edmund Burke's *Reflections on the Revolution in France* is described as "a spiteful and dastard but too successful attempt to *put a spoke in the wheels* of knowledge and progressive civilization, and throw them back for a century and a half at least" (*HW* 19:273).[62] And then there is Coleridge. Taking issue with the contemptuous allusion, in *The Statesman's Manual,* to the emergence of a modern "READING PUBLIC," which diets at "the two public *ordinaries* of literature, the circulating libraries and the periodical press," Hazlitt demands:

> For what have we been labouring for the last three hundred years? Would Mr. Coleridge, with impious hand, turn the world "twice ten degrees askance," and carry us back to the dark ages? Would he punish the *reading public* for their bad taste in reading periodical publications which he does not like, by suppressing the freedom of the press altogether, or destroying the art of printing? He does not know what he means himself. Perhaps we can tell him. He, or at least those whom he writes to please, and who look "with jealous leer malign" at modern advantages and modern pretensions, would give us back all the abuses of former times, without any of their advantages; and impose upon us, by force or fraud, a complete system of superstition without faith, of despotism without loyalty, of error without enthusiasm, and all the evils, without any of the blessings, of ignorance. (*HW* 16:106)

In each case Hazlitt's strategy is the same: to turn the older authority into a figure of paternal *ressentiment,* whose "jealous leer malign" seeks to dampen the aspirations of youth, to block "modern advantages and modern pretensions." This critical maneuver might itself be taken as an expression of *ressentiment* or envy; but its intentions are active and liberating, rather than reactionary and illiberal. *Ressentiment* turns into a *resistance* to the "envious commands" imposed by the tyrannical father-figure.[63] And Hazlitt's specific challenge to Coleridge here allows us to grasp, finally, the nature of the difference between the two greatest Romantic critics. In *Biographia Literaria* Coleridge wants to believe in the possibility of transcending the material conditions of contemporary critical practice by establishing "fixed canons of criticism," principles that would be independent of the sordid burden of history. Hazlitt, by contrast, readily acknowledges the new public sphere of journalistic criticism to be historically, as well as politically, necessary, despite its manifold divisions and discord. If "the standing pool of criticism" (*HW* 11:28) has its surface ruffled by envy and other unruly passions, this is just one instance of how "the still-life of letters" acquires political significance within the public sphere. It is such frictions that might set "the true revolutionary leaven" to work. As Hazlitt says in one of his most arresting sentences, "a little of the alloy of human frailty may be allowed to lend its aid to the service of humanity" (*HW* 17:40). By the same logic can he appropriate the language of envy and reinscribe it as a positive force within the discourse of criticism.

Philip W. Martin

Authorial Identity and the Critical Act: John Clare and Lord Byron

Lord Byron poh—the man wot rites the werses
And is just what he is and nothing more
—*John Clare,* Don Juan

Criticism in the Romantic period is a practice intricately caught up with politics, both in the sense of our being able to identify party or ideological positions in its particular discourses, and in the broader sense of politics as a set of relations existing between institutional structures—in this case those of writer, critic, and audience. My main focus in this chapter is on the politics of criticism in this wider sense, taking as a specific example John Clare's "imitation" of Byron.

Clare's late poems *Child Harold* and *Don Juan,* and chiefly the latter, are critical acts themselves, as any discourse that is a palimpsest of a kind must be, writing over another text even while evoking its presence and therefore presuming to mediate that original text to its reader. As will be seen, however, this is not the only dimension of criticism that is alive in Clare's palimpsest poems, since they bear within them the signs of his own fraught relations with the reviewers. They also have a fascination as repositories of Byron's critical heritage: Clare's toying with author identity follows a predominant tendency in Byron's reviewers to scramble or unscramble the poet and the persona, or the poet and the hero. Clare's tacit but witting reference to that history is perhaps more resonant than he knows: his deliberate confusion of authors in these poems raises questions about the point of textual origin, but more, provokes the larger question, axiomatic in the Romantic expressive paradigm, of how authorial identity is rendered or granted.

Clare's interest in plagiarism has been remarked before and is easily documented. Here, in these late Byronic poems, he resumes a vigorous imitative energy to engage combatively with the Romantic tradition of individual inspiration. The place of the poem's beginnings is now another text; the scene of writing changes its imaginary site, from the abstract and private notion of the authorial intelligence or the "genial spirit," to that which is material and public. Accordingly, the figuring of readership within Clare's poems runs counter to that dominant tradition within Romanticism which declares the poet "a man speaking to men," or indeed, the originator of words scattered "among mankind." That sense of the poem issuing from a private place to an undifferentiated audience, posterior or contemporary, is displaced by a model that represents writing as essentially intertextual and public. Clare writes within and out of Byron's most famous and notorious poetry, a poetry wherein the phenomenon of Byronism was constructed (in *Childe Harold*) and then most ironically metamorphosed (in *Don Juan*). These poems, beyond all others that Byron wrote apart from *Beppo,* display the theater of authorship itself; more importantly, *Don Juan*'s theater includes the materialization of an audience in its modes of address which figure—albeit aggressively—a homogenous reading public held together by its protocols of reading. Writing within this arena, Clare in his late poems does not therefore ask simple questions about author identity, but complex ones about the symbiosis of "author" and "audience."

How is it then, that authorial identity can be figured in the Romantic public text, or—in elaborate pretense—conferred in the text's playing to an audience? As Jerome Christensen's recent study of Byron has shown, Byron's career as a public poet is an ideal place for that question to be situated. Christensen argues that "Byron's public life begins in contention: a state of obligatory reciprocity between the aristocratic poet and the self-confirmed arbiters of culture" and he goes on to demonstrate how the passage into the "symbolic order" of authorship is compounded by George Gordon's accession to his title, at which point his naming as "Byron" is caught up with the aristocratic imperative of the motto "Crede

Byron."[1] Christensen's subtle analysis sits easily alongside Peter Manning's case for *Beppo* as a poem that remakes Byron's name through strategies of anonymity.[2] These arguments are at one in their highlighting of the public dimensions of author identity and the necessity of understanding the idea of authorship in what has been called elsewhere a "pragmatic poetics of audience."[3]

By "authorial identity" therefore, I do not allude to the presupposition—which so easily obtrudes into the reading of Romantic poetry—that there is a real self somehow struggling to be expressed. Indeed, much of the problematizing within Romantic poetry itself, even without the interventions of modern critical theory, seems set on disturbing or displacing that very notion, and Clare too absorbs the contemporary habit, writing Byronic poems that deconstruct the popular notion of the poet's subjectivity. "Authorial identity" here refers to something far more public, more akin perhaps to Stephen Greenblatt's notion of self-fashioning: the making of a reputation for authors through the act of critical interpellation in which their own declarations of selfhood play a part; the hailing of an author with sets of attributes which in turn become textual agencies or characteristics in subsequent poems and their criticism.[4] Such a currency has bequeathed us "Byron" as a big signifier, more deeply developed in its connotative than its denotative function, and "Clare" as a slightly smaller one, perhaps given that relatively little has accrued in the cultural fund from which such connotative reference derives.

The politics of Romantic reviewing consists of this process of the making and breaking of public identity. The poetry's traveling between writer and reader is intercepted by that voice of authority which, as Jon Klancher points out, constructs an audience. It is worth adding to this that just as audiences are made out of readers, so authors are made out of writers.[5] Romantic criticism is not monolithic in opinion, but its warring voices function together to speak for and of authors and audiences. Characteristically, it assumes a plural authority that is simultaneously able to adopt the mask of democracy, a guise which enables such criticism to persuade the reader of its representative or majority opinion. To refuse the identity asserted by critical interpellation is a formidable if not impossible task: theoretically, it is to exert the writer's citizenship against the autocratic powers that deny those rights in declaring authors and audiences to be bound together or split apart by the very notion of a public taste. Yet it is this feeling of fellow-citizenry, I suggest, that causes Clare to bind himself to Byron, and the act simultaneously marks out a late attempt and perhaps a political displacement of a kind, to recover that subversive intent discernible in all the canonical Romantic writers at various points in their lives.[6]

The issue of identity, then, is always charged with these relations of power and control, relations that Clare, in his poem *Don Juan* brings to the foreground in a most spectacular way:

> Lord Byron poh—the man wot rites the werses
> And is just what he is and nothing more.[7]

The manifold complexities of these lines and their allusions will be returned to. At this point I wish only to note how they might interleave with equivalent lines of resistance in Byron, where the writer interpellates his own author in playful opposition to that simulated by the reviewers:

> But I am a nameless sort of person
> (A broken Dandy lately on my travels) . . .[8]

Such passages in Byron are well known, and have been the subject of extensive commentary, so that now few would quarrel with a description of *Don Juan* as a highly self-reflexive poem, a poetical *Tristram Shandy,* as Hazlitt was quick to observe. Even so, the situating of this textual feature within the context provided by the habits of Romantic critical reviewing is less readily assumed or acknowledged, so that while we know *Don Juan* as a self-reflexive aesthetic construct, we are not so familiar with it as a poem thoroughly integrated into the field of social practice supplied by the reviewing habits of the day. To move the poem into this context is hardly contentious. It places on us an obligation to investigate the status of some of its commentary, to question whether the poem, broadly, is in dialogue with its imagined reviewers or not.

The main focus of my argument here, however, will not be on this matter, but on Clare's identification of Byron's poetry as a textual region antipathetic to the overbearing invasions of critical reviewing which tended to center on the question of authorship and identity. Beyond that, I will be suggesting that this critical bid to construct author identities, in reaction to and against authorial personae, is tied up with the question of politics. Both Clare and Byron, in different ways, found themselves depoliticized authors from an early stage. Marilyn Butler has argued that in Byron's case this was achieved by the reading that produced the Byronic hero as a "sanitized" figure . . . "drained of ideological content" whose possible political significance is displaced by an essentially psychological curiosity.[9] Byron's heroes, most obviously Childe Harold, have a potentially political resonance (in *Childe Harold* this develops well beyond the putative stage, of course) that is muted by a critical concern with ethics and metaphysics. In Clare's case the depoliticization is to be seen more materially, as his patrons demand that the "indelicacies" of the first edition of *Poems Descriptive* are removed for the second edition, "indelicacies" which not only have a political significance in their vernacular impropriety but also in the polemic against "wealth" in the first published version of the poem "Helpstone." *Don Juan*—and in this instance I use the title to refer to a textual locus that is constituted by Byron's poem and Clare's—is the place at which the repoliticizing strategies of writing occur. For both poets, it is a textual region in which a display of risqué innuendo undermines critical control or interpretation, in which the author observes himself in the moments of his textual construction, and most importantly, a place in which part of that self-fashioning involves the articulation of political polemic.

For Byron, of course, those writing strategies are fully tested in the public arena, and the evidence of their successful disturbances is there to be seen: in the farcical affair of Roberts and the Grandmother's review (*BLJ* 6:213); in Murray's nervousness and John Hunt's assumption of publication (a material political change of a particularly important kind); in Hazlitt's devastating and insightful remark that in *Don Juan,* Byron "would force them [the public] to admire in spite of decency and common sense—he would have them read what they would read in no one but himself . . . he is equally averse to notice or neglect, enraged at censure and scorning praise." (*HW* 11:76). Clare's poem is of a different order in that it was never published: I am less concerned in this case with its public effect, therefore, and in discussion I will concentrate on the identification of a writing strategy that derives from a regard for a hypothetical audience.

Don Juan is in one sense the end point of a prevalent Romantic anxiety attending the act of publication. Some consideration, therefore, needs to be given to the beginnings of Byron and Clare and the construction of author identities, in particular in the announcements made about their poetical selves. Clare's neglected poems *Child Harold* and *Don Juan* have their determinants, I suggest, in his anxiety about critical reception, his realization of "a critical presence or audience as an otherness within discourse"[10] and in a concomitant desire to inhabit the Byronic oeuvre as a location that offers resistance to a critical tyranny. That desire has its origin in Clare's awkward inauguration as a major poet with the publication of *Poems Descriptive* in 1820, and in particular, his unhappy relations with his patrons over the censorship of the second edition. The issue is nevertheless much broader. Clare was to make a myth out of Byron's independence, preferring to see him as a writer unimpaired by the politics of patronage. Byron's early relations with Lord Holland, however, indicate that the public self Byron was conceiving in 1812 was one highly dependent on patronage. As I argued above, Clare's implicit reference to Byron's reception mobilizes a history larger than the myth he cherished.

It might readily be forgotten that Byron's ambitions for a place in public life in 1812 were focused on making an entry into politics. At this time he was making considerable efforts through Lord Holland to ease himself into the Whig oligarchy. Two days before making his maiden speech on the frame breakers in the House of Lords, Byron's anxiety to receive the seal of moderate Whig approval through Holland is clear:

> I believe your Lordship does not coincide with me entirely on this subject, & most cheerfully & sincerely shall I submit to your superior judgment & experience, & take some other line of argument against ye. bill, or be silent altogether, should you deem it more adviseable.—Condemning, as every one must condemn the conduct of these wretches, I believe in ye. existence of grievances which call rather for pity than for punishment.—I have ye honour to be with great respect, my Lord, yr. Lordship's
>
> most obedt. & obliged Servt.
>
> BYRON
>
> P.S.—I am a little apprehensive that your Lordship will think me too lenient towards these men, & *half a framebreaker myself.* (*BLJ* 2:165–66)

Pleased with his public display as politician ("I have had many marvellous eulogies"), Byron made a private and anonymous debut as a domestic political poet, publishing his "Ode to the Framers of the Frame Bill" in the *Morning Chronicle* on March 2. Eight days later, *Childe Harold* appeared, and Byron had already sent Holland a copy with an apology for his defamation of Holland and the Whig *Edinburgh Review* in *English Bards*. The moment of *Childe Harold,* then, is the moment at which Byron's political self-fashioning is subverted by a poetical self-fashioning. So significantly, for the poet himself and later for Clare's identification of him, that poetical self-fashioning and what Greenblatt calls (following Clifford Geertz) its "control mechanisms" produce the Byronic "authentic" self, a self beyond the trappings of outward show:[11]

And dost thou ask, what secret woe
I bear, corroding joy and youth?
And wilt thou vainly seek to know
A pang, ev'n thou must fail to soothe?

It is not love, it is not hate,
Nor low Ambition's honours lost,
That bids me loathe my present state,
And fly from all I Priz'd the most:

It is that weariness which springs
From all I meet, or hear, or see:
To me no pleasure Beauty brings;
Thine eyes have scarce a charm for me.

It is that settled, ceaseless gloom
The fabled Hebrew wanderer bore;
That will not look beyond the tomb,
But cannot hope for rest before.

What exile from himself can flee?
To Zones, though more and more remote.
Still, still pursues, where-e'er I be,
The blight of life—the demon, Thought. (*Childe Harold,* I.837–60)

"What exile from himself can flee?" The question rhetorically confirms the ineluctability of authentic selfhood while the whole lyric, with equal insistence, remarks that the authenticity is readable even while its historical detail defies hypothetical textualization. Despite the elaborate but somewhat confused framing of speakers that produces this lyric as the Childe's, Byron's public took up the idea of an essential and individual autonomy to be located in the poet behind the poetry. Thus even though *Childe Harold*'s complexity consists of a performing self which paradoxically nominates an actual self that is permanently undisclosed, darkly hidden, the Byron phenomenon of 1812–16 depended partly on the reading audience's sense of access to that essentiality.

That *Childe Harold* and its success created a dominant persona for Byron is a commonplace, but the various coordinates of this event are easily ignored. *Childe Harold* was published at a moment of great provincial unrest. Disruptions in British trade with Europe and America led to the serious recession compounded by high food prices following bad harvests. Luddites were on the move, breaking up machines in the east Midlands, south Lancashire, and west Yorkshire, and there were food riots.[12] Secret committees were formed in the North to promote and protect acts of insurrection; there were murders and arrests. The large riot in Manchester in April 1812 which saw a mob of three thousand take over the town hall may seem a long way from the success of Byron's poem in London in the same month, but in a way, it is not. As Byron hesitatingly enters the public realm of political discourse in the House of Lords, he attempts to situate himself, in the letter to Holland, in a safer class context than that intimated by his speech: he wishes to be inside the Holland House circle ("I am a little apprehensive that your Lordship will think me . . . *half a framebreaker myself*"). The success of *Childe Harold* intervenes to displace that emergent political persona lodged insecurely on the wrong side of moderate Whig policy, and allows him into that circle. The politics of the subsequent verse tales of 1812–16 in locating injustice and the oppressed as subjects for foreign policy or foreign governments effectively espouses freedom in groups away from home. At the same time, the poet as subject emerges as a free spirit of liberal and independent thought. The ideological effect of Byron's interpellation, the process of his recognition through the reviews and his public success, is to reposition his discourse of unrest. Simultaneously, his attempt to secure Whig patronage of the highest pedigree is made redundant; his public identity is of another kind, and his putative relation to Holland as a father figure makes little sense in the new relations of power induced by celebrity.

In this way Byron's patron for his entry into politics is replaced by the patronage of the reviews that undertook to construct his new reputation:

> Who Childe Harold was, we are wholly at a loss to inform the inquirer. We only know that his satiated appetite is said to have made him selfish, gloomy, discontented and suspicious; and we are warned against supposing that any real personage is represented by him. In some trivial and local particulars, it is indeed admitted that grounds might exist for such a notion; and certainly those tourists, who have visited Newstead Abbey, will easily recognise its likeness. . . . No effect is produced, no incident created, by this imaginary *Childe,* who in the whole poem does nothing but go over the ground which Lord Byron traversed, write verses very much in the style of the detached pieces

at the end of the volume, and make remarks and observations which might with equal possibility have occurred to his Lordship's own mind. Indeed, when we read of him, we involuntarily think of the author . . .[13]

By the end of the second decade, this notion of Byron as a "distempered spirit" had gained a considerable hold, and the interpellation of the author as a congeries of emotional trauma had become a settled habit.[14] Indeed, to some reviewers, the idea of Byron's emotional transparency made him unique: "There is something quite new and peculiar, indeed, in the whole career of Byron. . . . He seems to have identified his character with his writings; his poetry, at least a considerable portion of it, is a mirror in which are reflected the movements of his soul."[15] Byron's *Don Juan* might be profitably read as a refusal to comply with such a construction. Clare's identification of this poem, and *Childe Harold* (which inaugurated this version of the author) as the manuscripts for his palimpsests was particularly appropriate for the problematization of authorial identity. For in one sense these poems had confounded the critics: as *Childe Harold* had encouraged the emergence of the pageant of the bleeding heart, so *Don Juan* had exploded it. Clare's experience with the reviewers had been markedly different in detail, but equally powerful in effect, and to one in his circumstances, probably more so.

Clare's entry into the arena of Romantic writing in 1820, with his first volume *Poems Descriptive of Rural Life and Scenery,* was as nervous and as tentative as that of any other of the Romantic poets. In addition, his commodification as a "peasant poet" adds a further dimension, the manipulation of a class heritage that simultaneously was being put into a reversed charge for Keats, the "cockney" poet. The details of Clare's beginnings have been well documented elsewhere[16] but the same uneasy passage can also be marked out by a different series of indicators: those of Clare's writing as he confronts the prospect of the authorial self, the nomination of his name as writer. The manuscript book that Clare bought from Henson the bookseller allowed him to translate his writing practice into a hypothetically public realm. The book has a hand-drawn inscription on its first page, as follows:

A Rustic's Pastime
in Leisure hours;
J. Clare;
1814[17]

Evidently a mimicry of a printed book, the manuscript book presents the spectacle of the public self held within the province of private experience. In one sense, this is a fantasy which surrenders independence in the conventions of writing it adopts, yet maintains it with the signature, the marking out of the book as Clare's property, because it is in his hand, and remains, literally, in his hands. Nevertheless, the conventions begin to speak for Clare and construct him as a writer. First a certain anonymity is established by the indefinite article: an anonymity both surrendered and retained in the inscription of the name, "J. Clare"—the initializing of the Christian name being an erasure of the self already known, significant I think, in the context of the reclamation of that self exemplified in one of the last poems Clare ever wrote, "To John Clare," in which he addresses John Clare as "Honest John." The priority of identity is thus given to that signified by "A Rustic" and the effect of this, in turn, is to declare a strong relation to a tradition of bucolic poetry with a pastoral genesis: poetry is the pastime that succeeds labor.

Of course it might almost go without saying that the regularity of rustic life implied by this title was a long way from the conditions of Clare's life in this period. Regular employment in the fields was almost impossible to find, although some work at hay time and harvest could be secured. The effects of enclosure in creating a temporary wage-labor force and an unemployed sector are commonly understood; equally familiar perhaps is Clare's inveighing against such effects and the enclosure of his district by an act passed in 1809. Out of work in the years 1810–14, Clare tried to enlist twice in the local militia (the second time successfully); he probably joined "catchwork gangs," and he worked as a gardener.[18] According to his own account in the "Autobiography," he found it very difficult to write under the eye of his employers. Before his poems were published in 1820, he was forced to seek employment in Rutland as a lime burner (sometimes having to work right through the night to clear his debts) and again, as a gardener. In all probability, most of his poetry was written in times of unemployment.[19]

What we are confronted with here is evidently a kind of self-fashioning: the distance between Clare's real circumstances and those connoted by his inscription in the manuscript book I adduce not to complain of the "falsity" of literature, but to demonstrate the extreme self-consciousness that attends Clare's nomination of himself as author. The provinces of cultural control are here clearly marked out: the author constructed upon the title page is neither a confused identity nor a delusion, but a spectacle of a kind, evolved in the act of writing itself. Later in his life, indeed, in

1821, Clare was to complain that his being sought out as a celebrity was nothing less than a peep show.[20]

The manuscript elaborates this further and yet opposes it too, in an undated fragment evidently included as an address or preface. I will place this in sequence with the other early announcements of Clare contrived to attend his entry into the public realm: the address in Henson's prospectus and the erased dedication from *Poems Descriptive.*

> As the ensuing Trifles are nothing but the simple productions of an Unlettered Rustic their faults and Imperfections will undoubtedly be nothing more than what might be expected—as correct composition and Gramatical accuracy can never be lookd for from one whose mental facculties (such as they were) being continually overburthend and depressd by hard labour which fate ordained to be his constant employment—It is hoped that the unnoticd Imitation should any occur (being unknown to the author) will not be deem'd as Plagarisms as the humble station of life in which providence has placed him has ever debarred him from Reaping that advantage of extending his knowledge.[21]

Here, held in tandem with the fashioning of a writer, is the image of the laborer: more, there is a sense of an oppressed self (the writer) struggling to emerge from the conditions in which "Providence" has cast him. Notably, these conditions do not denote the jocund rustic, but an oppressed class—the *overburdened,* the *depressed.* This is a complex interpellation. The conventions dictate the deferential and apologetic mode which hails the writer as uncomplaining or at least fatalist (the conditions are the result of providence) but the descriptive vocabulary speaks for a position of exploitation and excess beyond the norm. If Clare's self-fashioning demonstrates an imperfect handling of the conventions, or more, the desire to preserve both selves in writing, then Henson's advertisement censors out that part of his discourse that threatens its deferential aspect with an ironic inflection. In the prospectus, Clare is interpellated as a figure worthy of indulgence. Here there is no sense of an oppressed and struggling writer, but an illegitimate mode of writing:

> The public are requested to observe, that the Trifles humbly offered for their candid perusal can lay no claim to eloquence of composition, (whoever thinks so will be deceived,) the greater part of them being *Juvenile* productions; and those of a later date offsprings of those leisure intervals which the short remittance from hard and manual

labour sparingly afforded to compose them. It is hoped that the humble situation which distinguishes their author will be some excuse in their favour, and serve to make an atonement for the many inaccuracies and imperfections that will be found in them. The least touch from the iron hand of *Criticism* is able to crush them to nothing, and sink them at once to utter oblivion. May they be allowed to live their little day . . .[22]

Clare was not long content to allow this apparatus to speak for him. When Octavius Gilchrist wrote the dedication for *Poems Descriptive,* he wrote to Taylor to decline it on the grounds that it was "too Refined and Elegant to flow from the pen of a Clown," a gesture which suggests either a sharp-edged irony or his preference for the illegitimate mode of the peasant poet. In this letter, Clare included his own dedication to his patron, Lord Milton, a dedication apparently orthodox in its declarations of dependency:

> To the Right Honourable Charles William Lord Viscount Milton These artless Rural Delineations are most humbly and unostentatiously inscribed with the gratitude of the Northamptonshire Peasant who feeling the blessings of his Lordships benevolence to an helpless and afflicted Parent thus dares to declare his admiration and thankfulness.[23]

The nature of this genuflexion, nevertheless, is to mark conspicuously Clare's economic position, alluded to doubly in his nomination as peasant and his allusion to Lord Milton's unlucky aiding of his father (who, at this time, incidentally, was receiving parish relief).[24]

Clare's attempts to speak for himself within what he took to be the conventions demanded of him were never printed. Taylor was unhappy with this dedication and took it out. Clare's introduction to the literary world was implemented by Taylor himself in an introductory essay to *Poems Descriptive,* and by Octavius Gilchrist in an essay in the *London Magazine,* "Some Account of John Clare, an Agricultural Labourer and Poet." Neither of these essays set out to sentimentalize Clare. They both include details of his straitened circumstances and his family's difficulties. Other voices attending Clare's first publication nevertheless took some hints from these essays to produce a version of the poet with a powerful contemporary mythology:

> There nature's dictates, unadorn'd by art,
> She sweetly tells; and powerful, doth impart

Those moral precepts—in such simple strain
We read—we wonder—and respect the swain.
Hail! native Genius! bred in lowly vale . . .

(Eliza Emmerson)

Hail! Pleasing Poet; though distrest, and poor,
Thy richer Genius Nature can display;
And though unskill'd in deep and classick lore,
Her varied Beauties faithfully portray.

(anonymous)[25]

While there are clear signs in these dedicatory poems of the sense of the "mute, inglorious Milton," and even clearer signs of the gifts of artlessness to be nurtured by gradual acculturation that derives from Beattie's *The Minstrel,* elements of both formulae combine with the Wordsworthian notion of the poet as Nature's child. Thus it is that Clare's contemporary culture speaks for him in the moment of his public inception, despite his own erased attempts to preface his poetry through conventions that shaped him as a laborer and a poet.

Within a month of the first edition of *Poems Descriptive,* as is well known, a small controversy evolved about the volume's "indelicacies": among them, its attack on wealth and enclosure in "Helpstone," and the use of colloquialisms in "My Mary" (where Clare mediates Cowper through Burns—or so it seems). The passages objected to might both be realized as integral parts of that class heritage which Clare attempted to preserve in his awkward prefaces, and the attempts to remove them offer remarkable evidence of how the struggle for control of an author's fashioning can be enacted in the arena of class struggle. Lord Radstock, author of *The Cottager's Friend* and an apparently zealous patron of Clare, wrote to Eliza Emmerson:

> You must tell him—to expunge certain highly objectionable passages . . . wherein, his then depressed state hurried him not only into error, but into the most flagrant acts of injustice; by accusing those of pride, cruelty, vices, and ill-directed passions—who are the very persons, by whose truly generous and noble exertions he has been raised from misery and despondency. . . . [N]o, he must cut them out; or I cannot be satisfied that Clare is really as honest & upright as I could wish him!—tell Clare if he has still a recollection of what I have done, and

> am still doing for him, he must give me unquestionable *proofs,* of being that man I would have him to be.[26]

Clare finally capitulates to the pressing demands of Radstock and Emmerson (the latter telling him roundly that "gratitude should now be your theme") and writes to Taylor (who, interestingly, expressed his willingness to stand by Clare and reprint the originals) requesting that certain erasures should be made, in complaining terms: "D-n that canting way of being forced to please I say—I cant abide it and one day or other I will show my independence more strongly than ever."[27]

That defense of independence is at once a statement which takes us to the center of early nineteenth-century cultural production and a passage into Byron's writings, for it is reminiscent of Byron's letters defending *Don Juan,* and indeed of his defense of Pope.[28] The idiom of Clare's letters of this time, oddly, bears a remarkable similarity to that of Byron's, but the simple point I wish to stress is the kinship between Clare's illusion of independence and Byron's. Historically, what we are witnessing in the lionizing of Clare in 1820 is a particularly interesting example of the struggle for writing's control; particularly interesting because in Clare's case there is the representation of a kind of originary writing alongside his censored poems and erased prefaces. Clare was offered to the public as an example of artlessness and spontaneity: his poems, say his impresarios, are written on scraps and tucked into his hat in the fields, or pushed into cavities of the cottage wall, whence they are taken to be used as spills for the fire.[29] These are representations of a secretive and primary form of poetic discourse, the evidence of natural genius and creativity, which features, ironically, will figure in Clare's commodity value and fetishization. This spontaneity, moreover, has also to be controlled by the anxious manipulations of patronage, an institution that might seem almost anachronistic in 1820, but was nevertheless important to Clare, who needed its influence for his sales.

In the light of his uncomfortable entry into the public realm and the official culture of his day, Clare's belated description of Byron as the poet who "is just what he is and nothing more" has a resonance of some consequence. Precisely how Clare read Byron must remain a hypothesis, yet speculation can be led in part by what Clare writes about Byron in his essay "Popularity in Authorship," published in the *European Magazine* in 1825. There his reading of Byron as a scourge for the instruments of cultural control is made perfectly clear:

> by a desperate daring he overswept petty control like a rebellious flood, or a tempest worked up into madness by the quarrel of the elements, and he seemed to value that daring as the attainment of true fame. He looked upon "Horace's Art of Poetry" no doubt with the esteem of a reader, but he cared no more for it in the profession of a poet than the weather does for an almanack; he thought of critics as the countryman thinks of a magistrate: he beheld them as a race of petty tyrants. . . . He gained the Parnassus of living applause by a single stride, and looked down as a free-booter on the world below, scorning with seeming derision the praise that his labour had gained him.[30]

This may be derivative, but not slavishly so. Clare articulates Byron in the language of the rural working class; writing poetry is labor, and the critics are country justices. It is a striking moment in Clare's essay, yet the idiosyncratic description might guide us toward a recognition of what both poets have in common. For in a sense, Clare is right about Byron. He knows from his own experience how writers and their writings are fashioned for consumption, and he perceives how the idiom of Byron's writing might offer modes of resistance to the process. So it is that Clare is moved to inhabit Byron's works in 1841, and it is fitting that he does so at precisely the same moment that he makes a bid for freedom from institutional control by walking out of Matthew Allen's asylum.[31] Neither poem can be described as simply imitative of Byron. *Child Harold* has moments that recall, if somewhat vaguely, parts of Byron's poem, and interestingly, Clare drops the alexandrine in the last line of the stanza, which has the occasional effect of rendering the Spenserian verse in the behavior of ottava rima. Yet the shape of the whole poem is distinctive, being broken up by a plethora of interspersed songs and lyrics. *Don Juan,* similarly, is marked out by its differences: it is more pointedly vulgar and misogynistic, and its engagement with contemporary politics, as will be seen, is distinctive.

To read these poems as imitations based on bad guesses will offer less than to read them as occupations of the poetry of resistance. Primarily these poems use the authorial signature to deny the expectations attached to authorial character. Thus Clare writes Byron's poems: the author interpellated by the procedures of early-nineteenth-century poetic production as the unlettered and honest "natural" genius denies the validity of the claim with the signature of Byron, and creates a province of writing in which signification resists the collapsing of its meanings into the authorial biography, the poetic persona. Clare's use of Byron is therefore the co-opting of a powerful and impossible signature to displace textual ownership. For as Clare does not merely emulate Byron, so too he does not eradicate himself, or that selfhood that has been made for him. Rather, he enters his own reputation and biography into this new textual region, within which it can be defamiliarized, or indeed, recast. Thus in *Don Juan,* where the mobility of Byron's text finds further exaggeration, Clare might enter Byron's original—"Don Juan was Ambassador from russia / But had no hand in any sort of tax" (ll.215–16)—and come out of it in the subsequent verse in the references to Allen's asylum, which in itself is part of the political and social satire against corruption:

> Truth is shut up in prison while ye're licking
> The gold from off the gingerbread—be lythe
> In winding that patched broken old state clock up
> Playhouses open—but mad houses lock up (ll.243–49)

In the same section of the poem there is the elaboration of the parallel between the two authors:

> Now this day is the eleventh of July
> & being Sunday I will seek no flaw
> In man or woman—but prepare to die
> In two days more I may that ticket draw
> & so may thousands more as well as I
> To day is here—the next who ever saw
> And In a madhouse I can no mirth pay
> —Next Tuesday used to be Lord Byrons birthday
>
> Lord Byron poh—the man wot rites the werses
> and is just what he is and nothing more
> Who with his pen lies like the mist disperses
> & makes all nothing as it was before
> Who wed two wives & oft the truth rehearses
> & might have had some twenty thousand more
> Who has been dead so fools their lies are giving
> & still in Allen's madhouse caged and living.(ll.255–70)

July 13 (the "next Tuesday" referred to here) was not Byron's birthday but Clare's: the confusion indicates an identification and a split. Clare is, and is not, Byron. The stanza identifies the birthday not as a celebration of birth, but as a date contemplated within a meditation of impending death. In the madhouse there is nothing to celebrate, "no mirth," no beginnings perhaps, only ends. But in a sense, Clare's birthday, because it is now Byron's (and Byron is dead) is a thing of the past; a commemoration. Clare's birthday is now a remembrance of that which is gone, the life of the public poet of the 1820s perhaps, fixed in Clare's mind, quite plausibly, by his chancing on Byron's funeral the day *after* his own birthday in 1824.[32] Byron's significance to Clare as a figure of independence, asserted so strongly in the stanza that follows, is that which is now presented by the presence of his own birthday, and thus the celebration of the John Clare that is becomes the commemoration of the Lord Byron that is no more. Yet so, interestingly, the succeeding stanza might reverse this in its assertion that this death is also only confinement: Byron "has been" dead but is "in Allen's madhouse caged and living." So the presence of Clare's birthday becomes, through the series of imaginary relations that the poem establishes, the revival of the Byron that is within him—the independent poet of truth fighting against endemic cant, the free dispersal of "lies" by "fools." It is a motif that recurs continually in Clare's *Child Harold* and *Don Juan.*

How striking it is, whatever the implications of this identification, that Clare's description of Byron in the opening line of the second stanza quoted above is rendered in the writing of the unlettered poet. Thus the interpellation of Byron is simultaneously an interpellation of self according to the outmoded expectations of Clare's lionizing public. It becomes therefore a most ironic piece of self-fashioning that simultaneously opens up a sequence of idiomatic puns. Lord Byron writes verses and corrects wrongs; the unlettered poet writes without respect for conventions, either of class ("Lord Byron poh") or spelling. But if Clare, in a way, is now Byron, reinscribing the script of *Don Juan,* then there is also the new identity of being "just what he is and nothing more," that wonderfully cryptic tautology. Interestingly, what is repeated here is the grammar of Clare's most famous poem about identity, "I am," the insistent grammar of the subject without a differentiated object, the subject which repeats itself as predicate. The distinctive quality of this grammar in *Don Juan* is that its meaning does not depend on the implied presence of the difference felt in isolation: "I only know I am" gains a certain coherence from the poem's other statements, such as "my friends desert me like a memory lost." Thus "I am" represents a state of being that is in a relation of otherness to social life.[33] There is nothing comparable to this in *Don Juan:* the fashioning of Byron/Clare had nothing else to it, for the act of writing is all there is. Moreover, the ambiguity of the lines permits a reading that sees writing as a kind of self-definition with no further referential function. Verses might really be "werses"; poetry might purge away lies by "dispersing" them, but it might equally disperse them in the sense of dissemination, so that writing is a form of lying, the shrouding of truth in deception:

Who with his pen lies like the mist disperses
& makes all nothing as it was before

And if all is nothing through writing, but there was nothing there before it, then there is only writing, a negation of all but the act itself, which therefore gains primacy over the notion of authorship. Thus texts engender authors, and not the other way around. The authorial name—in this reading—becomes an irrelevance—"Lord Byron poh." This idea of the author's figurative signature being interchangeable or merely an indicator of the act of writing can be found elsewhere in Clare's discourse of apparent derangement. When he was visited in the Northampton asylum by G. J. de Wilde, the editor of the *Northampton Mercury,* de Wilde challenged his assertion that he had written some of Byron's and of Shakespeare's poetry, to which Clare retorted, "It's all the same . . . I'm John Clare now. I was Byron and Shakespeare formerly. At different times you know I'm different people—that is the same person with different names."[34]

Clare's inhabitation of Byron's poetry also brings us back sharply to the question of politics. First, each poem makes space to discourse on the nature of poetic utterance and its making. While this is most obvious in the inherited self-reflexivity of *Don Juan, Child Harold* has a polemical edge which again argues for poetry as the repository of independently held truth, an edge announced in its opening stanza. Simultaneously, the stanza seemingly enacts an intriguing repression of the politicizing polemic that complains of culture's policing:

Many are poets—though they use no pen
To show their labours to the shuffling age
Real poets must be truly honest men
Tied to no mongrel laws on flattery's page
No zeal have they for wrong or party rage
—The life of labour is a rural song
That hurts no cause—nor warfare tries to wage

Toil like the brook in music wears along—
Great little minds claim right to act the wrong (ll.1–9)

As Clare's editors remind us, the entry here is in fact into Byron's poem "The Prophecy of Dante," and the familiar Romantic claim that there are poets who do not write, but the most notable point about this stanza is its swerve into the "rural song," and what that signifies. Certainly, the claim is for the poet's independence, but poetry is still *labor,* and that predicates the idea that work itself is a disinterested creativity. It is only "great little minds" which in the very act of embracing ethical rectitude cause injustice. It is an opinion that the poem has difficulty in sustaining in its autobiographical strand, which even while it indulges visions of retreat in alienated solitude, also meditates on the injustice of the public:

Fame blazed upon me like the comet's glare
Fame waned & left me like a fallen star
Because I told the evil what they are
& truth & falsehood never wished to mar (ll.426–29)

Here is the clear evidence of Clare relating his presence in Byron to his early career, and it may be that in entering the two Byron texts he rives the Byronic tendencies. *Child Harold,* elaborating a subjectivity that is detached and alienated, depoliticized in its dwelling on disappointed hopes, is a poem that uses the madhouse emblematically, to figure the confinement of its predominant consciousness. *Don Juan* is utterly different. There the madhouse is the denial of speech and individuality, which can yet be resisted by the adoption of a deeply politicized voice:

Long speeches in a famine will not fill me
And madhouse traps still take me by the collar
So old wig bargains now must be forgotten
The oil that dressed them fine has made them rotten (ll.77–80)

The references are to the collapse of the Whigs in 1841, and it is very likely that the "old wig bargains" to be forgotten are the Whig promises of reform and assistance to the poor: in 1841 the Chartists were making alliances with the Tories to oust the Whig aristocracy.[35]

These astute and topical political references testify to *Don Juan*'s temporal certainty; it is a poem of its time and place, not an ephebic imitation. And while we might speculate that its political urgency derives in part from Clare's willful adoption of a Byronic persona, there is little doubt that its affiliation binds Clare with the oppressed of the hungry forties:

Lord what a while those good days are in coming—
Routs Masques & Balls—I wish they were a dream
—I wish for poor men luck—an honest praxis
Cheap food & clothing—no corn laws or taxes (ll.45–48)

I wish the Whigs were out of office &
Pickled in law books of some good atorney
For ways and speeches few can understand
They'll bless ye when in power—in prison scorn ye
& make a man rent his own house and land (ll.98–102)

"In prison" Clare's political identification is with those disillusioned with the Whigs, perhaps even with the Chartists, who at this time were considering common ownership and reviving that great radical tradition of a land plan offering independence, ownership, and subsistence, finally formalized in the Chartist Co-operative Land Society in 1845. Resettlement on the land was a part of Chartist thinking in 1841, and it does not seem too unlikely to suggest that the poet of "Helpstone" would find himself drawn toward such a politics. The references to people having to rent their own houses and land might therefore be quite precise; their topicality runs counter to the dehistoricized claim for the life of labor and rural song at the opening of *Child Harold*. There is of course a huge incidental irony in Clare's writing as Byron in 1841 to celebrate the final demise of the Whig oligarchy, since the very authorship he is moved to inhabit had its beginnings when Byron was struggling to achieve Whig patronage, only to find that his poetry's success made it largely superfluous. There is something fitting too in Clare's restitution of Byron's poetry to a context of domestic unrest.

Beyond the coincidences, this odd and unexpected connascency of Clare and Byron is consistent with an interactive writing practice that derives from, or relates closely to, the conditions of criticism that prevailed in the Romantic period. We know well enough that the writings we call Romantic are interactive: the movement is commonly characterized by reference to its authors' writing in response or reaction to one another. The question of Romantic criticism might regard this textual interchange as an important focus: the boundary of the Romantic text is not absolute, but continually open to an invasion that has a critical motive in the broadest sense. Thus, the "Immortality Ode" or the "Dejection Ode," if regarded separately, might be seen to be critically incomplete. In an utterly different way, but offering a similar symbiosis, the third canto of *Childe Harold* might not stand without the presence of Wordsworth. These relations do not always depend on permissions or agreements. Clare's writing of poems bearing the titles of Byron's most famous works might be one of the most remarkable and surprising examples of this kind of critical interaction, yet the act can also be understood as a part of that ubiquitous "radical uncertainty" to which Klancher has drawn attention in discussing the early-nineteenth-century writer's relation to the contemporary audiences.[36] The new anxiety, so evident in the numerous apologetic, self-effacing, or combative prefatory apparatuses, is productive of a taut self-consciousness attending the act of writing itself. So it is that the question of criticism in this period turns not only on the compilation of new aesthetic categories, but also on the interactive procedure itself, as authors write against and for critics, or even in and out of each other's texts.

Caught in the dilemma of writing poems about selfhood that were also generative of a public identity collectively fashioned by the material practices attending publication, Romantic self-fashioning is both a myth and a reality. Writing's representative function allows writers to create textual selves over which they have more control than those identities constructed for them as authors. Yet as Greenblatt reminds us, that notion of a self outside of social practice (a "real" or extra-cultural self as opposed to a self in culture perhaps) is as great an illusion as that which sees selves solely produced with the imprimatur of an overarching ideology, and is always likely to be produced, antithetically as it were, by a formalist overstressing of the persona's role.[37] Clare's inhabitation of the Byronic oeuvre takes the interactive critical exchange between authors (where one text is written against or in relation to another) beyond its common location to a point at which the question of how authors are constructed around texts, and in relation to each other, becomes intriguingly confused. This is not a parodic relation, nor a directly imitative one, but one that questions how authorial identities are formed and sustained. Most importantly, it is a relation that deconstructs the dichotomy of self and persona in favor of a pointed identification of the author as one who writes: a disestablishment, therefore, of Romantic solipsism. Clare writes as Byron to declare Byron's identity as the man who writes the verses "and nothing more." Whatever else the puns suggest, they continually draw the reader back to this blunt and subtle assertion, while their idiom tellingly indicates the presence of Clare's own authorial history, and reminds us that all poets, lettered or unlettered, are fashioned in the politics of a distinctly public criticism.

Nigel Leask

Toward a Universal Aesthetic: De Quincey on Murder as Carnival and Tragedy

I

The 1987 supplement to the *Oxford English Dictionary* relieves De Quincey of a previously assigned responsibility for inaugurating the term *aesthetic* in English, at least insofar as the word pertains to a judgment of Taste.[1] As late as 1971, the *OED* was erroneously attributing this first usage to a passage in his dark satire "On Murder Considered as a Fine Art," in which he wrote "Everything in this world has two handles. Murder, for instance, may be laid hold of by its moral handle . . . and *that,* I confess, is its weak side; or it may also be treated *aesthetically,* as the Germans call it—that is, in relation to good taste" (*DQW* 13:13). In the light of the *OED* supplement's correction (taking *aesthetic* in this, rather than in its strictly Kantian sense),[2] we discover that it is *Coleridge,* not De Quincey, who first employed *aesthetic* in English in an October 1821 article for *Blackwood's Edinburgh Magazine.* In his third "letter to Mr Blackwood," Coleridge laid out his desideratum that the magazine (founded four years before in 1817) be "a Philosophical, Philological, and Aesthetic Miscellany." In a long footnote, he apologized for the unfamiliar word—without, like De Quincey in the "On Murder" passage, mentioning its German provenance—but defended it as being "of more reputable origin" than the term *belle-lettristic* or *tasty,* the latter corrupted by "milliners, tailors . . . and dandies." Coleridge glossed this "useable adjective" as signifying "that coincidence of form, feeling, and intellect, that something, which, confirming the inner and the outward senses, becomes a new sense in itself, to be tried by laws of its own, and acknowledging the laws of the understanding so far only as not to contradict them."[3]

There is a certain justice in the fact that the term *aesthetic* should have made its English debut in a widely circulating literary periodical in the context of a programmatic account of social and cultural distinctions. This is more understandable in the light of Jon Klancher's study *The Making of English Reading Audiences,* with its illuminating account of the role of early-nineteenth-century periodicals in establishing the cultural distinction between "readership" and "audience." Following Pierre Bourdieu, Klancher demonstrates that "social divisions among classes both constrained the use of signs and resulted from the use of signs."[4] As if in endorsement of Klancher's thesis, Coleridge was firm in equating the newly defined sense of the "aesthetic" with a social "profit of disinterestedness" in the formation of *Blackwood's* select Tory readership,[5] by linking it with the principle of method he had adumbrated in the "Essays on Method" in the 1818 *Friend.* "There is reason to hope," he wrote, "that the term *aesthetic,* will be brought into common use as soon as distinct thoughts and definite expressions shall once more become the requisite accomplishments of a gentleman." Coleridge's harking back to the "energetic days . . . in the starry court of our *English*-hearted Eliza, when trade, the nurse of freedom, was the enlivening counterpoise of agriculture, not its alien and usurping spirit," marked a bid to counterbalance the shallow materialism of the new plutocracy by a gentlemanly standard of taste anchored in a national—or Shakespearean—literary canon. He elicited from Shakespeare's exemplary aesthetics of distinction in the "wit combats of Benedict and Beatrice and Mercutio" the lesson that "in the sparks and crackling of mental electricity, in the sportive approaches and collisions of ordinary intercourse . . . are stronger indications of natural superiority, and, therefore, more becoming signs of the accompaniments of *artificial* rank, than apathy, studied mediocrity, and the ostentation of wealth."[6]

Despite his scruples about lowering himself to write for *Blackwood's*—or any popular periodical for that matter—Coleridge clearly felt constrained to the rather self-defeating task of legislating the aesthetic for the magazine's conservative, middle-class readership. He had struggled to define the politics of readership in his *Lay Sermons* and *Biographia Literaria,* and was clearly not yet ready to abandon the public sphere in favor of the "National Church" or "Clerisy" which he would outline in the 1829 *Constitution of the Church and State.*[7] Despite the lambasting he had received at the hands of the *Blackwood's* reviewer John Wilson in 1817, he now felt more confident addressing the magazine's Tory readership for whom a professional ethic and the accumulation of cultural capital, rather than inherited social and economic status, represented the royal road to power and prestige. The learned wit of Coleridge's "idea of an inkstand" in the fourth letter of his *Blackwood's* article and his spirited discussion of Wordsworth in the fifth letter fitted well with the combination of erudition and playful irony that were the new magazine's hallmarks. However, the heavy dose of thinly disguised Fichtean and Schellingean metaphysics that he doled out in the second letter (redolent of the densest passages in chapters 12 and 13 of the *Biographia*) risked alienating this readership, even considering what Jon Klancher calls *Blackwood's* "imperializing mental energy . . . a full-blown ideology of the power of mind itself."[8]

In the same month that Coleridge's article appeared, the second installment of De Quincey's *Confessions of an English Opium Eater* was published in the pages of *Blackwood's* great rival, the *London Magazine.* The *London* had recently been taken over and refurbished by the publishers Taylor and Hessey after its former editor John Scott had been killed in a duel with a representative of the editors of *Blackwood's,* following an attack on its Edinburgh rival. De Quincey had recently fallen out with *Blackwood's* and arrived in the metropolis, desperately short of money and, despite his personal hatred for its former editor Scott, seeking employment with the *London.* After a humiliating (and unsuccessful) appeal to Coleridge to repay an earlier gift of £300, an indigent De Quincey hastily penned the *Confessions,* which he exchanged for hard cash.[9] De Quincey (and the editors of the *London*) were quick to capitalize on its success, and he produced a succession of articles for the magazine over the next few years, including the much-neglected *Letters to a Young Man Whose Education Has Been Neglected* in 1823.

In these *Letters,* his recent humiliation perhaps still smarting, De Quincey launched a rather facetious attack on Coleridge as author of the

Biographia and *Lay Sermons*, but also (more immediately) as the dispenser of transcendental metaphysics to readers of the *London*'s Scottish rival, *Blackwood's Magazine.* With an overliteral pugnacity, the first letter challenged Coleridge to a journalistic boxing match, exhorting him to return to poetry and to "leave transcendentalism to me and other young men" (*DQW* 10:21–22). Jonathan Bate has recently drawn timely critical attention to the *Letters* by suggesting that they, rather than the *Confessions* (as I have previously argued elsewhere), respond to Coleridge's politics of authorship as laid out in the *Biographia.*[10] Bate, however, overlooks the fact that, given their magazine context as well as their reactive style, form, and content, the *primary* target of the *Letters to a Young Man* would seem to have been Coleridge's *Blackwood's* article rather than the *Biographia* itself. Even their title seems to evoke Coleridge's final "Letter to a Junior Soph, at Cambridge" rather than the imaginary correspondence of *Biographia,* chapter 13, as Bate would have it. De Quincey's direct reference to Coleridge's "celebrated" *Blackwood's* article several years later reinforces the point.[11] There is an even more compelling reason for linking the two articles, however, and one that brings me back to the main current of my argument. Both are concerned with the social and political ramifications of the *aesthetic,* which they name as such for the first time in English literature.

Defending literature as a trade against Coleridge's insistence in chapter 11 of the *Biographia* that literature should be pursued as a gentlemanly pastime, supplement to a professional career, De Quincey in the *Letters* seeks to promote the image of an all-round intellectual plying his trade in the public sphere of the higher journalism. Coleridge's existential and intellectual failings are introduced to support De Quincey's argument by default. In a tacit defense of his own current involvement in the study of political economy (which he knew to be Coleridge's bête noir) he denies the *sufficiency* of literature as an intellectual pursuit to the exclusion of all others, "even when the mind is so far advanced that it can bring what has hitherto passed for merely literary or *aesthetic* questions under the light of philosophic principles" (*DQW* 10:14). De Quincey's fears concerning the increasingly abstract and rationalized nature of modern imaginative literature (not merely the discursive "literature of knowledge") is closely related to his critique of Coleridgean aesthetics and his attempt to propagate what he described, in the same essay, as a literature of *power.* To summarize: it is evident that the *Letters to a Young Man* (and not the 1827 "On Murder" essay, as the OED supplement has it) contain De Quincey's own first use of the word *aesthetic,* italicized but untethered from its German context. Preceding "On Murder" by four years, it appears in the course of De Quincey's critique of Coleridgean aesthetics, and in particular Coleridge's attempt in *Blackwood's* to promote a gentlemanly standard of taste among an elite sector of the reading public.

Four years later, in the February 1827 issue of *Blackwood's* (for which, a veritable Vicar of Bray, De Quincey was again writing), he published two captivating essays, "The Last Days of Immanuel Kant" and the first part of "On Murder Considered as a Fine Art." Three more essays on murder were to follow, in 1839, in 1851 (the little-known "Philosophy of Murder" in *Tait's Magazine*), and finally in the "Postscript" prepared for the selected edition of his works in 1854. De Quincey's "Murder" essays have never been considered in relation to his dispute with Coleridge in the early 1820s concerning the bearing of the term *aesthetic*, and the case I want to make here is that they represent an ongoing critique of Coleridge's politics of authorship closely related to the magazine context in which both writers had been working. John Whale has drawn attention to the importance of this "polite magazine context" for the early "Murder" essays, suggesting that the 1827 "lecture on murder" "exhibits [the] familiar self-congratulatory tone of the periodical magazines, especially of *Blackwood's*," representing both "an overt attack on the public and . . . an implied satire on the dilettanti readership of [the magazine]."[12] Given De Quincey's former partisanship of the *London* in the 1823 *Letters to a Young Man* and other articles, and his visible disagreement with Coleridge about the social bearing of literature, one might add to Whale's argument the contention that De Quincey's ironic send-up of *Blackwood's* dilettantism was also a veiled attack on Coleridge, who in 1821 had envisaged the magazine as a "Philosophical, Philological, and Aesthetical Miscellany." Seen in this light, De Quincey's exhortation to his readers to consider murder *aesthetically* (*his* second, and only the *third* recorded general usage in English, counting Coleridge's), self-consciously participates in what Klancher terms "a troubled contention over power, signs, and the function of culture itself" in the process of being distilled into "the discourse of Romantic imagination."[13]

II

The characteristic irony of the early "Murder" essays depends largely, as John Whale has shown, on the gentlemanly persona of the "lecturer" familiarly addressing a coterie audience in the typical *Blackwood's* manner—except that *this* audience has become "the Society of Connoisseurs in Murder. They profess to be curious in homicide; amateurs and dilettanti in the various modes of carnage; and in short, Murder-Fanciers" (*DQW* 13:8–9). The 1827 essay and the additions of 1839 and 1851 all tread a tightrope between comedy and horror, representing a carnivalesque satire of an aesthetic doctrine that De Quincey saw as formalistic, class-specific, and cerebral. In the 1854 "Postcript" De Quincey for the most part dropped the ironical mask. He admitted (defensively) that the satirical extravagance, the "mere aeriality of the entire speculation" of the essay and supplement, "furnishes the surest means of disenchanting [the reader] from the horror which might else gather upon his feelings" (13:71). In the "Postscript," the mask of satire is replaced by tragedy; in the words of Joel Black, he now sought to "conjure up a nonrational, amoral, purely aesthetic world of sublime, inescapable terror."[14]

In both the comic and tragic parts of the "On Murder" sequence, De Quincey sought to exemplify—at first negatively, and then positively—his own central idea of the "literature of power" (10:48), an idea whose sublime scope was frustrated by the effete coterie aesthetics of Coleridge and *Blackwood's Magazine.* De Quincey's target was thus not so much German aesthetics as Coleridge's particular interpretation of them; sharing Coleridge's enthusiastic partisanship of German literature, he sought rather to contest the latter's scruples concerning post-Kantian accounts of the sublime.[15] By developing the concept of the literature of power both in theory and in his prose style, De Quincey sought to remedy the shortcomings of a narrowly defined *sensus communis* as the basis for aesthetic judgment, particularly evident in contemporary notions of tragedy.[16] De Quincey's reservations concerning Coleridgean aesthetics are paralleled (although in the context of a discussion leading to very different conclusions), by G. S. Gadamer's later critique of the Kantian school in *Truth and Method:* "In Germany, the followers of Shaftesbury and Hutcheson did not, even in the eighteenth century, take over the political and social elements contained in *sensus communis* . . . . [I]n the removal of all political content it lost its real critical significance. *Sensus Communis* was understood as a purely theoretical faculty, theoretical judgement, on a level with moral consciousness (conscience) and Taste. Thus it was fitted into a scholasticism of the basic faculties."[17]

I will argue later in this chapter that De Quincey's dissatisfaction with the "Germano-Coleridgean" tradition was expressed in a powerful counterinterpretation of Greek tragedy that deliberately veered away from Shakespeare, the customary focus of romantic discussions of tragedy. However, the young De Quincey did nevertheless develop his critique of Coleridgean aesthetics in his one celebrated piece of Shakespeare criticism, the 1823 essay "On the Knocking at the Gate in *Macbeth*." Although this proved a seedbed for the central satirical idea of the "Murder" essays, it would, as we will see, be significantly qualified in the 1854 "Postscript." In the Ratcliffe Highway murders of 1812, executed by the fiendish John Williams, the "same incident of a knocking at the door soon after the work of extermination was complete did actually occur which the genius of Shakespeare had invented" (*DQL* 82). The 1827 "On Murder" essay develops the simple idea, broached in 1823, of treating Williams as a great romantic artist: "In 1812 Mr Williams made his debut on the stage of Ratcliffe Highway, and executed those unparalleled murders which have procured for him such a brilliant reputation" (*DQL* 82). In the "Knocking at the Gate" essay Shakespeare the tragedian and Williams the murderer compete uneasily for the laurels, and despite De Quincey's bardolatry in the penultimate paragraph ("Oh! mighty poet!—Thy works are not those of other men, simply and merely great works of art; but also like the phenomena of nature, like the sun and the sea, the stars and the flowers" [*DQL* 83]), one feels that Williams and not his dramaturgical namesake has stolen the show.

De Quincey's analogy here between the artist and the "phenomena of nature" (as much a parody of Coleridge's bardolatry in the Shakespeare lectures as a eulogy on Shakespeare himself) picks up a troubling indeterminacy at the heart of the aesthetic tradition he was addressing. Eighteenth-century theorists of the sublime such as Burke and Kant (in his theory of the "dynamic sublime") had focused largely on sublimity in relation to natural phenomena rather than human actions either "real" or represented, as in the case of tragedy. They thereby tended to subordinate the ethics to the aesthetics of power. As Joel Black puts it, "once natural violence was considered as a possible source of aesthetic experience, what was to prevent human violence, which inspired perhaps even greater terror, from making aesthetic claims as well?"[18] De Quincey was certainly not the first writer to capitalize on this problem, and there is doubtless considerable justice in Black's suggestion that Schiller (who sought explicitly to consider tragedy in relation to the Kantian sublime) was a major source. But there is another source nearer home.

In the 1827 essay, De Quincey's "Lecturer" cited Coleridge's "ideal of an inkstand" (see note 11) as the inspiration for his thesis that "even imperfection itself may have its ideal or perfect state" (*DQW* 13:16). De Quincey has developed his account of the murderer as hero by taking a hint from another Coleridge text, the latter's discussion of the sublimity of the evil genius, or "individual of consummate wickedness" in essay 16 of *The Friend.* The sense that throughout the "Murder" essays De Quincey is elaborating Coleridge's own notion of the possible "ideality of imperfection" is supported by the fact that he introduced the figure of Coleridge twice at crucial stages in his argument. First, Coleridge's aesthetic enjoyment of a fire at a piano-forte maker's in Oxford Street is archly justified by De Quincey: "Virtue was in no request. On the arrival of the fire-engines, morality had devolved wholly on the insurance office" (*DQW* 13:14). But Coleridge's enjoyment of a sublime *natural* phenomenon (a fire, presumably an accident) is relatively easier to justify, even if premised upon another's misfortune, than his sense of *wonder* at the sublime malice of murder described in the 1854 "Postscript." Here, De Quincey has Coleridge comment upon the murderous genius of John Williams in terms that closely echo the latter's thoughts about power and sublimity in *The Friend.* Although unsurprising in relation to his discussion of tragic villains like Iago or Macbeth, Coleridge's sense of wonder here is a response to power unmediated by dramatic form, and therefore suggestively proleptic of De Quincey's ironic discourse in the "Murder" essays as a whole. "Coleridge" tells De Quincey that although "as a philosopher" he has not "shared in the prevailing panic," the Ratcliffe Highway murders "threw him into a profound reverie upon the tremendous *power* which is laid open to any man who can reconcile himself to the abjuration of all conscientious restraints, if, at the same time, thoroughly without fear" (13:75; italics mine).

Coleridge had in fact presented this idea (more cautiously) in the *Statesman's Manual* and the second chapter of the *Biographia Literaria,* distinguishing two distinct modes of genius, with two distinct kinds of power. Whereas "Absolute Genius" manifested itself primarily in the world of the arts and the intellect, "Commanding Genius" showed itself rather in the world of practical affairs (e.g., politics and warfare), facilitating great acts of construction but also appearing in its most destructive form in the "mighty Hunters of Mankind, from NIMROD to NAPOLEON" (*CLS* 65–66). In the *Friend* essay mentioned above, Coleridge described this evil version of "Commanding Genius" as being motivated by "*systematic* vice. . . . [T]he abandonment of all *principle* of right enables the soul to chuse and act upon a *principle* of wrong, and to subordinate to this principle all the various vices of human nature" (*C Friend* 1:121). Coleridge's active genius must be guided by conscience just as (he tells us in the *Biographia*) the secondary imagination must be policed by the "conscious will" (*CBL* 1:304). De Quincey's satirical strategy in the "Murder" essays is simply to deny Coleridge's carefully drawn distinction and treat *Commanding* Genius in terms which for Coleridge would only have been appropriate to the "disinterestedness" of *Absolute* Genius. Confounding art and life, De Quincey dismissively implies that the distinction itself is symptomatic of the rational and ethical prerogatives which, since Dr. Johnson, have plagued critical attempts to moralize the power of Shakespearean tragedy. In the "Knocking at the Gate" essay, the tragic power of *Macbeth* was shown to be a product of imaginative identification with Macbeth and his wife, not pity or sympathy for their victims. The "poet," De Quincey tells us, "must throw the interest on the murderer: our sympathy must be with *him,*" for in the murderer—*not* his terrified victim—"there must be raging some great storm of passion,—jealousy, ambition, vengeance, hatred,—which will create a hell within him; and into that hell we are to look" (*DQL* 83). But in the 1827 essay the emphasis has changed. If in "The Knocking at the Gate" he had illustrated his thesis concerning *Macbeth* with reference to the Ratcliffe Highway murders, he now reverses the priority, building his aesthetics of murder upon the foundation of Aristotle's theory of tragedy: "the final purpose of murder, considered as a fine art, is precisely the same as that of tragedy, in Aristotle's account of it; viz., 'to cleanse the heart by means of pity and terror'" (*DQW* 13:47). De Quincey now seeks the Romantic sublime in crime rather than literature.

This collapsing of the distinction between "Absolute" and "Commanding" Genius in "On Murder" exploits what De Quincey seems to have considered a central contradiction in Coleridgean aesthetics. In his discrimination of Absolute and Commanding Genius, Coleridge had illegitimately introduced an alien, ethical criterion into the discourse of power, thereby inhibiting (in De Quincey's view) the representation of sublimity. If one can conflate the work of art with the genius of the artist to the extent to which Coleridge did in the *Biographia* ("What is poetry? is so nearly the same question with, what is a poet? that the answer to the one is involved in the solution of the other" [*CBL* 2:15]), could one not judge the murderer—provided he was "systematic" or disinterested, unmotivated by gain or lust—in the same aesthetic terms as one judged the murder when "virtue was in no request" (*DQW* 13:14)?

In the interests of a literature of power, De Quincey sought to turn some of Coleridge's more unguarded statements about aesthetic disinterestedness against the ethical agenda underlying his general philosophy of art. In his 1814 essay "On the Principles of Genial Criticism," Coleridge had after all insisted that "The BEAUTIFUL is . . . at once distinguished both from the AGREEABLE, which is beneath it, and from the

GOOD, which is above it: for both these have an interest necessarily attached to them: both act on the WILL, and excite a desire for the actual existence of the image or idea contemplated: while the sense of beauty rests gratified in the mere contemplation or intuition. . . . The Beautiful, therefore, not originating in the sensations, must belong to the intellect: and therefore we *declare* an object beautiful, and feel an inward right to *expect* that others should coincide with us" (*CBL* [1907] 2:239, 242). Even as Coleridge moved from the Kantian premises of "Genial Criticism" to the Schellingian idiom of the 1818 "On Poesy or Art," his doctrine of disinterestedness insisted on distinguishing the beautiful from the good: "[Beauty] may be present in a disagreeable object, in which the proportion of the parts constitutes a whole; it does not arise from association, as the agreeable does . . . It is not different to different individuals and nations . . . nor is it connected with the ideas of the good, or the fit, or the useful" (*CBL* [1907] 2:257).

It seems clear from De Quincey's own hint that Coleridge's theory of "Commanding Genius" is an important spur for his celebration of the murderer Williams as an artistic genius: "like Aeschylus or Milton in poetry, like Michael Angelo in painting, he has carried his art to a point of colossal sublimity; and, as Mr Wordsworth observes, has in a manner 'created the taste by which he is to be enjoyed,'" (*DQW* 13:12). In carnival mood, De Quincey plays off one kind of Coleridgean genius against another, satirically confusing the artist (absolute genius) with the murderer (commanding genius), the art critic with the murder connoisseur, Coleridge himself with the "Williams Lecturer." Coleridge's Kantian doctrine of aesthetic disinterestedness, adapted to promulgate the gentlemanly aesthetic adumbrated in the 1821 *Blackwood's* article, readily exposes itself to De Quincey's inflationary "ideality of imperfection," except that an inkstand has become a brutal murder. De Quincey's "commanding genius" exercises a systematic, disinterested power of destruction. In a parody of Coleridge's celebrated doctrine of aesthetic indirection (associated most notably with his remarks on the moral of *The Ancient Mariner* and Iago's "motive-hunting of motiveless malignity" in *Othello*), De Quincey at one point has his "gentleman amateur" give, as his motive for cutting the throat of the Mannheim Baker, "no other reason . . . [than] that you put alum in your bread" (*DQW* 13:40). The calculated confusion of categories satirizes not just a body of aesthetic doctrine but also (as I suggested above) the polite magazine context of his own—and Coleridge's—public address. The tension between terror and wit—the sublime and the ridiculous—translates Coleridge's carefully policed and exclusive aesthetic into the terms of the "literature of power," here via bathos in the register of the *grotesque,* and later (in 1854) in the aggrandized form of *tragedy.*

III

The chance was a good one,
and the mob was made aware of it,
for catching the wolfish dog in the high noon and carnival of his
bloody revels—in the very centre of his own shambles.
(*DQW* 13:113)

In his essay "Hysteria and the End of Carnival," Allon White comments on the virtual elimination of traditional carnival as a real social practice in nineteenth-century Europe. However, he adds, the "disjecta membra of the grotesque body of carnival found curious lodgement throughout the whole social order of bourgeois life."[19] De Quincey's "Murder" essays might be seen as an instance of one such lodgement. The "theorization" of the art work within "a scholasticism of the basic faculties" in post-Kantian and particularly Coleridgean aesthetics and anxieties concerning the definition of *sensus communis;* the regulation of the theaters in early-nineteenth-century England[20] and the "impossibility" of a modern catharsis (to be addressed below in relation to De Quincey's *Antigone* essay); the delegitimization of state violence in the reform of the penal code and the abolition of public execution; the proletarianization of lower-class women and male anxieties concerning the decline of the patriarchal family;[21] all these mark aspects of social desublimation against which the "Murder" essays work in constructing a "literature of power."

At one point in his article, White describes another carnivalesque "lodgement," the hysterical fantasy of Frau Emmy von N. (one of Freud's patients) in terms of the ritual combat of Carnival and Lent. "The anorexic figure for Lent—a figure represented as emaciated, a kill-joy, old, and female, a cold-blooded figure of humourless fasting and sexual abstinence—is invariably the victor."[22] In De Quincey's "Murder" essays the combat between Carnival and Lent is fought in a curiously literalized battle between Art, and Philosophy with its moral-rational claims; here, however, "Art" is the victor, Descartes, Spinoza, Hobbes, Malebranche all fall victims to the murderer's art, the last-named murdered by another philosopher, the "poetic" Bishop Berkeley. Leibnitz dies of "vexation that he was not murdered" (*DQW* 13:34). Kant, whose philosophical "demands of unconditioned veracity" in guiding an assassin to his quarry is described by De Quincey as aiding and abetting a murder, has himself *nearly* fallen victim to a murder (*DQW* 13:34). His would-be murderer—a man of discerning taste—at the last moment decided against murdering the Lenten figure of the Prussian philosopher who "could not possibly look more like a mummy when dead, than he had done alive" (*DQW* 13:35). De Quincey himself delivered the literary coup de grâce denied Kant by his would-be assassin in "The Last Days of Immanuel Kant," published in the same issue of *Blackwood's* as the first "Murder" essay. Here, complained the (Kantian) Henry Crabb Robinson, "[the author] has made much of the bodily constitution of a great man, with no allusion to his mind or philosophy."[23]

Even more noteworthy in this carnivalesque fascination with the bodies of great minds is the figure of Coleridge, the fire-fancier "too fat to be a person of active virtue, [but] undoubtedly a worthy Christian" (*DQW* 13:14). De Quincey here puns on the word *virtue,* which in a gesture miniaturing the drift of his whole essay, is translated a couple of pages later into "virtu" ("Virtue has had her day; and henceforward, *Virtu,* so nearly the same thing as to differ only by a single letter . . . *virtu,* I repeat, and Connoisseurship, have leave to provide for themselves" (*DQW* 13:16–17). Ostensibly commenting on the threshold of Coleridge's goodness (his virtue), De Quincey punningly suggests that were it not for his "grotesque body," the poet/philosopher might have made a successful "virtuoso" in the practice of arson (and even murder?). In a later essay entitled "Conversation and Mr. Coleridge," De Quincey imagined Coleridge as the "unhappy murderer" of his brother Frank and cruelly indulged himself at the former's expense by picturing the philosopher as a guilt-ridden fratricide.[24] But Coleridge's *failed* fratricide is surely the issue here; after all, his famous critical "desynonymization" of Fancy and Imagination in the *Biographia* is premised upon his virtuosity as a *reader* of Wordsworth's poetry, a virtuosity for which he has paid with his own poetic creativity. As he put it elsewhere, "I have too clearly before me the idea of a poet's genius to deem myself other than a very humble poet; but in the very possession of the idea I know myself so far a poet as to feel assured that I can understand and interpret a poem in the spirit of poetry" (*CM* 1:482).

Analogously, De Quincey's narrator (the "John Williams Lecturer") admits, "As to murder, I never committed one in my life"—although he does confess to a botched job on a thieving tom-cat (*DQW* 13:53). De

Quincey's connoisseur-narrator is a carnivalesque satire on Coleridge himself, just as his "virtuoso" Williams (namesake of both Shakespeare and Wordsworth) stands in the same relation to the narrator as Wordsworth to Coleridge in the *Biographia.* The narrator's authority as a connoisseur of carnage is based upon his failure as a practitioner or virtuoso, just as Coleridge's critical authority in the *Biographia* is premised upon his "failure" as a poet, eclipsed by Wordsworth's genius. The obese Coleridge is however a far more interesting target for De Quincey's rhetorical "assassination" than the spindly, Lenten Kant, or any other "pure" philosopher, precisely because of his complicity, his double existence in the worlds of both criticism and creativity. De Quincey's assertion in the *Letters to a Young Man* that transcendentalism "does not prosper in his [i.e., Coleridge's] hands" is balanced by his wish that, relieved of the burden of legislating the aesthetic, he might produce another instance of the "literature of power": "he will thus be more at leisure to give us another *Ancient Mariner*" (*DQW* 10:21–22).

As with his treatment of the fastidious Kant in the "Last Days of Immanuel Kant," De Quincey *embodies* Coleridgean theory in "On Murder"; in contrast to Kant, Coleridge's fleshiness invites the parodist's attention, like the Mannheim Baker's voluminous throat "fancied" by the English "amateur." The Lecturer's encomium on the "Augustan Age of Murder" (*DQW* 10:35), an age that reached its apogee with the Ratcliffe Highway murders, is tinged with the melancholy intimation (anticipating George Orwell's) that the present marks the decline of the English murder.[25] Not only the "spurious class of mere political or partisan murders" (*DQW* 10:36) but also the introduction from Italy of poisoning "no better than wax-work by the side of sculpture" (*DQW* 13:39)—echoing Coleridge's celebrated distinction between "imitation" and "copy"—has compromised the nobility of modern murder. In a brilliant parody of Coleridge's fears of the "plebification of knowledge," De Quincey's connoisseur (in the 1851 sequel to the "Murder" essays) laments the "march of intellect operators in chloroform and new improved strangulators."[26] De Quincey also parodies Coleridge's demand (made most prominently in chapter 21 of the *Biographia*) for a "fair and philosophical criticism" based on philosophical principles, in contrast to the "present mode of conducting critical journals" (*CBL* 2:107). Stung by the quixotic nature of this demand in the faction-ridden world of the reviews, De Quincey parodies it in the Lecturer's lofty standard of taste, capturing the characteristic *Blackwood's* tone of "an expert condescending to the act of public communication."[27] He refuses to pander to the sensation-seeking "reading public" in his aesthetics of murder: "As to old women, and the mob of newspaper readers, they are pleased with anything, provided it is bloody enough. But the mind of sensibility requires something more" (*DQW* 13:46).

IV

Our attention has been turned, by the current of events, to the general nature of men and things; and we cannot call it heartily back to individual caprices, or head-strong passions, which are the nerves and sinews of Comedy and Tragedy.

William Hazlitt's diagnosis of "modern tragedy" (in an essay of the same title published in the *London Magazine* of April 1820)[28] singles out the dramatic writings of Coleridge, Wordsworth, Godwin, and Southey as instances of the imaginative failure of Romantic tragedy. Coleridge's "spurious tragedy" *Remorse* exemplifies for Hazlitt the abstraction and paradox of contemporary tragedy, creation of "a florid poet, and an ingenious metaphysician, who mistakes scholastic speculation for the intricate windings of the passions, [who] assigns possible reasons instead of actual motives for the excesses of his characters."[29] George Steiner, developing Hazlitt's critique, locates the Romantic evasion of tragedy in its obsession with *remorse,* ultimately traceable to the revolutionary and meliorist ideologies of the 1790s: "Dramas of remorse cannot be ultimately tragic. . . . [B]ecause the individual is not wholly responsible, he cannot be wholly damned. Rousseauism closes the door to hell."[30] The absence of "power" that De Quincey diagnosed in Coleridgean aesthetics—and parodied in the "Murder" essays—is related to a similar conviction that remorse robbed tragic action of its sacramental and ritual meaning and, in the spirit of the Enlightenment, "explained it away" in secular or political terms.

If De Quincey's diagnosis of the abstraction afflicting contemporary tragedy is recognizably akin to Hazlitt's (and, I suggest in passing, Shelley's), his turn to the annals of crime in search of a viable substitute for the "Dark Sublime" missing from English Romanticism introduced a new element into nineteenth-century literature. "The police spoils all," Hazlitt proclaimed in 1818, "and we now hardly so much as dream of a midnight murder."[31] Not, however, the author of "On Murder Considered as a Fine Art," inspired by the popular response to the Ratcliffe Highway murders. Setting himself apart from the critical elitism adumbrated in Hazlitt's "Whether the Fine Arts Are Promoted by Academies" essay (echoing, from an unexpected political quarter, Coleridge's ideal of an "aesthetical" readership in the *Blackwood's* article), De Quincey would baldly assert in 1854 that "the tendency to a critical or aesthetic valuation of fires and murders is universal"—in stark contrast to the "aristocracy of taste" propounded by Coleridge and Hazlitt (*DQW* 13:72). As early as 1818 he had defended his editorial policy of cramming the columns of the *Westmoreland Gazette* with assize reports and grisly murder stories because of their "powerful and commanding interest" to all ranks of society, because they taught "social duties in the most impressive shape . . . not in a state of abstraction . . . but exemplified (and, as the logicians say, *concreted*) in the actual circumstances of an interesting case," and because they were "the best indications of the moral condition of society" (*DQW* 13:95). Despite his special pleading here, De Quincey's interest in crime, like his later "idolatry" of Greek tragedy, distinguishes him sharply from other English writers of the age.[32] The rational analysis of motivation and the moral interest of remorse is replaced in De Quincey by a fascination with revenge and a desire to sacrifice the criminal to a fate as ghastly as the crime he has perpetrated. In John Barrell's words, De Quincey demands "a whole mouthful of teeth for a tooth."[33]

De Quincey's 1854 "Postscript"—building on earlier fiction such as "The Avenger" and "The Household Wreck"—marks what is perhaps a unique moment in nineteenth-century criminal literature, resisting both the moral and political telos underpinning Romantic tragedy, and the growing challenge (in the 1840s and 50s) of the new genre of detective fiction, which placed the reassuring figure of the detective between the criminal and a bourgeois reading public. To quote Joel Black, "where romanticism had glorified the outlaw or outcast as a social rebel, the age of realism rationalized the criminal subject in literature as *Reason* in the figure of the detective: this is what Foucault calls 'the appropriation of the criminal in acceptable terms.'"[34] What then is the inspiration for the undeniable tragic power of De Quincey's murder narrative in the 1854 "Postscript"?

In the years between the 1839 "Supplement" to the "On Murder" essay and the "Postscript," De Quincey sought to elaborate and deepen his earlier *satirical* aesthetics of murder by means of a study of Greek tragedy. This bore fruit in his "Theory of Greek Tragedy" (1840), "The *Antigone* of Sophocles" (1846), and "The Theban Sphinx" (1850). The aesthetic lessons learned from Greek tragedy—a genre, it should be remembered, centrally concerned with the question of revenge—were translated into modern prose narrative in the "Postscript" itself. In a recent essay entitled "The Bacchic in Shelley," Michael Rossington has underlined the conservative interpretation of Greek tragedy in the work of Romantic critics like A. W. Schlegel and J. G. Lockhart (the latter, significantly, published his articles on Greek tragedy in the early issues of *Blackwood's*), who sought to associate classical culture with social authority. For Rossington, Shelley represents perhaps the most successful contemporary challenge to this critical hegemony. *Prometheus Unbound,* refiguring and "orientalizing" Greek tragedy by dwelling upon subversive Bacchic elements suppressed in classical theory, "asserts a radical instability which upsets Greek classicism and the aesthetic taste which it bequeathes."[35]

De Quincey, for whom Greek tragedy was closely linked to the Dark Sublime explored in the *Confessions* and its "sequel" *Suspiria de Profundis,* sought a counter-interpretation analogous to Shelley's "Bacchic," although one motivated by different political goals. The first step in this critical revision was to question the conventional wisdom which downgraded Greek in relation to Shakespearean tragedy, as exemplified in an 1808 lecture by Coleridge at which De Quincey had been present.[36] With the one brilliant exception of the "Knocking at the Gate" essay (based on *Macbeth,* the most "Greek" and "monochromatic" of all Shakespeare's tragedies), De Quincey had disappointingly little to say about Shakespearean tragedy in general, maybe in part because he had so *much* to say about Greek. René Wellek's statement that De Quincey's "whole strong anti-Hellenism [is] apparent in his discussions of Greek religion and literature throughout his writings"[37] has been extremely misleading to critics. It might more truly be said of Coleridge, who, like Schlegel and Lockhart, relegated the pagan Greek drama to a position below the Christian, "romantic" tragedy of Shakespeare: "However great their progress in the development of . . . outward & even of moral Beauty . . . we cannot concede [to the Greeks] a higher character than that of a refined & elevated Sensuality" (*C Lects 1808–19* 1:438–39). Contrast this with De Quincey who, characteristically at odds with Coleridgean judgment, confessed in 1840 that "the one sole section of the Greek Literature as to which I profess myself an enthusiast, happens to be the Tragic Drama, and here only I myself am liable to be challenged as an idolator" (*DQW* 10:364).

De Quincey's writings are crowded with the vengeful murderers and accursed victims of Greek tragedy; Orestes in the *Confessions,* tormented by the Furies and comforted by his devoted sister Electra (*DQL* 35–36); the child of "the superb Medea," murdered in his innocence by his mother in the nursery at Corinth, in *Suspiria de Profundis* (*DQL* 138); and most memorably, the pariah king Oedipus, guilty of "acts incestuous, murderous, parricidal," and yet paradoxically innocent of all crime (*DQL* 130n), and his daughter Antigone, willing to make herself "a houseless pariah, lest the poor pariah king, [her] outcast father, should want a hand to lead him in his darkness" (*DQW* 10:365). The quality of his interest in these somber narratives of sublime murder and revenge makes De Quincey (more than the "Bacchic" Shelley of *Prometheus Unbound* and *The Cenci*) a progenitor of the Dionysian Nietzsche of *The Birth of Tragedy.* Nietzsche, meanwhile, stands closer to De Quincey than the hellenizing Matthew Arnold of *Culture and Anarchy,* liberal heir to the Schlegel and Lockhart school.

In his 1840 *Blackwood's* essay entitled simply "Theory of Greek Tragedy," De Quincey offers his most detailed, and I think most problematic, account of the relations between Greek and Shakespearean tragedy, forms which "stand so far aloof as hardly to recognize each other under any common designation" (*DQW* 10:343). One of his most telling accounts of the distinction is found in his remarks on the "mise en abîme" or "introvolution" in *Hamlet.* The "play within the play," described by De Quincey as being "rough and horrent with figures in strong relief, like the embossed gold of an ancient vase" (*DQW* 10:345) is differentiated, in the mind of the modern reader or spectator, from the fluidity and relative verisimilitude of Shakespeare's main text. In his "mise en abîme" Shakespeare has "swollen, tumefied, stiffened, not the diction only, but the tenor of the thought": by the "short gyrations" of its scenes, so different from the "free sweep and expansion of his general developments" in the rest of *Hamlet,* he has purposely "[stilted] it, and [given] it a prominence and an ambition beyond the scale which he adopted for his ordinary life" (*DQW* 10:345). However, De Quincey's critical purpose here is not so much to offer another insight into Shakespeare's dramatic technique (although he does so very effectively) as to construct an analogue—the play within the play—to explain "the original phasis under which we contemplate the Greek Tragedy." As a paradigmatic "literature of power," Greek tragedy was "ultra-human and Titanic," its actors massively aggrandized and idealized, "a life below a life" (*DQW* 10:345–47). Like the crowded cityscapes and mysterious oriental rituals of De Quincey's opium dreams, tragedy on the Greek stage was "projected upon the eye from a vast profundity in the rear; and between this life and the spectator, however near its phantasmagoria might advance to him, was still an immeasurable gulf of shadows" (*DQW* 10:347).

The deep "recess" and "life of shadows" that for De Quincey characterize the Greek tragic stage and the opium dream alike is evidently a psychic space, a site where the "deep deep tragedies of childhood" are metamorphosed into a "literature of power." The importance of "recesses" and "pictures within pictures" in dreams or neurotic fantasies is of course a psychoanalytic commonplace: De Quincey's scholarly "analogue" here of the play within the play in *Hamlet*—an attempt to convey the *ambience* of Greek tragedy in relation to the modern—discovers itself as a ruse to draw attention away from the *function* of the mise en abîme in Shakespeare's drama. De Quincey has nothing to say about the way in which Hamlet *deploys* the play—itself a crude murder narrative—to discover the king's guilt, to reveal him as a fratricidal murderer and a perpetrator of incest. Just as Hamlet deploys the play within the play, so De Quincey deploys the mise en scène of Greek tragedy itself in distancing and idealizing the traumatic narratives that reverberate throughout his writing, most commonly in the "dream architecture" of the *Confessions* and *Suspiria de Profundis*.[38] Greek tragedy may be in itself morally castrated, shorn of a Christian sense of infinitude, but in a world in which (as Hillis Miller has indicated[39]) the "'disappearance of God' has left only the immeasurable space and time of His vacant creation," it at least represents a powerful magnitude which displaces vacuity. As such, it configures that "false" aesthetic which Coleridge discerned in Klopstock's *Messiah,* the "arithmetical sublime . . . mistak[ing] bigness for greatness" [*C Lects 1808–19* 2:427). For De Quincey, Greek is to Christian tragedy what Coleridge's "Commanding Genius" is to his "Absolute Genius," the enactment of physical rather than moral power. Translated into the sphere of ethics, Coleridge's "arithmetical sublime" adumbrates the difference between "the mighty hunters of mankind" whose power is built upon systematic vice, and the "absolute" artist "bring[ing] the whole soul of man into activity" (*CBL* 2:15–16), the difference we saw De Quincey eliding in his parodic aesthetics of murder.

De Quincey's idea of Greek tragedy is dependent upon his selective development of part of Schlegel's theory, namely the latter's praise (following Winckelmann) for its statuesque, rather than picturesque, perfection: "We can only become properly acquainted with the tragedies of Sophocles, before the groups of Niobe or Laocoön."[40] This may have been reinforced in conversation with Coleridge, who had introduced the idea to an English public in the ninth of his 1811–12 lectures on Shakespeare and Milton (*C Lects 1808–19* 1:348–49). De Quincey took his cue from Schlegel's remark that the movement of the Greek tragic actors represented "a succession of plastic attitudes . . . [like] so many statues in the grand style endowed with life and motion,"[41] an idea we will see him applying in the narrative of the 1854 "Postscript." In all the Greek plays, he argued, "certain great *situations*—not passion in states of growth, of movement, of self-conflict—but fixed, unmoving *situations,* were selected; these held on through the entire course of one or more acts. . . . The story of the tragedy was pretty nearly involved and told by implication in the *tableaux vivants* which presided through the several acts" (*DQW* 10:349).

Developing his idea of the stiffened, stilted language and the short scenic gyrations of the play within the play in *Hamlet* in relation to Greek tragedy, De Quincey argued that the 150 to 180 lines of iambic hexameter verse composing the dialogue in each act sufficed merely to unfold a situation, but not to develop a character. Because the whole point of the tragic drama for De Quincey was to create an atmosphere of sublime power rather than a moral interest, a sense of "life in a state of remotion, unrealized, and translated into a neutral world of high cloudy antiquity" (*DQW* 10:349), the characters were in no way individualized or portrayed as moral agents. Sounding for a moment more like Hegel than A. W. Schlegel, De Quincey argued that the characters of Antigone and Creon were for a Greek audience idealized, monochromatic figures from a remote antiquity, "entirely passive to the moulding and determining power of the situation" in which the tragedy placed them. Hence De Quincey's indifference to tragic ethics, which Schlegel had represented as the struggle between "inward liberty" and "external necessity,"[42] and which Coleridge had interpreted as a primitive anticipation of Christian revelation. Picking a quarrel with the Schlegels and Coleridge, he denied that Fate had any ethical relevance in Greek tragedy: "Fate was therefore used, not for its own direct moral value as a force upon the will, but for its derivative power of ennobling and darkening" (*DQW* 10:351). "A prophetic colouring, a colouring of ancient destiny, connected with a character or an event," he affirmed, "has the effect of exalting and ennobling" (*DQW* 10:350).

Fascinated by the ritualistic character of "religious awe" in Greek tragedy, De Quincey seems to have understood catharsis in an almost sacramental sense. He had after all been present at the second of Coleridge's 1808 lectures on the "Principles of Poetry," in which the religious origin of tragedy was established in the choric hymns that "accompanied an established sacrifice to one of the Hero-Gods . . . It first appeared as the Hymn of the Goat, the victim offered to Bacchus, as God of the vine"

(*C Lects 1808–19* 1:44). Unlike the English tragedians, the Greek never represented murder on stage, but nonetheless the primitive origin of the genre lay in the ritual murder of a heroic scapegoat. Although De Quincey dismissed the Dionysiac sacrifice as "an idolatrous rite" and "sacrificial pomp" (*DQW* 10:345), his explanation of catharsis has more in common with Freud's in *Totem and Taboo* than with Aristotle's cryptic account in the *Poetics*. The hero has to suffer the tragic guilt that is heaped on his shoulders by the chorus; in reality the guilty party (in Freud's version of the story, the band of brothers who have murdered their father), the chorus nevertheless present themselves as impartial spectators.[43] In "Theory of Greek Tragedy" De Quincey followed Schlegel in his characterization of the chorus: it "stood on the level of a sympathizing spectator, detached from the business and the crash of the catastrophe; and its office was to guide or to interpret the sympathies of the audience" (*DQW* 10:359).

Yet the role of the chorus is more complicit, less comfortable than De Quincey would have it here. In his essay on the "Brocken-Spectre" in *Suspiria de Profundis* he compared the Greek chorus to the mysterious psychic projection which he termed the "Dark Interpreter." The function of both is "not to tell you anything new, *that* was done by the actors in the drama; but to recall you to your own lurking thoughts—hidden for the moment or imperfectly developed, and to place before you . . . such commentaries, prophetic or looking back, pointing the moral or deciphering the mystery, justifying Providence or mitigating the fierceness of anguish, as would . . . have occurred to your own meditative heart—had only time been allowed for its motions" (*DQL* 157). The murderous dissimulation that Freud discovered in the Greek chorus has its analogy in a rejected draft for *Suspiria* in which De Quincey is far more explicit in representing the fiendish character of the Dark Interpreter. The fragment cites the testimony of the English murderer Symons who, "as he rushed on his hellish career, perceived distinctly a dark figure on his right hand, keeping pace with himself. . . . [A] fiend would be a poor, trivial bagatelle compared to the shadowy projections, *umbras* and *penumbras,* which the unsearchable depths of man's nature is capable, under adequate excitement, of throwing off, and even into stationary forms."[44] The Dark Interpreter—the Romantic avatar of the Greek tragic chorus—is at once a figure of identification and displacement, an agency for playing out a sense of inadmissible guilt in the symbolic locus of tragic art. It "stimulates" and "ventilates" profound natures, "revealing the worlds of pain and agony and woe possible to man—possible even to the innocent spirit of a child."[45] In the final section, we shall see De Quincey using the choric Dark Interpreter in the "witness narrative" of the 1854 "Postscript" as a refined alternative to the strategy of narrative identification proposed in his 1823 *Macbeth* essay.

Before turning to the "Postscript" itself, however, I will conclude by glancing at De Quincey's extraordinary notion of the stagecraft of the Greeks. In the "Theory of Greek Tragedy," he suggested that the statuesque nature of Greek drama, in part a product of the religious awe and veneration that surrounded the performance, was also a necessary result of the enormous physical size of the Greek theaters. In a theater seating 30,000 people such as the Athenian, every citizen had the right of accommodation, "a pledge of grandeur" unthinkable in the modern theater and one that required the physical aggrandizement of the bodies and features of the actors: "Hence the cothurnus to raise the actor; hence the voluminous robes to hide the disproportion thus resulting to the figure; hence the mask larger than life, painted to represent the noble Grecian contour of countenance; hence the mechanism by which it was made to swell the intonations of the voice like the brazen tubes of an organ" (*DQW* 10:346).

In common with other Romantic critics, De Quincey had no more faith in the modern theater as a vehicle for "the literature of power" than he had in the "polite magazine context" of *Blackwood's* or the other periodicals in which he was constrained to write. A case in point is his 1846 essay "The *Antigone* of Sophocles, as Represented on the Edinburgh Stage," a review of a contemporary attempt—one of the first of its kind—to stage a translation of *Antigone* with music by Mendelssohn. Apart from the popular actress Miss Helen Faucit's surpassing Antigone, the performance failed to convince the theater critic for *Tait's Edinburgh Magazine*. The theater felt more like the boudoir of Antigone than a regal hall in Thebes, the Coryphaeus "seemed . . . no better than a railway labourer, fresh from tunnelling or boring, and wearing a *blouse* to hide his working dress," and Mendelssohn's attempt to re-create the music of ancient Greece struck De Quincey as better suited to a Liverpool synagogue than to the tragic stage. In short, the whole thing collapsed into a sad burlesque of the original, not through any fault of the revivers, but rather because "the limitations of our theatres, arising out of our habits and social differences, had made it impossible to succeed" (*DQW* 10:386). Nevertheless, still inspired by his idea of Greek tragedy, and moving beyond the ironic bathos within which tragedy seemed necessarily constrained in the nineteenth-century space of representations (evident both in the *Antigone* review and the earlier "On Murder" essays), De Quincey turned to the tragic muse one last time in the powerful "Postscript" of 1854.[46]

V

The 1854 "Postscript," nearly sixty pages of impassioned prose bearing the marks of the elderly De Quincey's "nervous malady" (*DQW* 13:124), links up the aesthetics of murder explored in earlier writings with his later theory of tragedy. It enacts what the earlier "Murder" essays satirically assert, namely that murder can be represented aesthetically; Williams's murders are described in the course of the "Postscript" as "so complex a tragedy" (*DQW* 13:80), a "bloody drama" (13:85), a "tragic drama" (13:91), a "piteous tragedy" (13:93), and "this hideous tragedy" (13:104). A. S. Plumtree has suggested that in De Quincey's compelling account of the murder of the Marr and Williamson families (the McKean murders at the end are really a coda to the rest of the essay) he deployed the narrative method described in his critical exegesis of the knocking at the gate in *Macbeth*.[47] Let us put this to the test by examining the manner in which the narrative squares with De Quincey's theory of tragedy.

Mary, the Marr's servant girl, is sent out from their hosiery shop on the seedy East-End Ratcliffe Highway late one Saturday night to buy oysters for the family supper. While she is away, John Williams, an erstwhile shipmate of Marr, visits the shop and brutally murders Marr, his pretty young wife, a young apprentice-boy, and the couple's young baby, which had been lying asleep in its cradle in the basement kitchen. Williams shatters the skulls of his victims with a ship's carpenter's mallet and then cuts their throats for good measure. Just as he is completing his gory task, Mary returns and knocks on the front door. The passage in which we experience the moment of terrified suspense in the persona of Mary is justly famous, and I will quote only part of it: "On the stairs . . . was heard a creaking sound. Next was heard most distinctly a footfall; one, two, three, four, five stairs were slowly and distinctly descended. Then the dreadful footsteps were heard advancing along the narrow passage to the door. . . . The very breathing can be heard [De Quincey's shift into the present tense heightens dramatic effect] of that dreadful being who has silenced all breathing except his own in the house. There is but a door between him and Mary" (*DQW* 13:88). Mary has become Macduff knocking at the gates of Dunsinane; or at least *nearly,* for reasons which will be evident in a moment. It is a tribute to the power of De Quincey's narrative that Dostoyevsky based his account of Raskolnikov's murder of Alena Ivanovna and her sister Lizaveta in chapter 7 of *Crime and Punishment* on this passage, in particular the moment when the murderer stands by the door watching the bolt rattling as it is shaken from outside by Koch.

Despite the superficial similarities noted by Plumtree between Mary's and Macduff's knocking on the door, Joel Black is surely closer to De Quincey's design in pointing out the significance of his shift of narrative focus.[48] Despite his earlier exhortation (in the *Macbeth* essay) to the poet "to throw the interest on the murderer" (*DQL* 83), De Quincey's narrative differs significantly from both Shakespeare's and Dostoyevsky's inasmuch as it "chooses to leave [the murderer's] reaction to the servant's knocking a mystery, and instead presents the climactic doorway scene from the perspective of the terrified servant girl outside the door."[49] De Quincey's recourse to a "witness narrative" here attests to the influence of the choric perspective of Greek tragedy (associated above with his mysterious idea of the "Dark Interpreter") rather than the Shakespearean identification with the murderer proposed in the 1823 *Macbeth* essay. Moreover, the narrative structure of the "Postscript" is peculiarly static in its monochromatic intensity, the account of the murders only given after the event. Like the Greek tragedians, De Quincey doesn't actually represent murder "on stage." The scene is a tableau vivant of Mary listening to Williams on the other side of the door; a similar effect is achieved in the relation of the Williamson murders when the killer is watched rifling through the drawers by a petrified journeyman, lodger in the Williamson household (*DQW* 13:100), or in that of the boy who pretends to be asleep in the room where McKean cuts the throat of the maid Elizabeth Bates (*DQW* 13:121). In *Macbeth,* by contrast, the knocking on the door disturbs Macbeth and Lady Macbeth just as they have completed their grisly task—and we hear it with *their* ears, just as we follow Raskolnikov's murders, in all their nauseating detail, as a serial narrative which climaxes in the disturbance from outside—"the human has made its reflux upon the fiendish" (*DQL* 85).

The whole atmosphere of the "Postscript" is thus statuesque rather than picturesque, redolent of the "advancing phantasmagoria" and the "immeasurable gulph of shadows" characteristic of the Greek stage, "frozen into marble life." De Quincey narrates the Marr murders as "a tragic drama [which] read aloud its own history, and the succession of its several steps—few and summary" (*DQW* 13:91). In the second murder, the narrative tension achieved by juxtaposing Williams's ransacking of the downstairs rooms with the journeyman/witness's frenzied activity in tying together sheets to enable him to escape from the first-floor window is described in choric terms: "Like chorus and semi-chorus, strophe and anti-strophe, they work each against the other. Pull journeyman! pull murderer! Pull baker! pull devil!" (*DQW* 13:107). This self-conscious choric narrative has the effect of highlighting Williams's "artistry" rather than his psychological condition, making the reader identify with the witness/critic rather than the murderer as was proposed in the *Macbeth* essay.[50] The mind of the murderer is now left a sublime mystery, a "force of nature," frustrating any attempt at psychological "explanation," while the reader is enlisted into the company of Freud's "band of brothers" whose choric function disguises their complicity. As De Quincey had expressed the "hypocrite lecteur" theme in the first "Murder" essay, translating from Lactantius, "the hand which inflicts the fatal blow is not more deeply imbrued in blood than his who passively looks on . . . nor can that man seem other than a participator in murder, who gives his applause to the murderer, and calls for prizes on his behalf" (*DQW* 13:11).

De Quincey's portrait of Williams is itself an exercise in grotesque aggrandizement, a hang-over from the carnivalesque tone of the 1827 and 1839 essays; the common Irish sailor of the newspaper reports has been completely transformed. The fresh complexion heightened by wind and weather and the sandy hair have turned to "a cadaverous ghastliness, extraordinary hair [tinted bright yellow with dye used to paint high-caste horses in a macabre Punjabi religious ritual—Williams has just returned from a sea-voyage to India] and glazed eyes" (*DQW* 13:98). The sailor's clothing has been replaced by a dandyfied silk-lined surtout, and in the Williamson murder, the predator wears a new pair of creaky black boots. No attempt is made to develop Williams as a character, to offer any motive or explanation for his actions. The suggestion of sexual jealousy is raised, but attributed to popular rumor. Williams appears to have no remorse for his crimes, and even his suicide seems more an attempt to cheat the authorities than a symptom of a stirring conscience. All his energy is absorbed in the act of murder; in the "ultra fiendishness" of his aesthetical rigor, the escape of Mary or the Williamsons' journeyman or the sleeping girl is a flaw in the formal perfection of his crimes. For this mighty hunter of mankind (to appropriate Coleridge's phrase) "the household ruin [must be] full and orbicular" (*DQW* 13:89). Williams has become a tragic hero-villain from the Greek drama, complete with grotesque tragic mask "larger than life," "voluminous robes" (under which, like Raskolnikov, he conceals the murder weapon as he walks through the busy streets of the city) and even, on his feet, a creaky patent-leather cothurnus.

Albert Goldman, in one of the best critical accounts of the "Postscript," has remarked De Quincey's weakness as a "real fabulist": his inability in this or any other of his narratives to convey character, action, or plot, or to create "a world of living people engaged in significant actions."[51] But what is maybe a weakness in stories like "The Household Wreck" or "The Avenger" becomes a positive strength in swelling the sordid Ratcliffe Highway murders to a tragic magnitude. Without noticing the links with De Quincey's theory of Greek (not, I think, Shakespearean) tragedy, Goldman suggests that "a close reading of the 'Postscript' will show that it is not essentially a narrative of actions involving characters who have motives, passions, and personalities; rather it is a rhapsody of horror swelling to three great crescendoes [the three tableaux vivants], in which the theme of impending disaster is expressed with overwhelming power."[52] De Quincey's critical theory of Greek tragedy, his fascination with "that slumbering life of sculpture, as opposed to painting, which we have called a life within a life" also describes his own peculiar power here as a writer of fiction (*DQW* 10:357). In "Shakespeare," an article published in the *Encyclopaedia Britannica* in 1838, De Quincey defined dramatic "character" as that "distinction between man and man, emanating originally from the will, and expressing its determinations, moving under the large variety of human impulses. The will is the central pivot of character; and this was obliterated, thwarted, cancelled, by the dark fatalism which brooded over the Grecian stage" (*DQW* 4:74). Little wonder that he chooses to disguise the historical Williams in the mask of Greek tragedy.

I have suggested that the "dark sublimity" of the "Postscript" applies some of the aesthetic methods of Greek tragedy to popular prose narrative, legacy of De Quincey's earlier contention with Coleridgean aesthetics. It is in "impassioned prose" as a vehicle for the literature of power that De Quincey seeks to reincarnate the tragic sense, unsatisfied by stagy reconstructions of Sophocles in the Edinburgh theater or gentlemanly aesthetics addressed to a polite magazine readership. De Quincey's theory of Greek tragedy exposed the Coleridgean—and one might say paradigmatically Romantic—aesthetic to a Dark Sublime which sundered power from the ethical norms of a Coleridgean clerisy and a voluntaristic definition of culture. Even in the field of theory, notwithstanding the continuing prestige of the "Romantic ideology," it would never fully recover, and De Quincey's challenge to the Kantian/Coleridgean aesthetic would echo and reverberate in the counter-romanticism of the Nietzschean Dionysus and the Freudian Oedipus. The view of De Quincey as a Romantic tyro is thus a misconception that has been fatal to his subsequent reputation; the very fact of his involvement in the English coinage of the term *aesthetic,* the starting point of my essay, should rather lend force to the maxim that the owl of Minerva flies only at dusk.

The resilience of De Quincey's Dark Interpreter in keeping pace with the spirit of the age is attested to in the 1854 "Postscript's" revisionary portrait of the historical moment of Romanticism as a sublime configuration of power and violence diminishing the Victorian present. The "colossal sublimity" of Williams's murders, located at the watershed of the "Augustan Age" of murder (before the long decline into a dreary present of march-of-intellect poisoners) assists in the construction of a Victorian myth of the Romantic era—its "burden of the past." It even allows De Quincey, like the Greek tragedians, the historical distance necessary to metamorphose the sordid facts of the Ratcliffe Highway case into a narrative of power. As such, it troubles the Victorian religion of progress, including (the irony is sustained) the progress of crime. Like the extension of the franchise, or the proletarianization of women, or the diffusion of "useful knowledge" among the working classes, the poisoning that seemed to De Quincey to mark mid-century crime was "capable of working upon whole cities and communities" undetected, an insidious "secret ministry."[53] It is not surprising to find De Quincey linking poison—at once a parody and a symptom of social *desublimation*—with women, notably "unnatural mothers" and "English working wives."[54] What a contrast (he implies) with John Williams, "the most aristocratic and fastidious of artists" (*DQW* 13:79), unashamed of the "primitive" bludgeon and knife, but at the same time "a sort of martinet in the scenical grouping and draping of the circumstances in his murders" (*DQW* 13:110). As Josephine McDonagh notes, Williams as the agent of "household ruin" is also (perversely) "the protector of family values, or moral respectability, a Mary Whitehouse with a knife, a murderous moral majority."[55]

The narrative treatment of the Ratcliffe Highway murders in the 1854 "Postcript" is thus conceived as a salutary antidote to the "prevailing style of crime" as well as to the prevailing style of literature. For the problem with the contemporary epidemic of poisonings, "The Philosophy of Murder" tells us, is that you "cannot get up an excitement in the case of poison; it is a plain-dress drama without scenery or properties." Murder, no longer cathartic, "infuses balm into the minds of the unhanged assassin" when it should rather satisfy "the morbid taste for the terrible . . . one of the most natural and *universal* of tastes."[56] What holds true for modern murder also holds true for modern punishment. De Quincey's account of the cathartic and ultimately prophylactic agency of the murder *narrative* clearly associates it with the abandoned practice of public execution, the Hobbesian "shadow of the gallows." Reacting to the state's withdrawal from the enactment of legitimate violence, De Quincey's narrative attempts a compensatory relocation of violence in the murderer and popular reactions to the murderer. According to Randall McGowan, the goal of the reformed nineteenth-century criminal code "was to make the horror of crime exceed the horror of punishment; this was the only way to satisfy Lord Holland's injunction that the compassion likely to be produced by the punishment should not exceed the indignation generally excited by the perpetration of the crime."[57] If the carnivalesque "lodgement" we discerned in the earlier "Murder" essays parodied the brittle legislative norms of Coleridgean aesthetics, then the "Postscript" (in which carnival violence is transformed into tragic violence) serves to reinforce the law itself by "*staging* . . . the normally *repressed poles* of the fundamental binary structures underpinning a culture."[58]

One of the most effective ways in which De Quincey creates a sense of the tragic magnitude of the Ratcliffe Highway murders is by evoking the public reaction to the news of each crime. It is as if only the tragic aesthetics of murder could recover—in the mid–nineteenth century—the intensity and *universality* (the true *sensus communis*) of the tragic catharsis of the ancients. De Quincey's aesthetics of murder thus acts as a surrogate not only for the abandoned practice of public execution but also for the political violence of the revolutionary mob which haunted the Victorian imagination and which the "Postscript" struggles to exorcise. His evocation of the London panic takes its place with great nineteenth-century mob scenes like the storming of the Tolbooth in Scott's *Heart of Midlothian* or the insurrection of the sans-culottes in Carlyle's *French Revolution:*

> The frenzied movement of mixed horror and exultation [when news broke of the second Ratcliffe Highway murder]—the ululation of vengeance which ascended instantanously from the individual street, and then by a sublime sort of magnetic contagion from all adjacent streets—can be adequately expressed only by a rapturous passage in Shelley [De Quincey quotes from canto 12 of *The Revolt of Islam*] . . . In fact, the deadly roar of vengeance, and its sublime unity, *could* point in this district only to the one demon whose idea had brooded and tyran-

nised, for twelve days, over the general heart . . . The chance was a good one, and the mob was made aware of it, for catching the wolvish dog in the high noon and carnival of his bloody revels—in the very centre of his own shambles. (*DQW* 13:112–13)

If the mobs of Scott or Shelley or Carlyle are impelled by the revolutionary enthusiasm of 1789 or 1793, De Quincey's (retrospectively) Romantic mob is driven wild rather by a series of private murders. His authority here is no less a figure than Robert Southey, who had informed the young De Quincey that the Williams murders ranked "amongst the few domestic events which . . . had risen to the dignity of a *national* interest" (*DQW* 13:124). The apolitical aesthetics of murder are at once a stimulus and a sedative for those "working poor, Scottish and English," whom De Quincey had long regarded as "latent Jacobins, *biding their* time" until the revolution that he feared was approaching.[59] In the conclusion, John Williams is transformed from the Romantic artist of the "Knocking at the Gate" essay to the role of a public scapegoat whose own *remorselessness* (a quality that measures his distance from *properly* Romantic hero/villains) finds a multiplied echo in the vengeful ululations of the aroused mob. In this way the aesthetics of murder fills the vacuum left by the "secularization" of punishment and resublimates the public sphere without engendering a political rationalization of the mob's thirst for revenge, its metamorphosis into revolution.

Perhaps it is no accident that in describing the enormous crowd of London laboring poor who attended the funeral of the Marr family, following their cortege to the cemetery with "horror and grief" (it might have been "pity and terror") written on their countenances, De Quincey estimates their number at 30,000—the very capacity of the Athenian tragic theater, as he has told us in the "Theory of Greek Tragedy" (*DQW* 10:346). The "romantic" blood sacrifice of murder (like that of war in De Quincey's eponymous essay, "a counter-venom to the taint of some mortal poison" [*DQW* 8:373]) engenders a truly universal taste, a genuine *sensus communis,* which tacitly rebukes the partiality and subjectivism of Kantian and Coleridgean aesthetics. Without a political object, De Quincey returns to the patriotic rhapsodic mode of his 1849 essay "The English Mail Coach," in which the secret word "Waterloo and Recovered Christianity" unites the beleaguered nation (*DQL* 228), a comparable exercise in Romantic retrospection.

When Williams is captured after making a series of fatal mistakes, he hangs himself in his prison cell before he can be brought to trial, thereby sealing off the circle of his "ultra fiendishness." Having cunningly evaded the humiliation of public justice, he is buried in a manner which, while acknowledging his status as a homicide and suicide, also confirms the ritualistic, tragic significance of his diabolical career. De Quincey, recollecting no doubt how tragedy originated in the sacrifice of a goat, or scape-goat, to Dionysus, describes the burial of Williams with particular relish. Williams as the "Dark Interpreter" of Coleridgean genius is at once the focus for De Quincey's dangerous fantasy of a universal aesthetic and of a Romanticism (retrospectively) reconstituted in terms of power. It is fitting, therefore, that public revenge should pursue him beyond his death and seek to fix him in an unquiet grave: "Williams . . . was buried in the centre of a quadrivium, or conflux of four roads . . . with a stake driven through his heart. And over him drives for ever the uproar of unresting London!" (*DQW* 13:124).

II

Romanticism in Criticism

❦

Drummond Bone

The Question of a European Romanticism

Extending consideration of the idea of Romanticism beyond the British literary scene assists, among other things, the formulation of a history for a modern critical question: is *Romanticism* the name of a historical entity, or merely a word that became an idea and has now outlived its usefulness? We have a sense of its meaning when applied to a broad tract of cultural history, but does its use reveal a unity hidden in diversity, or only conceal real diversity? Discussions of *Romanticism* that decouple their concerns from the historical usage of the word must assume its reality as a concept;[1] yet discussions that tie themselves strictly to the word can often seem to ignore its common-sense sense—ignoring, for example, Goethe in Germany, Byron in England, the Symbolists in France. The problem of *Romanticism*'s ontological and even historical status is in absolute terms probably without an answer, but it is a question that can still be meaningfully asked. The complication is exacerbated by the fact that writers of the Romantic period itself were intensely interested in the relationship between multifarious particularity[2] and transcendental unity, both in their desire to seek some unifying substance and, *per contra,* in their suspicion of totalizing structures. The modern debate therefore mirrors a debate integral to its subject. Nowhere does it seem more challenging than in the idea that Romanticism was a Europe-wide phenomenon, which under the name of Transcendentalism later spread also to the United States. That Romanticism did transcend national boundaries is almost a cliché of criticism, and yet such a view must presume that the entity exists, and in this presumption has already taken one side of the debate.

Does it make sense to talk of a Europe-wide Romanticism, transcending particular authors or groups of authors and particular texts?[3] The question can be approached by entering the analogous contemporary debate over the relationship of the individual to the Universal in the period following the French Revolution. I shall deal mainly with German and British artists, but even here the sheer weight of the material might at least suggest that a conundrum raised in the late twentieth century has some relation to the concerns of the period itself.

The earliest usages of the word *romantic* that seem to bear on current critical usage suggest the centrality of transcendence. They derive from the "expansive effect that romances exerted upon the imagination of their readers . . . affording the boundless freedom of wild nature" which is found in the earliest usages of the adjective with their roots in the name of popular narrative verse.[4] In his notes for a lecture series in 1812–13 Coleridge distinguishes "the Poetry of the Antients . . . from that of the Moderns; or, the differences of the *Classical* from the *Romantic* poetry." The force of this distinction is characterized by an earlier note (of 1808?): "Ancients—the Finite, & therefore Grace, Elegance, Proportion, Fancy, Dignity, Majesty,—whatever is capable of being definitely conveyed by defined Forms or Thoughts— The Moderns, the infinite, & indefinite as the vehicle of the Infinite—hence more to the Passions, the obscure Hopes and Fears . . . Sublimity."[5] Coleridge is leaning directly on A. W. Schlegel's *Lectures on Art and Literature,*[6] but the question of influence does not concern us here; the important point is that both should speak so confidently of the Romantic as a will to escape the confines of the finite material world, and wander in the freedom of the infinite sublime. Coleridge also knew Friedrich Schlegel's Aphorism 116 from the *Athenaeum* of 1798: "Romantic poetry is a progressive universal poetry. . . . It alone is infinite, as it alone is free."[7] He found it natural to Europeanize his mind, just as A. W. Schlegel translated and lectured on Shakespeare as a Romantic; Friedrich spread his net even wider, as we shall see, and lectured on the Hindus and on comparative philology not solely for their own sake but as enactments of Universalism. All characterize the modern and the Romantic as spiritual and transcendent. Here, then, it is easy to speak of a broad movement: it is historically self-evident, and its existence is as it were anticipated by the theories in which it manifests itself.

At the same time the context of these usages also tends to suggest an infinity of inner space, a psychological depth whose floor vanishes to reveal not a quiddity but an allness. Schlegel: "It is individuality which is the original and eternal within man; personality doesn't matter so much. To pursue the education and development of this individuality . . . would be a divine egoism"; "God is each truly original and exalted thing, therefore the individual himself to the highest power."[8] Coleridge: "Romantic Poetry . . . appealed to the Imagination rather than to the Senses, and to the Reason as contemplating our outward nature, the workings of the Passions in their most retired recesses"; he characterized his aim as "to establish not only the identity of the Essence under the greatest variety of Forms, but the congruity & even the necessity of that variety," for "the Spirit of the Romantic Poetry, is Modification, or the blending of the Heterogeneous into an Whole by the unity of the Effect."[9] It is this insistence on the inner that led to Abrams's characterization of Romanticism as an expressivist aesthetic, in contradistinction to classical mimesis.[10] But Coleridge's "inner workings" are common to all mankind, their representation is an agent of the revelation of harmony, and Friedrich Schlegel's artists "who just wanted to write a novel" and "have by coincidence expressed themselves" have also expressed the divinity. Schlegel's insistence on the "psychological" point of view, the facing of "unnatural lusts, gruesome tortures, shocking infamy, and disgusting sensual or spiritual impotence"[11] is a yea-saying not to the different or individual in itself, but to the individual as a manifestation of the All, or at best (from the individual viewpoint) to the individual as the necessary form of the All. M. H. Abrams, it might be thought, was himself blinded by the vogue for psychoanalytic and psychological essentialism into thinking that the innerness of the Romantics was the same as post-Vienna twentieth-century innerness. This would be to oversimplify the case, for of course he is well aware of the spirituality rather than the personality of Romantic expressivism, but nevertheless the discourse of *The Mirror and the Lamp* now seems heavy with an idea of personal expression which has certainly gone from later Romanticisms. Frequently, then, the theory of individuality is a vehicle for Universalism.

Inasmuch as de Staël brought the idea of Romanticism, though not exactly the word, to Britain—and to a more or less baffled Byron in Switzerland shortly before he came across it again in Italy—she brought with it the ambiguity of differentiation and the search for universals.[12] For her distinction between literature of the North and literature of the South, like that of the Schlegels between ancient and modern, was in a crucial sense serving not a real discrimination, but a quasi-scientific reductionism. The interest lay, in other words, not in the reality of distinctions, but in the idea that taxonomy revealed a hidden order in the seemingly random. This explanatory drive, like Friedrich's comparative studies, has a curiously late-medieval quality to it. Things are linked or separated in reference to grand generalizations which are themselves, not in substance but in form, the most powerful elements in her writing. It is the *scale* of the intellectual endeavor that is communicated, and that carries what we might want to call its Romanticism.[13] A more explicitly medieval note, but a related one, is struck by Novalis in his essay *Christendom or Europe,* when the modern secular political unit is compared unfavorably to the ancient Holy Roman Empire—or rather, to Novalis's idealized conception of it.[14] On the face of it this is straightforwardly mystical, but the lurking ambiguity is brought into focus if we place it alongside Fichte's *Address to the German Nation.* A Universal emptied of historical particularity is ripe to be filled with whatever farmyard material happens to be available—and in this case it was to prove highly toxic, for the dehistoricized political unit turned into the mystical union of people, which in turn metamorphosed into the mystic inviolability of the nation state.[15] The intellectual maneuvre is the same as Friedrich's with the individual discussed above (though it can be seen throughout the period—Wordsworth's solitaries are a prime example[16]), in which the core of individuality in fact lies in the infinite divine. That itself has its roots in Fichte's explanation of the self, though it does some violence to Fichte's more careful argument.[17] The movement, then, from seeing unity at the heart of diversity is reversed, and a single individual (state or person) is endowed with the full force of the One.

In this way the Romantic love affair with the medieval, or geographically with the exotic—in particular the Orient—can be seen not as a love affair with the Other, but as a love affair with the self masquerading as the Other.[18] The individuality of the self is dissolved by the dehistoricized or despatialized, but is then reinscribed with all the weight of the Universal behind it. Another way of putting this would be to say that mysticism is typically in the service of the self. Perhaps the *locus classicus* of this experience is the end of Wagner's *Tristan and Isolde,* as Nietzsche with characteristically uneasy percipience noted: does Isolde at the point of death flow out into the overwhelming All (as the words literally say), or does the audience not experience rather the identification of the All with Isolde's self, a grandiose triumph of the Ego? It is a fine point, and the music dissolves some tensions (individualities into unities—specifically tonal), but inscribes others (it differentiates Isolde rhythmically).[19] My aim here is not to adjudicate, and it may be that others are happy to read de Staël, for example, as making a genuine discrimination. But certain ways of thinking do seem to produce characteristic knots, and politically this confusion of individual and Universal has a sinister subsequent history.

In their attitude toward language itself there can also be a universalizing tendency. Even in Schlegel's *On the Language . . . of the Hindus,*[20] a study intended to be "a scrupulous investigation," one can sense an almost moral approval behind the "richness and fertility" of the Indian and Greek languages as compared to the Amer-Indian, because in the latter "the inflections are formed by supplementary particles, instead of inflections of the root, [and thus] have no such bond of union" as in the former. The roots in American languages "present us with no living germ," whereas in the inflected languages all words "bear the stamp of affinity, all being connected in their simultaneous growth and development by community of origin." Although he admits that this very difference seems to argue against the notion that languages themselves have a single common root, one can sense his regret. The "apparent richness" which is in truth "utter poverty" in the noninflected languages could be compared to Shelley's impatience with the "copiousness of lexicography," and his belief that "the grammatical forms which express the moods of time, and the difference of persons and the distinctions of place are convertible with respect to the highest poetry."[21] Language should not be an expression of the individual, but of the One. Schlegel would "reject all immaterial differences of outward form"—in English the word *immaterial* has an irony that may survive from the original—and Shelley laments that in translating *Faust* "even with all the license I assume" he cannot render the original (which clearly is not a matter of form, since literalness obscures rather than reveals it).

Schlegel's search for "a real language" is motivated by the desire to "stop rummaging about for words,"[22] and not surprisingly perhaps it leads him to a belief that "incomprehensibility" is the sine qua non of real, that is immediate and total, communication. This worrying idea drains value from meaning, while asserting the fundamental importance of Meaning. In Shelley's "Epipsychidion" words "obscure" their subject. In Keats's "Ode on a Grecian Urn," famously, "Heard melodies are sweet, but those unheard are sweeter."[23] To turn to a visual analogy, the differentiation of color "stains" the "white radiance" of eternity in Shelley's "Adonais," and in "Mont Blanc" the parti-colored rainbow is "earthly" while the waterfall is "ethereal."[24] In this radical view of language as differentiation, and of differentiation as the opposite of communication (since in the moment of communication difference dissolves), language inscribes the failure of communication. This paradox became an attraction for poststructuralist critics because it seemed to dramatize Derrida's analysis of Western culture as obsessed with both the "necessity and the impossibility of total communication" (as Schlegel put it) or "of Presence" (as Derrida himself would put it).[25] But the Romantics who were so obsessed, like Schlegel—and unlike the critics who were to be obsessed with the obsession—saw irony (to which we shall return) not as the deconstruction of an immaterial content, but as the deconstruction of the material form that was traditional language (that is, as another path to the Universal). The critics and the poets form yet another rather disconcerting set of chiastic twins.

This vertiginous inversion of Universal and individual is not, however, always so dizzying. The fundamentally individualist politics that underlie *Lyrical Ballads* and the autobiographical impulse of both *The Prelude* and Coleridge's "Conversation" poems support an individualist strand to their metaphysics, and neither is totally outweighed by the Universalizing tendency, though that too is there. Here we are not often giddily wrenched about in mirrors—though some recent critics write rather as if they were. "This Lime Tree Bower My Prison," for example, separates the ecstatic diction of the second paragraph from the conversational tone of both beginning and end. In doing so it allows the end to balance gently (as opposed to vertiginously) the very specific noise of the rook (a bird of communities, though here alone) and the specified address to Charles with the transcendent moment of shared experience, when the body of the rook dissolves in the light of the sun (the word "crossed" ringing symbolically as well as pictorially) as both look on.

My gentle-hearted Charles! when the last rook
Beat its straight path along the dusky air
Homewards, I blest it! deeming its black wing
(Now a dim speck, now vanishing in light)

Had cross'd the mighty Orb's dilated glory,
While thou stood'st gazing; or, when all was still,
Flew creeking o'er thy head, and had a charm
For thee, my gentle-hearted Charles, to whom
No sound is dissonant which tells of Life.

The last line's negative formation ("No . . . dissonant" as opposed to "All . . . harmonious") only accentuates the gentleness.[26]

The important question might be how far this kind of discourse negates the Universalizing possibility. It is certainly a question that is beginning to be addressed in current criticism. For the emphasis on the quotidian which has recently been argued as central to a Romantic anti-canon, particularly of woman poets, draws attention away from transcendence. Moreover, it accentuates different poems within the canonical poets—Shelley's "Letter to Maria Gisborne," for example, seems more important—and perhaps also emphasizes prose at the expense of poetry. Dorothy Wordsworth's *Journals* are popular not only because of the renewed interest of feminist criticism, but because of the related interest in particularity as a significant textual feature alongside transcendence. Mary Wollstonecraft's autobiographically specific *Short Residence in Sweden* is now as much studied as her theoretical *Vindication of the Rights of Woman.* The question is as much one of tone as abstractable "message." It is perfectly possible to interpret Coleridge's closing lines above as an archetypically transcendent moment, but rather more difficult to read it (literally, aloud) as such. Indeed, if we are disposed to give close attention to that surface so despised by Schlegel and Shelley (and Blake, who not only desired to write but insofar as he was an etcher literally did write by "the infernal method . . . melting apparent surfaces away"[27]), we will inevitably find difference, and in finding difference, be less disposed to the transcendental, and accordingly to the idea of a "Universal Poetry" or a Universal Romanticism. Insofar as the quotidian interest is an interest in the material, it runs against Romantic transcendence.

Walter Scott's name is not usually mentioned (yet) in this context, but his attempts at historicism, and the early Waverley novels' suspicion of the very exoticism that made them popular, their pragmatic insistence on milch-cows over moonshine (as in Waverley's own carefully undercut progress to the Highlanders' camp[28]), might seem to suggest that the arch-Romantic, blamed by Twain for almost precisely the political sickness associated with German Romanticism in this century, as hinted at above, was himself struggling to be historically specific rather than romantically transcendent.[29] Compared to the novelists of the Gothic tradition he clearly succeeded, but equally clearly *Waverley* was not read as a warning against other-worldly Romanticism, but rather as a romantically nostalgic lament for Romanticism's passing (Romanticism must always be elsewhere if it is conceived as transcendent, either in time or place). In the same vein it is not necessary to see Jane Austen in terms of the enlightenment to explain her empiricism—or indeed her latent materialism. For the secular and the quotidian, the opposite of the transcendent and the political, is part of Romanticism (if Romanticism is a useful idea, which of course the secular argues it is not, or not very . . .). One can argue that Austen's endings, her marriages, are themselves an escape into a Universal—in which case they constitute presumably a Romanticism against her will. As soon as one introduces the term one is locked into these labyrinthine reversals. Read only *Waverley* or *Mansfield Park* themselves and they would probably never occur. But no critic can be so innocent.

Of the twentieth century's canonical figures in the period, Byron and Goethe are the main examples of the emphasis on material specificity at the expense of Universal identity. From their own cultures' perspective, neither is seen as unequivocally Romantic, and indeed Goethe, partly because of the cultural and linguistic connotations within German of the terms, is seen by his countrymen rather unequivocally as classical. Yet from an international perspective the creators of Manfred and Childe Harold, of Werther and of Faust, are quintessentially Romantic. But again, late Byron and late Goethe share a secular ironic relativism which is sympathetic to the twentieth century, and in that sense they represent a more radical turn of mind than can be ascribed to the Universalists of the self-styled Romantic movement in Germany, or those poets who had the term thrust upon them in Britain. If the term *Romantic* is a synonym for a revolution of thought, it is more proper to apply it to Byron and to Goethe than to many of their contemporaries, yet paradoxically it is a revolution which has little to do with transcendent categories such as Romanticism. For the ironies of Goethe and Byron are not totalizing, they are not Schlegel's "irony of ironies," but live rather happily in the plural—ironies.

Irony as a figure foregrounds form and therefore particular expression, whereas the Romantic theory of irony foregrounds the retreat of particular meaning. Romantic irony involves exactly the same twist as we have seen in the invertibility of the individual and the Universal, in that content (now "Meaning") is led surreptitiously back to underwrite the seeming dominance of form. Romantic irony is the possibility of infinite expression behind one form. Not so the actual ironies of Byron and Goethe. It is equally a mistake to identify these last with the ironic tropes of the Enlightenment, for they articulate a material texture of ironic thought, and not the distance of a mistaken or overweening expression from an ideal truth. The elegiac gentlemen of *Westostlicher Divan, Beppo,* and *Don Juan,* close-focused, materially sensual, write from a world in which creation is parasitic, parodistic, and in which life is self-created—and none the worse (or almost none the worse) for it. Goethe's *Faust,* even in part 1, rewrote a "universal," a people's, tragedy, as art—a self-consciously produced artifact. In *Beppo* and *Don Juan* likewise, and even more strikingly perhaps in *The Vision of Judgment,* there is no meaning without art; the social criticism rarely seems to stem from the presumption of some ideal attainable in another or prelapsarian world. If we adopt the perspective of late Byron or middle-to-late-period Goethe, we shall find it hard to deny that the two had a great deal in common, yet we shall also have to argue against the idea that they partook of something called Romanticism. If we accept the perspective of Universalizing Romanticism, on the other hand, then it is early Byron and early Goethe who will attract us, and *there* they will be seen to have a lot in common too.

If Byron's and Goethe's "Romanticism" is modern, why is it that they are, or have been, less fashionable among poststructuralist critics? The answer may already have been touched on: they leave the deconstructionist less work to do; they are not so inextricably bound up with the bad faith of the metaphysics of Presence (as the deconstructionists would have it). There is also another, perhaps less comfortable thought. One of the most glaring of universal taxonomies is that which defines Western culture as the culture obsessed with a Romantic nostalgia for Presence. But for those interested in dinner menus or excuses for drinking, late Byron and Goethe may make welcome if inexplicable exceptions to that generalization.

To say that Delacroix and Turner are both Romantic painters would make little sense from a Goethean perspective. But the even more apparently bizarre comparison of an artist to a poet, say Turner to Shelley, which was frequently made by contemporary reviewers, would make every sense from the standpoint of a Schlegel, for whom the medium is only a barrier to the "activity." One can, on the other hand, at least attempt specified comparisons across the arts. The dissolution of certain kinds of visual structure in the later Turner (perhaps even the impermanence of his paintings' media) might for example parallel the dissolution of certain kinds of musical structure in, say, the Schubert of *Schwanengesang* (notably in the tonality of "Die Stadt").[30] Nevertheless, from the finale of Beethoven's Ninth Symphony onward, the idea of the union of words and music as a point at which specificity and Universality in some way meet without destroying the qualities of either[31] grows toward Wagner's *Gesamtkunstwerk* (the ideal union of music, words, and theatrical realization), which might then be taken as the *ne plus ultra* of Romantic synaesthesia, allowing comparisons of any medium with any other through their common participation in art.[32] Music (with a material medium only as a notation, and timeless in the sense that it exists only for an instant) had indeed, long before the *Gesamtkunstwerk,* become almost a synonym for all Romantic art. It seemed the ideal of an art communicating without reference to particular space and time.[33] From the musical craftsman's point of view such a position might be well nigh absurd—though Wagner certainly wrote as if it were not. As Shelley believed that any great poetry was convertible into any other great poetry with respect to time, so, particularly through music, any art became convertible into any other art with respect to its medium.

The comparativist impulse, whether among languages or among arts—whole communicating systems—has a healthy history in the Romantic period, and this will not surprise us.[34] Yet this impulse can be seen either as Universalising or as reductive of the richness of individual experience. Or to put it the other way round, the individualist imperative seems to bring with it an equal but contradictory universalising imperative. Modern critical thinking is caught in the same dilemma. The desire to allow everything its own space seems contrary to the need for explanation, and there is an urgent need for explanation. The idea of a European Romanticism presupposes the idea of Romanticism—and no matter how commonsensical this may seem, it may only be an index of how the Universalising aspect of what we call the Romantic period has penetrated our way of thinking at the expense of the radically individualist. We should perhaps remember that this way of thinking has not had the happiest of historical consequences, and that we may find ourselves uncomfortably aligned with some of the period's own more unnerving ideals.

Susan J. Wolfson

Romanticism and the Question of Poetic Form

❦

Beyond Formalism and Back Again

A determination to move "beyond formalism" gave the title to a collection of essays published by Geoffrey Hartman in 1970. Yet, five years onward, he found himself "more rather than less impressed . . . by how hard it is to advance 'beyond formalism' in the understanding of literature."[1] This tenacity draws its strength from divergences and contradictions in the very definition of "form" and the applications of "formalism"—themselves significant legacies of Romanticism's own sophisticated debates about poetic form and its relation to other cultural forms, even to matters of social and political performance.[2]

The emergence of formalist criticism in this century, about fifty years ago, revived an important Romantic aesthetic, namely that poetry requires recognition as a composition in form. Against a then-dominant emphasis on content (manifest or repressed), polemicists such as R. S.

Crane argued that in poetry, nothing "is matter or content merely, in relation to which something else is form. . . . [E]verything is formed, and hence rendered poetic."[3] This is why W. K. Wimsatt called the domain of poetry "more than usually verbal": it is "hyperverbal" in the way its forms of composition are "supercharged with significance."[4] At the historical moment of these polemics, Wimsatt was tactically promoting a logocentrism of "words taken in their fullest, most inclusive and symbolic character" and of the poem itself as an "iconic solidity" with "a fullness of actually presented meaning" (231), and Crane was seeking a neo-Aristotelian analytic to identify the determining "principles of structure" in "particular configurations" (184). We need not share these agenda to appreciate the perspective that they provide on how the formal elements of poetry (as a European contemporary, Jan Mukařovský, put it) work as "an indirect semantic factor" by calling attention to form itself.[5] Not only is this attention a surprising common ground in the diversity of mid–twentieth-century theory, it concentrated the critical energies and polemics of Romanticism, which frequently took shape in a formalist poetics where choices of form and the way it was managed had as much resonance as words themselves.

The formal investments of poetry are one reason that it has proven so difficult for criticism to get "beyond" formalism. Hartman diagnosed his own addiction as an inability to discover a "method to distinguish clearly what is formal and what is not"[6]—a perplexity that others have felt. René Wellek and Austin Warren concede as much in the midst of *Theory of Literature*—an earlier, and for a while very influential, brief for the "intrinsic study of literature."[7] Their call for a study of the "work of art" as "a whole system of signs, or structure of signs, serving a specific aesthetic purpose" was set against their dissatisfaction with the old dichotomy between "form as the factor aesthetically active and a content aesthetically indifferent." They wanted a way to "distinguish between words in themselves, aesthetically indifferent," and the means by which words become "aesthetically effective" (140–41). Their solution was predicted by (though not attributed to) a Romantic, Coleridge: a cutting across and replacement of the dichotomy of form and content with a theory of "'form' [as] that which aesthetically organizes its 'matter'" (241), the means by which "aesthetically indifferent elements acquire aesthetic efficacy" (141).

This notion of aesthetic agency was valuable for focusing attention on poetry as a discourse defined, if not necessarily privileged, by its formal actions. At the same time, however, this aesthetic designation and its presumption of historical neutrality unwittingly forecast the terms in which midcentury formalism, along with the Romantic texts to which it is indebted, would be discredited.

Formalisms, Antiformalisms

The effects of designating aesthetic agency, the rationale of mid–twentieth-century formalist criticism, were at once integrative and isolationist. Even as form was linked, both in technique and as a troping of tradition and convention, to semantic work, the insulation of criticism from contextual claims also suppressed attention—with no small sacrifice—to the way formal choices and actions are also enmeshed in networks of social and historical conditions. To assess the effect of this twentieth-century formalist criticism on the study of Romanticism and its formalisms, we need to review the general scene onto which it emerged.

Modern formalist criticism was itself a revaluation. The first powerful reviews of Romanticism, a century before, had read in it an antiformalism symptomatic of intellectual and moral failure. Charles Kingsley's protest is typical: "A poetry of doubt, even a sceptical poetry, in its true sense, can never possess clear and sound form, even organic form at all. How can you put into form that thought which is by its very nature formless?"[8] The patent reference was to Coleridge's German-into-English elevation of "organic form" over the "mechanical regularity" of "predetermined form" and his grounding of this aesthetic in nature rather than culture: its processes are "innate," taking shape as "it developes itself from within. . . . Such is the Life, such the form" (*C Lects 1808–19* 1:495). I shall have more to say about the subsequent designation of this aesthetic as a synecdoche for Romanticism; for now, I am concerned with the critical revelation of the first part of Kingsley's charge: how an interpretation of Romantic poetic form as a quality of thought drew attention to form as something other than subordinate device. The displays of form itself were deemed significant.

For serious Victorians, the significance was default. Arnold implies this in opposing Romantic expression, with its "source in a great movement of feeling," to the poetry of "high seriousness," identifiable in "the noble and profound application of ideas to life . . . under the conditions immutably fixed by the laws of poetic beauty and poetic truth."[9] The language of laws evokes a formalism not just of technique but of intellectual judgment and social consequence. Thus, even his praise of Wordsworth hints at an art without "formal philosophy": "[T]he accident . . . of inspiration, is of peculiar importance. It might seem that Nature not only gave him the matter for his poem, but wrote his poem for him. He has no style. . . . Nature herself seems . . . to take the pen out of his hand, and to write for him with her own bare, sheer, penetrating power" (Preface to *Poems of Wordsworth*, xix, xxii, xxiv). Mere philosophy in the neoclassical mode was not the antidote, however, as Arnold's famous judgment on Dryden and Pope makes clear: "Though they may write in verse, though they may in a certain sense be masters of the art of versification, [they] are not classics of our poetry, they are classics of our prose" (*APrW* 9:181). Even so, he was not prepared to work the issue from the other side, that is, to define an aesthetic domain releasing literature both from the social obligation of applying its ideas to life and from the didactic function of limiting those ideas to "profound, permanent, fruitful, philosophical truth" (*APrW* 3:266). This would be the task of A. C. Bradley's inaugural Oxford Lecture on Poetry, "Poetry for Poetry's Sake."[10]

In a pivotal rethinking of poetic function, and with critical attention to poetry as a verbal form, Bradley disputed the traditional "antithesis of substance and form" (13) to contend that their identity is "the essence of poetry." He carefully resisted both "the heresy of the separable substance" (17) that deemed form "negligible" to sense, and "the formalist heresy" (24) that subsumed content into sensuous effect. He insisted instead that "if substance and form mean anything *in* the poem, then each is involved in the other" (15–16). However much one may "decompose" a poem "and abstract for comparatively separate consideration [the] formal element of style," the actual "experience" of reading never lets one "apprehend this value by itself," but forces attention to the fact that "style is . . . a significant form" (19). This claim for form as "significant" moved the discussion past the terms of power and relapse wielded by Kingsley and Arnold; it verged on a semantics of form.[11]

American formalist criticism was impelled by a similarly polemical sense of form as the constitutive element of literary language. This focus may seem insular now, but it was radical in light of then-prevailing modes of analysis, as John Crowe Ransom's prophetically titled *The New Criticism* makes clear. By 1913 Sir Sidney Lee was describing literary scholarship as a study of "the external circumstances—political, social, economic—in which literature is produced," and by the 1940s Ransom was feeling that the study of literature per se had been lost to contextualism, which he summed as "critical theory": "Most critical writing is done in the light of 'critical theory,' which unfortunately is something less than aesthetics."[12] While he did not consider how "aesthetics" might bear a theoretically (and ideologically) cast light, he was alert to what might be lost without aesthetic attention. When the New Criticism of the 1940s devoted itself to the "intrinsic study of literature" (the urging of Wellek and Warren), it also took contextualism—in particular historicism—as its heuristic antithesis.

For their part, Wellek and Warren went to work defining various "fallacies" of interpretation, ones for the most part based on protocols of "causal" explanation from "extrinsic" reference (to authorial intention, biography, historical and social contexts, popular and critical reception, textual genetics). Cleanth Brooks's approach to reading in *The Well Wrought Urn,* a primer of New Criticism, openly resisted the sway of "historical background" and "literary history." In an atmosphere that had made it seem that reading literature in relation to "historical context" was "the only kind of reading possible," he proposed "to see what residuum, if any, is left after we have referred the poem to its cultural matrix" (x) and to assume "that there is such a thing as poetry, difficult as it may be to define," against the view of literature as "synonymous with 'anything written in words'" (216–17). In this criticism's assertion of its "newness," a prevailing contextualism was reformed into a view of the text as a discrete artifact, following its own dynamics of "formal structure and rhetorical organization" (218). When Brooks contended that "form and content cannot be separated" because "form is meaning," he meant that form as well as language could signify.[13]

We can see why reactions against New Criticism (and the Romantic poetics of "organic form" that seemed complicit) routinely charge it with being antihistorical and fixated on "mere" technique.[14] Yet the critiques usually elide the dialectic *with* historicism marked, for instance, by Brooks's interest in the residuum "left *after* we have referred a poem to its historical context" (x, my italics).[15] Brooks was not rejecting contextual reference; he was testing whether there is anything in literary—more specifically, poetic—organizations of language that could not be restricted to this information. There is an important difference, of course, between his idea of history as objective "background" and theories of history and literature as mutually implicated in cultural poetics (or, in some analyses, of history as the suppressed referent of literary process). But it is important to recognize that Brooks did not say that studying poetry refused history and culture, only that the former required different kinds and sequences of attention.[16]

It was not formalism per se that discredited New Criticism; it was its strategic displacement of context "to make the study of the work of art the center of interest" (Wellek and Warren, 140) and its regard of form as the product of a historically disinterested, internally coherent imagination. This is what motivated Jerome McGann's influential but somewhat restrictive judgment of the purpose of literary form: "unlike non-aesthetic utterance," it offers social evaluations "to the reader *under the sign of completion*" (his emphasis). Formalists take this sign "as their object of study," he says, and he urges us to see both the "experience of finality and completion" and the representation of "the poem as transhistorical" as effects of a specific discourse of "historical totality": "its integral form is the sign of this seeming knowledge—and it persuades its reader that such a totality is not just a poetic illusion, but a truth."[17] McGann viewed events of poetic form as worth attention only as part of a nearly deterministic "ideological formation." Formalist analysis, like any "specialized" approach, will matter only insofar as it can, indeed "must," find its "*raison d'être* in the socio-historical ground."[18] The critical task was to show how "social forms" shape "forms of consciousness," "forms of thought," and "forms (or 'structures') of feeling"—and to expose the uncritical complicity of these forms with an "ideological form."[19]

This critique of literary form as an ideological totality was not interested in closer reading for local lines of resistance. But another contemporaneous movement against (if not beyond) New Critical formalism used subversive close reading "to reveal the existence of hidden articulations and fragmentations within assumedly monadic totalities," in Paul de Man's words.[20] Where New Criticism rejected a determinate reference to the "intention of the author" in "judging . . . a work of literary art,"[21] de Man redeployed intention, applying it to New Critics themselves. That "poetic language, unlike ordinary language, possesses . . . 'form'" struck him as a "prefigurative structure" for formalist criticism. The difference, he proposed, is merely temporal, the poetry constituting the "foreknowledge" of the critic and so orienting, by a "dialectical interplay," the "intent at totality of the interpretative process."[22] The peculiar strength of New Criticism for de Man was the way, even as it promoted a formalism of totalized understandings, it focused on events within the "distinctive structures of literary language (such as ambiguity and irony)" that contradicted "a purely empirical notion of the integrity of literary form." This contradiction was a kind of prefigurative structure, in turn, for de Man's theoretical interests. He saw the "internal evolution" of New Criticism as self-deconstructing but simultaneously prevented from integrating its subversive insights "within a truly coherent theory of literary form" by the unfortunate collusion of its theory of the intentional fallacy with a blindness to its own critical intentionality.[23]

De Man's challenge to the New Critical "theory of signifying form" (which sees language as containing, reflecting, or referring to experience) with a theory of how "form . . . can constitute a world" would eventually lead him to suggest the usefulness of an evolved formalism for social and ideological analyses.[24] But it was not in rapport with him that Marxist and new-historicist critiques were describing the ideologically motivated "constructing functions" of literary form. Although Terry Eagleton, like de Man, was interested in events of incoherence, inconsistency, and self-contradiction in literary form, his investment was different. For him, these events showed the "ideological struggles" displaced by the "naturalising, moralising, and mythifying devices" of form invading literary production. "Marginalised yet . . . querulously present," these struggles either compel "organic closures" to "betray their *constructing* functions" or "inscribe" such structure in "self-contradictory forms," "fissures and hiatuses." The literary project of "formal displacement" thus ruptures into a texture of "formal discontinuities," and it is these events that constitute a literary work's "historical meaning."[25]

For both de Man and Eagleton, formalism is still regarded under the sign of "specious form" and organicist ideology, itself an inheritance of the Romantic poetics of "organic form."[26] Ruptures were taken to be signs of ideological contradictions that it was the business of criticism, operating against poetic coverups, to discover and expose. What is missing from the story thus told is any sense of how Romantic formalism itself was involved in this kind of critical project. While it is true that Romanticism is the historical moment when organicist theory received forceful and elaborate articulation, "organic form" is not the whole story of formalism, either in Romanticism or in the full text of New Criticism. The centrality of "organic" form in recent critiques reflects only the partiality with which the official rhetoric of New Criticism appropriated Romanticism—and, not coincidentally, the (still) seductive sway of Romanticism's own most idealizing formulations.

The Fortunes of Formalism and the Fate of Romanticism

About Romanticism, twentieth-century formalist criticism is nothing if not ambivalent. On the one hand, Romanticism seemed antithetical—by virtue of the contextualism called for by its historical moment; by the fact of its own formation as a revolution against, or at least a reform of, inherited forms; and even internally, by the reference to intention and biography demanded by its poetics of expressiveness: "It is not so much a historical statement as a definition to say that the intentional fallacy is a romantic one," Wimsatt and Beardsley remark in a key position paper on the latter point.[27] And it was to Romanticism—not as an aesthetic ideology but as a cultural event—that Wellek and Warren attributed the overwhelming contextualism that had taken hold of literary study in their day: "Modern literary history arose in close connexion with the Romantic movement, which could subvert the critical system of Neo-Classicism only with the relativist argument that different times required different standards. Thus the emphasis shifted from the literature to its historical background" (139). And thus formalism took as its antithesis a leagued Romanticism and historicism—with the convenience, as Fredric Jameson observes, of repudiating "its radical tradition and return[ing] for [its] models to Metaphysical and Cavalier poetry."[28] On the other hand, formalism kept returning to Romanticism's theoretical writing, especially Coleridge's. The crucial attraction was an idea of literary or, more particularly, poetic language distinguishable from ordinary language by its internally coherent "organic form," a principle by which opposites could achieve unity by force of a specific aesthetic agency—a "shaping spirit of Imagination," in Coleridge's terms.[29]

This split view of Romanticism—as an inimical contextualism and as a progenitor of theoretical formalism—patterned the way its poetry got discussed, discounted, or evaded altogether for the sake of (sometimes as a condition of) other critical agenda. Tuned primarily to a theoretical affiliation with Romanticism, New-Critical reading of the poetry was sporadic, anomalous, or in effect, reformist. New Criticism preferred a few well-formed poems (not the long ones and fragments), displaying tension, irony, and paradox—texts that accord with their admired canon of similarly well-wrought Renaissance, metaphysical, Victorian, and modern lyrics. Brooks's statement that in the best Romantic poems "form is meaning" found its best demonstrations in a sifting of songs, sonnets, and odes, and in these genres, primarily early Blake, early Wordsworth, and Keats.[30] The broad consequence for Romantic study is recollected by one student of those days, Jonathan Culler: "Those of us who had been nurtured on the New Criticism and thought Donne and the moderns the supreme examples of poetic achievement were inclined to find Romantic poetry the aberration of an age and sensibility out of tune with our own. The Romantics, we had heard, thought poetry a spontaneous overflow of feeling rather than a verbal construct, an expression of personality rather than an impersonal and comprehensively ironic form."[31] It took a return to literary history via Abrams's *The Mirror and the Lamp* to show

Culler and his generation that "a whole series of contemporary critical concepts" (i.e., New Criticism) "had in fact been formulated by Coleridge and other Romantic critics" (150); and it took yet another turn, with de Man and against Abrams, to reveal "a self-deconstructive movement" within Romantic theory of the terms privileged by New Criticism (152).

The initial lack of attention to the Romantic poetics of form in any terms other than "organic form" was exacerbated by subsequent resistances to formalism altogether and a sweeping critique of organic ideology. Poetic forms became features to be seen through, read beyond, around, or against. This is not to say that there were not several very fine and still valuable late- or post-New-Critical studies of form in particular poets, but these were local forays, tactfully assimilating attention to form to other frames of analysis (biography, literary history, genre, philosophy) rather than asserting its value in the face of its emerging detractors.[32] The polemical studies, by contrast, assaulted formalism and were determined to reorganize the reading of Romanticism in defiance of it. This "challenge to formalist dogma," notes Christopher Norris, "went along with a revived interest" in "the ethos of Romanticism"—the very contextualism that earlier formalist critics wanted to set aside.[33]

The new contexts were various—phenomenology, intertextuality, historicist analysis, rhetorical theory—but each marked its resistance to formalism by shifting the discourse of form away from device and technique. Myth criticism, in Northrop Frye's influential application of it to Romantic poetry, did recognize literature as an "autonomous verbal structure" but submerged specific forms into the "original hypothetical form" of all "discursive verbal structures" given by "conceptualized myth."[34] Not only did this criticism, in Hartman's apt description, translate poetic form into a "mediated form called allegory" but it subsumed the "allegorical forms" into "archetypes." Nor was Hartman's own philosophically tuned reading of Romantic poetry particularly formalist: avoiding "minute stylistic or structural analysis," he focused on the "structures of consciousness" reflected in verbal figures, literary modes (epitaph and inscription), and "rhetorical form[s]" such as surmise.[35] The psychoanalytic studies of Romantic writers appearing alongside Hartman's and Frye's typically elided literary form, except as a signifier of deeper truths which, while not exactly imageless, were felt to have little to do with specific formal choices, beyond the choice of imaginative literature itself as a form of expression and displacement. Even the most text-based of such criticism, Harold Bloom's reading of ratios of influence, revision, and tropological displacement in Romantic poetry, just glanced at form to note how the centrality of the prized "lyric form" courted "the shadow cast by the precursor." So baleful was Bloom's view of the "impasse of Formalist criticism" that colleagues such as Hartman regarded him as fundamentally "anti-formalist"—a stance that Bloom flaunted a few years later in the opening essay for *Deconstruction and Criticism,* "The Breaking of Form": conceding his "own lack of interest in most aspects of what is called 'form' in poetry," he proposed that "poetic meaning" gleams in "the breaking apart of form." About the only formalism surviving this breakup, remarked Frank Lentricchia, was Bloom's own, his "desire to totalize literary history."[36]

And about the only large-scale accounts of Romantic forms in these decades saw them as agents of occlusion. De Man read Romanticism the way that he read American formalism—as a rhetoric that displaced, or at least remained strategically blind to, the knowledge that poetic language is always "constitutive . . . unable to give a foundation to what it posits except as an intent of consciousness."[37] In general, deconstructive readings inverted New Critical designs. De-privileging the unity vested "in the 'achieved' or 'coherent' form of a literary work," they sought "to see *through* literary form to the way language or symbolic process makes or breaks meaning."[38] These readings concentrated on subversive tropes and intertextuality, and tended not to see how form, too, might be involved in this critical activity. So, too, marxist and new historicist critiques cast Romanticism as an aesthetic ideology intent to proffer its poetic forms as autonomous unities signifying knowledge authorized by nature rather than determined by history and culture. "Organic form" (and its taint of New-Critical renewal) was the summary for Romanticism, its formalist poetics, and its dominant critical tradition. It was "*The* Romantic Ideology"—in the broadcast of McGann's influential study by that title.

As with deconstruction, the critic's charge was to expose the complicity of poetic form with this ideology. In "the privilege accorded by the Romantics to the 'creative imagination,'" Eagleton told readers of *Literary Theory,* his terms at once echoing McGann's and parodying Coleridge's,

> [T]he literary work itself comes to be seen as a mysterious organic unity, in contrast to the fragmented individualism of the capitalist marketplace: it is "spontaneous" rather than rationally calculated, creative rather than mechanical. . . . At the centre of aesthetic theory at the turn of the eighteenth century is the semi-mystical doctrine of

the symbol. For Romanticism, indeed, the symbol becomes the panacea for all problems. Within it, a whole set of conflicts which were felt to be insoluble in ordinary life . . . could be magically resolved.[39]

Eagleton is concerned primarily with the imprint of this doctrine on the post-Romantic novel, whose forms of displacement he sees complicit with the emergence of "organicist" social theory: both discourses evoke the "spontaneous unity of natural life-forms" in order to "denote symmetrically integrated systems characterised by the harmonious interdependence of their component[s]."[40]

What is problematic for Romanticism in this critique is the equation of poetic form with harmony, symmetry, and unity, and thus a categorical insulation from the conflicts discovered and contemplated by historicist theory (and its own use of "organic" formulations).[41] Even so, this view spread to Romantic studies. If Hartman once found fault with formalist criticism for its reluctance to "demystify" the "disinterestedness of form in 'To Autumn'" by "discovering behind its decorum a hidden interest,"[42] readers such as McGann, David Simpson, and Marjorie Levinson were offering urgent divestments, pointedly casting the lexicon of form into a syntax of ideological analysis. Simpson reviews Coleridge's theory of organic form as a "discursive response to the material basis of culture and political life in early nineteenth-century England," one marked by the contentiousness of "wars, civil rights trials, food riots, radical and reform movements."[43] Applying this analysis to the canonical poetry (and, unlike Simpson, evading questionings and ironies), McGann and Levinson "demystify" the textual processes to expose an "ideological formation," arguing that the literary form masks "the contradictions inherent in contemporary social structures and the relations they support."[44] The critical terms are emphatically reform(al)ist. What is "inherent" is not a shaping principle of poetic form but, in Levinson's words, the contradictions in social structure that the "manifest theme and *achieved* form" of the text occludes (my italics). Thus seeing the poem as "formally a sort of allegory by absence" of what is "outside or social," the new historicist must reverse the older formalism and "set . . . form *against* content"—against, that is, the social exterior.[45]

Helpful as these readings are in historicizing Romantic poetry, there is a tendency in McGann and Levinson (at least) to limit accounts of poetic form to the organic, the unified, the achieved, the stable. Everything factitious, contradictory, and unstable is credited to the world "outside" the poem, or readable in its form only as the rupture of organicist desire.[46] This kind of reading misses how canonical Romantic texts such as "Tintern Abbey" or book 1 of *The Excursion* expose rather than conceal the constructedness (not only aesthetic, but social and ideological) of their designs of unity, how visibly strained (not magical) their forms of reconciliation often are, how even the theoretical ideal of organic form (as so unlikely a critic as Abrams has noticed) contends with a discourse on will and voluntary purpose (*Abrams ML* 173). Donald Wesling is not alone in viewing the idealizing as "a calculated overstatement of a literal impossibility," a "hyperbole" deployed as a "rationale for innovation in the patterning of poetic language."[47] This hyperbole may be "the primary myth of post-Romantic poetics" (2), but it is far less consolidated in Romanticism itself, whose debates alternately indulged and critically tested it. Some poems do turn from social conflict, or use their forms to exile and displace disruptive knowledge; but others, far from concealing the problematic of formalism, provoke it anew, as a condition of their very composition.

This contentious and internally divided poetics is also a Romantic legacy. It even fissures the well-wrought urns of New Criticism—and in these events helps explain the uncanny return of formalism, in different guises, to those who meant to move beyond. In *The Well Wrought Urn,* one of the texts credited with bearing the mystified formalist ideology of Romanticism into modern critical thought, Brooks means to draw on Coleridge's famous definition (in *Biographia*) of imagination as an agent of unity and reconciliation: "poetic structure" is "a structure of meanings, evaluations, and interpretations; and the principle of unity which informs it seems to be one of balancing and harmonizing connotations, attitudes, and meanings" (195). This process of "unit[ing] the like with the unlike" (195) is no magical sleight for Brooks, however; it confronts and strains under "pressure" and "stresses" (198, 203). In some Romantic odes, he sees the "thrusts and pressures exerted by the various symbols" being "played, one against the other," sometimes "perversely," with their language "under the pressure of context," "warped into new meanings" (210); words in poetry bear no discrete meaning but are "a potential of meaning, a nexus or cluster of meanings," so that even when they form a statement, this is "warped and bent . . . deflected away from a positive, straightforward formulation" and rendered "perverse" (211). Almost counterintuitively, Brooks's own words slip into warps and bents. Citing Coleridge's description of the imagination as a "power" which "reveals itself in the balance or reconcilement of opposite or discordant qualities," he reports that among these are "*sane*ness with difference" (18, my italics)—an erratum (or, given its persistence in every edition, a misreading?) yielding the spectral suggestion that in "difference" looms the *in*sanity of semantic heterogeneity—of everything that resists and subverts the organization of poetic form. In the shadow of Romanticism, this verbal slip looks like a return of the repressed, a concession of the motives impelling the well-wrought turns of New Critical argument.

Romantic Formalisms

The restlessness of Brooks's formalism is, in some ways, a late reverberation of the polemics about form that defined Romanticism. For a long time the prestige of Romanticism and a sense of its modernity were strongly allied, both ideologically and stylistically, with its rhetoric of resistance to form, the declarations sounding even at times like antiformalism. Whether cast as a progressive "experiment" and "innovation" or allied with "liberty" and "revolution," the rhetoric claimed modernity by troping imposed or inherited forms as tyranny or, at the very least, the strictures of unexamined prestige, custom, or habit. Wordsworth revokes Dryden's argument that the discipline of verse form "put[s] bounds to a wilde over-flowing Fancy," by asserting that all good poetry is a "spontaneous overflow of powerful feelings" and by recoiling from "the bondage of definite form."[48] German Romanticism celebrated a poetics of "chaos," "the infinite," and "the unformed"; and the infiltration of this energy, if not its extremism, was evident in English texts.[49] Hazlitt had no trouble retrospectively linking the formal practices of "the Lake school of poetry"—indeed, attributing this school's very origin—to the cataclysm of the French Revolution. Not only did radical politics parallel Laker aesthetics, they were seen as complicit. A change in poetry "went hand in hand" with "the change in politics," the one as "complete, and . . . as startling" as the other: "According to the prevailing notions, all was to be natural and new. Nothing that was established was to be tolerated. . . . [K]ings and queens were dethroned from their rank and station in legitimate tragedy or epic poetry, as they were decapitated elsewhere; rhyme was looked upon as a relic of the feudal system, and regular metre was abolished along with regular government."[50] In the historical moment of 1818, this extravagant satire was calculated in part to embarrass the conservative political evolution of Wordsworth and Coleridge. But the retrospect is not just a local barb; it is a register of how poetic form, in both Revolutionary and Regency England, was politicized.

This politicizing, with its seventeenth-century precedents, was decisively reinvigorated by Romanticism, and is more central to its practices than the antiformalism with which it was retrospectively associated. The poet of Blake's "London" uses his rhymes strategically to evoke the "mind-forg'd manacles" of social institutions and their internalization as mental prisons, and in *Jerusalem* Los famously declares, "I must Create a System, or be enslav'd by another Mans."[51] This rhetoric extended to the sheer presence of poetic form as a promise of revolution, at least in perception. Coleridge describes Wordsworth's poetry in the 1790s as "awakening the mind's attention from the lethargy of custom" and "the film of familiarity" (*CBL* 2:7). With bolder verbs, Shelley argues that poetry at once "purges from our inward sight the film of familiarity" and "strips the veil of familiarity from the world,"[52] forecasting the critical agency that Russian Formalism, almost a century later, would attribute to aesthetic deformations of the familiar.[53] In the Romantic phase, of course, these actions invest poetic form as a dissolver of customary constructions rather than (as in Russian theoretical politics) their agent of exposure. What poetry "lays bare" for Shelley is not a formal artifice but an intuition beyond form: "the naked and sleeping beauty which is the spirit of its forms" (*SW* 7:137). And for Coleridge poetry dispels the film of familiarity in order to reveal those "wonders of the world before us" that, in effect, defy critical analysis in their capacity "to excite a feeling analogous to the supernatural" (*CBL* 2:7). By contrast, in the pre-Revolutionary ferment in which Russian Formalism emerged, the value of defamiliarization was not to unveil the extraordinary but to expose the ordinary, showing its devices and motivations.[54] Nonetheless, even in English Romanticism, a political application is potential, insofar as the unveiled spiritual scene evokes new senses of power and a higher law. Echoing Isaiah 6:10 and Jeremiah 5:21, Coleridge heralds an impending revolution in perception: in "consequence of the film of familiarity and selfish solicitude we have eyes, yet see not, ears that hear not, and hearts that neither feel nor understand" (*CBL* 2:7); and Shelley, already confident of dispelling this film, claims that the poet's unveiling at once renders "the familiar world . . . a chaos" and "creates anew the universe" (*SW* 7:137)—powers that promote the poet, at the close of his *Defence,* to legislator, however unacknowledged his temporal effect may be.[55] For both Shelley and Coleridge, there is a sensation of the capacity of poetry, by the sign of its unfamiliar forming of language, to put historically contingent knowledge in a different perspective and to interrogate its hold.

So influential has this discourse been in readings of Romanticism that

Wesling deems it a "watershed": for the first time a preexisting and prescriptive inventory of forms "is consciously seen as in contradictory connection with what is regarded as poetic" (2–3). Romanticism's modernity, he argues, is its "break-up of formal rhetoric, the transfiguration of figures" (9). Wesling is self-consciously overstating these actions and overspecifying their point of occurrence; even so, his gesture attests to the impressive force of Romanticism's self-definition against traditional forms. Yet the deeper truth is that its poetic formalism had a complicated literary and cultural context, where the politics of liberation from custom contend with the resources of tradition, or at least the necessity of some kind of form. Los's system is still a system, one in which his "fury & strength" now has the power: "Obey my voice & never deviate from my will" (*BE* 152). And if Romantic writing sometimes invests poetic forms and language with a distinctive aesthetic agency, it may also expose the consequences of making this investment. Idealizing theory is strained by internal contradictions, and the most stridently polemical declarations are shadowed and cross-illuminated by practices that register conflicting attitudes—both about what it means to seek expression in poetry and about the systems of value involved in this search.

The terms of these debates define and invigorate each other in specific sites, even as they expose the range of attitudes in the age. There are Coleridgean efforts to distinguish the "superficial *form*" by which any construction in rhyme and meter may be called poetry (*CBL* 2:11–12) from poetic form, an organization of "genius," traditional resources, and material constraints, developed by a "shaping spirit of Imagination" (*CPL* 1:293; *CPW* 1:366). The word *spirit* in this phrase, though it denotes for Coleridge a force of internal necessity, alerts us to Romanticism's involvement with classical notions of form as the opposite of content, as a principle that precedes it, is discrete from it, shapes it, conveys it. In this aspect, form bears authority by its abstraction and precedence—whether in Platonic terms, as the originary ideal of any specific manifestation (hence the idealizing poetics of symbol); or in Aristotelian terms, as the common property of a category (hence the poetics of generic form).[56] This signifying of impersonal value persists in the "New Formalism" of the 1980s, whose practitioners regard traditional poetic forms as a kind of antidote to the immediacy of self and culture and thus a "mediation between public feeling and private expression."[57] In the decade of *The Well Wrought Urn,* a similar sense subtended the antimodernism of Allen Tate, who insisted (in his pointedly titled *Reason in Madness*) that "the formal qualities of a poem are the focus of a specifically critical judgment because they partake of an objectivity that the subject matter, abstracted from the form, wholly lacks." Nothing shows Frost's kinship with this tradition more than his famous comment to Brooks and Penn Warren: "I'd as soon write free verse as play tennis with the net down. I want something there—the other thing—something to hold and something for me to put a strain on; and I'd be lost in the air with just cutting loose." For Frost, poetic performance is a play with and against external forms, a "thing" other than "me." In similar terms, a self-confessed "last Romantic" states a formalist antipathy to free verse as an inhibition of self-expression: "Because I need a passionate syntax for passionate subject-matter," writes Yeats, "I compel myself to accept those traditional metres that have developed with the language. . . . I must choose a traditional stanza, even what I alter must seem traditional."[58]

Although the first Romantics do not always polarize form this way, they show an attraction to the metaphysics, even as they attempt to conceive of a commerce between abstract principle and specific event, or imagine a poetics of mutual incorporation. Inclining to the neoclassical theory of the generic principles imitated by literary form, Wordsworth claims in the Preface to *Lyrical Ballads* that his poems represent "the passions of men . . . incorporated with the beautiful and permanent forms of nature" (*WPrW* 1:124); years later, in *The Excursion,* we hear his Wanderer speak of the way "the Forms/Of nature" embody a "pure principle" (IV.1208–13),

> And further, by contemplating these Forms
> In the relations which they bear to man,
> [We] shall discern, how, through the various means
> Which silently they yield, are multiplied
> The spiritual presences of absent things. (IV.1230–34)

Coleridge, too, voices such principles. Although he concedes the necessity of specific forms for contemplation—"Something there must be to realize the form, something in and by which the *forma informans* reveals itself"[59]—he insists on the translucent abstraction towards which individual forms tend and from which they derive their power: "'*Forma formans per formam formatam translucens*' is the definition and perfection of *ideal* art"—"The forming form shining through the formed form" (*CBL* 2:215). Such plays on the word *form* and these distributions of its references encourage shifts between metaphysical form, embodied form, and poetic form, and between notions of form as inherent and informing and as outward and superficial—as if all these investments could have open congress with one another in a capacious mimesis.[60]

But impasses are conspicuous throughout, perhaps with most anguish in Shelley, the poet whom Wordsworth judged "one of the best *artists* of us all . . . in workmanship of style" and "one of the greatest masters of harmonious verse in our language." The poignancy of such mastery for Shelley's art is its repeated reach beyond writerly forms to "the eternal, the infinite, and the one"—the realm his *Defence* designates as the true origin of the poet's authority and the ultimate frustration of his art (*SW* 7:112). Shelley idealizes the mind as "the mirror upon which all forms are reflected and in which they compose one form" (Preface to *Prometheus Unbound*, 115), and in one phase of *A Defence* speaks of poetic form as "the creation of actions according to the unchangeable forms of human nature, as existing in the mind of the creator" (*SW* 7:115). In this mimesis, multiple and changeable forms signify abundance. Thus the poet of "Hymn to Intellectual Beauty" dedicates himself as "one who worships . . . every form containing" this ideal (II. 81–82), and the poet of "Epipsychidion" extends this philosophy to social conduct, resisting the sepulchral confinement to "one object, and one form" of the "heart that loves, the brain that contemplates,/The life that wears, the spirit that creates" (II. 169–73). Yet these and a host of other poems lament even as they theorize this pluralism of forms, sensing that multiplicity is the reflex of an inaccessible unity. In a bewildered search for "one form resembling" the "veiled Divinity" of a fleeting apprehension (II. 252–54), the poet's forms lapse into refiguring his frustration:

> The winged words on which my soul would pierce
> Into the height of love's rare Universe,
> Are chains of lead around its flight of fire——
> I pant, I sink, I tremble, I expire! ("Epipsychidion," ll. 587–91)

Felt as leaden constraints, poetic words are at one only with the world of dead matter.[61]

The language of "Form"—whether evoking an ideal origin or describing a representative model—has double operation in these scenes: it at once casts an ideal and, in its frustrations, exposes an unstable rationale for poetic formalism. Despite an overcredited claim (represented by Antony Easthope) that "Romantic theory is founded on precisely [its] misrecognition" of representation and that it left "unproblematized as aesthetic, formal and natural" the construction of its "poetic discourse,"

Romantic texts are more various than monolithic, and their poetic practices are alert to form as a construction. It is hardly the case, for instance, that exemplary texts such as Wordsworth's Preface show how "at a stroke, all the specific forms of enunciation that make poetry poetry are rendered accidental" and "dismissed."[62] If he defines "poetry" as "the spontaneous overflow of powerful feelings" (*WPrW* 1:126), he also pauses more than once over what its deliberate forming in meter signifies. He is, moreover, very aware of the signifying value of form per se in his experimental poetics, and what is at stake in an overt refusal of traditional contracts about poetic form. In a vocabulary keyed to the lexicon, Wordsworth states his terms directly at the start: if "it is supposed, that by the act of writing in verse an Author makes a *formal* engagement that he will gratify certain known habits of association," the subversion he has undertaken "to *perform,*" he flatly states, will seem aberrant (122, my italics). While his myth of "rural occupations" as incorporating "the passions of men . . . with the beautiful and permanent forms of nature" (124) had its own illusions, Wordsworth's commitment to it entailed certain decisions that he knew would be provocative. Even a Whig radical, Charles James Fox, complained about seeing the measure that conveyed the lofty meditations of "Tintern Abbey" also used to write the humble tales of "Michael" and "The Brothers": "I am no great friend to blank verse for subjects which are to be treated with simplicity," he grumbled to Wordsworth.[63] The affront was calculated, however: Wordsworth had originally tried "Michael" as a ballad, a "low" form, then decided to democratize his blank verse. This is a move that reverses Eagleton's and Easthope's polarities: far from obscuring the artifice of form, Wordsworth motivates his commitments to confront and reform certain codes in the institution of literature, and to challenge, thereby, implied class claims and associations.

At the same time, these polemics are beset by internal contradictions, especially about the rationale for metrical composition per se. Noting that "the act of writing in verse" signifies a "formal engagement" with readers (I think the pun is deliberate) to "gratify certain known habits of association" (122), Wordsworth warns of their disappointment. Yet the one habit of association that he preserves is the status of "metrical language" as an "exponent or symbol" of the poetic contract: every one of the volume's poems is shaped with a standard meter and pattern of rhyme. Not only does the presence of these habitual forms contradict the Preface's polemically "modern" insistence on the spontaneous and organic origination of poetry, but in 1800, there was a further political embarrassment in this metrical standard's seeming collaboration with any number of conservative eighteenth-century theorists. A contrary essay published in 1796 in the liberal *Monthly Magazine* asked, "Is Verse Essential to Poetry?" and stayed to answer, "Whatever is the natural and proper expression of any conception or feeling in metre or rhyme, is its natural and proper expression in prose."[64] The question is infused with politics: it is only the elitism of certain poets, this essay contends, that effects the "exclusive appropriation of the term *poetry,* to verse" (453). Possessing "arrogant assumption," this "ambitious race" of writers, "not satisfied with holding the almost undisputed possession of the first division in the ranks of literary merit, have . . . conjured up a wall of separation between themselves and other writers. Fancying the inhabitants of this consecrated inclosure a privileged order, they have been accustomed to look down, with a kind of senatorial haughtiness, upon the prose-men, who inhabit the common of letters, as a vulgar, plebeian herd" (453). The "monopoly" of verse over the domain of poetry is not only an "arbitrary" sign of privilege in the "republic of letters" (453), this essay proposes, but ultimately a dispensable one. Having cited metrical composition as the ally of a dubiously "consecrated inclosure," it proceeds to undermine the "solid foundation" of meter's value both as sign and agent of poetry's "privileged order." The strategy is to expose the self-subverting irony of the terms of privilege by converting class distinction into generic constriction, revealing protective "inclosure" as imprisonment: verse "confin[es] the productions of the muses within the enclosure of measured lines" (453) and poetry is falsely "confin[ed] within the narrow inclosure of metre" (455). The analogy to class politics is not casual, for in the 1790s the privileged orders, alarmed by the Revolution abroad and reverberations at home, were retrenching and shoring up their vulnerable privileges. The term *inclosure* is particularly charged, for this decade was also witnessing an acceleration in the enclosure of open fields and common lands, acts of definition and discrimination that at once served the interests of landowners and produced widescale misery in the dispossessed "plebeian herd."[65]

In addressing the aesthetic difference obtruded by metrical composition, Romantic poets found themselves debating questions of vital import—about the origin of poetic form and the status of poetic language, as well as about the agency of poetic form in examining other cultural forms. Questions about the significance and function of meter pressed on just about every poet with an inclination to theorize.[66] Where Wordsworth contended that there "neither is, nor can be, any essential difference between the language of prose and metrical composition" (despite his having written every poem in meter), Coleridge (despite valuing "organic" over "mechanical form") flatly announced, "I write in metre, because I am about to use a language different from that of prose" (*CBL* 2:69). And he made this commitment an aspect of "Genius" itself:

> Imagine not I am about to oppose Genius to Rules—No!—the Comparative value of these Rules is the very cause to be tried. The Spirit of Poetry like all other living Powers, must of necessity circumscribe itself by Rules, were it only to unite Power with Beauty. It must embody in order to reveal itself. . . . This is no discovery of Criticism—it is a necessity of the human mind—& all nations have felt & obeyed it, in the invention of metre, & measured Sounds, as the vehicle <& Involucrum> of Poetry. (*C Lects 1808–19* 1:494)

Shelley's *Defence* turns out to include a defense of meter, too. Meaning to set aside the "vulgar error" of distinguishing "between poets and prose writers" and to consider only "the distinction between measured and unmeasured language," he had to concede that most poets, at least, have chosen to express their harmonies of imagination in "arrangements of language, and especially metrical language" (*SW* 113). And Keats, despite his insistence that "if Poetry comes not as naturally as the Leaves to a tree it had better not come at all" (*KL* 1:238–39), appeals to the cultural standard of poetry as measured verse when he begins his rhymed and artfully stanzaic "Lines on Seeing a Lock of Milton's Hair" by calling Milton "Chief of organic Numbers"—the epithet insisting on measure, whatever the organic justification.[67] Byron's formalism not only signed on to the metrical contract but flaunted a fondness for the additional form of rhyme: "Good workmen never quarrel with their tools," he declares (*Don Juan* I, 201), implying that failure to rhyme is not only a default of craft but a contamination of genre.

These senses of poetic form as material and constructed operate in complicated and unstable alignment with theories of informing principle (and there is a classical basis for this instability as well).[68] A revealing crux is blank verse. Milton famously called it liberty from bondage, and Dryden's debaters variously disagreed (it is "Wild and Lawless"), agreed (verse is "constrain'd" and "fetter'd" by rhyme, even by meter), found it "nearest Nature" in its imitation of "ordinary conversation," or depoeticized it (it is "more properly" *Prose Mesurée*).[69] Some critiques today, focusing on the discourse that opposes blank verse to "Art and Order" and allies it with "Nature," see a covertly ideological practice that conceals the status of the form as a production and thus conspires, as in the ideology of "organic form," with mystified interests. This is Easthope's line. Yet in blank-verse practice after Milton, the issue was precisely its artifice. Dryden stresses the artistry as much as the illusion, calling it "Poetick Prose," "measur'd Prose"; Byron thought it the most difficult, not the most natural, to write; and eighteenth-century theories of elocution frequently insisted that it had to be recited so as to distinguish it from prose.[70] In this line, too, Wordsworth argued that "as long as verse shall have the marked termination that rhyme gives it, and as long as blank verse shall be printed in lines, it will be Physically impossible to pronounce the last words or syllables of the lines" without "giv[ing] them an intonation of one kind or another, or to follow them with a pause, not called out for by the passion of the subject, but by the passion of the metre merely" (*WL 1787–1805* 434).

This sense of a radically formal agency erupts in such famous claims as Wordsworth's equation of poetry with the "spontaneous overflow of powerful feelings," for it turns out that it is guided by what has been previously "formed" in "sensibility" (*WPrW* 1:126). There are also, even within the same authorial canon, sometimes even in the same work, events of poetic form that shape meaning in a play and interplay of formal elements.[71] This productivity even manages to figure into one of Romanticism's most innovative, seemingly antiformalist projects: autobiography. Its subjective poetics seem the vital antithesis of fixed form (originary, spontaneous, organic); but Wordsworth, for one, stages the subject in important ways both as constituted and made legible by form—a texture refuting Easthope's claim that Romanticism epitomizes the illusion of "the subject appear[ing] fully present to itself in a signified without a signifier, a represented without means of representation," in language "virtually untrammelled" by its "specific forms of enunciation" (123). An early draft of *The Prelude* displays just this canny trammeling, and not merely by force of the reflexiveness of writing as a poet about becoming a poet—the "contradiction and complexity . . . inscribed in the very form of Wordsworth's text" that even Eagleton regards as "a condition of [its] superior value."[72] It does this with what Eagleton calls "a certain curvature in the ideological space" that Wordsworth shapes with the word *form* itself.

This word first appears in the verse in the same paragraph in which the autobiographer tries to formulate the import of several immediately previous recollections of boyhood thefts. Each theft, he reflects, had recoiled in an arrest of the self by a formative discipline:

The mind of man is fashioned & built up
Even as a strain of music: I believe
That there are spirits, which, when they would form
A favored being, from his very dawn
Of infancy do open out the clouds
As at the touch of lightning, seeking him
With gentle visitation[.] quiet Powers!
Retired and seldom recognized, yet kind,
And to the very meanest not unknown;
With me, though rarely,
They communed: others too there are who use,
Yet haply aiming at the selfsame end,
Severer interventions, ministry
More palpable, and of their school was I.[73]

Just as palpable is the work of form, signaled by the placement of the word itself at the turn of the line, and framed by the way the paragraph that ends with "I" begins with a figure of self as the intentional formation of other powers. The poetic "I" comes into being in form cast as a system that precedes it, takes possession of it, and defines it. Yet this is no smooth or untroubled formalism. For one, the analogy to musical composition is shifty: as a strain in music, the self is composed—fashioned and built up by formal relations; but since the author of this passage is himself a composer, these spirits and powers of formation, although projected as external in agency, also imply his present act of autobiographical fashioning. The powers that form the mind, that is, are staged in a scene of which the poet's mind is not just a reflector but the formulator. This kind of reflexivity animates many sophisticated autobiographies; what makes Wordsworth's enactment distinctive is the way his verse form itself operates as a trope for its formalism: the lines above appear in the manuscript as blank-verse sonnet stanza.[74] Although later versions do not preserve this form, the textual archeology is telling, for it shows how deeply Wordsworth's autobiographical investigation is tuned to a sense of self as a composition of forms.[75]

In the Romantic poetics of liberation from custom and its idealizing of organic form, a natural evolution might have been free verse. That Romantic writing did not go this far attests to its energizing and self-defining engagement with poetic form in traditional contours, even as this engagement generated its critical interrogations of these forms, their conventions, and the formalist aesthetic itself.[76]

Tilottama Rajan

Phenomenology and Romantic Theory: Hegel and the Subversion of Aesthetics

❦

I

The effects on the study of Romanticism of the recent shift of interest from literary criticism to what is called *theory* are well known. Not only has theoretical commentary increasingly dominated the analysis of Romantic texts in the eighties; these very texts had already provided a major site, in the early work of Jacques Derrida and Paul de Man, for the development of a contemporary theory that makes universal claims for its elaboration of a crisis in the thinking of such categories as representation, the subject, and history. Since Romanticism has in some sense this originating status, it is logical to suppose that the problems played out in literary texts would have been theorized in the prose of the period. Thus the shift described has also had an impact, less often noted, on the study of Romantic criticism. It has expanded our sense of what constitutes the field, producing a displacement of interest from essayists such as Hazlitt and Lamb to a more philosophically self-conscious German tradition that includes Schopenhauer, Hegel, and Nietzsche, and whose concerns are consistent with those of theory rather than literary criticism. Romantic artistic and literary theory has a proximate relationship to semiotic and language theory: a major concern from the eighteenth century onward, but not a strong presence in literary criticism of the period. It has a similarly proximate relationship to other branches of philosophy, such as metaphysics and epistemology. As theory, it does not deal with individual texts or artifacts, but its reflection on larger matters such as the subject and history is mediated through specifically artistic concerns with author(ity), with the status of representation, and with form and genre. Romantic theory[1] can thus be defined as a field that lies midway between philosophy and criticism: a field that includes what used to be called aesthetics, but that is focused on more than simply the study of the beautiful. Indeed, we can define it partly as a sub-version of aesthetics concerned with what happens when art fails to be beautiful, fails to achieve what Hegel calls the "adequate embodiment of the Idea"[2] through a harmonious fusion of form and content. This sub-version generates what I shall call phenomenological aesthetics, as a mediation between organicism and idealism on the one hand and deconstruction on the other.

Theory as distinct from criticism is by no means new, being the concern of such classic studies as M. H. Abrams's *The Mirror and the Lamp* (1953). The pedagogical canon that we might use in studying Romantic theory has, however, changed considerably, albeit in a somewhat ad hoc manner, as a result of the use made by Derrida, de Man, and others of writers such as Rousseau, Nietzsche, Hegel, and more recently Schelling, to discuss such issues as the figurality of representation and the identity of the subject. That the (re)construction of a Romantic theoretical discourse has been a byproduct rather than a goal of the contemporary undertaking has two important consequences. To begin with, theory has been deflected into philosophy, and has been drawn away from its potential middle ground as a sub-version of aesthetics with practical ramifications for the study of Romantic texts. This middle ground can nevertheless be found in the very precursors who have given contemporary theory its identity as philosophy. Secondly, the recovery of a Romantic theory has often involved its transposition into contemporary terms. Such transposition can take the ahistorical form of an allegory, in which a set of Romantic terms is made to stand for an equivalent contemporary vocabulary, as when the dialectic between Apollo and Dionysus in Nietzsche's *Birth of Tragedy* is glossed as a version of the dialogue between *logos* and *différance.* Alternatively it can take the form of a teleology (recuperative or dismissive) in which Romanticism is seen as a shadowy type of contemporary truth. Before we dismiss such procedures as anachronistic we should recognize that they are within the spirit of Romantic theory itself. Thus Friedrich Schleiermacher argues for the importance not only of historical reconstruction but also of a "divinatory reading" that treats a text as part of an ongoing process in which it is intertextually continued by subsequent texts. Such a reading would see as entirely legitimate the reconception of nineteenth-century theory in the light of the "contemporary" theory to whose development it has contributed. William Godwin makes a similar point when he speaks of a text as having a "tendency," and Shelley too alludes to such readings when he describes poetry (which for him means creative thinking generally) as a lightning which has as yet found no conductor (*SW* 7:13).[3] Nevertheless, there are also disadvantages to the genetic practice of making Romantic theory an embryonic version of its most recent contemporary counterpart. Not the least of these is a certain condescension. We risk unduly restricting our sense both of what Romantic theory is, and of the possibility that it may itself have produced an autonomous and still influential theoretical vocabulary concerned with the spaces between idealism and deconstruction.

The two contrary figures in the genetic reading of Romantic theory have been Nietzsche and Hegel. With some exceptions, readings of Nietzsche have approached him as a precursor of poststructuralism, whether because he already recognized the figurality of representation seen by de Man as endemic to language, or because he had already deconstructed concepts such as 'origin' and 'history,' replacing them with notions such as 'genealogy' and 'power.'[4] While it is recognized that the Nietzsche of *The Birth of Tragedy* is more "Romantic" than the author of the fragments collected as *The Will to Power,* this difficulty is often dealt with by a teleological reading of Nietzsche's own career that valorizes the later over the earlier texts, or (as in the work of de Man) by a reading that flattens out the corpus by treating the early texts as always already "late." The case of Hegel is somewhat different. With the exception of Fredric Jameson, Hegel is treated as a philosopher of absolute knowledge whose system is beset by problems that it cannot contain, and who foreshadows despite himself recognitions that are not fully articulated until the twentieth century.[5] Unlike Nietzsche, who was initially seen as a precursor of existentialism and has been appropriated into literary theory only in the past two decades, Hegel had already been assimilated into literary and art criticism much earlier in the century by theorists such as Georg Lukács,

Walter Benjamin, Arnold Hauser, and Wilhelm Worringer. Ignoring these hermeneutic continuations of the *Aesthetics*, and using the influential readings of *The Phenomenology of Spirit* by Alexandre Kojève and Jean Hyppolite[6] for their own purposes, Derrida and de Man have cast Nietzsche as a thinker of demystification, but have read Hegel against the grain so as to convert him into what he should be. Hegelian desire, foregrounded in Hyppolite's and Kojève's analyses of the master-slave dialectic, has been made into the mystified precursor of Lacanian desire, and given a metonymic and linguistic rather than a dialectical and historical character. I shall go on to suggest how Hyppolite's focus on desire as a crucial element in Hegel's phenomenology can intertextually illuminate the historical typology of forms correctly isolated by an earlier tradition as Hegel's chief contribution to aesthetic theory. At the same time the further reduction of Hegelian to Lacanian desire seriously distorts him, by extracting a seemingly deconstructive theory of negativity from the phenomenological project of which it is a part.

The same allegorical and teleological tendencies are evident in the reading of other nineteenth-century aestheticians now being appropriated into the field of theory. In contrast to interpretations that recognize Kierkegaard's Romanticism but critique it as mystified, or ones that see him as part of a Hegelian aftermath leading to deconstruction, Sylviane Agacinski actually does locate him within an alternative (in this case) Heideggerian tradition.[7] However, in this reading too Kierkegaard is discussed selectively and made to serve the agendas of twentieth-century continental philosophy. It is perhaps impossible to recover earlier theory for the present by reading intertextually, without being guilty of selective distortion. But it is also important to recognize the multiple lines of influence or critical genealogies that join earlier theoretical discourses to more than one contemporary approach, thus providing us with more than one means of intertextual access to Romantic theory. In what follows I shall argue that we need to approach Romantic theory in phenomenological as well as deconstructive terms. Rereading it through deconstruction has already sensitized us to the fact that the Romantics did not view expression and representation as unproblematic, and that they often saw the identity of the text (and of the subject who is its origin) as displaced in the gap between signifier and signified, or form and content. But it is also true that representation remains for the Romantics the form of content, and that the much discussed "crisis in representation" is often approached through a typology of signs and forms in which even deconstructive forms such as allegory are expressions of states of consciousness.

My focus here is on how Hegel develops in the *Aesthetics* a thematics and semiotics of modes concerned with the non-identity of form and content as expressions of an artistic consciousness that can be historically situated. In current terms I am therefore concerned with the reinscribing of deconstruction within the phenomenology of a subject-in-process: a methodological symbiosis that may well strike contemporary readers as idealistic, but which, for precisely that reason, can provide a way of approaching Romanticism. Or to describe this symbiosis differently—as an approach that provides a first site of emergence for deconstruction but that also exists as an autonomous theoretical practice in the nineteenth century—phenomenology can provide a way of recovering and reinscribing certain concepts traditionally associated with Romantic aesthetics, but discarded from the critical lexicon in the aftermath of both the New Criticism and deconstruction, either because they seemed or were made to seem too naive. These include the notion of art as expressive rather than mimetic; the idea of artistic forms as organisms rather than artifacts, and thus as objects that must be understood as temporary transcriptions of processes operating within and through them; and the related notion of the subjective and the autobiographical as crucial to understanding the overdetermined relationship between the work of art and its "life-world."

Hegel's approach is at once a crystallization of much contemporaneous thinking, a radicalization of phenomenology whose significance we have yet to appreciate, and a seminal influence on subsequent theory. It is best described as "phenomenological" because the term is his, and the method of his *Phenomenology of Spirit* is also that of his *Aesthetics*. For Hegel the word *phenomenology* describes the attempt of Spirit to achieve self-understanding and self-identity through the cultural forms in which it is objectified; the fact that the thing-in-itself or "Idea" can be known only as it appears in phenomena and *is* nothing other than its appearances; and finally the fact that consciousness is not an essence but a process, and is fundamentally historical. But although I shall use the word *phenomenology* in a specifically Hegelian sense, the term in its broader senses is also relevant to Romantic theory. For precisely because the word does not refer to a clearly delimited set of critical practices, it can also serve as a terminological envelope for various tendencies in Romantic theory linked within a network rather than a unified body of assumptions. Indeed, because the term *phenomenology* designates in this century approaches as diverse as those of Georges Poulet, Maurice Blanchot, Wolfgang Iser, and Georg Lukács, it can be used as a means of intertextual access to a nineteenth-century field that includes figures as different (and indeed self-differing) as Schleiermacher, Shelley, Nietzsche, and Hegel.

In its broadest sense phenomenology attempts to isolate the (in)variant structures of consciousness, and phenomenological criticism studies art as an expression of consciousness. Although the latter is not necessarily antiformalist, it moves beyond or behind formalism, often locating art works in a "Lebenswelt" or in the life-processes which are the site of their emergence. The study of art works in terms of consciousness rather than genre connects with what used to be a traditional description of Romanticism as concerned with processes rather than products. The "consciousness" in question may be that of the author who produces the art work, as in the hermeneutic concept of "psychological" reading. Alternatively, it may be that of the reader who appropriates the art work, as in the hermeneutic concept of "applicative" reading, and in the frequent references to a literature of "power" rather than "knowledge," definable as effect and affect rather than simply as semantic content. Correspondingly the term *process* is also a highly open category. It can and does refer to the creative process. But it can also go beyond individual authors to locate them in a milieu, which may be an intellectual context characterized by a certain "spirit of the age" (as in Dilthey's *Schleiermacher Biography*), or may be a culturally and geographically distinct milieu (as in the work of writers like Herder, who initiate what later becomes ethnology and anthropology). "Process," in other words, is not necessarily an idealist concept complicit with what Jerome McGann critiques as the Romantic ideology in his book of that title (1983). It can also involve an understanding of the very cultural and historical processes valorized by ideological critique.

Phenomenology, as this brief survey indicates, can be either an idealism or a materialism. Correspondingly, it may either simplify or complicate the category of consciousness, identifying it with an unmediated interiority, or with the externalization of this inwardness through its displacement in the forms in which it becomes present to itself. Indeed, we can distinguish two tendencies within modern phenomenological criticism having to do specifically with its treatment of form and representation, and thus with the problem of mediation and the (im)possibility of a consciousness fully present to itself in what Hegel calls the 'Idea.' Typical of the first tendency is Poulet, who avoids all discussion of genre or language so as to achieve unmediated access to the author's consciousness. In thus "bracketing" the structures that mediate between consciousness and the world, or author and reader, he follows the transcendental phenomenology of Edmund Husserl in seeking an *epoché* or moment of pure consciousness prior to its articulation either in language or the language of the world. Like Shelley at certain points in *The Defence of Poetry,* Poulet seeks a "conception" free of "expression," or as Derrida puts it in his critique of phenomenology, a "layer of pure meaning, . . . of prelinguistic or presemiotic . . . meaning whose presence would be conceivable outside and before the work of *différance.*"[8] On the other hand Lukács, whose work is strongly influenced by Hegel, makes form central to a study of modes like the epic and the novel as expressions not of individual but of cultural consciousness. Forms for Lukács are expressions of consciousness. But it is only in the epic, as the supreme expression of what Hegel calls the "adequate embodiment of the Idea," that this consciousness becomes "the present and *in-different* being" associated by Derrida with phenomenology.[9] Insofar as even epic is the product of a particular society, there is in fact no such thing as a consciousness unmediated by the material forms in which it produces and objectifies itself.

Romantic theory is broadly phenomenological in approaching genres as modes of consciousness rather than analyzing their mechanical features. It is also phenomenological in being concerned with processes rather than products: both the process (individual or cultural) from which the artwork emerges and the process it stimulates in the reader. This orientation is evident in Shelley's nongeneric use of the word *poetry* to indicate a spirit or disposition that can equally well express itself in the prose of Bacon or the life of Jesus Christ, and that communicates itself to the reader as a lightning that has yet to find a conductor. It is also evident in Schleiermacher's hermeneutics, which argues for the anchoring of a "grammatical" reading concerned with semantics and syntax, and of a "technical" reading concerned with form and structure, in a "psychological" reading that connects and crosses two processes: the creative process in which texts have their genesis and the reading process which allows a "divinatory" reader to understand the author better than he understands himself.[10]

The linked concerns with process and consciousness ultimately compromise any sense of artworks as finished products identical with themselves in their function as containers of meaning. For not only are the contents of consciousness in excess of the form to which they are reduced, but these "contents" are already overdetermined by a complex cultural and intellectual context. Moreover, precisely because they are in flux, they are open to being reinscribed in the reading process, as each generation, in Shelley's rendition, returns to a text to develop "new relations" left unnoticed by the blindnesses that had facilitated the insights of their predecessors (*SW* 7:13). Nevertheless, it would be inaccurate to suggest that the identity or non-identity of the consciousness assumed by "process-thinking" has always been rigorously worked out. Indeed, the attraction of a phenomenological vocabulary for the Romantic mind may well be that it creates an "overlap" between opposed positions that allows one not to have to choose between idealism and materialism, or between the identity and non-identity of consciousness and its products. These positions would instead be complementary, accounting for the same phenomenon from different perspectives. Thus the non-identity of a text (which we would now see as deconstructing it) would, from another perspective, be what gave it its organic quality as an expression of a process and thus, in a sense, its "identity."

To put it differently, it may not be productive for an understanding of Romantic phenomenology to discriminate rigorously between the two tendencies noted in its modern equivalent. Rather, the attractiveness of "phenomenology" as a way of approaching Romantic texts may be precisely that by combining these tendencies it puts the aesthetic and ontological program of idealism under erasure while also holding it in reserve. Shelley's way of negotiating this paradox is to syncretize idealism and its unraveling: a strategy facilitated by the paratactic syntax and structure of the *Defence,* which gives each tendency its own space without having to reconcile them. Hegel's approach to the aporia between idealism and materialism is different, but no less Romantic. *The Aesthetics* constructs the history of art as a story about the impossibility of embodying or indeed defining the Idea, while preserving the empty category of the "Idea" as a desire without which history cannot exist. Thus on the one hand, Slavoj Zizek, reading Hegel through Lacan, has correctly pointed to the radical character of Hegel's phenomenology as a deconstruction of (post)Kantian idealism. Where Kant still posits the "Idea" negatively as the failure of "phenomenality" and "representation" to reveal it, Hegel's position is "that there is *nothing* beyond phenomenality, beyond the field of representation. The experience of radical negativity, of the radical inadequacy of all phenomena to the Idea, . . . this experience is already *Idea itself as 'pure,' radical negativity.*"[11] On the other hand, negativity is always related to the desire for an (im)possible identity, which is to say that deconstruction is always part of a phenomenology in which spirit tries to understand itself through its failure to coincide with itself.[12]

In focusing on Hegel's *Aesthetics* as a *summa* of Romantic phenomenology, I shall suggest that it brings together three important strands in previous and subsequent theory, and that it operates simultaneously in several different critical registers: offering a theory of form and representation, a theory of history, and a theory of reading or a cultural hermeneutic. Considered in relation to contemporaries such as Schiller and the Schlegels, Hegel inherits and advances the study of artistic modes as modes of cultural consciousness. But reading him from a more current perspective, we can see that these modes radically complicate the very concept of "consciousness," for what they express is the non-identity of a consciousness that can only produce works in which there is a discrepancy between form and content, or which produces classically complete works only to find the very concept of completeness inadequate. A theory of modes, which I shall go on to examine in the next section, is thus combined with a metaphysics and semiotics of non-identity to which I return at the end of this chapter. This non-identity, however, must be seen in terms of the increasing tendency of Romantic hermeneutics to treat works of art as (un)finished products that must be situated in an ongoing process. Schleiermacher's insistence on the need to go beyond a grammatical and technical reading of a text had already suggested a possible discontinuity between form and content, in which the form of a text does not entirely express its content. This content may be what we would now call a transcendental signified, but it may also be indeterminate, or we might say "overdetermined." Historicizing the categories of Romantic hermeneutics, Hegel reads works of art which do not quite come together as incomplete expressions of a 'Spirit' that has not yet adequately defined or embodied its 'Idea,' being a lightning which has still found no conductor. He thus places the non-identity of consciousness and the forms it produces within the wider horizon of what Fredric Jameson calls the political unconscious.

II

Hegel's single most important contribution to aesthetic theory is his analysis of artistic forms and cultural practices in terms of the structures of consciousness they express. He thus postulates three basic modes of art: the symbolic, the classical, and the romantic. These modes are analyzed in a vocabulary that is at once proto-materialist, idealist, and semiotic. Thus they are forms of praxis or work through which 'Spirit' *(Geist)* "produce[s]" itself in the material world (*HA* 1:31). They are also names for different relationships between "inwardness" and its "external manifestation" or between the Idea and its embodiment (1:77, 301). Finally, they also construct varying relationships between "theme" and "execution" or form and content (1:96). Hegel's approach to the concept of "mode" is phenomenological in three important senses: it isolates the invariant structures of the major forms of consciousness; it links these forms within the process of Spirit's attempt to produce and understand itself in the world; and it therefore sees consciousness as fundamentally historical, so that the thing-in-itself is knowable only as it appears in material phenomena.

As a narrative that tries to move toward closure, the *Aesthetics* is a kind of quest and tells the story of Spirit's attempt to achieve identity with itself through the forms in which it objectifies itself. Briefly, Hegel defines the forms of art as "the different ways of grasping the Idea as content" or "the different relations of meaning and shape" (1:75). Meaning and shape are fused in the classical, but the two other modes reflect varying asymmetries between inside and outside. Thus symbolic art, which is produced during the earliest phase in the phenomenology of mind, fails to achieve identity with itself because of a deficiency in self-consciousness which results in the Idea still being "indeterminate" (1:76). In the final phase of Romantic art, on the other hand, the Idea is fully developed, but external forms have become inadequate to embody it. Theoretically, the goal of art is the classical "union of meaning with its individual configuration" in beauty, which produces a corresponding "unity of the artist's subjective activity with his topic and work" (1:101, 299, 602). Hegel, however, is essentially interested in dis-integrated art forms, so that his narrative not only is a failure, but also seems to desire its own failure. For when Spirit transcends the symbolic's inability to make the Idea concrete, by achieving in classicism "the adequate embodiment of the Idea," this moment of pure presence proves limiting and must in turn be displaced by the Romantic, as a form in which the Idea once again cannot be made present by its representation. I shall return later to the significance for the subversion of aesthetics of Hegel's self-consuming narrative. For the present I am concerned with what makes the *Aesthetics* phenomenological rather than purely idealistic. That Hegel joins two theoretical discourses, semiotic and expressive, is a point that can hardly be overemphasized. Abrams, as is well known, distinguishes Romantic theory from the mimetic and pragmatic theories that precede it and characterizes it as expressive, and thus oriented toward the subjective (*Abrams ML* 21–26). David Wellbery isolates a very different strain in the theory that precedes the Romantic period. He sees the Enlightenment as producing a semiotically based theory, concerned (albeit very differently from poststructuralism) with representation and with the nature of signs, although he continues to see the theory that replaces it as expressive.[13] The point, however, is that Romantic theory is also semiotic, and that while Abrams is correct, both 'expression' and 'subjectivity' are far less naive concepts than have hitherto been recognized. Expression, in other words, can occur only through the mediation of form. Or put differently, expression *is* form, which means that consciousness cannot occur without representation and *is* its various representations. Equally important is the fact that Hegel overlaps a metaphysical with a linguistic vocabulary, entwining the problem of the Idea and its embodiment with the problem of content and form or signified and signifier.

Crucial to this marriage of the expressive and the semiotic is the category best described by the English term *mode*. Hegel's phenomenology of modes can be located within a larger spectrum of (post)Romantic criticism that includes, in the early twentieth century, the work of Lukács, Worringer, and Benjamin. The approach survives in our own time in early essays by de Man such as "The Rhetoric of Temporality" (1969), where the seemingly rhetorical terms *symbol* and *allegory* actually function within a thematics of the signifier that sees language (rather than form) as the category that mediates between the subject and the external world. But the formalization of this approach into a critical terminology may well begin with Friedrich Schiller, who combines a philosophical and cultural thematics with semiotic description in distinguishing naive from sentimental poetry. Thus for the naive mind nature is unproblematically present, whereas the sentimental mind can only represent nature through a language in which the sign remains "forever heterogeneous and alien to the thing signified."[14] In distinguishing these two forms of art Schiller substitutes for the notion of genre (*Gedichtart*) the more flexible concept of mode of perception (*Empfindungsweise*), as a disposition that can occur across genres, such that the elegiac can be present not only in the elegy but also in drama and epic.[15] Whereas genres are substantives, modes of perception such as the naive and the sentimental are nongeneric qualifiers or adjectives that have to do with affective and philosophical content, and with form as a concretion of content. Put differently, genre is a purely formalist category that studies external features of a text, but the mode of perception subsumes the formal within the phenomenological so as to study art forms as expressions of states of consciousness.

The influence of Schiller raises the question of the connection between 'mode' and the related but more purely idealist and expressive concept of 'mood' (or *Stimmung*). Stanley Corngold, in isolating the latter as an important concept in Romantic aesthetics, places Schiller's essay in an "arc" that begins with Kant's *Critique of Judgment* and continues through Nietzsche's early texts into the work of Heidegger. Whereas in Nietzsche mood "enacts the being 'outside' of articulated understanding," in the preceding Romantic-Idealist tradition going back to Kant it is "regularly viewed as 'inside'" and as possessing "no correlative domain of objects."[16] Corngold thus places Schiller within a purely idealist tradition concerned with feeling as distinct from what I am calling "consciousness," which is necessarily intentional, conscious *of* something and thus oriented to the outside world. The modern equivalent of *Stimmung* would be the Geneva school notion of "inscape": the inner essence of a work of art grasped through a critical *epoché* that brackets off the text's formal and structural features, and that completely dissolves what Schleiermacher calls the "technical" in the "psychological" reading. Whereas a mood (whether it is purely inward or on the boundary between inside and outside) would not be accessible to any kind of formalist description, a mode would describe a state of consciousness through a correlative domain of stylistic and structural features. Thus it is important to note that Schiller does not foreground the word *Stimmung* as Heidegger does, and that his discussion blurs the boundary between mood and what I am designating by the English term *mode,* or between feelings (such as anxiety and dread, to take Corngold's examples[17]), and neogeneric categories such as the elegiac and the idyllic. The term emphasized by Schiller is *Empfindungsweise,* which is sometimes cognate with *Gefühl,* but is also linked to *Empfindungsart, Art des Ausdrucks,* and *Dichtungsart.* This term, in turn, is cognate with *Gedichtart* or genre: a term that Schiller is not rejecting but reinscribing.[18] The boundary between mood and mode is observed in Heidegger's *Being and Time* and in the schoolboy essay "On Moods" by Nietzsche that Corngold discusses, both of which associate mood with feeling. But it is likewise blurred in *The Birth of Tragedy,* where the Apollinian and Dionysian are moods that are correlated with specific formal and material characteristics of artistic forms such as drama, epic, and sculpture, and where these forms are also placed within a post-Hegelian phenomenology of art that is teleologically oriented not toward the revelation of the Idea but toward its deconstructed inverse: the "incarnation of dissonance."

That *mode* has its genesis in *mood* and is thus a transposition of the latter into the concept of genre is an important point. But the difference between the two is the difference between an idealist aesthetics committed to the expression of interiority, and a more radical phenomenology in which conception exists only as it is expressed and displaced in language and form as sites of engagement between the subjective and the objective. The concept of mode is distinguished in four interrelated ways from that of mood. To begin with, modes are expressions of a self that is, in part, culturally produced, and is not simply in itself in its own interiority. Although the naive and the sentimental express and elicit certain feelings, they also reflect specific historical and material conditions having to do with the transition from an agrarian to an industrial society, and thus the disappearance of nature from experience and its return as an idea. Secondly, these sociocultural conditions are analyzed in terms of relations between the subject and the object as well as between the Idea and its instantiation (both linguistic and historical). The vocabulary that accompanies the discussion of modes therefore tends to be philosophical rather than affective, and posits a reflective rather than pre-reflective subject: a subject or metasubject that (mis)recognizes itself in the forms through which it produces itself. Although these vocabularies are mixed in Schiller (and also in post-Hegelian theorists such as the early Lukács), the post-Kantian philosophical context of Schiller's distinction is more explicitly drawn out by Schelling when he integrates his predecessor's terms into his *Philosophy of Art.*[19] Thirdly, discussions of a "mode of perception" are always correlated with discussions of aesthetic form: a move that shifts the emphasis from interiority to its objectification. Schiller's naive and sentimental are modes of perception that have literary correlatives in epic, on the one hand, and elegy and idyll on the other. Nietzsche's equivalents for these modes in *The Birth of Tragedy* are the Apollinian and the Dionysian, which become the basis for assessing cultural forms as diverse as ritual, epic, music, tragedy, Socratic philosophy, and opera. Hegel likewise analyzes specific art forms such as allegory, sculpture, and painting in terms of his three fundamental modes of consciousness. Finally, and because of its greater emphasis on the outside as constituting rather than simply interfering with the inside, the concept of mode results in a criticism that is "narrative" rather than "lyric." Hegel studies the various modes of art as part of a historical sequence oriented toward, but never achieving, the revelation of the Idea in concrete form. Schiller does not simply describe his two modes of feeling in and for themselves but places them in a historical sequence that is proto-Hegelian. The Apollinian and the Dionysian likewise underwrite a literary history that plays itself out in what we can best describe as a deconstructive dialectic.

Hegel does not use the word *Empfindungsweise,* employing the term *Kunstform* and sometimes *Gestalt* to designate both modes of perception and the artistic forms they generate. Nevertheless if Schiller, Nietzsche, and Heidegger are linked by their use of the word *Stimmung,* Schiller, Hegel, and the Nietzsche of *The Birth of Tragedy* are also part of an intersecting tradition linked by common procedures if not by a shared terminology. They participate in what Wellbery calls a "theory type" with its own distinctive "physiognomy."[20] In its broadest form this theory type would include the post-Hegelian tradition in art criticism studied by Michael Podro, a tradition concerned with art forms as expressions of cultural "attitudes" or of what Heinrich Wölfflin calls a "Lebensgefühl."[21] More narrowly, it would also be characterized by a "metasemiotics of culture,"[22] by a concern with signs and media of representation linked, however, to a philosophical thematics. In such a metasemiotics (traces of which survive as recently as Derrida's *Of Grammatology*) signs and forms are sites of negotiation between the inside and the outside, the finite and the infinite, body and soul, and also deception and truth. The implication of signs in ontological issues is what allows this theoretical tradition to study cultural attitudes not only through the content of a work of art but also through what Jameson calls "the form of content," or the symptomatic deformation of content through its representation. Finally, in its narrowest and specifically Romantic form, this theory type is characterized by the construction of metasemiotic systems of the arts that are part of a historical typology. These historical systems include Nietzsche's *Birth of Tragedy,* which narrativizes Schopenhauer's typology of the arts, in which art forms are classified according to their proximity to the will. Hegel's is the most ambitious of these typologies, with later rewritings of the theory type such as Kierkegaard's *The Concept of Irony* (1842) and Lukács's *The Theory of the Novel* (1920) often being sub-versions of a single phase in the Hegelian system.

We can further define the theory type as a system organized in terms of two levels, related somewhat like *langue* and *parole.* First of all, there are pre-formal categories that describe a way of feeling and perceiving: these include the naive and the sentimental; the symbolic, the classical, and the romantic; or the Apollinian and the Dionysian. The intertextual genesis of this *langue* lies both in a vocabulary of moods (such as the sublime and the beautiful) and in Goethe's nonhistorical distinction between symbol and allegory—the naive, the classical, and the Apollinian all being versions of Goethe's symbol.[23] The double genesis explains why this terminology functions in the three registers of the affective, the philosophical, and the semiotic, by condensing within a single term a reference to a certain state of consciousness, to a relation between the universal and the particular or the subject and the object, and finally to a relation between form and content or the signifier and the signified. This *langue* in turn generates particular art forms such as sculpture and music, and more narrowly epic and drama.

But the theoretical formation discussed here is characterized by more than simply the construction of a two-tiered system in which modes of awareness generate typologies of art forms. For Schelling, to whose *Philosophy of Art* I shall return, constructs such a system but describes it as "scientific" rather than "historical." Thus it is the historicization and narrativization of these systems that is crucial for our purposes. These systems do not simply distinguish modes from each other; they also tell a philosophical and semiotic story about the attempt of consciousness to achieve identity with itself through the forms in which it produces itself and becomes aware of itself as other than itself. Their narrative character is crucial to their participation in what I am calling a radical phenomenology that puts the very concept of the Idea at risk. For narrative is not only the scene of the Idea's working out and accomplishment, its attainment of a dialectical strength and materiality lacking in the lyrical form of mood criticism. It is also the scene of the Idea's testing through the repetitions and returns, the paradigmatic overlaps, that disrupt the syntagmatic movement of the story to its conclusion. Narratives, as D. A. Miller, has pointed out, are driven not simply by a desire for closure but also by the discontents with which closure seeks to deal,[24] and the accommodation of which results in complications that put any closure under erasure. We can note two such discontents in the *Aesthetics* that consciously suspend its logocentric project of an art that is the adequate representation of the Idea. The first involves the repetition of the symbolic as the romantic. On the syntagmatic axis of the text's plot, the romantic is obviously designed as a dialectical recuperation of the problems posed by the symbolic. But the disturbing similarity of the two on the paradigmatic axis results in a haunting of the romantic by the symbolic, so that we are never sure whether the Idea exists but cannot be represented or whether it is always indeterminate, a "*mere search* for portrayal [rather] than a capacity for true presentation" (*HA* 1:76). The second of these discontents is the concave dialectic that displaces the classical synthesis from the end to the middle, thus creating a split valorization both of classical completion and of its undoing in the romantic. For the classical fails because it limits the Idea to a concrete form, but the romantic also fails because it is unable to make the Idea concrete. The two are involved in relationships of mutual inadequacy that are not so much resolved as apocalyptically deferred through the highly overdetermined metaphor of the death of art.

III

The radically phenomenological as opposed to idealist character of Hegel's *Aesthetics* will become clearer if we distinguish it from Schelling's *Philosophy of Art,* which does not have the form of a narrative but rather of an anatomy of criticism.[25] Like Hegel, Schelling posits three forms of art: the schematic, the allegorical, and the symbolic. The first two are roughly parallel to Hegel's terms "symbolic" and "romantic," in that they reflect differing imbalances between the universal and the particular, or the Idea and its embodiment. The third of these, the "symbolic," corresponds to what Hegel calls the classical, in that its "subject not only signifies or means the idea, but *is itself the idea*" (*ScP* 151).[26] Schelling's system, like Hegel's, expands Goethe's influential distinction between symbol and allegory into a three-part schema. His version, however, does not so much intimate a historical dialectic as confer a logical symmetry on his system, with the symbolic being the normative center in a spatialized system: the aesthetic equivalent of the "potence" in *The System of Transcendental Idealism* which achieves the "indifference" of the real and the ideal.[27]

Like other post-Kantians, the early Schelling seeks to account for the real and the ideal in one unified system. Accordingly he uses the principles of "duplicity" and "triplicity" to arrange the individual art forms, positing two series (the real and the ideal), each of which is elaborated through three "potences," which take form as the three modes of representation: the allegorical, the schematic, and the symbolic. Thus music, painting, and plastic art comprise the real series in which matter is made a symbol of the Idea, while lyric, epic, and drama form the ideal series. Each of these individual forms is in turn divided into submodes according to the principle of triplicity, so as to introduce several further permutations. While art divides and differentiates itself into various forms when appearing in finite situations, it is one in the absolute, where the forms make up a kind of macropoem which, in Shelley's words, all artists "like the co-operating thoughts of one great mind, have built up since the beginning of the world" (*SW* 7:12). Although Schelling includes a phenomenology of art as it is disseminated through the various modes of its appearance, this phenomenology is therefore ultimately subsumed into an essentialist idealization of 'Art.' Particular forms may express a disjunction between the ideal and the real. But this disjunction at no point calls into question the essence of Art as the synthesis of the particular and the universal. I shall not consider here the question of whether Schelling's *Philosophy of Art,* like other compulsively systematic texts, is structurally overdetermined by the excessive relationship between its overall conception and the parts in which it is executed. More important are the characteristics that distinguish it from Hegel's *Aesthetics.* Schelling describes his system as "scientific" rather than "historical" (*ScP* 8–12), and it is developed in a purely deductive way by using the categories of triplicity and duplicity to subdivide each other according to a logic that precedes the actualities of cultural history. Like other texts in Romantic aesthetics such as Schiller's *Letters on the Aesthetic Education of Man* (1793), Schelling's system is generated by a desire to press beyond Kant's sense of a radical incompatibility between sensible presentation and the ideas of pure reason, and thus beyond his sense that the absolute cannot be known. Schelling, from this point of view, is one of the exemplars of what Philippe Lacoue-Labarthe and Jean-Luc Nancy term the literary absolute: the belief that the absolute (which Hegel deferred beyond art to philosophy) can be adequately realized in art (a category for which literature, seen as itself a form of theory, provides the model).[28] For Schelling it does not matter that the individual art forms prove to be sites of a discrepancy between the Idea and the phenomenon, or that his system itself is an inadequate embodiment of its Idea, being schematic rather than symbolic. The Idea and its embodiment are simply the same thing seen from the two perspectives of the eternal and the finite, which are thought synchronically rather than experienced temporally as the perpetual deferral of their coincidence. The inadequate embodiment of the Idea is therefore never the defeat of art or, worse still, of the Idea itself. Correspondingly, Schelling also sees no incompatibility between art and philosophy, insisting that the work of art is the highest objectification of philosophy (*ScP* 13).

Abandoning the Jena Romantics' (dia)logocentric concept of an aesthetic absolute, Hegel on one level remains within post-Kantian idealism by projecting a philosophical absolute. But on another level he allows the death of art to become the paradigm for the death of "god."[29] For the Romantic is the undoing of the classical as the incarnation of the Idea, and knows itself in Hegel's system to be no more than an idealization of radical negativity. In theory the project undertaken in *The Phenomenology of Spirit* (1807) was to have been merely preparatory, and phenomenology was to have been superseded by logic. At the core of phenomenology is a sense that the *logos* or Idea is not a transcendental signified, having no existence apart from its appearances in language and the language of events, which do however produce the Idea as its noncoincidence. Phenomenology was to have been to Hegel a means to an end, the end of Logic, which was also in a different sense the end of art and the end of history. But after writing the *Logic* between 1810 and 1812, Hegel returned to phenomenology in lectures on art given between 1818 and 1828, repeating and doubling back upon his own career so as to interrupt its projected linearity. The teleological conception of Hegel's work is thus suspended within the recursiveness of its execution, within the *Gestalten* it assumes in his own canon as the (in)adequate embodiment of its Idea. The only way to read Hegel's work as summed up by the ideas of "logic" and *logos* would be to read his corpus synchronically, as though the whole preceded its component parts, which could therefore be executed out of sequence. But whereas the early Schelling writes a logic of art, diachrony is at the very core of Hegel's thinking. The *Logic* may provide the paraphrasable content of Hegel's work, but phenomenology is its mode of production and its containing form.

Hegel's corpus can be experienced diachronically by the reader as an interrupted and deferred teleology. Alternatively it can be reconstructed in terms of a different kind of synchrony in which the phenomenology and the logic coexist and displace each other. It is useful in this context to recall Dominick LaCapra's suggestions about the reading of Sartre's career. As against Sartre's own narrative, which makes his later work a dialectical completion of *Being and Nothingness,* LaCapra suggests that the parts of an authorial corpus should be reconceived in terms of a "supplementary interplay that permits a process of mutual grafting not entirely accounted for by a notion of dialectical totalization."[30] Instead of being seen as part of a preconceived dialectical design, the phenomenology and the logic can be seen as "sectors" in which the project of the latter is problematized by Hegel's inability to leave phenomenology behind: his compulsion to return to it in the *Phenomenology of Spirit,* the *Philosophy of World History,* and the *Aesthetics.* As the (im)possibility of the Idea, phenomenology is the haunting of Spirit by matter, an idealism that provides a philosophical cover for valorizing not the Idea but its displacement in material and phenomenal forms.

This tension between the idealism of the philosophical absolute and phenomenology as the displacement of idealism by its absent body is played out in Hegel's ending of his narrative with the death of art. Hegel's goal is identity and his norm for art is 'beauty,' or the organic integration of form and content. This concept of the aesthetic as the beautiful is also related to the ideal of mimesis as the making present of representation. For mimesis is the disappearance of form in content, of the signifier in the signified. The centrality of beauty and mimesis in the discipline of aesthetics have to do with the normative role of classicism in Western thinking until the point when Nietzsche wrote *The Birth of Tragedy*. But as we have seen, the art that comes closest to Hegel's ideal does not interest him, while the art that does interest him conforms neither to his goal of identity nor to his concept of art. Ostensibly by proclaiming the end of art (not its literal end but its closure), Hegel protects both a traditional aesthetics and a philosophy of identity. For the end of art accommodates both his discontent with an art conceived classically as the embodiment of the Idea in sensuous form, and his apprehension at the problem posed for a philosophy of identity by Romantic art. The figure of the death of art is, however, highly overdetermined, since it is scarcely likely that one would write twelve hundred pages on something whose value is only as a relic of the past. On some level what is at issue here is the death not of art but of an art associated with beauty and mimesis, and the birth of an art conceived phenomenologically as the self-production of a non-identical consciousness that remains still in process. Moreover, the art that Hegel renounces is in some sense homologous with logic, which is a return to classicism at a further point on the dialectical spiral. Although on the syntagmatic axis of its teleological plot Hegel's corpus therefore moves toward a resolution of the crisis in representation figured by Romanticism, on the paradigmatic axis the end of classicism has already figured the coming into being of the Idea as the embodiment not only of a content but also of a discontent.

The *Aesthetics* is thus the scene of a simultaneous rethinking of philosophy and art through each other. As already suggested, Hegel puts idealist philosophy (and philosophy itself as an idealism) under erasure. Because he thinks the possibility of the Idea through the history of art, which raises the question of its embodiment or representation, he is driven to concede that the Idea is pure negativity. For art proves to be philosophy as phenomenology: a deferral of philosophy as logic and *logos* that can itself be deferred only by the liquidation of art. More important is the fact that the *Aesthetics* also contains a radical redefinition of art itself that undoes the twin idealisms of beauty and mimesis, as well as the Jena circle's recuperation of the "romantic" in a "literary absolute." In effect Hegel valorizes art forms that consciously fail to achieve organic unity and thus do not cohere as acts of representation: either those in which the inwardness of content cannot be embodied as form, or those in which there is a conspicuous excess of form as that which has not been said in content. That the *Aesthetics* is thus a sub-version of aesthetics, as phenomenology is a sub-version of idealism, can hardly be overemphasized. Its unique quality emerges if we read it intertextually through the lines of influence that link Hegel to various twentieth-century theoretical traditions, each of which picks up on a different aspect of his work. The early critical appropriations of Hegel are already quite diverse, though linked by their sense that his major contribution was a theory of artistic modes as modes of consciousness. Some post-Hegelians, such as Lukács from *The Theory of the Novel* to *The Meaning of Contemporary Realism,* follow not only his approach but also the teleological story that accompanies it. Others, like Wilhelm Worringer in *Abstraction and Empathy* (1910), extract Hegel's phenomenological approach from the Eurocentric narrative which causes him to devalue symbolic in relation to classical art, recognizing that his contribution is not the narrative itself, nor the analysis of all art forms in terms of a single metatheme, but rather a hermeneutics of art forms as expressions of distinct cultural and philosophical physiognomies. Yet others, like Arnold Hauser in *The Social History of Art* (1958), elaborate the materialist potential of this cultural hermeneutic.

Focusing on the concept of mode, these continuations of the *Aesthetics* (with such exceptions as Benjamin's *Origin of German Tragic Drama* [1922–23] and Kierkegaard's *The Concept of Irony* [1842]) assume a straightforwardly expressive relationship between consciousness and form. This is true even when the consciousness in question is (as in Lukács) an unhappy consciousness. Lukács, Worringer, and Hauser are not concerned with the diacritical way in which different forms are related by mutual deficiency within a narrative of non-identity, and thus with the ramifications of Hegel's focus on representation for a philosophy of identity. This second aspect of Hegel's thought has been developed within a philosophical rather than a critical tradition, and has therefore not been taken back into a reading of the *Aesthetics*. I refer to the mid–twentieth-century Hegelians whose emphasis on the *Phenomenology* rather than the *Logic* and whose linkage of 'identity' to 'desire' and to the unhappy consciousness were crucial to the transposition of German idealism into French poststructuralism, and thus to a rereading of Hegel in a contemporary key. Central to this rereading is the characterization of consciousness in terms of a desire that metonymically transfers itself to a series of substitutive objects, none of which can do more than signify the absence of what Lacan, in his version of Hegel's absolute knowledge, names the 'phallus' as ultimate goal of the subject presumed to know. But here it is necessary to distinguish the treatment of Hegelian negativity in Hyppolite and Kojève themselves from its reduction to Derridean *différance* and Lacanian desire. Interiorizing the dialectic within philosophy and psychoanalysis, and abstracting negativity both from the subject and the object, contemporary theory reduces it to a movement of language in relation to itself. As Judith Butler points out, Lacan not only dissociates desire from any sense of subjective agency, he also denies that desire can be "materialized or concretized through language."[31] By making the signifier no more than a position in an empty series, he dispossesses the means by which desire signifies itself of historical value. The French Hegelians, on the other hand, are still social theorists as well as philosophers, concerned with the "labor of the negative," as Hegel himself was concerned with art as a form of work by which the subject produced himself in the objective world. For Hyppolite, although desire is the non-identity of the subject with his work, this non-identity is defined Romantically as the "very existence of man, 'who never is what he is,' who always exceeds himself and is always beyond himself" and who in that sense "has a future."[32]

Without attributing to Hegel the positivism of subsequent mode theory, a reading of the *Aesthetics* must therefore recognize two things neglected by an assimilation of negativity into deconstruction, and implicit in the earlier appropriations of Hegel into literary and art criticism. To begin with, the self-representation of the subject in language and form is always productive as well as reflexive. Secondly, the alienation of the signifier from the signified formalized in symbolic and Romantic art remains the semiotic expression of a problem that must be referred back to the structures of (historical) consciousness. Within the tradition we have been discussing it is perhaps Kierkegaard's *Concept of Irony* that comes closest to deconstruction. Kierkegaard's text is a sub-version of Hegel that concentrates on the one mode his predecessor could not accommodate in his philosophical romance. It does not simply recognize the alienation of the Idea conceded by Schelling's concept of the allegorical or Hegel's categories of the symbolic and the Romantic. It enacts the unconscious of the *Aesthetics* to perform the very deconstruction of the related concepts of inwardness and the Idea, which persists only as the *desire* that there be a teleological redemption of infinite absolute negativity. As the negativity of the Idea, irony cannot contribute to "the content of personality." Even so, for Kierkegaard irony can be understood only in relation to subjectivity, as a mode of consciousness that signifies the (im)possibility of self-presence and absolute knowledge: "It has the movement of turning back into itself which is characteristic of personality, of seeking back into itself, terminating in itself—except that in this movement irony returns empty-handed."[33] From this point of view the persistence in the early Derrida of a post-Hegelian thematics of presence and absence, interiority and externalization,[34] under the cover of deconstructing this vocabulary which he still inhabits inversely, may well inscribe the profound (dis)continuity between phenomenology and deconstruction.

Be that as it may, Kierkegaard provides a model in the Romantic tradition for the containment of deconstruction as part of a phenomenology of the sign. At the level of content he may carry out a deconstructive critique of philosophical idealism. But this critique has the form of a phenomenology and of a hermeneutic, so that the effect of his text lies not in what it "says" but in the persistent (and "Romantic") difference between its "theme" and "execution." If Kierkegaard entwines deconstruction with phenomenology, Hegel embeds phenomenology in history, thus making artistic modes not just expressions of consciousness, but sites of negotiation between consciousness and its own historicity. Through art, consciousness produces itself in the world and thus produces itself as historical. Art for Hegel is therefore a praxis whose inevitable failures in representation must be read symptomatically as expressing the contradictions of their historical moment. This sense of art as historical and of history as incomplete is a pervasive feature of Romantic process-thinking, and surfaces in such notions as the "spirit of the age" or in Shelley's notion of poets as "mirrors of the gigantic shadows which futurity casts upon the present" (*SW* 7:140). The historical sense, however, is often idealized through the figure of a 'spirit,' with Shelley's statement being exceptional in the way its imagery captures the sense of a historical unconscious. Participating in this idealism, Hegel also moves beyond it in two ways: in the linkage he constructs between historicity and form, and in his *systematic* theorizing of the relationship between form and content in terms of the concept of negativity.

Although he does not deal with the *Aesthetics,* Fredric Jameson in *The Political Unconscious* comes closer than anyone else to articulating this negativity, by reading Hegel and the contemporary tradition that develops from and against him in a genuinely intertextual manner. On the one hand, Jameson revisions Hegel by approaching him not only through Hyppolite but also through Althusser and Lacan, so that the world-historical spirit is refigured in terms of the radical negativity of the political unconscious. On the other hand, he is concerned to bring to light Althusser's own unconscious, by focusing on the inescapable organicism of his concept of "structural causality," given that an "Althusserian exegesis . . . requires the fragments, the incommensurable levels, the heterogeneous impulses, of the text to be once again related, but in the mode of structural difference and determinate contradiction."[35] Using Jameson's analysis of Hegelian history as an intertextual gloss on the *Aesthetics,* we can argue that Hegel's unique contribution is to construct a theory of modes that accounts for both "expressive" and "structural" causality, and thus for idealism as well as deconstruction. Whereas other theorists of mode see form as a straightforward expression of content, Hegelian exegesis[36] approaches the text as an overdetermined structure in which form and content function as 'semi-autonomous' parts. Long before Althusser and Pierre Macherey, Hegel's use of the categories "symbolic" and "Romantic" thus requires a symptomatic reading of the text in terms of what Jameson calls the "content of form" and the "form of content."[37] Jameson's categories, like Hegel's, are ways of expressing what is not expressed. For in locating overdetermination in the structure as well as the content of a work, they locate the work's meaning not simply in its paraphrasable content, but also in what it does not say: in the philosophical assumptions embedded in a form that may say something different from its content, as well as in the deformation of content by the structural or syntactic shape it assumes. The resulting theory of art both is and is not expressive. For in focusing on asymmetries between form and content, Hegel displaces the concept of 'expression' from a semantic to a syntactic level, so that the work does not express its Idea, but does express the contradiction that in(forms) it. Furthermore, this asymmetry between the form and content of a work is the source of its negativity: its deferral of any hypostasis of its Idea through mimesis and beauty. Because the symbolic and the Romantic fail as acts of representation, they can be read as what Jameson calls "symbolic resolutions": art forms that embody their Idea inadequately, so as to mark the limits of a resolution overdetermined by its historical moment. As symbolic resolutions they do nevertheless perform the labor of the negative, and here it is important to recall Hegel's linkage of negativity to a series of artistic forms, as distinct from Zizek's attribution to him of a theory of pure negativity. For forms are positive in that they temporarily give form to the Idea. Focusing on how art posits the Idea, but in forms that do not cohere, Hegel opens the work to its historical unconscious: to its contradiction by what it has not said, but also to its continuation into what it has not yet said.

Frederick Burwick

The Romantic Concept of Mimesis: Idem et Alter

In explaining the shift from art as imitation to art as expression, M. H. Abrams began his chapter on "Romantic Analogues of Art and Mind" by citing Wordsworth's definition of poetry as a "spontaneous overflow of powerful feelings." Abrams was certainly right in arguing that Wordsworth's metaphor revealed the new emphasis on creativity as the expressive "overflow" of the mind. Unfortunately, one of the consequences of Abrams's profound and influential *The Mirror and the Lamp* (1953) has been the tendency to presume that once the lamp began to glow the mirror was shattered. Although it was not his intent to ignore the subtle interplay of imitation and expression by positing only an either/or possibility, Abrams did stress the ways in which the claims of mimetic representation were compromised and subordinated in Romantic poetry by the insistence on the primacy of mind and emotion.

When, for example, Wordsworth declared, "I have at all times endeavored to look steadily at my subject," Abrams opposed what he considered the mistake in accepting this statement as the poet's "recommendation for objective accuracy and particularity" (*Abrams ML* 53). Although Wordsworth ranked observation and description first among "the powers requisite for the production of poetry," he nevertheless relegated passive observation to subservience. Attention to the particular object of the sense should assist, not usurp, the mind's active and transforming powers. After praising faithful description, Wordsworth went on, Abrams reminded us, to limit its use: "The ability to observe with accuracy things as they are in themselves, and with fidelity to describe them, unmodified by any passion or feeling existing in the mind of the describer . . . though indispensable to a Poet, is one which he employs only in submission to necessity, and never for a continuance of time: as its exercise supposes all the higher qualities of the mind to be passive, and in a state of subjection to external objects."[1]

As metaphor for the creative process, the mirror implied an unwarranted and restricting passivity. By suggesting that mental reflection was no more than a repetition in the mind of images received through the senses, the mirror metaphor seemed to affirm the empiricist denial of innate capacities of the mind. Rather than simply reflect an external object, according to Wordsworth, the poetic image should reveal as well the alterations imposed by the perceiver; in "The White Doe of Rylstone," he wrote, "objects . . . derive their influence . . . not from what they are actually in themselves, but from such as are bestowed upon them by the minds of those who are conversant with or affected by those objects."[2] Holding up the "mirror" to nature was rendered poetically suspect because it might define the poetic act as a surface reflection. What had invalidated the mirror as metaphor was not the rejection of the mimetic principle per se but only the notion that the mirror might be deemed, kindred to the Lockean metaphor of the tabula rasa or camera obscura, as an instrument capable of recording only the external data of the physical world without contributing any modifying peculiarities of its own. To avoid these passive connotations, of course, the poet might insist on the dynamic attributes of the reflecting medium. In order to animate mimetic reflection, the poet need only reveal the magic in the glass. The trick could still be performed with mirrors.

For the purpose of Abrams's investigation, art as imitation is said to be promulgated by an objective and empirical philosophy, while art as expression is seen as an effort to fulfill the expectations of a subjective and idealist philosophy. Acknowledging the radical opposition between these two philosophical positions, Coleridge also observed their essential relationship. Philosophers, he wrote in the *Biographia Literaria,* either begin by positing the mind, and then must pursue the task of accounting for the world of things; or they begin by affirming things, and then must explain how we come to have ideas about them (*CBL* 1:255–60). Coleridge, it will be recalled, proposed a reconciliation of these Platonic and Aristotelian traditions by beginning with the moment of cognition, the coalescence of subject and object. Were such a philosophical union possible, the barrier between "imitation" and "expression" might well collapse.

Historically, of course, the concept of mimesis had been forwarded by both Platonic and Aristotelian philosophies. In Plato's *Republic,* the concept of art as imitation fared rather poorly, for the account of the three beds—the bed as idea or "essence," the bed made by the carpenter, and the bed represented in a painting—left the artistic imitation "thrice removed . . . from the truth" (Book x). This is the text cited by Abrams to document the "lowly status" of imitation in Plato's realm of Ideas (*Abrams ML* 8–9).

As Plotinus had argued, the case for mimesis might be revised by granting that the artist, no less than the carpenter, was capable of conceiving the idea of the bed. The artist might then inform the real with the ideal (*Enneads* 5:8).[3] Plotinus knew, of course, that Plato scorned only the imitation of external appearances. Plato was resisting an older philosophical confidence in the sensuous and emotional basis of knowledge.[4] In order to establish that the philosopher, not the poet, had the advantage in defining the sources and province of knowledge,[5] Plato denied that the descriptive images of art or poetry were adequate in representing truth. He also dismissed the Pythagorean application of the mimetic principle to a speculative mode of analogical reasoning: "as the eyes are framed for astronomy so the ears are framed for the movements of harmony" (*Republic* VII.530d). To advance the primacy of ideas in the *Republic,* he objected to mimesis in the arts, which under the pretense of enacting "deeds and experiences" could accomplish no more than "copying the appearance."[6]

One act of imitation, however, not even Plato could avoid: language itself is mimetic. In the *Cratylus,* Plato discusses primitive and derived signs as the two means by which language communicates.[7] Primitive signs, communicated by bodily gesture or vocal mimicking, seek to "imitate the nature of the thing" they represent; derived signs elaborate the scope of communication by the use of conventions accepted within the community. The mimesis of language has the potential danger that the derived can be confounded with the primitive, and that either may be misapplied (423–27). "Images," Cratylus concedes to Socrates, "are very far from having qualities which are the exact counterpart of the realities which they represent" (432d). Because the names of things are untrustworthy as a source of knowledge, we must study the forms rather than the names. Language does not reveal forms, but to the extent that it exposes its own incapacity, it may prompt the mind to seek for enduring forms amidst the very Heraclitean flux of unreliable images (438d–440c).

In the *Republic,* he cites Homer's turn from direct narrative to dialogue as "narration through imitation." By representing another "in speech or bodily bearing," the poet is imitating a character. While an epic may thus intersperse narration with imitation, the drama is fully imitative. Plato then raises the question whether "we are to suffer our poets to narrate as imitators or in part as imitators and in part not, and what sort of things in each case, or not allow them to imitate at all." The irony, although not intentional, is that Plato presents this inquiry not as narration but as imitation. In the home of Cephalus, Socrates discusses with Glaucon, Adimantus, and several others the conditions of an ideal state. Plato remains fictively absent from the dramatic scene. Yet it is just such a maneuver that is seen as a threat to the ideal state. If imitation is to be tolerated, it must not be allowed to represent anything that is base or shameful. From ridiculing the extravagance of a speaker willing to "imitate anything and everything," the province of acceptable imitation is soon so curtailed that only the voice of the wise and good man is deemed a fit subject for imitation. But such should be the voice of the narrator, obviating any need for recourse to the dangerous subterfuge of imitation (*Republic* III.392–98).

Greek drama did not pretend to overwhelm an audience with stage illusion, nor did Greek poetry strive to copy nature. The intent was, rather, to present and enact human thought and feeling. Crucial to dramatic and epic, no less than to lyric poetry, was the informing harmony and rhythm of music. Indeed, music was for Plato the most important of the mimetic arts. While he may scoff at the imitation of appearances, Plato valued the imitation of form. Thus in the *Philebus* he praises the beauty of form as superior to "the beauty of a living creature or a picture" (51c).

Although he wanted to banish the poets from the Republic, in the *Laws* he declared that mimetic arts provide a sound educational foundation for the state (653a). The mimetic arts—music, dancing, poetry, drama, painting, sculpture—are essential to education because they reveal the beauty of form (*Laws* 397a–b, 400d–401a). Indeed, they are mimetic arts for Plato precisely because they imitate ideal form. The formal elements of composition—order, rhythm, harmony, balance, proportion—all derive from ideal perfection. They complement the teaching of reasoned knowledge by revealing the pleasure in the good, true, and beautiful. The simple ability to perceive and delight in rhythm, melody, and order teaches those who experience the pleasure to pursue with love its informing principles (653e–655a, 664e–665e). In language, the relationship of the signifier to the signified should be sustained with the same moral commitment to the rightness of representation as is expected in the mimetic arts (*Cratylus* 430).

Having opposed mimesis as Pythagorean metaphor for the relation of sensed things to general and characteristic forms, Plato went on to adapt it as metaphor for the task of imitating unsensed forms. But what does an "unsensed form" look like? How does the artist, or the critic, know if the imitation is correct? When he discusses mimesis in the *Laws* (643c, 655d, 705c, 706b, 713b, 798d–e, 815a, 816a, 898a), he offers two criteria for judging the rightness of the imitation: one cultural, the other intrinsic. On the one hand, he calls upon the elders of the chorus to judge, for they are "better educated" and have familiarity with the harmonic scales. On the other hand, those who are to judge must be "keenly sensitive to rhythms and melodies" (670a-e). There is a factor of self-correction in the very principle of imitating form: the success of the imitation becomes evident as the attributes of harmony are made more harmonic, as the melody becomes more melodic.

What one judges, in other words, is the artist's degree of success in striving to imitate the ideal. Upholding both criteria, Plato urges that the community should rely on the good and wise man in their midst who has the knowledge to judge how well the form of beauty has been imitated.[8] That a "true imitation" might reveal nature and form in artistic representation is conceded in the *Sophist* (236). Discussing the way in which the ideal becomes real (*Timaeus* 29), Plato compared the physical universe to a work of art. Both involve the sensuous embodiment of the ideal in the real. In this comparison, the Neoplatonists (and with them, Coleridge too) recognized the exaltation of artistic mimesis as replicating the very process of divine creation.

Because Aristotle's account of mimesis is concerned with the real rather than the ideal, one might expect him to affirm the imitation of appearances that Plato had denounced. Nevertheless, when Aristotle states that the purpose of the drama is to provide an "imitation of human action," he specifies that what is to be imitated is mental rather than physical.[9]

The crucial action is the *proairesis* rather than the *praxis*. It is not enough simply to depict the physical movement of a character upon the stage. The playwright must reveal the motives of the movement, the predication of action in thought *(dianoia)*: a character must respond, deliberate, and choose (*Poetics* 1449b36–1450b15). Like Plato, Aristotle considers rhythm and harmony formative elements in the mimetic arts. Unlike Plato, he does not explain the imitative drive as aspiring toward ideal forms. He grounds it, rather, in the natural inclinations evident in the make-believe improvisations of children: "Imitation is natural to man from childhood, . . . he is the most imitative creature in the world, and learns at first by imitation" (1447a14–1448b24).

These two principal concepts of mimesis—imitation of ideal form, imitation of the processes of thought—both persist in the Romantic period. Indeed, several of the Romantic philosophers endeavored to combine the two. Coleridge, as previously noted, prepared for such a reconciliation when he suggested that a philosophy might avoid the traditional opposition of mind and matter by grounding itself in the cognitive union of subject and object. If imitation is to represent objectively the phenomena of subjective experience, then it must somehow counter its own objective form. In Romantic aesthetics, therefore, mimesis was understood as a transformation in which an essential sameness is retained in spite of the otherness of its material meditation. The union of form and thought in the creative process, as explained in the aesthetics of Schleiermacher and Hegel, is identity in difference. In the critical essays of De Quincey this mimetic principle is called *idem in alio*. Coleridge, as he himself often stated, derived his formulation of the *idem et alter* from Philo Judaeus.

As translator of Plato, Schleiermacher was fully aware of the changes that had taken place in the presentation of mimesis in the later dialogues, especially *Timaeus* and the *Laws*. Like Plato, he argued the essential identity of aesthetic and ethical judgment, and, again like Plato, he recognized both cultural and intrinsic grounds for judgment. In order to extend the province of judgment in the practical arena of human activity, he required a more ecumenical, less hegemonic arbiter than Plato's "wise and good man." The ethical and aesthetic responses to art, he believed, were not only generally accessible within the culture, they also defined the cultural identity. The simultaneity and reciprocity of identity and difference, which Schleiermacher began to propound in his system of ethics in 1812, were further elaborated as significant constitutive elements in his aesthetics and hermeneutics.[10]

In its rational appeal, art does not simply invite us to compare the imitation with the object imitated; it should reveal something about the representation of images. Similarly, in its affective appeal, art should do more than reproduce an object that excites the senses; it should also examine the conditions that inform or influence the sensual relationship. Because pleasure in an object gives rise to desire for the object, Schleiermacher grants that art reciprocates through "diese Nachbildung des in der Natur Wohlgefallenden" (25–26).[11] Each genre has its own means of satisfying mimetic desire. While some genres might be properly defined by locating the mimetic principle in the idea, others by centering it in the mediation of affective response, neither account adequately defines imitation in the arts.

Schleiermacher therefore proposes to address mimesis in the very activity in which the work of art is produced (29–30). Only if art is a free activity can an aesthetic experience also be ethical (35). Art may persuade or influence, but it does not force or dictate. To be sure, the affective response cannot always be controlled by the will, but the individual can choose whether to engage or continue the exposure to unwanted modes of sensual or emotional appeal. Even affective art exists in and through its intellectual mediation. As mental activity, it is perceived by the individual as familiar or strange. Identical activities are those that are shared and in which an entire community may participate. They are to be contrasted with those activities that are strange and different because they are peculiar to an individual or belong to a foreign experience.

This dialectic of identity and difference is studied in several interrelated contexts. It has certain kinship, for example, to the distinction between the general and the particular in Enlightenment aesthetics, but rather than laud the former and condemn the latter,[12] the dialectic requires both. Advancement in thinking is possible only through the contributions of difference which extend the range of identity. The primary impulse is the maintenance of an enduring community ("bestehende Gemeinschaft") and the suspension of difference ("Aufhebung der Differenz" [51–53]). Schleiermacher acknowledges, however, that the tension between identity and difference is ineluctable.

The identity of an idea is altered in expression by the difference in language. No matter how malleable the medium, it will impose some change upon the artist's conception. That very difference, however, may render the conception more identical to the thinking of the audience. Thus he proclaims that the place of the work of art is always the artist's people ("der Ort des Kunstwerks ist immer sein Volk" [54]). Just as identity may subsist in difference, the inverse may also be true:

> Why cannot one turn the matter around and say, thinking contains within itself a national difference even though its identity presupposes it; and why cannot one also turn it around in art and say, it is in general identical but it differentiates itself in reality? and if one can thus turn it around, then the opposition does not persist but is suspended; the difference remains, but not as an attribute useful for generically separating the activities. (54)[13]

Because he does, indeed, want to use identity and difference to discriminate the functions of mimetic activity, he cannot annul the dialectic by allowing the terms to become interchangeable. As free activity, art does not seek to bring others into accord with its own presumptions. Difference persists because art always respects difference. The difference that sets one nation apart from others may be thoroughly imbedded in language, but it is the effort of thinking to overcome this difference ("es ist ein Bestreben des Denkens, diese Differenz aufzuheben"). The dialectic continues because difference abides in art, identity in the epistemic laws that govern the thinking of all humanity ("die Gesetze des Denkens für alle Menschen" [55]).

Art may represent the activities of the inner self, whether intellectual or sensual; or it may seek to show these activities in their relation to the external world. The former begins with identity and encounters difference in the artistic medium; the latter begins with difference and seeks to reveal identity in the act of apprehension. Mimetic activity in all the arts (poetry, music, dance, painting, etc.) involves this fundamental opposition (56). Just as the place of the work of art is among the people, the place of the mimetic activity is always in the mind.

Because the finished work of art is the imitation of the inner image ("die Nachahmung des innern Bildes"), Schleiermacher argues the primacy of the inner image ("das innere Bild ist das eigentliche Kunstwerk"). Granting that the work of art is inevitably altered in its physical realization, he contends that the reshaping of the inner image still precedes, even as it consciously accompanies, the act of externalizing (57–59). To demonstrate this primacy of the inner image, Schleiermacher offers a variation on Diderot's paradox of the actor:

> If we ask why the movements of an angry person, for example, are not as much a work of art as when an angry person is represented on the stage, it will become evident that the movements of the angry person want measure and for that reason are without beauty. For it is the

> primary prescription of art that its matter be measured. To be sure, there is something in human movement which we call grace, and if a person who possesses natural grace really becomes angry, that person's movements will never be as unbeautiful as another's. But should those movements bear the character of deliberation and measure, thereby giving the impression of art, then we would say that he is no longer the angry person, but that he has internalized the external image of the angry person, and his conscious awareness now mediates and controls the movements. The angry person himself lacks this control. (60–61)[14]

The conscious awareness of the inner image is manifest in all aspects of the aesthetic experience. It directs the production and informs the reception of the work of art. Even in its external difference, art reveals its inherent identity. Always recognized as an immanent activity, art is never confounded with reality (61).

There is no solipsism in Schleiermacher's definition of art as imitation of an inner image. He has made it clear that the inner image has its identity not in individual difference but in the artist's participation in the community. The artist, however, is not thereby doomed to repeat what is already known. Whether drawn from internal or external being, the artist's image is no copy. Just as no two people will perceive the same object in the same way, the inner image is different in its very conception (64–65). As already acknowledged, it is further altered in its production. Just as we may rightly anticipate certain familiar features, expressions, gestures to be realized by a sculptor in making a memorial statue of an admired fellow citizen, we may nevertheless have our expectations pleasingly fulfilled in an unanticipated way when the statue is unveiled. A composer may both meet and contradict a listener's expectations with an innovative adaptation of a conventional musical phrase. The difference in the identity, the identity in the difference, both contribute to the compelling power of art.

Thinking, in its usual modes, presumes identity; it seeks to reconcile, to bring into harmony, whatever difference it may encounter. Another mode of thinking, which deliberately presumes and maintains difference, is skepticism. Aesthetic thinking shares with skepticism a deliberate disbelief. Artistic truth is inherently different because it has no validity outside of art (61–62). The work of art, Schleiermacher declares, exhibits its own fictive reality and does not causally engage in events outside itself. We may recognize a fictional character as drawn true to life, but such a character does not, like Pygmalion's Galatea, step forth from art into life. The truth of a fictional character—the accuracy with which human thought and action are represented—is still a truth that is confined to the work of art. The apparent paradox of a fictional truth derives, in Schleiermacher's terms, from the capacity to discover identity in art's persistent difference (63). Precisely because it provokes no such tension of identity in difference, a copy is merely a mechanical reproduction and not a work of art (64).

Having discriminated the essential activity of art from its end product, Schleiermacher locates each in its own ontic *Ort:* the place of the work of art is the nation; the place of art itself is in mental activity. The work of art, in its place among the people, is thus immanent activity. He discusses the various genre and modes of art in terms of the ways in which they engage the activity of the mind.

Although the truth of art is conditional and speculative, it is a truth that may well be amplified and allowed to dominate our experience of the work of art. The sense of difference is suspended *(aufgehoben)* in order to experience the identity. Art that seeks to engender a sense of identity in difference emphasizes the receptivity. Another sort of art invites the audience to share in the artist's productivity. To accomplish this, the artist requires a constant attention to difference, subordinating the sense of identity (65–66).

The emphasis on receptivity is important to art that is concerned with representing human character or action, a *Lebensmoment.* The attention is to identity, the recognition of self in other. Character, no matter what change, development, or reversal of fortune it may undergo, is presumed constant. There is one "I," one consciousness that attracts the interest of the reader or spectator. The medium of receptivity art is thus consciousness: it is an art in which we witness *Bewußtsein.* The emphasis on productivity, in which the artist endeavors to represent the creative process itself, is a self-reflexive mode that requires awareness of difference. Process, after all, always involves a transmutation, a becoming other. The medium of productivity is a reenactment of the artist's thinking. Rather than participating in the consciousness of a character, the reader or spectator enters into the creative activity of the artist (68–69).

Crucial to Schleiermacher's purpose, it will be recalled, is his effort to demonstrate that the aesthetic experience is also ethical. It is therefore necessary to show that the activity of that experience is always a free activity. At the very outset (35), he admitted that in its receptive mode art may excite involuntary sensual or emotional responses that are ethically objectionable. At that moment, he argues, we may reject the work of art on ethical grounds. In his subsequent exposition, it becomes evident how the ethical and aesthetic grounds correspond: the work is deemed objectionable, after all, because it has no place in the national identity. He confesses, however, that the productive mode of art is far more problematic to his case for free activity.

The problem is that artistic creativity may arise in those darker regions of mind beyond the reign of conscious, volitional control. Within the identity of consciousness there is a ferment of difference. This strangeness within the self emerges in dreams. As manifest in dreams, it is involuntary and irrational, but nonetheless creative and potentially productive. To some degree, art is always the waking dream of the artist ("das wachende Träumen des Künstlers") and owes at least a part of its origin and being to a difference that resists subjection to the will. Only through waking effort may the artist tame the defiant difference of the dream. As represented in art, the dream sheds its chaotic irrationality and becomes the object of a willed and ordered activity (80–85). The dream and fantasy, in Schleiermacher's aesthetics, are accorded a high value precisely because they reveal in the very psychological immediacy of their subject matter the power of art to reconcile identity and difference.[15]

The two major thrusts of all art—to represent difference through the propagation of ideas and images, to represent identity by engendering a sense of consciousness and mental presence (85–86)—are both subject to a restraint (Hemmung) that reveals, rather than retards, its free activity. To liberate itself from the disorder and abandon of wild chaos, whether the exterior sources of anarchy and excess or the uncontrolled interior wellings of irrationality, art must exercise the will and exemplify the freedom of an ordered and measured world.

Hegel, too, responds to Plato in his presentation of identity and difference in imitation, and he shares with Schleiermacher an emphatic concern with negative powers ("die ungeheure Macht des Negativen").[16] Mimetic desire, after all, might release rather than control irrational otherness, the alterity within our own identity. The Mandaean Gnostics told of such a terror: When the Uthras plot the creation of a world, Abathur enters into the darkness where he beholds "his face in the black water, and his likeness and son is formed unto him out of the black water."[17] The sensual and material demiurge is thus born, *idem et alter*, in the act of mirroring.

For Plotinus, the soul participates in divine identity and the intellect is caught up in difference. He thus locates the demiurge, similar to the

Mandaean Gnostics, in sense perception and material thought. Adapting from the *Timaeus* (35a), Plotinus believes all souls to be a part of the Universal Soul. In the divine division, material bodies were generated within the Universal Soul, and each body took with it a partial soul. The soul thus is attracted in two directions: identity and difference. The movement toward identity approaches true being (Ὄντος); the movement toward difference lapses into nothingness (τὸ μη ον). The more one enters into the self and makes images of the self, the more one strays into the indefinite and treads upon emptiness (*Enneads,* 3:9 §3).

Although Hegel recognizes the formative influence of *Timaeus* on Plotinus, Philo, and the Alexandrine philosophers (*Vorlesungen über die Geschichte der Philosophie,* 18:57, 264; 19:24, 61), he avoids the appeal to cosmic mimesis as a model for artistic mimesis (*Timaeus* 29). He is no less wary of the materialist trap of empty images. The one leads to pure idea, with no content; the other to mere copies, with no meaning or "truth." The Neoplatonic fascination with the sensuous embodiment of the ideal in the real, if it is to have any abiding value as a metaphor or analogy, must confront the essential difference in artistic imitation. In divine creation, so it is assumed, material being is actually animated with a vital soul. The mere mortal artist, however, can at best create only an appearance of such animation.

Drawing upon Plato's *Parmenides* (146–47), Hegel asserts that each being is posited as a "something" against the "other," while every "other" is itself a "something." Identity and difference, therefore, coexist only in reciprocal negation (*Enzyklopädie der philosophische Wissenschaft,* §§42–48). Revising the argument from the *Sophist* (255–56), Hegel internalizes into self-reflective being what for Plato had been only a matter of a shifting frame of reference. The reciprocal negation of identity and difference takes place within consciousness.[18] Identity defines itself in terms of what is different. But in each encounter with difference, identity changes. Difference becomes familiar and is absorbed by sensation and thought into identity.

The drive to comprehend one's own identity, Hegel explains in his *Vorlesungen über die Ästhetik,* is inextricable from those desires stimulated by the external world. As the individual consciousness explores the internal and external unknown, the work of art provides a way of recording its discoveries. Mimetic desire is fulfilled in the consummation of the sensual and intellectual. The sensual aspects of the work of art are necessary to its presentation, for even the pure intellectual ideal must, as art, be represented to eye or ear through some material media. By the same token, the mind must also be engaged through the sensual mediation of art. Because it is mediated rather than immediate, the sensual presence of art is only an illusory appearance *(Schein).* The work of art is thus poised, as it were, some place between the intellectual and the sensual. The very mediation of art as appearance *(Schein)* engages the activity of the mind as well as the senses: "das Sinnliche in der Kunst [ist] *vergeistigt,* da das *Geistige* in ihr als versinnlicht erscheint" (13:61).[19]

To what extent is the mental activity subject to rational control? In his discrimination of talent and genius, Hegel dismisses the notion that "in artistic production all consciousness over its own activity is not only superfluous, but even a disadvantage" (13:46). The cult of genius, as forwarded by Herder and Goethe in the 1770s, claimed that creativity arose out of inspiration or enthusiasm. Hegel insists upon reflection, effort, and practice as necessary for artistic accomplishment. Reflection, he readily grants, entails a study of consciousness and its capacities of memory and phantasy. Images of experience are, of course, available through the memory, but the phantasy provides the artist a far richer source of profound and moving human imagery. Talent may be trained and disciplined, but phantasy, as a natural activity of the mind, is not the product of rational control: "Phantasy . . . has a manner at the same time of seemingly instinctual Production, in which the essential imagery and sensual appeal of the work of art must be present subjectively in the artist as natural attribute and natural drive and must also belong to the natural side of humanity at large as unconscious effect" (13:63).[20]

What Hegel denies to the inspiration of genius, he may thus seem to grant to the spontaneous workings of phantasy (13:363–73). He insists, however, that in the production of the work of art even the images of the phantasy, which well up instinctually from the unconscious, must be subjected to the intellectual and self-conscious control of the artist. Although the phantasy does, indeed, open a secret door through which the dark images of the unconscious enter into dreams, in the artistic consciousness the images of phantasy are wed with the images of waking experience to produce symbol (inner-directed) or allegory (outer-directed). The fascination with the dream is what Hegel finds characteristic in the art of India (12:176–77; 13:434–46). In European art, the tendency has been to valorize symbol making (10:266–68; 13:363–64, 430–48).

Imitation in art, as the mere reproduction of what is already available in nature, Hegel considers a redundant and superfluous activity. Even if the eye or ear is temporarily deceived by an illusion, delight in the mimicry seldom outlasts the moment of surprise when the deception is discovered. Unless the imitation has something more to reveal about subjective processes of perception or imagination, the mere objective replication cannot please (13:65–70). The purpose of art to imitate nature should not be understood as an alternative at odds with the purpose of art to arouse the passions. Both work together, as Horace would have it, "to teach and delight." The truth that art teaches, for Hegel, is the truth of human consciousness (13:70–82). Even when the artist turns to external nature as if determined to present in "still life" a mere accidental collection of homely and, in themselves, uninteresting items, the translation from object to appearance is what may convey significant "truth." Not the content nor its reality, but the reenactment in pigment on canvas of the play of light and color is what reveals the perceptual moment: "die Kunst ist Meisterschaft in Darstellung aller Geheimnisse des sich in sich vertiefenden Scheinens der äußeren Erscheinungen" (14:227).

The polished glaze of pottery, the transparent sheen of glass, the shimmering translucence of a grape, the reflection and refraction of rippling water, the effects of moonlight, or the glaring sun, all require not only a scientific scrutiny of optical causes and physiological effects, but also a mastery of the medium in which that causality is to be re-created. Light and color do not work in and through the painter's oils as they do in the objects to be represented on canvas. Thus when a peculiar glint of light seems to flash forth from the edge of a depicted vase, we may peer closer to behold nothing more than a strategic daub of white pigment. Or the water drops glistening in apparent beads on the surface of an apple may, at close look, lose their illusion of three-dimensional transparence and turn into mere painted streaks of red, yellow, green, and blue. To render the dynamic movement of light and color, even in a "still life," is to grapple in a static medium with the fleeting attributes of perception. Such, too, is the complexity of a smile or a glance on a human face, the thought or feeling in a momentary expression. Its "momentary" nature, without appearing fixed or frozen, must nevertheless be captured in the static image on the canvas (14:227–28). In confronting such extensive demands to represent the truth of inner consciousness, the *Schein* in the *Erscheinung,* the artist succeeds only by fidelity to the essential subjectivity of the perceptual act. Where objective mastery fails, as it must, to replicate fully the physical phenomena, a sensitive reenactment of the subjective attributes of the experience will enable the viewer to comprehend and, in the personal subjective response, complement the aesthetic moment.

Light, Hegel wrote in the *Enzyklopädie* (§317), is revealed as identity in difference: it reflects, refracts, diffracts, illuminates, and variously reveals iridescence and color. Its identity is always manifest only in its becoming other (9:226–29). But the same is true of mind, as the processes of self-reflexion and sensory apprehension are exhibited to consciousness (*Phänomenologie des Geistes,* 3:559–74). Identity and difference, he argues in his *Vorlesungen über der Philosophie der Religion,* also defines the immanence of God (17:241–99). Or, rather, the mystery of divine immanence gave rise historically to a mode of philosophical analysis based on the dialectics of identity and difference. That historical development, which commenced at the time of Christ's birth, was forwarded principally in the works of Philo of Judaea. Philo, drawing from his studies of Pythagoras and Plato, transformed his exegesis of the divine Logos into a full-fledged philosophical system. In the midst of nothingness, τὸ μη ον, is the presence of the divine Father, Ὄν. His Identity is negative, for it is His determination to be negative, a one-sided abstraction, the potential moment of conception. That potential is expressed in the λόγος, the Word as rationally determined activity. In the Word, Identity becomes Difference. In the comprehension of the Word, σοφία, Identity informs Difference (17:237–39).

The mimetic tensions of identity and difference, elaborated by Schleiermacher in his lectures on ethics and aesthetics, and by Hegel in his lectures on aesthetics and the philosophy of religion, had also been pondered by Schelling in his lectures on the philosophy of art in 1802–3. Although they each grappled with the notion of *idem et alter* in their own manner, the Romantic philosophers and critics found it relevant in accounting for the mimetic act.

Pertinent historical antecedents to the Romantic versions of *idem et alter* may be traced in logic and rhetoric as well as theology. In the *Sophist,* the very passage upon which Hegel constructed his account of *Anderssein,* Plato demonstrates that in arguing by contraries it must be observed that some oppositions are not discrete, that τὸ ταὐτόν (the same) and τὸ θάτερον (the other) may coexist or even interchange.[21] Indeed, the concepts of sameness and difference may shift fields of designation: If sameness refers to identity and difference to otherness, then it may be said that both refer to change. Since all things change, one of the common attributes of all things, a part of their sameness, is that they are all in the process of becoming different (254–59). In arguing by opposites one should be alert to the ways in which the field of reference may be altered. By substituting the field of reference, Socrates points out to the Eleatic Stranger, one can argue that great is small or that small is great (259c-d).

The seeming paradox is produced only because the terms are relative. The words remain the same.

When Aristotle discusses "the one" and "the many" in the *Metaphysics* (book 10), he also notes that "same" and "different" are relative terms. Although it is possible to establish many categories of meaning, "so that everything is either the same as or other than everything else," the terms are not contradictory. The opposition of "same" and "different" remains bound within a given ontology: the meaning is predicated in reference to existing things (1054^{b}, 14–23). *Otherness,* unlike *difference,* is not a term limited to definite and existing being. Thus "the other or the same," τὸ ἕτερον ἢ ταὐτό, may open into the nonexistent, τὸ μη ον, and indefinite speculation.

To assume the coherence of being may be a simple mental act, but its logical consequences easily lead into a philosophical entrapment. "But being—what is being?" Heidegger asks. "It is its self," he answers. "Subsequent thinking must learn to experience this and to say it. 'Being'—that is not God and not a universal ground."[22] The ontological dilemma arises in the attempt to ground being in something outside itself, to derive being from nonbeing, the ontic from the meontic. Insisting on the identity of being as "its self," Plotinus discovered, does not resolve the dilemma (*Enneads* 6:8–9). What is to be done with Heidegger's "not God" and "not universal ground"? Even if the identity of being is said to exist independent of nonbeing, is the nonbeing the same or different? Philosophers, at least those determined to save the cosmos from sundering chaos, devise strategies for assimilating difference into identity: "Omne quod est, est idem sibi ipsi et alteri aliud" (Everything that exists is the same to itself and other to the other).[23]

The concept of rhetorical imitation, traditionally advanced with reference to Quintilian's *Institutions of Oratory* (book 10, ch. 2), presumes that the something new will be added to form or content, manner or matter.[24] "Imitation per se is not sufficient" (§4), Quintilian argued, adding that "it is even dishonorable to rest satisfied with simply equaling what we imitate" (§7). To imitate, one must also be true to the power of judgment which informed the original. "Nothing improves by imitation only" (§8). Quintilian recommends, therefore, not slavish replication, but sameness with difference. It was to this concept of rhetorical imitation, then, that the poets of the Renaissance appealed when they sought to break away from the constraints of convention. The dominance of Petrarchan conceits in the sonnet prompted the liberating countermovement of the anti-Petrarchan. Gascoigne's "Lullaby" is an apt example of rhetorical imitation as an experiment with new content in established forms.

The *idem et alter* was also appropriated into theological explanations of the divine mystery of the Trinity. The divine Identity manifest in the Father, Son, and Holy Ghost is sameness in difference. It is to this tradition that Coleridge refers when he introduces the concept in the *Biographia Literaria.* As part of his argument on the reconciliation of the opposing traditions of idealism and materialism, Coleridge presents ten theses borrowed from Schelling.[25] He observes that even in the act of self-representation, when a spirit seeks its own identity in self-consciousness, there is a necessary act of forming the subject into an object. The argument, of course, harkens back to Kant's postulation of the "Das: Ich denke" as the phenomenal awareness of the self (the noumenal self, as *Ding-an-sich,* remains inaccessible to consciousness).

While the immediate provocation for Coleridge's remarks is Schelling's exposition of Kant in *Abhandlungen zur Erläuterung des Idealismus* and *System des transscendentalen Idealismus,* he was already familiar with the Neoplatonist arguments on positing the self. Thus in the very context of his extrapolation from Schelling he inserts the statement that "the spirit (originally the identity of object and subject) must in some sense dissolve this identity, in order to be conscious of it: fit alter et idem" (*CBL* 1:279). In his marginalia to Jacob Böhme, Coleridge explains the Triunity of the Word that is God, the Word that is with God, and the Word become flesh (John 1:1, 14): "with God" is the copula that unifies the trinity, the *Idem et Alter* of God become other (*CM* 1:690). And in a gloss on Arianism, he cites again the "*Hic* et *Alter*" in arguing "the *alterity* of the Son to the Father" (*CM* 2:33). Because he wants to affirm the primacy and originary identity of God, the "thisness" from which is generated the Son "as self-subsistent indeed but not self-originate," he must object to the description of Christ as "aliud et aliud" (actually "aliud ab alio") in Tertullian's *Adversus Praxean* (9).

Coleridge much preferred the designation *Deus idem et alter,* "named in imitation of the Jewish Philosopher." As he acknowledges in the *Opus Maximum* (MS B3, ff. 263–64), he found "God's co-eternal idea of himself" clearly expressed in the works of Philo.[26] Thomas McFarland, in his account of Coleridge's reading of Philo, cites the passage on the ὁ θεοῦ λόγος, the "'world descried by the mind'" (*De Opificio Mundi* VI, §21) as representative of Philo's attempt "to prevent pantheism by separating deity and world." Why should Coleridge translate from Greek to Latin in referring to the "Deus alter et Idem"?[27] With scholarly caution, McFarland rightly ponders "the pertinence of Coleridge's Latin formula."[28] The explanation may simply be that Coleridge used the familiar Latin phrase from the commentaries on Philo. The divine unity of αὐτός (self) and ἕτερος (other) is echoed by Nicholas of Cusa in his many names for God: "Deus idem absolutum" (God the absolute same), "Deus oppositio oppositorum" (God the opposition of opposites), "Deus autem, quia non aliud est ab alio"[29] (God, on the contrary, because he is not other from the other). Even with the revival of the Greek texts in the sixteenth century, scholarly discussion of Philo still drew upon the Latin translations.[30] Once scholars had access to texts other than the Eusebian extracts, they began to notice that Philo's thought often seemed at odds with the Christian dogma into which it had been received. The Greek text was indispensable in pursuing Philo's debt to Plato.[31] For Coleridge, the central debate concerned the relation of the Philonic to the Johannine Logos.[32]

The divine creation is not merely an external expression of the divine identity, it is consubstantial with that identity. In a letter of April 1818, Coleridge cites Philo in explaining the doctrine of divine immanence:

> The only possible mode of conceiving God as at once infinite and yet personal, is that of assuming that in the former sense it is God, as τὸ θεῖον, in the latter sense only Ὁ Θεός: that these are bonâ fide distinct—and the contra-distinction of God from all finite Beings consists of God's having the *ground* of his existence in himself, whereas all other Beings have their *ground* in another. Therefore God alone is a self-comprehending Spirit; and in this incommunicable *Adequate* Idea of himself (Λόγος) his Personality is contained—πρὸς τὸν Θεόν (very ill translated by the preposition, with) καί Θεός. Philo has asserted the same, and anxiously guards against the misconception that the Logos is an Attribute or Personification or generic or abstract term.—*Est* enim, et est Deus alter et idem.

Because Philo posits the Logos in distinguishing between the divine idea and the divine creation, there is an obvious similarity with the Gospel of John. Coleridge recognizes that, as in Plato's account of the artist's bed thrice removed from ideal bed, the doctrine of God's Word had immediate implications for the concept of mimesis and the poet's word. The Philonic-Johannine Logos, rather than setting the real apart from the ideal, affirmed their essential unity. The image in a mirror, Coleridge observes, may reflect the external appearance but is not informed by the creative presence:

> St John effects the same by interposing the account of *John,* a concrete, a man, and then adds—*He* was not the Logos. Can any thing be conceived more absurd than to affirm that John was not one of God's *Properties?*—In the beginning of this Mahogony Table was redness; and this Redness was in indivisible approximity to the Table, and was the Table—There was likewise a Looking-glass in the same Parlour—But this Looking-glass was not the Redness, of which I am speaking—&c.

Whether John was directly indebted to Philo, or Philo to John, or both to some other source familiar to the Hellenic Jews of the period, had stirred a debate among theologians.[33] Coleridge favors the arguments giving the credit to Philo.

> Now Philo & John were Contemporaries—either therefore Philo learnt the doctrine from the Christians, of which there is no proof or probability—or (of which there are many proofs) he wrote long before John wrote the Gospel. In the latter case John could not have used words so familiar to all the Hellenistic Jews for whom his Gospel was written, in a sense utterly different, and without giving them the least hint of this change, without intentional delusion. Rationally or irrationally, the Logos in his time meant a personal Being. (*CL* 4:850; cf. 632, 803)

When God molds man in His own image (Genesis 2:7), the Logos (in Philo's exegesis, "the first principle, the archetypal idea, the pre-measurer of all things") retains its identity even in that difference which is "a mixture of the corruptible and incorruptible" (*Quaestiones et Solutiones in Genesin,* §4). Philo's Logos become man is exalted in John's Logos become Christ. For Philo, only the spirit that God breathed into the mortal flesh is incorruptible and self-sufficient. For John, the very body of Christ partakes of the divine presence.

In citing Philo on the immanence of the Divine Logos, Coleridge affirms the advantage of also interpreting the Johannine Logos as "literally and mysteriously Deus alter et idem" (*CLS* 95). The "I am" of the Johannine Christ (the Way, the Light, the Bread, the Vine) is accessible precisely because of its double nature as I-Thou. Coleridge thus extended Philo's doctrine to other circumstances in which he wanted to acknowledge the pervasive presence of an informing will, whether in the disparate multitude of people that make up a society, or the disparate impulses and drives that make up an individual:

> Each man in a numerous society is not only coexistent with, but virtually organized into, the multitude of which he is an integral part. His *idem* is modified by the *alter.* And there arise impulses and objects from this *synthesis* of the *alter et idem,* myself and my neighbour. This, again, is strictly analogous to what takes place in the vital organization of the individual man.[34]

The self in which the emotions are at strife with the reason is a self in which "individualization subsists in the *alter*" rather than "confined to the *idem.*" The individual, no less than the state, can be disrupted by recalcitrant alterity. Coleridge thus uses identity and difference, as does Schleiermacher, to refer both to an interior and to an exterior Other. Granting that the "Body Natural" is the obvious analogue to the "Body Politic," the inherent correspondence informing both bodies, Coleridge asserts, is "the Divine Alterity, the Deus Alter et Idem of Philo."[35] The Logos as informing I-Thou dialogue is not only necessary to the idea of God and the possibility of religious experience, it is also as crucial to the artist as it is to the statesman, and to the individual as it is to the community.

Philo pursued such relationships in his exegesis of the biblical text: "The Lord God, seeing that the wickednesses of men were multiplied upon the earth and that every man intended evil in his heart diligently all his days, God had in His mind that He had made man upon the earth, and He bethought Him . . ." (Genesis 6:5–6). Opposing "careless inquirers" who find evidence in this passage that God changed his mind about his own creation, Philo asserts that error and change are human rather than divine attributes. He therefore proposes a distinction between the ways in which God and man may be said to have something "in mind." God, as eternal identity, conceives the universe of things. His thought is our reality. Things appear in perpetual flux as they gradually reveal to human perception the divine idea. All change is immediately present in God's mind. The mind of man, as a part of process, is itself subject to change. It is man, not God, who changes his mind. When God speaks, His word is absolute unity, at once signifier and signified. Unfortunately, the human mind habitually comprehends only duality, always separating idea from thing (*Quod Deus immutabilis sit,* §§83–84). In spite of being caught up in constant change, human consciousness may perceive the idea of God's immutable identity. As divine idea, its identity is present even in the alterity of the material world and the mortal mind. Through meditation and through dream, the human mind can experience the divine Idea (*De Vita Contemplativa* and *De Somniis*).

Although Philo in his *Legum Allegoriae* supports an allegorical interpretation of the Bible, reverberations of his argument are evident even when Coleridge opposes allegorical reading of the Bible. Commenting, for example, on the connection of faith with power proclaimed by Christ in the "faith as a mustard seed" passage (Matthew 17:20; Luke 17:6), Coleridge responds that there is "no proper allegorism in Scripture/ ταυτο εν γενει, αλλο solum in gradu αλλα σγορει" [the same in kind, but differs only in degree] (*CN* 3:4183). What Coleridge in *The Statesman's Manual* calls symbol, in contradistinction to allegory (*CLS* 30, 79), is not at odds with the sense of allegory advocated by Philo.

Allegorizing Hebrew scriptures, as practiced by Hellenic Jews seeking to establish themselves among the educated Greeks, had already in Philo's day resulted in a disregard for the sabbath and an indifference to the Mosaic laws. Philo opposed the loose humanistic allegorizing that severed the letter from the spirit; he insisted, instead, on immediate revelation, *Deus idem et alter,* in the scriptural word. Because the human mind dismantles all words into signifier and signified, the essential oneness of the divine word would be lost to human comprehension if God were not capable of communicating His identity even in the alterity of human language. What Philo calls "allegorical" exegesis is actually an attempt to retrieve the underlying meaning (ὑπόνοια) from an apparent meaning (φανερά). Because "God is not as man" (Numbers 23:19), the effort to make God comprehensible gave rise to anthropomorphic narratives.[36]

These narratives, by telling of God in human terms, make the Scriptures generally accessible, even "for the ways of thinking of the duller folk" (*Quod Deus immutabilis sit,* §11). However, biblical language also conveys more profound meaning to those who inquire into the inherent symbol (σύμβολον). While Eden is presented as if it were a geographical place with physical qualities of sensual luxuriance, Philo urges that we read the account of Paradise "symbolically." "Paradise should be thought a symbol of wisdom," and the rational soul a garden in which "the Creator planted His ideas like trees" (*Quaestiones et Solutiones in Genesin,* §§6, 8). Philo's allegorical reading, compatible with Coleridge's account of symbol, proposes to interpret the divine Logos as immanent even in the fragmentation of human language.

Less compatible with Coleridge's thought, however, is the "nothingness" which for Philo is the consequence of self-knowledge. Coleridge praises the power of the will to achieve that state of philosophic insight which he calls the "heaven-descended KNOW THYSELF!" From Plato through Plotinus, γνῶθι σεαυτόν involved a discipline of the mind toward self-perfection. For Philo, although it still requires meditative discipline, the end is recognition of inadequacy and imperfection: to know the nothingness of the mortal condition (*De Mutatione Nominum,* §54) and of the self (*Quis Rerum Divinarum Heres,* §30). To know that one knows nothing, as Socrates described the γνῶθι σεαυτόν, means to Philo that one must desert the nothingness of the mortal mind and seek the Divine Mind. When Abraham most knew himself (ἔγνω ἑαυτόν), Philo puns, then did he most disown himself (ἀπέγνω ἑαυτόν) (*De Somniis,* I, §§57–60). He who flies from his own νους (mind) flees to Absolute Νους (Mind) (*Legum Allegoriae,* III, §§29, 48). The language is similar to Coleridge's account of the finite I AM and the infinite I AM. But Coleridge did not want to abandon the former in order to find the latter. He required the very opposite. When he claims self-knowledge as "the postulate of philosophy and at the same time the test of philosophic capacity," Coleridge refers to the awareness of material knowledge as "the coincidence of an object with a subject" (*CBL* 1:252) and he anticipates that act of the imagination, "co-existing with the conscious will," through which the "finite I AM" perceives its participation in the "Infinite I AM" (1:304).

The leap is possible, for Philo no less than for Coleridge, because of *Deus idem et alter.* Philo repeats this concept of the infusion of identity into difference in *De Opificio Mundi* and *De Decalogo.*[37] Most relevant to Coleridge's thought, however, is the passage in which Philo describes the reconciliation of opposites in the divine act of creation: "He called the non-existent into existence and produced order from dis-order, qualities from things devoid of quality, similarities from dissimilars [ἐξ ἀνομοίων ὁμοιότητας], identities from the totally different [ἐξ ἑτεροιοτήτων ταυτότητας], fellowship and harmony from the dissociated and discordant, equality from inequality, and light from darkness."[38]

In defining the poetic imagination as "that synthetic and magical power" which "reveals itself in the balance or reconciliation of opposite or discordant qualities: of sameness and difference; of the general, with the concrete; the idea, with the image; the individual, with the representative" (*CBL* 2:16–17), Coleridge too lists in series the opposing elements unified in the creative act. Coleridge most probably also recollected here Schelling's argument that the artist, in unifying subject and object in the work of art, accomplishes what the philosopher can only posit. In adapting his theses from Schelling in chapter 12 of the *Biographia,* as noted above, Coleridge could easily assimilate Schelling and Philo into one argument. In his account of the "reconciliation of opposites" in chapter 14,[39] he clearly found Philo's presentation more immediately pertinent than Schelling's statement that the artist works with the "opposition of things" to achieve a "reconciliation of all powers."[40]

Philo's doctrine of the Logos as instrument of divine mediation is no less pertinent, Coleridge recognized, to aesthetics. At once signifier and signified, idea and reality, the Logos mediates God's activity in the world. Philo complicates the relationship by describing hierarchies of intermediary powers. A λογισμός is a finite manifestation of the infinite, a fragment of the divine creative act. Were it not for this doctrine of intermediaries, even Coleridge might have shuddered at the pretension of replicating in the finite I AM the universal creativity of the infinite I AM. To claim as one's own the seminal power of the divine Word (Λόγος σπερματικός; *Quaestiones . . . in Exodum,* II.68) is a self-deluding hubris to which Coleridge recognized his own frail susceptibility: "rationes spermaticæ—λογοι ποιητικοι—[spermatic reasons—creative words] O Formidable Words! and O Man, Marvellous Beast-angel! Ambitious Beggar, how pompously dost thou trick out thy very Ignorance, within such glorious Disguises that thou mays't seem to hide in order to worship it!" (*CN* 3:4136).

Through the intermediaries, God descends to human consciousness and man is elevated by divine thought.[41] Coleridge thus seeks to redeem mediation from megalomania. Just as the divine mind is mediated in nature (ὑπὸ τοῦ μεθορίου λόγου [under the limiting word]), the mind of the artist is mediated in the work of art. But the mind of man can create only in and through the mind of God. The reality we behold in material nature is an imitation of God's idea. Although there is no reality outside of God's idea, as the mediating Logos it may also inspire the mortal mind (*Quaestiones . . . in Genesin,* IV.29; . . . *in Exodum,* II.68, 94). When Coleridge declares that "Art is the imitatress of Nature" and "the Mediatress, the reconciliator of Man and Nature," he has granted the artist the capacity not only to imitate reality, but to imitate as well the divine act of creativity. While this passage, from Coleridge's lecture notes "on the relations of Genius to Nature in the Fine Arts," draws extensively from his reading of Schelling, it is nonetheless relevant to Coleridge's own peculiar account of artistic imitation as a mediation, *idem et alter:*

> In all Imitation two elements must exist, and not only exist but must be perceived as existing—Likeness and unlikeness, or Sameness and

> Difference. All Imitation in the Fine Arts is the union of Disparate Things.—Wax Images—Statues—Bronze—Pictures—the Artist may take his point where he likes—provided that the effect desired is produced—namely, that there should be a Likeness in Difference & a union of the two—*Tragic Dance.* (*CN* 3:4397, ff 50–50v)

Imitation as mediation is a "Tragic Dance," for the artist experiences the limitations of the finite mind entrapped in its mortal body. Art strives against those limits and succeeds insofar as in imitating nature it imitates as well the process of divine mediation. The key to "the Mystery of Genius in the Fine Arts," Coleridge suggests, is that "*Body* is but a striving to become Mind—that it is *mind,* in its essence." In this "Tragic Dance," the more successful the endeavor, the more the artist knows the failure.

For De Quincey, too, the co-presence of identity and alterity is a crucial attribute of art. He first posits the *idem in altero* in a note to his translation of Lessing's *Laokoön.* To the passage in which Lessing ponders the effects of the human form robed and disrobed in sculpture, De Quincey adds his own account of identity and difference. Although he is fully aware of the precedents in Athenian, Hellenic, and Roman art, he also knows that contemporary sculpture has favored draped representations of the human figure. Yet even in his own time, Canova and Thorwaldsen endeavored to make the robes appear to disappear. In spite of the moral pretense that demands drapery, "reason, conscious of an impotence to satisfy its moral need, has recourse to the *parergon.*"[42] Mimetic desire is fulfilled only in making the drapery reveal rather than conceal. To render transparent the opacity of stone, the sculpted body is enveloped yet exposed in diaphanously light and clinging garments.

De Quincey does not claim that attitudes about the body had become prudish, nor that "modesty" might be violated. But he does employ subtle irony in suggesting that opposition to a display of the undraped body may have come about because nudity is such an unusual condition and "we are too little familiar with the undraped figure to be able so readily in that state to judge of its proportions." In insisting that "neither the grace nor the majesty of the human figure is capable of being fully drawn out *except* by drapery," he claims his aesthetic ground in the association of sameness with difference. The human form is enhanced by "the great power of drapery under the law of association," and by the similarity and contrast between flesh and cloth. In "the original adaptation, neither accidental nor derivative, of drapery to the human figure," there is a power manifest in "repeating the flowing outlines of the human figure in another and more fluent material." This conjunction is the source "whence arises the pleasure, subtlest of all in nature, and the most effectively diffused, of similitude in dissimilitude." Nevertheless, the draped figure is less appropriate to sculpture than to painting.

> That drapery is not essential in sculpture, and that the highest effects of sculpture are in fact produced without it, is in some measure dependent on this very law of the interfusion of the similar and the dissimilar; for, in order that any effect should be felt as the *idem in altero,* it is necessary that each should be distinctly perceived; whereas, in sculptural drapery, from the absence of shading and of colouring, the "alterum" is not sufficiently perceived *as* an "alterum." There is another and transcendent reason for the ill effects of sculptural drapery, into which the former reason merges. For why *does* sculpture reject colouring; and why is it that just taste has always approved of the sightless eyes in statues? Manifestly, on the general and presiding law which determines the distinctions of the statuesque from the picturesque. The characteristic aim of painting is reality and life; of sculpture, ideality and duration. Painting is sensuous and concrete; sculpture abstract and imaginative. (*DQW* 11:195–96)

In entering into Lessing's exposition, De Quincey reiterates Lessing's "distinctions of the statuesque from the picturesque."[43] Lessing did not use the Latin phrase *idem in altero,* but, in a passage De Quincey omits from his translation, he did recognize an inevitable difference in artistic imitation: "One imitates in order to make similar; can one make similar, however, if one makes more changes than necessary? Moreover, if one does this, the intention is clear, that one did not want to make similar, that one therefore has not imitated."[44] The Laokoön problem is complicated by the inherent differences in the verbal and visual media. Because the mimetic process is different for each, radical transformations are entailed should the poet imitate the artist, or vice versa.

In spite of a polemic opposition to Lessing's text, De Quincey is fair in his summary of Lessing's argument. He leaves out major sections of the essay, but retains the essential points about the temporality of poetry and the spatiality of the visual arts. In his note on the *idem in altero,* however, he raises his own peculiar set of concerns about sameness in difference. When the note goes on to discuss problems in the representations of Christ, it becomes obvious that De Quincey—like Coleridge, not like

Lessing—thinks of imitation in terms of the doctrine of the Logos. The contrasting ground of representation in sculpture and painting, De Quincey asserts, is expressed in metaphysical terms by the *esse* and *existere* respectively. Thus the crucified Christ has been a subject for sculpture, while the living Christ "has been perpetually painted and but rarely sculpted." The reason, De Quincey asserts, derives directly from the mystery of the Logos:

> For in this mysterious incarnation, this entrance of Deity within the shade of time and passion, we must recollect that the divine is the true nature of Christ, and the human his superinduced nature; consequently it is to his human nature, as in this case the preternatural, that our attention is called. Life, therefore, or being in time,—which is here the uppermost idea,—fits the conception of Christ to painting. But, if the case had been reversed, and a nature originally human were supposed to have projected itself into eternity, and in some unspeakable way have united itself with the Deity, the divine nature would, in this synthesis of the two natures, have been the preternatural or superinduced, and the human nature the ground. Such a conception would be adapted to sculpture; and some such conception is in fact embodied in the sublime head of Memnon in the British Museum, in which are united the expressions of ineffable benignity with infinite duration. (*DQW* 11:196)

De Quincey goes on in his translation to present Lessing's claim that imitation does not entail blind adherence, that the artist has "room enough left for originality of thought to be manifested in his deviations from his archetype." Lessing's notion of original deviation within the constraints of imitation, however, is not shared in De Quincey's presumption of an immanence of the ideal in the real. De Quincey's account of the ground and the superinduced also explains why he has formulated the relationship *idem in altero* rather than *idem et alter.*

Insisting on coequivalence, Coleridge relied on the separate identity of the "I AM," as McFarland has most thoroughly demonstrated, to keep the immanence in the "it is" from spawning pantheism. In spite of his religious affirmation of the Trinity, De Quincey presents the relationship as if it were a dialectic in which mind either asserts its primacy over matter, or is subsumed in matter. In the Neoplatonic tradition it was frequently debated whether the rational principle remains a discrete ideal or somehow animates material being. Plato himself, as Billings has observed, combined "sound, consistent, logical thought with the fervor and imagination of the religious teacher and maker of myths."[45] Philo's doctrine of intermediaries should not be interpreted as an account of mythic underpowers, the Λόγος (Word) become λόγοι (words), which are diminutions of the divine presence. Philo, whose biblical exegesis endeavors to retrieve anthropomorphic representations of God, affirms that the divine idea is often manifest in anthropomorphic symbols. Adapting from *Timaeus* (36), Philo interprets the biblical description of the two Cherubim and "the sword of flame which turns every way" (*Genesis* 3:24) as symbols for night and day united by the moving sun, but also for the principles of sameness and difference (τὸ ταὐτόν and τὸ θάτερον) united by the divine Logos (*De Cherubim* 21). While the logoi are truly thoughts in the mind of God (*De posteritate Caini* 89–93), they are understood only as revealed to human mind (*De Somniis* I.69–70; *De Plantatione* 30–31, 83–84). When De Quincey explains the *idem in altero,* he is concerned with what happens to an idea under the influence of the imagination and of the medium in which it is expressed.

That the medium itself must be different is a part of his definition as first presented in his translation from Lessing. Twenty years had elapsed when De Quincey revived the concept in his essay on Sophocles' *Antigone.* Perhaps the discussion of Sophocles in Lessing's *Laokoön* came to mind and, with it, the recollection of the problem of "sameness in difference" in artistic representation. On this latter occasion, he conjures a Bosio-like sculptor who can move a viewer to tears "by exhibiting, in pure statuary marble on a sepulchral monument, two young children with their little heads on a pillow, sleeping in each other's arms." De Quincey's point is that the same scene would fail to achieve its emotional effect if it were done in wax. The difference would be wanting, for wax mimics the flesh all too well (*DQW* 10:369).[46] Madame Tussaud's wax figures seem astonishingly lifelike. But what is their effect? They make us gasp for a moment, then we peer more closely to see how the eyebrows are attached. The representation is too direct and immediate; we are compelled to seek for difference.

Because difference is readily evident in the artistic medium, the viewer is free to explore the identity. To be sure, we can focus on the medium in order to assess the skill and style of replication, but we can easily accept the manner of imitation and turn our attention to what is imitated and thus move emotionally and imaginatively into the aesthetic space of the work of art. The sculptor thus achieves the more profound effect: "He has expressed the *idem,* the identical thing expressed in the real children,—

the sleep that masks death, the rest, the peace, the purity, the innocence,—but *in alio,* in a substance the most different: rigid, non-elastic, and as unlike to flesh, if tried by touch, or eye, or by experience of life, as can well be imagined" (*DQW* 10:369). Joseph Addison, who thought Italian opera trespassed against the principles of mimesis, allowed, according to De Quincey, "no room or opening for any mode of imitation except such as belongs to a *mechanic* art." He failed to appreciate the need for difference, the first principle of the fine arts: "the object is to reproduce in the mind some great effect through the agency of *idem in alio.* The *idem,* the same impression, is to be restored, but *in alio,* in a different material,—by means of some different instrument" (*DQW* 10:368). The union of sameness in difference, then, exhibits the transforming presence of the mind in the matter. The viewer not only requires the leverage of aesthetic difference, the efforts at mimetic representation disappoint without it. On the other hand, the viewer has a far greater capacity to appreciate difference than the instance on verisimilitude generally recognized.

Far from disrupting illusion, the artifices of difference enable the artist to infuse into the work precisely those elements that are not attributes of external appearance. What Italian opera and Greek tragedy have in common is their reliance on elaborate conventions to explore depths of thought and feeling. "The principle of the *idem in alio,* so widely diffused through all the higher revelations of art, it is peculiarly requisite to bear in mind when looking at Grecian Tragedy, because no form of human composition employs it in so much complexity" (*DQW* 10:370). The masks, the recitative, the chorus are not at odds with, but are the very means through which the mimesis of Greek tragedy is made possible.

In his review of Thomas Noon Talford's *Memorials of Charles Lamb* (1848), De Quincey launches into a critique on the use of quotations. While granting "that essentially it is at war with sincerity, the foundation of all good writing, to express one's thoughts by another man's words," he calls upon the *idem in alio* to justify the apt use of borrowed words. It is a propriety maintained by the *in,* as opposed to *et,* of De Quincey's formulation:

> A quotation that repeats one's own sentiment, but in a varied form, has the grace which belongs to the *idem in alio,* the same radical idea expressed with a difference—similarity in dissimilarity; but to throw one's own thoughts, matter and form, through alien organs so absolutely as to make another man one's interpreter for evil or good, is either to confess a singular laxity of thinking that can so flexibly adapt

> itself to any casual form of words, or else to that sort of carelessness about the expression which draws its real origin from a sense of indifference about the things to be expressed. (*DQW* 5:237)

The real test, and only justification, of the propriety of quotation is whether one comprehends the other's thought and can absorb it coherently into one's own prose. The practical purpose may be "simply to back one's own view by a similar view derived from another." But De Quincey wants something more—a meeting of the minds: not that one has been forced to "bend to another man's expression," but that, having engaged in a kind of dialogue, the one fully understands the other.

The transforming action of mind, De Quincey states, alters all ideas that pass through consciousness. "The great catholic principle of the *Idem in alio*" is not a principle superimposed upon the work of art, but one that is inseparable from its very birth. To describe the mimetic process whereby the author attempts to represent the images of childhood, De Quincey invites the reader to ascend with him the Brocken in North Germany. Because it serves as symbol for the operations of the mind, this narrative has much the same function as the two epic similes in Wordsworth's *Prelude.*[47]

De Quincey had never climbed the Brocken, but Coleridge had. The narrative tells of the famous Spectre of the Brocken, the illusion that Coleridge had hoped to see, but did not. To conjure the image of the absent phantom, De Quincey relies on the account in Sir David Brewster's *Natural Magic.* This recollection of someone else's experience, supplemented by still another person's experience, is not inappropriate to the case that De Quincey wants to make about the otherness of one's own experiences. To introduce "Dream-Echoes" of remote childhood, he presents this narration as "a *real* ascent of the Brocken" to be distinguished from the "spiritualizing haze which belongs . . . to the action of dreams, and to the transfigurings worked upon troubled remembrances by retrospects so vast as fifty years." Coleridge's experience is more "*real,*" and perhaps less "other," than his own "troubled remembrances."

De Quincey records the date of Coleridge's ascent, Whitsunday 1799. Coleridge, had he but seen it, might well have made some connection between the Spectre and the special observance of the Trinity on that particular day. De Quincey, for his part, did not neglect due reverence. When he makes the sign of the cross, the phantom repeats the gesture, not spontaneously but with "the air of one who acts reluctantly or evasively." Cast by the rising sun onto the clouds on the opposite peak, the illusion is no more obedient than the images in De Quincey's "spiritualizing haze." As Brewster explains, its appearance and movement is also affected by atmospheric refraction. Thus De Quincey blames the reluctance of his giant alter-ego on "driving April showers" which "perplex the images." His prayer, true to his formulation of the *idem in alio,* describes the phantom, not as external apparition but as engendered in his own perception: "Lo! we—I thy servant, and this dark phantom, whom for one hour on this thy festival of Pentecost I make *my* servant—render thee united worship in this thy recovered temple" (*DQW* 1:53). The imaginary servant then plucks a blossom, kneels before the altar, and raises his right hand to God. "Dumb he is," De Quincey concludes, "but sometimes the dumb serve God acceptably."

This "*real* ascent of the Brocken," composed of borrowed details about an illusory phenomenon, is the symbol De Quincey chooses to depict how his present mind beholds "the solemn remembrances that lie hidden below." It is a symbol both *of* and *about* sameness in difference: "The half-sportive interlusory revealings of the symbolic tend to the same effect. One part of the effect from the symbolic is dependent on the great catholic principle of the *Idem in alio.* The symbol restores the theme, but under new combinations of form or colouring; gives back, but changes; restores, but idealises" (*DQW* 1:51). The image of his former self as a child of six is no less elusive an apparition: a shadow engulfed in shadows, a self transformed by otherness. Art can do no more than retrieve, *idem in alio,* the phantom images of perception, memory, and imagination. For De Quincey, as for Coleridge, Schleiermacher, and Hegel, this is the only valid claim to be made for artistic imitation.

Lucy Newlyn

"Questionable Shape": The Aesthetics of Indeterminacy

❦

I

The connections between sublimity and indeterminacy are already apparent in Edmund Burke's critique of the "significant and expressive uncertainty" which characterizes Milton's description of Death in *Paradise Lost.* In a chapter of his 1759 *Philosophical Enquiry* headed "Obscurity," Burke quotes this passage in full:

> The other shape,
> If shape it might be called that shape had none
> Distinguishable in member, joint, or limb,
> Or substance might be called that shadow seemed,
> For each seemed either; black it stood as night,
> Fierce as ten Furies, terrible as hell,
> And shook a dreadful dart; what seemed his head
> The likeness of a kingly crown had on.[1]

"To make anything very terrible," Burke argues, "obscurity seems in general to be necessary"; and accordingly, in this description of Milton's, "all is dark, uncertain, terrible, and sublime to the last degree."[2] By drawing attention to the vagueness of Milton's ideas of power and grandeur, Burke establishes sublimity as a special type of indeterminacy: his observation can, however, be extended, to suggest a more general equation between powerful ideas and indefinite language.

In Romantic and post-Romantic aesthetics this equation is so recurrent as to be commonplace. More interesting is the significance of the figure of death—a figure that threads its way with remarkable consistency through eighteenth- and nineteenth-century commentaries on the sublime, reemerging as recently as 1984 in an essay by Jean-François Lyotard entitled "The Sublime and the Avant-Garde." Why should death, the epitome of closure, be appropriate to concepts of sublimity and indeterminacy? What is it that makes for such a close and (it seems) abiding configuration of ideas? Lyotard has claimed that the major stake of Burke's aesthetic is to show that "the sublime is kindled by the threat of nothing further happening."[3] Whereas beauty gives a positive pleasure, there is for Burke "another kind of pleasure that is bound to a passion stronger than satisfaction, and that is pain and impending death." This passion Burke calls "terror": "Terrors are linked to privation: privation of light, terror of darkness; privation of others, terror of solitude; privation of language, terror of silence; privation of objects, terror of emptiness; privation of life, terror of death."[4] This idea of privation survives as a feature of the twentieth-century sublime. What writers, painters, institutions presuppose, Lyotard argues, is that "words already heard or pronounced are not the last words. After a sentence, after a colour, comes another sentence, another colour"; and so we forget "the possibility of nothing happening, of words, colours, forms or sounds not coming; of this sentence being the last." What the sublime offers is the terror of privation itself: "What is terrifying is that . . . *it* stops happening."[5]

For Lyotard, then, the existence of the speaking, writing, or painting subject is at stake: the sublime challenges the subject with the death of meaning. In this respect, sublimity resembles extreme cases of indeterminacy—cases in which the interpreting subject is either baffled by a plethora of potential meanings into a state resembling anxiety, or satisfied to relinquish control over the making of determinate meaning. The task of bearing witness to the indeterminate is, as Lyotard claims, a peculiar feature of modernity; and his own essay bears this out. But his description of the convergence between presence and absence (pleasure and pain) in the sublime moment is nonetheless highly relevant to Romantic writing, where the basis for an *aesthetic* of indeterminacy is first established. Furthermore, the anxiety Lyotard characterizes as modern—an anxiety centering on the "threat of nothing further happening"—takes a form that is peculiarly subject-centered at the end of the eighteenth century. This is partly because the status of the subject is at this time deeply unstable—still locked into problems of authority and metaphysics, yet attempting to negotiate independence from a transcendental order; but also because the events following 1789 brought the "sublime" rather too close for comfort, giving urgency and immediacy to the meaning of terror.

Death is a figure particularly appropriate to the Romantic sublime because, while it threatens the subject with extinction, its very unknowability gives freedom to subjectivity. But the questions it poses are transhistorical; and its associations with indeterminacy go back much further than the Romantics, or even Milton. Thomas Docherty has shown how Augustine tried in the *Civitas Dei* to remove the fact of death from human experience by reducing the moment of death "to an imaginary point, a disappearing asymptote."[6] The crux of the Augustinian argument, much echoed in the seventeenth century, is as follows: "If a man is still alive, he is 'before death'; if he has stopped living, he is now 'after death.' Therefore he is never detected in the situation of dying, or 'in death.' The same thing happens with the passage of time; we try to find the present moment, but without success, because the future changes into the past without interval."[7] Donne dramatizes this concern with the temporal indeterminacy of death in his "A Valediction, Forbidding Mourning"; and numerous further examples suggest that the Augustinian argument persists into the eighteenth century.[8] As Docherty points out, however, the effects of such sophistry are counterproductive, since death is thereby merely *relocated,* "as a potent force in the imagination, all the more trenchant in an age when untimely death was prevalent."[9]

That Shakespeare shared this interest in death's indeterminacy is borne out by a scene which in all likelihood lies behind Milton's personification, and which has a peculiar potency for Romantic writers. It is a well-known scene, set on the ramparts of a castle in Denmark, where the ghost of a father appears before his living son. "Thou comest in such a questionable shape," Hamlet cries, "that I will speak to thee" (I. iii.43–44). The word "questionable," here, is ambiguous on a number of planes. Its metaphorical significance is "doubtful," or "indefinite"; but it also means, literally, able to be questioned.[10] A "questionable shape" could therefore be a shape so indistinct as scarcely to be a shape at all; but it could also be a shape definite enough to be visible—and if visible, Hamlet concludes, then maybe also audible (able to answer questions). His pun takes advantage of a slippage from the metaphorical to the literal; but it also plays with a sliding of the direction of reference, so that "questionable" describes both the shape's ontological status and the perceiver's relation to it. Further to complicate these ambiguities, there is a doubleness within the attitude of questioning, which can suggest a seeking of answers, but may also be an acknowledgment that reliable authority has broken down. This gives a moral resonance to the word "questionable," and implies that a doubtful shape may give answers that are not to be trusted.

What is one to make of the convergence here between ideas of closure and indeterminacy? It is a truism that death baffles human comprehension with alternating possibilities: to some holding out the comfort of completion, while unsettling even rationalists with the hope (or fear) of life in another form. The uncertainty it faces Hamlet with is unusual, though, if only because it appears in the shape of a ghost—a shape who ought not to be doubted because he speaks as the father, the bearer of authoritative meaning, but whose existence is dubious because (in Freud's terms) it suggests an "uncanny" confirmation of primitive animistic beliefs.[11] This makes it a scene of arresting significance in the context of post-Enlightenment thinking, because the Enlightenment had sought to banish superstition—to rid the mind of "notions of ghosts and goblins, of which none can form clear ideas" (Burke, *Enquiry,* 59). The transcendental order, too, had begun to be questioned, along with other modes of authority, other systems restricting the subject's freedom—all of which has a bearing on how we may suppose late–eighteenth-century readers to have responded to a ghost who takes the dubious shape of a father.

Shakespeare's interest in the indeterminacy of death is extended, however, before Romanticism begins, in *Paradise Lost.* Milton follows Hamlet by making death into a "questionable shape" both metaphorically (in that its form is insubstantial) and literally, in that Satan challenges it with questions:

> Whence and what art thou, execrable shape,
> That darest, though grim and terrible, advance
> Thy miscreated front athwart my way? (II. 681–83)

It is clear that what interests Milton is not just the cognitive uncertainty this "shape" registers, but the perplexity it induces in the perceiving subject about the relation between being, not being, and seeming to be—"substance might be called that shadow seemed, / For each seemed either." The collocation of "substance" with "shadow" carries a specific philosophical resonance: these are the terms that Plato had used to explore the uncertain basis on which suppositions about the nature of "reality" are founded, when the world of appearances is all the human mind has to go by.[12] In the seventeenth and eighteenth centuries, they are terms applied not just to the equivocal relation between seeming and being, but more specifically to questions about the correspondence between material and spiritual "reality." The (apparently substantial) world that human beings inhabit comes to be thought of as a shadow, or pale reflection, of a spiritual world beyond.[13] Milton's adaptation of this conundrum to the subject matter at hand thus introduces the possibility that death only *appears* to be certain and to have finality in this world. In an ideal world it would not.

Furthermore, Milton's questioning of appearances is given a political dimension, it being presumably no coincidence that he associates death (as Shakespeare had done) with regal authority: "what seemed his head / The likeness of a kingly crown had on." A biblical allusion may be intended here, to *Revelation* 6:2, where the first rider of the Apocalypse bears a crown and goes forth conquering.[14] But the topicality of regicide in Milton's line could imply a general observation about the nature of power. The words "seemed" and "likeness" suggest not just that death is frighteningly powerful (kingly) because it is vague, but that the ascription of power and authority to kings is itself dubious. In allegorizing indeterminacy to make a political point, Milton at the same time succeeds in making a political point about indeterminacy. It is a point crucial to the argument of this chapter—namely, that mystification is the secret of power—and one that Burke himself develops, even though he does not share Milton's antimonarchical viewpoint. ("Despotic governments" he claims, "are founded on the passions of men, and principally upon the passion of fear"; such governments maintain their power over a benighted people by keeping "as much as possible from the public eye" [*Enquiry*, 59].)

The interest Wordsworth shows in Shakespeare's "questionable shape" is somewhat different from Milton's, though important ingredients are shared. *The Prelude*'s "Waiting for Horses" episode does not explicitly invoke the ghost of Hamlet's father as a metaphor for the return of kingly power; but it does suggest the persistence of patriarchal authority, even in the face of extinction. Critics have noticed that the mist, "Which on the line of each of those two Roads / Advanced in such indisputable shapes" (*W Prel* XI. 380–81) suggests a subliminal connection between Hamlet and the orphaned Wordsworth, each confronted (though in the second case only metaphorically) by his father's ghost.[15] Much has been made of the passage in terms of Freudian ego-psychology, and much more could be developed, by pursuing a Bloomian line of enquiry. One might ask, for instance, if the "shapes" that move toward Wordsworth do not amalgamate into a kind of "familiar compound ghost" (T. S. Eliot's phrase)[16]—a conflation of Shakespeare and Milton, whose joint authority the poet must vanquish, if he is to clear imaginative space for himself. Such Bloomian conjectures would derive support from Wordsworth's repetition of the Miltonic verb "advanced" to describe the movement of the mist; and also from the fact that in this composite echo there is an important slippage of meaning (in which much anxiety might be uncovered)—from Shakespeare's "questionable" to Milton's "execrable" and finally to Wordsworth's "indisputable."

It scarcely takes Freudian or Bloomian methodology, however, to see that the drama of this Wordsworthian scene centers on the unstable status of the subject in relation to past authority, at a time when authority is itself under question. The episode can therefore be read, not just as an echo of Hamlet's psychological and metaphysical enquiries, but as an allegorical paradigm for the Romantic subject's equivocal relationship with power. More specifically, it can be read in terms of Wordsworth's attitudes to authority—the authority of the past, which he as reader subjects to question; but also his own authority as writer, in relation to future readers. This takes us into Bloomian territory, though the point I wish to make has to do not with any particular "anxiety of influence" (in relation to Shakespeare or Milton, for instance), but with an anxiety that the writing subject experiences, at the very point where its challenging of past authority brings an awareness of the *reader*'s power. Roland Barthes has claimed that "the birth of the reader must be at the cost of the death of the author."[17] If, on one level, Wordsworth appears to celebrate the possibilities that this prospect brings with it, still the reader's birth is accompanied by guilts, by reservations, and above all by fears. For when the status of past authority is contested, the writing subject itself becomes unstable: just as dubious as the past, and just as vulnerable to extinction.

In the "Waiting for Horses" episode, then, Wordsworth's guilty confusion between the anticipation of holiday and the death of his father offers a suggestive parallel with Barthes's formulation of the transference of power from author to reader. As the irrefutable fact of the father's death merges with the "intermitting prospect" of his son's future, a site of closure becomes an opening. The poet, "straining his eyes intensely" to discern the shapes of the advancing mist, figuratively enacts the reading process; and, in interpreting the mist as the figure of death, draws on his reading of past writers. If power could be transferred from "author" to "reader" as straightforwardly as Barthes claims, one might expect Wordsworth to underline his questioning of past authority by accentuating the dubiety of these advancing shapes. However, in the movement from Hamlet's "questionable" to Wordsworth's "indisputable," there is envisaged the awful applicability of death to Wordsworth himself; there is also implied a replenishing of the past with some of its threatened authority. The writing subject, seeking to ensure that its own voice will not be disputed by future readers, defends itself, thus, against an extinction it fears to be inevitable.

II

Burke is clearly not responsible for the underlying connections between indeterminacy, sublimity, and the figure of death; but it was his *Philosophical Enquiry* that succeeded in establishing Milton's description of Death as a touchstone for sublime language. His analysis points to the uncertainty of definition with which Milton achieves his sublime effects: "it is astonishing with what a gloomy pomp, with what a significant and expressive uncertainty of strokes and colouring Milton has finished his portrait of the king of terrors" (*Enquiry,* 59). For Burke, sublimity is associated with indefiniteness of language because the grandeur of mental conceptions appears to make them uncontainable by verbal forms. Whereas "a clear idea . . . is another name for a little idea" (63), the presence of unclear ideas creates an illusion of excess, by suggesting the expansion of tenor beyond vehicle. Emotional or intellectual intensity correlates with verbal insufficiency: the transcendent signified breaks free of the inadequate signifier, leaving the human mind baffled and terrified by the sense of a power beyond its own conception.[18]

In empowering linguistic insufficiency by making it the source of emotional and imaginative pleasure, Burke prepares the way for an interest in what the *reader* does with this uncertainty; this will be developed later by (among others) Coleridge and Wordsworth. But the importance of Burke's argument is more complexly related to Romanticism than such an account implies. A further significant feature of the passage I have quoted is its tense combination of openness and closure—a combination that is apparent when Burke makes a kind of oxymoronic play on the word *finished:* "with what a significant and expressive uncertainty . . . Milton has *finished* his portrait." In the context of the visual arts, the word *finish* is a technical term used of the varnish given to a painting when it has been completed. Its main function is to preserve the pigment from discoloration; but it also provides the painting with an even surface, thus preventing any accidental effects of light and texture, which might be distracting to the observer. It is, furthermore, a term applied to polished oil paintings, not to those pencil or watercolor sketches whose sublimity consists in their "unfinished" suggestiveness.[19]

Unexpectedly, then, Burke ascribes to the visual properties of Milton's "portrait" some of the definiteness that is antithetical to the sublime. Transferring this implied paradox into the context of writing, one can see the implications for reader-response. Although it may seem at first as though the "expressive uncertainty" Burke describes is an attribute of the portrait painter himself, the word "finished" closes off this possibility—handing the feeling of uncertainty over to the reader, and leaving the artist in control of his technically achieved effects. The tension here suggested, between a belittled and an empowered reader, takes on greater significance as one moves from the implications of Burke's practical criticism to the ideological ramifications of his thesis.

A connection between the grandeur of ideas and the insufficiency of language makes possible the internalization of sublimity as a function of the subjective mind, since it draws attention to the fact that, as Kant later puts it, "ideas of sublimity cannot be contained in any sensuous form."[20] But conversely, it is this very connection that allows ideas of power and grandeur to be sustained as potentially tyrannical forces, since human beings are thereby reminded of their littleness. Obscurity of image, and indefiniteness of language, are effective in intensifying an aesthetic that rests on the sense of terror, because *they diminish the power of the human subject in the face of supersensible ideas.* (In the same way, both superstition and religion maintain their hold on the otherwise rational mind, through ideas of greatness and incomprehensibility.) As appropriated by Burke, indeterminacy is therefore a means of mystification: bringing home to the reader a magnified sense of the power of God, it succeeds in closing off, or "finishing," the expansiveness of subjectivity.

Cowper's interest in the figure of death has a similar slant, even though it enlarges the space available for readers to construct meaning. Comparing Milton's description of Death with Spenser's, Cowper claims that the former is "incomparably more poetical" because of its "ambiguous nature": "Milton's is in fact an original figure, a Death of his own invention, a kind of intermediate form between matter and spirit, partaking of both, and consisting of neither. The idea of its substance is lost in its tenuity, and yet, contemplated awhile as a shadow, it becomes a substance."[21] Cowper's explicit concern is with the achievements of obscurity through poetic skill rather than with the role of the reader in making sense of confusion. But his scrutiny of the successive stages of image-definition followed by image-retraction contains astonishing potential as an account of figuration in general. Equally, it offers a description of the poetic process that is adaptable to a phenomenological account of reading, in which the speculative activity of the reader is foregrounded:

> The indistinctness of this phantom form is admirably well-preserved. First the poet calls it a shape, then doubts if it could be properly so called; then a substance; then a shadow; then doubts if it were either; and lastly he will not venture to affirm, that what seemed his head, was such in reality, but being covered with the similitude of a crown, he is rather inclined to think it such. (453–54)

Overlooking Milton's covert allusion to regicide—an allusion that takes its gruesome force precisely from the suggestion that there may be no head for the likeness of a crown to rest on—Cowper concentrates instead on the hesitancy and equivocation in Milton's poetic voice, and on the philosophical issues that are raised by his use of Platonic terminology. The thematic explanation he offers for this hovering between "substance" and "shadow" is at once critically ingenious and predictably didactic. He sees a moral point in representing death as "a being of such doubtful definition," since death "will have different effects on the righteous and the wicked. To these it is a real evil, to those only an imaginary one." His allegorizing of indeterminacy can thus be seen to follow strictly Christian lines: "the dimness of this vague and fleeting outline" is, he claims, "infinitely more terrifying than exact description, because it leaves the imagination at full liberty to see for itself, and know the worst" (453–54).

It will be evident, from the two instances I have examined, how readily appropriable is a model of linguistic indeterminacy to ideological ends. Burke is interested in obscurity as a source of terror, which the mind controls by aesthetic distancing, but to which it ultimately succumbs, under the oppressive sense of its own littleness. Cowper adapts the Burkean model, so that it reflects his own vividly imaginative grasp of the terrors of damnation. The "full liberty" that, in his view, is pleasurably experienced by the mind while it is facing the choice between images must come to an end, since it is only a liberty to "see for itself, and know the worst": a circumscribed liberty, in fact, not a license for subjective interpretation. Both writers assume that Milton is *in charge of his poetic effects,* and that the uncertainty produced in the reader serves the author's didactic and theological ends. Both writers, in other words, give indeterminacy a more than aesthetic function, presenting it as part of a grandly inscrutable design which is preconceived by the author as though he were God.

This subordination of sublimity to devotional purpose is more or less standard in accounts of Milton belonging to the later part of the eighteenth century. Indeed, after the publication in 1787 of Bishop Lowth's *Lectures on the Sacred Poetry of the Hebrews,* it becomes almost impossible to separate Miltonic sublimity from the generic attributes of prophecy as Lowth defined them. It is in the context, therefore, of biblical language and hermeneutics that indeterminacy is best understood at this period: its ideological ramifications derive from the subordination of poetry to religion. Lowth affirms that religion is "the original office and destination of Poetry," and that sacred poetry is superior to both nature and art. "Nothing in nature," he claims, "can be so conducive to the sublime, as those conceptions which are suggested by the contemplation of the greatest of all beings."[22] Acknowledging, as Burke does, the close connection between obscurity of language and sublimity of conception, he is more explicit in giving it the divinely authoritative dimension that underpins Burke's aesthetic.[23] He finds two different species of the sublime in the Bible: the first uses "the grandest imagery that universal nature can suggest," and yet "proves totally inadequate to the purpose," so that the mind "seems to exert its utmost faculties in vain to grasp an object, whose unparalleled magnitude mocks its feeble endeavors" (353). The second depends on a comparison between divine qualities and natural objects or human attributes; these latter, precisely by being inadequate or bathetic, allow for an enlightening comparison with the greatness of God: "From ideas, which in themselves appear coarse, unsuitable, and totally unworthy of so great an object, the mind naturally recedes, and passes suddenly to the contemplation of the object itself, and its inherent magnitude and importance" (364). Lowth thus adopts two routes for underwriting divine authority. Both kinds of language, grand and humble, are seen as inadequate to the purpose of describing God; and "sublimity" is the acknowledgment of human inadequacy, in the face of supersensible ideas. Here, as in Burke and Cowper, humiliation of the subject is built into the structure of the sublime.

III

With this theological slant to the aesthetic in view, the question to be asked of Romantic indeterminacy is what kind and degree of freedom it envisages for the reader. The answer may be difficult to construe, since ideology is more carefully disguised in Romantic writing than in the commentaries of Burke, Cowper, or Lowth.[24] Take, for example, Coleridge's account of Milton's Death, which appears as a digression in one of his Shakespeare lectures, and which he uses to illustrate "an effort in the mind, when it would describe what it cannot satisfy itself with the description of."[25] This "effort" (the index of an inadequacy that is built into the structure of the sublime) is aimed toward reconciling opposites and qualifying contradictions, "leaving a middle state of mind more strictly appropriate to the imagination than any other, when it is, as it were, hovering between images." Coleridge argues that this activity of "hovering" allows the mind to break down cognitive boundaries, and to discover its own subjective power in the refusal of closure: "The grandest efforts of poetry are where the imagination is called forth, not to produce a distinct form, but a strong working of the mind, still offering what is again rejected; the result being what the poet wishes to impress, namely, the substitution of a sublime feeling of the unimaginable for the mere image."[26] Coleridge's appropriation of indeterminacy is less heavily accented than Burke's or Cowper's, because sublimity has been internalized (much as it is in Kant's *Critique of Judgement*) through a concentration on the subject's *ideas* of greatness, as opposed to the grand objects themselves. There is, as a result, no terrified submission by human subjectivity to a power beyond itself, such as that embodied by mountains or God in the Burkean aesthetic. And yet the direction in which Coleridge's argument moves is markedly intentionalist: he underlines the fact that indeterminacy produces a result that "the poet wishes to impress," much as Burke had stressed the sublime effects with which Milton "finished" his portrait of the king of terrors. Coleridge's emphasis, like Burke's, is on the power of authorial imagination, not the flexibility of reader-response.

The broader implications of this passage become apparent if one sees it as part of a philosophical debate (going back into Locke's *An Essay Concerning Human Understanding*) about the relative merits of reason and imagination, or "judgment" and "wit." For Locke, judgment lies "in separating carefully, one from another, Ideas wherein can be found the least difference, thereby to avoid being misled by Similitude, and by affinity to take one thing for another."[27] Wit, on the other hand, proceeds in the opposite direction, perceiving likeness where it is not intended, and so producing ambiguity. Whereas the first requires vigilance—an activity of the will, to be clear that different signifiers point to different signifieds—the second is described by Locke as a lazy habit of confusion: metaphor, he says, "strikes so lively on the Fancy, because its Beauty appears at first sight, and there is required no labour of thought, to examine what Truth or Reason there is in it" (136). Not being "conformable" to truth or reason, wit is subversive of morality: its slipperiness makes it the vehicle of deceit.

Coleridge's analysis of indeterminacy retains the shape of Locke's distinction, but reverses its import. As soon as the mind is fixed on one image, Coleridge points out, "it becomes understanding"; but while it is unfixed and wavering between them, attaching itself to none, "it is imagination."[28] Descended from Locke's "wit," imagination is given a more emancipated role than Locke could have conceived for it, without taking on any of the connotations of laziness or deceit: indeed, the accent falls very heavily on the mind's "effort" and "strong working" while it wavers between opposite ideas. To make his anti-Lockean point, Coleridge depends heavily, and in two different respects, on Lowth's analysis of biblical language. First, he dignifies indistinctness by bolstering aesthetic with economic value—exactly as Lowth does in claiming that "while the imagination labours to comprehend what is beyond its powers, this very labour itself, and these intellectual endeavours, sufficiently demonstrate the immensity and sublimity of the object."[29] And secondly, Coleridge reshuffles the values of wit and judgment by giving wit some of the mystique of genius: a procedure Lowth adopts when he claims that finding out "some striking familiarity" between objects that "upon the whole have the least agreement" entitles the genius or fancy to "the highest commendation."[30]

Without explicitly invoking Lowth, then, Coleridge is dependent on his ideas: he could thus be said to draw indirectly on biblical authority to support Romantic ideology, assigning a lowly position to reason, and elevating the imagination as an alternative route toward the truth. Shelley will echo this realignment of Lockean categories when he writes, in *The Defence of Poetry,* "Reason respects the differences, and imagination the similitudes of things." So far so good, from a Lockean point of view; but Shelley continues by making reason the lowly servant of imagination, and (with a nod in the direction of Plato and Milton) by identifying the latter with an ideal world: "Reason is to imagination as the instrument to the agent, as the body to the spirit, as the shadow to the substance" (*SW* 7:109).[31] This reversal of values is made possible by changes in attitudes to grammar that take place during the latter part of the eighteenth century. As Tilottama Rajan has shown, the assumption that "fixed meanings are located in individual words" is at this period gradually eroded, and room is made for relationships behind and between words, as well as for "words referring only to other words."[32] These changes clear the way for a suspension of Locke's rationalist suspicion toward the duplicity of metaphor, and so for the validation of suggestiveness and ambiguity.

In chapter 13 of *Biographia Literaria,* indeterminacy makes its appearance, yet again, in the shape of Milton's Death: not, this time, to illustrate the imaginative power of Milton, but in order to claim this power on Coleridge's own behalf, and so to underwrite his hierarchy of values. The purpose behind the Miltonic quotation is well concealed. Coming as it does in the middle of an inserted letter (allegedly received by Coleridge in the course of writing *Biographia*), it appears as part of a critique of the structure and method he has so far adopted in his attempt to define imagination.[33] The letter complains that nothing Coleridge has said adds up to a logically coherent position; that there is a muddle at the center of his thinking, which leaves the reader baffled and unable to proceed. Apparently hostile, the complaining friend (here a model of the reader) makes a comparison between reading *Biographia* and entering a Gothic cathedral by moonlight. He begins by using devices of comic deflation, but these gradually give way to sublime poetic effects. The Miltonic juxtaposition of "palpable darkness" with "broad yet visionary lights" and the presence of "fantastic shapes" add up to an atmosphere of expressive uncertainty, into which Milton's Death can be introduced with ease:

> In short, what I had supposed substances were thinned away into shadows, while everywhere shadows were deepened into substances:
>
> If substance might be called that shadow seem'd,
> For each seem'd either! (*CBL* 1:301)

What appears to be a judgment on the confusion of Coleridge's thinking becomes, in the course of this description, and using the criteria Burke had evolved for discussing Milton's sublimity, a validation of his method. The presence of this Miltonic touchstone allows Coleridge to establish the imaginative credentials of his prose style, and to diminish the importance of consecutive reasoning in a context that calls for faith.

The structuring of chapter 13 is therefore more purposeful than even the most sophisticated of recent ironic readings have suggested. Tilottama Rajan claims that Coleridge "leaves his argument rhetorically unactualized and concludes with a merely embryonic definition of the imagination, lest the . . . process of elaboration and demonstration turn out to be a process of dismantling." The onus is then on the reader, she argues, "to restore the unity of the work."[34] She is right to emphasize Coleridge's suspicion of rationalist procedures; but she neglects the way in which Coleridge's ironic handling of the "spoof"-letter manipulates the reader, precisely through rhetorical actualization. For it is in the course of the letter itself, as it moves from the mock-gothic to the sublime, that the hostile reader learns to sympathize with Coleridge's authorial design; and it is the changing register of the letter which performatively underlines his crucial point, that imagination is best "defined" imaginatively. The inadequacy of Coleridge's philosophical argument comes to suggest as its own defense that logic is insufficient to the grandeur and incommunicability of his subject matter. This prepares the way for the *imagination* definition, which is itself antithetical to logical procedures. The conclusion of chapter 13 is thus strategically inconclusive—judiciously obscure. It demonstrates through untranslatable assertion, rather than proving through consecutive reason; and it makes its claims for the imagination by showing the powerlessness of philosophy in the face of religious belief.[35]

IV

It is perhaps unsurprising, in view of research recently undertaken by (among others) Elinor Shaffer and Anthony Harding, to find Coleridge fitting so readily into the tradition of nineteenth-century hermeneutics—exploiting its strategies to establish an audience that shares his ideology and sympathizes with his designs.[36] What happens, though, if one moves outside this closed theocentric circle, to look at more secular writers? Wordsworth, for instance, does not use the aesthetic category of the sublime merely as a function of divinity, but appears rather to offer notions of the unreachable as *substitutes* for God. In an early fragment, for instance, he describes how the mind retains "an obscure sense of possible sublimity," aspiring "with growing faculties" to an ever-receding goal, and strengthened by the consciousness that "there still is something to pursue."[37] And, in his Note to "The Thorn," he naturalizes a theological commonplace (along lines that are reminiscent of Bishop Lowth) by making a poetic virtue of inexpressibility. A "consciousness of the inadequateness of our own powers, or the deficiencies of language" accompanies any attempt to "communicate impassioned feelings," he claims. "During such efforts there will be a craving in the mind, and as long as it is unsatisfied the Speaker will cling to the same words, or words of the same character" (*WPW* 2:513). This unsatisfied craving, synonymous with inadequacy of representation, makes of the passion itself something unreachable or sublime.

What is the status of indeterminacy in this version of sublimity, and what freedom does it offer to the reader? The answer is best provided in terms of Wordsworth's affinities with Kant, rather than Burke. For whereas Coleridge follows a clearly Burkean line, in employing devices of self-defeat or bafflement to suggest the infinity of God, Wordsworth at several points (but most noticeably in book 6 of *The Prelude*) draws on a Kantian model of success-in-failure to reinforce the subject with ideas of its own potential greatness. Kant's analysis of sublimity centers on a perception of the inadequacy of nature to represent ideas of grandeur and, further, of the inadequacy of imagination to realize the totalizing conceptions of reason. The sublime experience is, in his view, one in which we are "pushed to the point at which our faculty of imagination breaks down in presenting the concept of a magnitude, and proves unequal to its task."[38] Far from signaling failure, however, this breakdown offers reassurance. Reason is confirmed in its paramountcy by the proof that it possesses supersensible intuitions, ungraspable by imagination: "The Subject's very incapacity betrays the consciousness of an unlimited faculty of the same Subject";[39] or, in other words, the inability of imagination to catch up with reason brings with it an awareness of reason's infinite potential; so the subject need not feel humiliated by its apparent "incapacity."

In analyzing the "bewilderment, or sort of perplexity" experienced by the traveler, on first entering St Peter's in Rome, Kant offers an account of sublimity which could be put alongside Wordsworth's "Crossing of the Alps." The sublime "object" that stimulates the mind into a feeling of sublimity is in the Kantian case man-made rather than natural; but it is the *right kind* of object, because its religious, cultural, and historical associations make it worthy of reverence. (In the same way, the Alps bear witness to the extraordinariness of human endeavor, and acquire a cultural status for Wordsworth over and above their "natural" grandeur.) Kant does not appear to be interested, as Wordsworth is, by the experience of anticlimax which excessive expectations of a sublime object may introduce; but he is interested in something analogous to anticlimax, which provokes a sense of incapacity in the mind. Entering St Peter's, the traveler is overwhelmed: "a feeling comes home to him of the inadequacy of his imagination for presenting the idea of a whole within which that imagination attains its maximum, and in its fruitless efforts to extend this limit, recoils upon itself, but in so doing succumbs to an emotional delight" (*Critique of Judgement,* 100). The failure of representation is experienced as a displeasure which is nonetheless pleasurable: "emotional delight" is thus provoked by the traveler's awareness of a disjunction between the totalizing conceptions of which reason is capable, and the limited sense-apprehensions achieved by imagination. This "failure" guarantees that "a feeling of a supersensible faculty within" has been awakened (97).

It is Kant's emphasis on the *recuperative* power of the subject that proves crucial to Wordsworth's version of the sublime, as his own handling of anticlimax bears out. In the "Crossing of the Alps" episode, the Kantian argument is pursued to its logical conclusion, with Wordsworth arranging for nature to let him down, so as to perpetuate his quest for the unattainable. In its initial impact, the moment of anticlimax is registered as displeasure; but, true to the Kantian pattern of recovery, the mind derives from this bewilderment or perplexity a reassuring guarantee that it is "lord and master" (*W Prel* XI.271). The unpleasurable frustration of desire thus makes possible the triumph of imagination; and it does so in such a way that the compensatory second stage is scarcely distinguishable from initial perplexity:

> Imagination!—lifting up itself
> Before the eye and progress of my Song
> Like an unfathered vapour; here that Power,
> In all the might of its endowments, came
> Athwart me . . . (VI. 525–29)

The temporal indeterminacy of this passage is essential to its meaning. Wordsworth seems at pains to emphasize the disjunction between past and present selves, by the use of alternating tenses: "I was lost . . . And now . . . I say" (VI. 529–32); but his imprecise use of the word "here" places the arrival of the "unfathered vapour" both in the present, as he writes, and in the past ("*came* athwart me"), at the geographical point where he was overwhelmed by disappointment. Whereas the first of these time schemes suggests an intervening or mediating consciousness of recuperation, the second has an effect of collapsing into each other the contrary feelings of anticlimax and recovery, thus underlining the suggestion that sublimity is *dependent* on insufficiency.

The arrival of the "unfathered vapour" on this sublime scene provokes speculation about a possible (subliminal) connection between the "Crossing of the Alps" passage and the "Waiting for Horses" episode I discussed earlier. Such speculation focuses on the presence of the advancing mist; on the identification of this mist with the orphaned ("unfathered") state; and on the oedipal implications of Wordsworth's recurring preoccupation with his father's death—an event he connects on both occasions with his creative growth. Beyond all this, there is a striking coincidence in the fact that the mist on the Alps comes "athwart" the poet, just as Death in *Paradise Lost* is described by Satan as advancing "athwart my way." Aside from the obvious fact that this echo gives the mist sublime associations, it also confirms the link I earlier established, between Wordsworth's literal father and his strong precursor, Milton. This adds a ghostly resonance to what is, after all, a scene of *self*-recognition:

> I was lost as in a cloud,
> Halted without a struggle to break through,
> And now recovering to my Soul I say
> "I recognise thy glory." (VI. 529–32)

Even with the utmost refinement of Freudian/Bloomian methodology, it would be cumbersome to unravel the oedipal significance of such obscure connections. I want, rather, to pursue the more general point, that this scene of self-recognition is also a scene of "usurpation"; and that Wordsworth's use of allusion and metaphor seems to invite allegorical interpretation. Like the "Waiting for Horses" episode, then, this one can be read in terms of an equivocal relationship with power, which induces in the writing subject an anxiety for its own permanence and stability. We have already seen how this "anxiety" manifests itself most strongly at the point where the power to displace past authority forces a recognition of the threat which reading poses for writing; and how the writing subject defends itself against such anxiety, by restoring authority to the past. In the "Crossing of the Alps" episode, a similar defense mechanism takes the more complex form of Kantian self-recuperation. The transference of power from past to present which Barthes describes in "The Death of the Author" is enacted, here, by the scrambling of temporal perspectives I have already discussed. It is also implied in the more brutal metaphor of usurpation, which refers in two directions at once: to Wordworth's sense of being overwhelmed by the authority of the past, and to his own access of power, as reader of that past. The moment of the "sublime" can be understood as the moment at which the writing subject *recuperates itself* precisely by *allowing itself to be overwhelmed:* the moment, in other words, at which the past conflates with the present, and "reading" collapses into "writing."

Such an interpretation becomes doubly plausible in light of the passage Wordsworth originally composed as a sequel to this one, but which actually appears in book 8 of the 1805 *Prelude,* as a simile for his entry into London. Wordsworth describes how a traveler, entering the Cave of Yordas during the day, "looks and sees the Cavern spread and grow, / Widening itself on all sides" (ll. 715–16), and, as his eye adjusts to the different light, "sees, or thinks / He sees, erelong, the roof above his head, / Which instantly unsettles and recedes" (ll. 716–18). The lines contain an allusion to the Virgilian trope of uncertainty, "aut videt, aut vidisse putat";[40] but more importantly, Wordsworth goes on to give this uncertainty a sublime dimension, by a reference to Milton's Death:

> Substance and shadow, light and darkness, all
> Commingled, making up a Canopy
> Of Shapes and Forms, and Tendencies to Shape,
> That shift and vanish, change and interchange
> Like Spectres—ferment quiet and sublime . . . (VIII. 719–23)

The Miltonic resonance is all the more powerful for the Platonic context in which it appears; and Wordsworth uses Plato's exploration of seeming and being to stage his own philosophical inquiry into the relation between a material world and its spiritual counterpart—understood, here, in terms of a bipartite treatment of visual impressions and imaginative projections. A close connection is thus made between visual indeterminacy and imaginative potency, which claims its "authority" from Plato, Virgil, Milton, and Burke.

The point in this digression that corresponds to the actual moment of crossing the Alps is the point at which obscurity "works less and less, / Till every effort, every motion gone, / The scene before him lies in perfect view, / Exposed and lifeless as a written book" (VIII. 724–27). Wordsworth's mention of "work" and "effort" recalls the dignity that Coleridge assigns to imagination by associating it with labor, and thus rescuing it from the Lockean charge of laziness: the Wordsworthian emphasis falls on a winding down of this imaginative effort, toward sterile immobility. The poet has here transferred the threat of extinction which occurs in the sublime moment into the context of writing itself, so that death once again makes its figurative appearance, as a premonition of the author's own demise.[41] But Wordsworth thinks on, beyond this death, into the act of "reading" which recovers the writing subject, and reactivates the creative process:

> But let him pause a while, and look again
> And a new quickening shall succeed, at first
> Beginning timidly, then creeping fast
> Through all which he beholds . . . (VIII. 728–31)

This recuperative process succeeds in moving the potential of subjectivity onto a higher plane, replacing "shapes and forms and tendencies to shape" with a train of images, appearing and disappearing in a "Spectacle to which there is no end" (VIII. 741). The simile as a whole conforms to the Kantian pattern of sublimation which we see also in *Prelude* book 6, as the poet's finite expectation is replaced by "something evermore about to be" (VI. 542).

There are several important senses in which this passage from book 8 may be compared with Coleridge's "spoof"-letter, in *Biographia* chapter 13. First, and most obviously, it offers an account of the unsettling but creative effect that darkness can have on visual impressions. Secondly, it invokes the Burkean aesthetic of indeterminacy, in order to give a poetic account of imagination. Most importantly of all, though, it is a digression—an interruptive mechanism—which builds into the narration of events a directive as to how they should be read. It does this through the use of a persona (the traveler) who passes from bewilderment to imaginative understanding in the course of the unfolding simile, and so offers a model of sympathetic reader-response. Just as the digression in *Biographia* provides a key to its hierarchy of values, so the "Cave of Yordas" simile establishes a method for understanding *The Prelude*'s overall design.[42] This design depends on the internalization of sublimity along Kantian lines: Imagination moves in to the place assigned by Coleridge to divinity, and the writing subject seeks to establish its own credentials.[43] It does so by using past and present selves to construct a pattern of gain-in-loss; and by making temporal indeterminacy the register of subjectivity's power.

Another simile, this time in book 4, provides a commentary on Wordsworth's narratorial procedures:

> As one who hangs, down-bending from the side
> Of a slow-moving Boat . . .
> Sees many beauteous sights, weeds, fishes, flowers,

Grots, pebbles, roots of trees, and fancies more;
Yet often is perplex'd, and cannot part
The shadow from the substance, rocks and sky,
Mountains and clouds, from that which is indeed
The region, and the things which there abide
In their true dwelling . . .
—Such pleasant office have we long pursued
Incumbent o'er the surface of past time
With like success. (IV. 247–48, 252–58, 262–64)

The presence of Milton's Death can be lightly touched on, as a reminder that Wordsworth's discussion of indeterminacy takes its place in a wider aesthetic debate.[44] More important is his extension of Milton's Platonic interest in the distinction between seeming and being, elaborated here through a sequence of confusions: between the underwater world and objects on dry land; between substantial things and their watery reflections; between imaginary shapes, and forms that have "real"—that is, material and tangible—existence. As a simile for Wordsworth's autobiographical method, this digression is used to affirm the interchangeability of past and present selves: reflections of the adult Wordsworth are perceived sometimes as gleams of his own image, sometimes as memories of his childhood self. Furthermore, these temporal/cognitive displacements are made the source of aesthetic pleasure to the narrator—"impediments that make his task more sweet." Whether we read the passage as a celebration of subjectivity, then, or as an exploration of the substitutions (words for things) on which language itself depends, the inability to part substance from shadow is experienced as gain, rather than as loss; and this simile (like the Cave of Yordas one) can therefore be seen to incorporate a Kantian scheme of self-recuperation.

Though possible and tempting, it would be less than responsible to interpret either of these two digressions as a modernist manifesto for the birth of the reader. Wordsworth's insistence throughout both is on the continuity (despite disruptions, obstacles, disappointments) of authorial consciousness. It is this insistence which reassures the subject, along Kantian lines, by showing how "the subject's very incapacity" discovers an "unlimited faculty *in the same subject*" (*Critique of Judgement,* 108). Although the traveler and the person in the boat appear as personas for the model reader, they are, to all intents and purposes, figures for the poet himself: writing is again collapsed into reading, just as the past conflates with the present in Wordsworth's account of imaginative recovery. For all its apparent openness, then, *The Prelude* defines an aesthetic of indeterminacy which is just as "closed" as Coleridge's, in *Biographia* chapter 13. Admittedly, Wordsworth's internalization of the sublime allows him to avoid the theological tenor of Coleridge's argument; but his disguised use of hermeneutic practice registers an anxiety for the status of the writing subject which is, if anything, stronger.

This is not the place for indeterminacy to find itself as a liberating medium for the reader. Instead, it is an early example of the paradox that Umberto Eco uncovers in modern writing: the paradox, that is, of *an open-ness which is designed.* Eco tentatively suggests that this phenomenon betrays an anxiety about the permissiveness of interpretation in an age which takes for granted the liberties of the reader: the modern artist, he claims, does not wish to "submit to 'openness' as an inescapable element of artistic interpretation"; and rather than do so, he "subsumes it into a positive aspect of his production, recasting the work so as to expose it to the maximum possible 'opening.'"[45] This suggestion bears a remarkable resemblance to the Kantian conversion of loss into gain, failure into success; and it coincides with my own suspicion that an aesthetic of indeterminacy may be one of the means whereby the encroaching power of interpretation is controlled, and the rights of the author defended.[46]

V

Romantic criticism anticipates the findings of twentieth-century semioticians such as Eco, by outlining two models of creativity—the open and the closed, the suggestive and the didactic—in its contrasting caricatures of Shakespeare and Milton. Shakespeare is associated with pathos and tenderness, Milton with the sublime; Shakespeare can enter fully into frailties, Milton stands aloof from them; Shakespeare is all relativism and humanness, while Milton is a synecdoche for the Judaeo-Christian God.[47] This polarization codifies an uncertainty about the direction in which Romanticism wishes to move its theories of authority and interpretation. An alignment with Milton would suggest that interpretation must have theological ramifications, since here the reader submits to the author in the same way as the subject is humbled by inscrutable divinity. But Shakespeare holds out a heuristic alternative—in which the reader gains independence from the author, just as the dramatic medium discovers freedom in its refusal of closure.[48] The evolution of aesthetics toward the latter of these two models is an inevitable by-product of secularization. During the Romantic period, a choice between them is much more than a matter of taste and personal allegiance: the whole future of subjectivity hangs in the balance.

I say that this polarization anticipates semiotics. And yet Romantic criticism is clearly *not* a scientific endeavor to understand writing as a system of signs, involving author and reader in a collaborative enterprise. Rather, it offers value judgments about different kinds of *creative genius,* resting on contrasting models of authority. It explores the tensions with which this chapter has been centrally concerned—tensions between closure and indeterminacy, authorial restrictions and interpretative rights; but it does so as though these were purely a matter of artistic characteristics, kinds of consciousness. Its observations begin and end with the author—and this remains the case, whichever kind of prejudice a given writer brings to bear on the question. Coleridge, for instance, strongly supportive of hermeneutic practices, is intent on mystifying Shakespeare and Milton equally, by aligning their two kinds of imagination with immanent versus transcendent models of divinity: "Shakespeare is the Spinozistic deity, an omnipresent creativeness," he claims; "Milton is Prescience; he stands ab extra" (*CTT* 1:125). Keats, approaching the problem from a purely secular angle, ascribes to *Shakespeare,* not himself as reader, the capacity to remain "in uncertainties, mysteries, doubts, without any irritable reaching after fact and reason" (*KL* 1:193), while he sees in Milton a denial and authoritarianism he finds stifling: "I have but lately stood on my guard against Milton, Life to him would be death to me" (*KL* 2:212). Wordsworth, somewhere in between these two positions, claims the works of Milton as one of the "grand store-houses of enthusiastic and meditative imagination," while Shakespeare, the epitome of "human and dramatic imagination," is equally valued as a role model (*WPrW* 3:34, 35).

So strongly does the "author function" maintain its stranglehold on Romantic criticism that it blinds writers to their own reading practices. For it is a striking fact about the reception of Milton and Shakespeare that, when one comes to look closely at Romantic poetry (rather than Romantic criticism) the division between kinds of imagination collapses entirely. As careful readers, the Romantics respond just as readily to Miltonic indeterminacies as to their Shakespearian counterparts. Even while exposing the closure of Milton's imagination in their critical observations, they are involved in revealing a quite different Milton—open-ended, ambiguous, negatively capable—when it comes to rewriting his poems.[49]

This reception-paradox offers an extreme example of the way in which

Romantic criticism controls indeterminacy by subduing it to authorial design, thereby reaffirming the primacy of the creative imagination. There is no contradiction of *ideology* between critical and poetic endeavors, since as we have seen Romantic poetry has an equally strong investment in affirming the status of the writing subject.[50] The paradox arises because different authorial imaginations are involved. Romantic criticism suffers from a sense of secondariness, and seldom moves beyond deferential obeisance toward such geniuses as Shakespeare and Milton. Romantic poetry, on the other hand, is concerned to establish its *own* primariness, its own originality—and this may well involve a more equivocal reading of those same authors.[51] That Romantic theory should go so much against the grain of its own reading practice is a measure of the extent to which Romantic writers are confused or threatened by the latent power of the reader. This in turn reflects the more imponderable problem Romanticism faces, in attempting to negotiate a stable place for the subject in relation to authority—especially the authority of the past.

Such confusion is obliquely registered by Charles Lamb, on those occasions when he attempts to rescue the idea of genius from its inevitable decline. His "Essay on the Tragedies of Shakespeare" is an example: here, Lamb is concerned to explain the disappointment that he usually feels on seeing Shakespeare performed—a disappointment he describes in terms strongly reminiscent of Wordsworthian anticlimax. The first tragedy he saw "seemed to embody and realize conceptions which had hitherto assumed no distinct shape." But, he goes on: "Dearly do we pay all our life after for this juvenile pleasure, this sense of distinctness. When the novelty is past, we find to our cost that instead of realizing an idea, we have only materialized and brought down a fine vision to the standard of flesh and blood. We have let go of a dream, in quest of an unattainable substance."[52] A Kantian would read the fall into materiality, here presented as loss, in terms of gain. Like the anticlimax of Crossing the Alps, disappointment allows for the perpetuation of an imaginative quest for the "unattainable substance"—"the something evermore about to be." But Lamb's point is that this imaginative quest will *always* be disappointed by seeing Shakespeare acted, because performance diminishes the suggestiveness of the words on the page. "What we see upon a stage is body and bodily action," he asserts; "what we are conscious of in reading is exclusively the mind and its movements" (98). Given this hierarchy of values, Lamb concludes that the only possible recuperation is to forget theatrical performance altogether, and return to the imaginative experience of reading the play itself. In case we are tempted to construe this as a defense of the rights of the reader—a modernist opening up of text to interpretation—we should recall the politics of theater at this time.[53] Lamb's claim that *King Lear* is "unactable" is more likely an elitist attempt to protect Shakespeare from the interference of vulgar popularization: to preserve the bard's genius as something that only the literate can appreciate, and, furthermore, to make that genius itself into something unapproachable or uninterpretable.

The outlines of Burke's mystificatory aesthetic are visible, then, even in Lamb's writing; but they are shadowed by irony—by a knowing awareness of the tendency to fetishize genius. With mock horror, Lamb recalls the first occasion when he looked at the manuscript of "Lycidas," only to discover that Milton was as fallible as other mortals:

> There is something to me repugnant, at any time, in written hand. The text never seems determinate. Print settles it. I had thought of the Lycidas as of a full-grown beauty—as springing up with all its parts absolute—till, in evil hour, I was shown the original copy of it. . . . How it staggered me to see the fine things in their ore! interlined, corrected! as if their words were mortal, alterable, displaceable at pleasure! as if they might have been otherwise, and just as good! as if inspiration were made up of parts, and those fluctuating, successive, indifferent![54]

Lamb blithely parodies Romantic clichés—inspiration, spontaneity, organicism—and affects a return to classical values (harmony, completeness, closure). But he is equally playful at his own expense: building up, to absurdity, his naive expectations; using Miltonic allusion ("in evil hour") to give bathos an epic dimension; and incredulously exclaiming at self-evident facts: "as if their words were mortal . . . as if inspiration were made up of parts." The irony is two-faced: what remains stable, and provides Lamb with a Kantian system of defense, is the perceived dichotomy between expectation and actuality, between imagination and the written word, between the sublime conceptions of Milton and the contingencies of language. The discovery that Milton was fallible and mortal can, after all, be turned to advantage—can be used to bear further testimony to the grandeur, authority, and unattainability of Milton's *imaginative* world; just as the apprehension of linguistic insufficiency can be built into the sublime.

The uncertainty of direction in Lamb's ironic voice continues, however, to tell its own story. It is as though he looks ahead into the age of postmodernism: an age that accepts the provisionality of language, relinquishes the concept of the author, and revels in the notion that words "might be otherwise, and just as good!"; an age that has institutionalized the fragment,[55] turned manuscripts and revisions into an industry,[56] and made indeterminacy itself into an obligatory feature of writing.[57] And, looking ahead to all this, it is as though Lamb perceives not only the strength of his own resistance to it, but also the pathos of that resistance. "As if their words were mortal, alterable, displaceable at pleasure": this, after all, is the very real anxiety that underlies Romantic writing, an anxiety that the reader will replace the author, that interpretation will threaten meaning, that the writing subject will assume the "questionable shape" of death. Perhaps it is an anxiety that twentieth-century criticism shares: why else are we so concerned to "define" indeterminacy?

John Beer

Fragmentations and Ironies

❦

To define or not define? Lucy Newlyn's essay leaves us still facing the question concerning Romanticism with which this collection began. Like some of the other contributions, also, it raises an issue that may help suggest an answer: that of the degree to which the thought of the period was characterized not by oneness but by fragmentation.

This loss of unity was characteristic not only of the thought but of the culture as a whole. In the preceding period something of the same kind had already been in train, though marked initially less by cultural fragmentation than by cultural divisions, the first signs of which may for our purposes be associated with the astonishing rise of mercantile activity in the late seventeenth and the eighteenth centuries and the consequent high valuation of individual enterprise. It is not fortuitous that in the 1740s, one of the most innovative decades in English literary history,[1] themes of individual liberty and responsibility were everywhere prominent.

From the seventeenth century onward, divisions in British culture evolved in various ways: that between the Royalists and Puritans was succeeded by one associated more closely with the landed interest and traditional Anglican establishment on the one hand and the new mercantilism on the other. The two elements could live fairly easily together, in that the wealth that was pouring in as a result of overseas trade was enabling its beneficiaries to purchase land and buy their way into the upper reaches of society, the members of which saw little reason to change their basic assumptions. It was rather as the urge of enterprise gave rise to industrial development and the growth of manufacturing towns that the new technology began to encourage new modes of thinking, based on questioning rather than on the following of received ideas and forms.

The divisions that were now springing up in England could be expressed geographically. For the old authority one might look to London, the cathedral cities, and the university towns. For the growing mercantilism one could still look to London, and then to the great Atlantic ports of Bristol and Liverpool (with their respective cultural satellite towns of Bath and Chester). The new industrialism, meanwhile, occupied great manufacturing towns such as Birmingham and Manchester and the smaller towns that were springing up around them.

It is in the last named centers that the signs of a cultural shift are particularly evident. The transactions of the Lunar Society of Birmingham and of the Manchester Literary and Philosophical Society alike bear witness to the wide-ranging interests of their members, and particularly to their appetite for knowledge of scientific advances. Much of the new thinking of the time was taking place in such industrial centers, often by individuals whose cultural interests were linked to interest in new technologies. In Staffordshire, for example, one need look only to Erasmus Darwin, the Wedgwoods, and Robert Bage, author of *Hermsprong,* to find evidences of this intermingling. A new kind of culture was emerging in the provinces by the end of the eighteenth century, in brief, often centered in the groups of educated people who met together for discussion of the latest developments in the arts and sciences. Their achievements are most characteristically represented in the work of Joseph Priestley in Birmingham, a man whose scientific interests were combined with advocacy of political freedom and service as a Unitarian minister.

Bristol, acting both as an outlet for exports from the manufacturing industries and as a point of reception for imports from abroad, was a particularly interesting center. The fact that its wealth owed much to the profitability of the sugar imported there prompted some of its inhabitants to organize opposition to the slave trade. When Thomas Beddoes set up his Pneumatic Institute and recruited as one of his first assistants the young Humphry Davy, the city became for a time a notable provincial center of science.

Yet although the cultural divisions in England might now run deep, they still did not amount to fragmentation. Those who regarded themselves as dissenters, whether religious or intellectual, would still have regarded themselves as inhabiting a common culture.

The impulse to unity and reconciliation is equally evident in responses to the French Revolution. The violent fractures in France during the 1790s were matched by a determination among forward-looking intellectuals in England that changes should be brought about by peaceful means. Although those who aligned themselves with the position of Joseph Priestley might be excited by the events across the Channel, they were unlikely to commit themselves wholeheartedly to the aims of the revolutionaries, yet still believed that the scientific enthusiasms they shared with the French philosophes could be turned to the service of social and political ideals. In place of revolutionary politics and the overthrow of the state by force they sought reform through the workings of parliamentary democracy; in place of the atheism or deism of the revolutionaries they remained committed to the ideals of the Christian gospel as interpreted by the Unitarians, who wished to eliminate from it all traces of the supernatural. The latter included among their number Dr. Price, whose discourse on the French Revolution disturbed Edmund Burke into writing his *Reflections*.[2]

Priestley's position appealed strongly to young men of the time who were looking for a more humane culture, especially to those who were writers. Charles Lamb was strongly attracted by Priestley and Unitarianism in the 1790s, while Hazlitt, whose father was a Unitarian minister in Shropshire, entered the Academy at Hackney at a time when it was in such total ferment following the French Revolution that it had to be shut down. A few years later the sympathies with intellectual and political dissent entertained by Charles Clarke, headmaster of the school attended by Keats, were communicated, at least obliquely, to his pupil.[3]

It was natural that this limited radicalism should have appealed strongly for a time to the youthful Coleridge, whose declaration of allegiance to "Science, freedom, and the Truth in Christ" manifested his respect for Priestley's threefold achievement and who was for a time thought of by some Unitarians as the rising star of their sect. It may also have encouraged the decision to make his home for a time in Bristol, where he lectured against the slave trade, initiated a reforming journal, made friends with the local Unitarians, came to know Humphry Davy, and generally aligned himself with progressive thinking. Like other young men of this persuasion, he could do so, at least for a time, without any sense of undermining contradiction.

In time, however, this mediating position proved inadequate to bridge what he was coming to see as a gulf between the attitudes involved, which harked back to a division between the natural and the moral. In *Biographia Literaria* he describes his subsequent condition of confusion:

> For a very long time indeed I could not reconcile personality with infinity; and my head was with Spinoza, though my whole heart remained with Paul and John. (*CBL* 1:200–201).

Initially, Coleridge's misgivings were palliated by the renewed enthusiasm for nature and her forms which came to him as a result of his dealings with the Wordsworths. The idea that nature herself, at her deepest, might actually assist the moral development of the individual was an attractive one, explored by both poets in *Lyrical Ballads* and by Wordsworth in the memories of his own childhood and youth recorded in the early books of *The Prelude.* Coleridge came to believe, however, particularly after his visit to Germany, that neither Unitarianism nor investigations into the significances of nature could offer the key to a unified culture; the problems he was trying to solve ran deeper, involving, among other things, an apparently irreconcilable gap between the physical constitution of human beings and their moral nature.

It was largely for this reason that he moved away from a position of near commitment to Unitarianism to the more independent position from which he hoped to resolve the sensed contradictions in his civilization. And at this point the stresses and strains in his thinking became still more serious. The young man who had been brought up an Anglican and for the first years of his life received local adulation as the gifted son of the Vicar of Ottery St. Mary, destined no doubt to become an ornament of the establishment, now recognized some of the logical implications of the attractive modes of free thinking in politics and religion he had been cultivating as a Unitarian and found it increasingly difficult to reconcile the two. As he tried to satisfy his various intellectual and emotional needs, his thinking was not only caught into fragmentary modes but began to generate writing that was itself riven, particularly in its poetic expression. In his work the concept of the "Romantic fragment" comes into its own.

In thinking about the fragment as a literary form it is helpful to turn to the work of Marjorie Levinson, who has thought with particular energy about its role in Romanticism. From her point of view the Romantic Fragment Poem (or RFP, as she prefers to call it) can be viewed in its English manifestation from the end of the eighteenth century onward as a new mode, with common identifiable features. In particular she is concerned to rescue it from the supposition that it should be read as a "'dynamic human disclosure' (organism, vision, or expressive overflow)," seeing it rather as "a motivated assembly incorporating available, even prefabricated material and units (for example gothic-tragic; coda-preface) and manipulating these in a determinate and determined fashion over time."[4] The reason for its emergence during the Romantic period, in her view, was the recognition by poets of their marginalized status in a mechanically dominated society, where they were expected to produce poems that were completed objects, to be consumed as such: "the binary alternative to reification-commodification was an aesthetic of presence, the dominant forms of which are familiar to us under the rubrics 'organic,' 'visionary,' and 'prophetic.'" In producing their fragments, she contends, the Romantic poets were moving beyond this set of alternatives in a manner that invited, and still calls for, a special kind of response, "completing the fragment in such a way as to estrange our procedures, and then, in a secondary and self-critical discourse, to describe the abyss one has just, through one's sympathy, abolished. In that abyss, where the poem '*manifests,* uncovers, what it cannot say,' resides the ideological imprimatur of the RFP—its special truth."[5]

For all its nobility this account sets together under one umbrella poetic achievements which call for further discrimination. Marjorie Levinson is not suggesting, of course, that the fragment began its existence as a literary form in the 1790s. The vicissitudes of artistic composition and preservation have meant that uncompleted works have always been around, but interest in them as a mode was particularly strong at the end of the eighteenth century. As Anne Janowitz has shown in detail,[6] it began with the ruins that presented their fragmentary forms everywhere in the landscape. The fragment, in this version, remained a part of that to which it had formerly belonged. The statue that was normally part of a temple would continue to be thought of in terms of the setting in which it formerly stood, the spectator who saw an arch among a set of ruins would visualize the whole building it had once helped to support.

Description of this interest as "Romantic" aligns it with the older use of the word as it flourished in the eighteenth century, connoting the growing feeling for the past as a locus of feeling. In this context—more accurately described, perhaps, as "gothic"—it could be linked with those fragments published in the eighteenth century which purported to be from Ossian or, in Chatterton's case, from the "Rowley manuscript." The popularity of such writings was due partly to the fact that by being read in the context of work from a writer of the past they acquired a borrowed authority.

Even when one considers the emergence of the fragment in its more consciously crafted version, it is still not true to say that the publication of *Lyrical Ballads* in 1798 marked its inauguration as a form. To suggest this is to ignore the evidence presented by Robert Mayo in an important but still little-noticed journal article forty years ago, showing that many of the forms we associate with the *Lyrical Ballads* were in fact familiar elements in the magazine poetry of the time. In the course of his discussion Mayo drew attention to the commonness of the "fragment," giving about twenty examples of poems with that word in their title during the ten years up to 1798. Their form he characterized as follows: "The aim of most fragments in the magazines was to explain little, but to suggest much. Many of them begin *in medias res* and end abruptly at some moment of violence or shocking revelation; others merely draw the curtain when the situation has been barely sketched, leaving the mind intrigued by the possibilities that have been opened up." His discussion of the apparent purpose of these poems also makes an important point: "Writers of Gothic fiction were devoted to the fragment as a form, since it allowed them to introduce marvels and mysteries without accounting for them. But the form attracted writers of other kinds of sentimental literature also, since it permitted them to explore the delicious possibilities of a single moment of experience without a clumsy apparatus of character, motivation, plot, exposition, and the rest."[7]

As one turns to previous literature the evolution of the fragment as a mode can be traced in detail. Its most important progenitor was Gray, whose forty or so poems include "The Triumphs of Owen. A fragment," "Agrippina, A Fragment of a Tragedy," "Hymn to Ignorance. A fragment," "The Alliance of Education and Government. A Fragment," and "Ode on the Pleasures arising from Vicissitude. A Fragment." Many of these descriptions were no doubt affixed by Mason, his posthumous editor, referring to the actual state in which the manuscripts had been left, but the fact that the published works contained such a notable array of fragments must have assisted the tendency for poets to characterize works of their own in this way and to find a possible virtue in incompleteness. In such imitations what was being set forth was less likely to result from an inability to conclude the poem than to be a construction foreseen from the start.

How, then, is the role of the mode in *Lyrical Ballads* to be judged? Marjorie Levinson draws attention to the fact that the poems presented there as "fragments" are offered "without benefit of authorial introduction, annotation or apology" and that the early reviews of the volume passed them over in silence. She suggests that this "speaking silence" signaled tacit acceptance of a new form. But on the evidence presented by Mayo, the silence would be due simply to the fact that the form was already familiar enough to render comment superfluous. And when one turns to the items in the *Lyrical Ballads* that are actually labeled "fragments" the picture shifts further. In the 1798 *Lyrical Ballads* the only point at which the word appears is in the subtitling of Coleridge's "The Foster-mother's Tale" as "a dramatic fragment." This was not the purely artificial use of the device that it might have been in the magazines; still less was it an invented form, since the passage was quite authentically an extract, taken from his drama "Osorio." In the expanded edition of 1800, moreover, the words "a dramatic fragment" were changed to "A Narration in Blank Verse," which hardly suggests that the term previously adopted had been of great significance to its author. In the new volume, on the other hand, Wordsworth introduced a further poem actually entitled "A Fragment." Although he explained that it had originally been designed as a preface to a ballad, his resort to the contemporary device may have been prompted by the presence of an unexplained element of the supernatural in the poem. Thirty-six years later, the word was to be given a more subordinate position: the full title would then become "The Danish Boy: A Fragment."

These examples show that the evidence for a devotion to the fragment as such in the collection is slender—all the more so since other items in the volume not so labeled might quite properly have been: the 1798 edition included Coleridge's poem "A Night-piece," and in 1800 Wordsworth included two extracts from his early version of *The Prelude*. Each of these has just the quality of "explaining little but suggesting much" which Mayo finds characteristic of the fragment as it had been appearing in the magazines. The term may also have been adopted on occasion as a cover for embarrassment. When he included his poem "The Happy Husband" in his 1817 collection, Coleridge subtitled it "A fragment." There is nothing particularly fragmentary about the poem itself, however, and he may simply have been wishing to divert attention from the fact that it concealed a reference to his earlier love for Wordsworth's sister-in-law Sara Hutchinson.

To isolate a particular form that can be labeled simply the Romantic Fragment Poem and under which one hopes to include some of the most significant productions of the age is, then, a hazardous enterprise. What is discovered from a study of actual "fragments" in the literature of the late eighteenth century is the emergence of a form seemingly fortuitous in its inception but subsequently acquiring a validity of its own by answering to the current fascination for the resonant incident or experience where observation breaks off, leaving a space for the operation of imaginative suggestion. But insofar as this effect seems to involve an element of deliberate cultivation it is not at all the same as that to be found in other major uncompleted texts of the Romantic period, where the fragmentariness proceeds rather as an undermining process from within.

The latter can be found, for example, in some of the most important poems in Coleridge's oeuvre, two of which are in fact the subjects of separate chapters in Marjorie Levinson's book. When Coleridge called "Kubla Khan" a "fragment"—as he did from the beginning—he had an interest in emphasizing the poem's incompleteness: by presenting it so and as a "psychological curiosity" he could avoid identifying himself closely with the occasional strangenesses in its language while also distancing himself from the arrogant implications of the concluding stanza. That does not falsify his description, however. "Kubla Khan" is in many respects *the* Romantic poetic fragment, betraying at every point underlying fissures that prevented the poet from proceeding into effortless completion of his project. It also differs from many of the poems already discussed to the degree that the fragmentariness was not designed by but forced upon its author.

The fissures inherent in the poem were at once political and moral. In political terms they reflect the varying current interpretations of the French Revolution. Thomas Paine had written "The palaces of kings are built on the ruins of the bowers of paradise"; and "Kubla Khan" can be read as a poem about that loss, describing both the tyrant's attempt to recreate the original paradise and the forces that prevent him from doing so—forces themselves figured as "huge fragments," vaulting like "rebounding hail."[8]

In the poem the only solution to such fragmentation is offered in visionary terms, through the apotheosis of the creative powers when the inspired genius of the last stanza succeeds effortlessly in creating the miraculous harmony that has eluded the tyrant of the previous stanzas.

Yet this creative power, once given expression, also falls back into the same perilous dialectic, since its exercise might well become an inhuman force, relapsing into the mode that Coleridge described as that of "commanding genius," its energies diverted as easily into war as into the creation of mighty works for the benefit of mankind (*CBL* 1:31–33).

The moral and political ambiguities that reverberate through the lines of "Kubla Khan" are equally evident in Coleridge's other poems of the supernatural at the time. His failure to complete "Christabel" can be ascribed to an inability to decide whether the plot of his poem should be developed in moral or imaginative terms. In orthodox moral terms the sinister Geraldine is simply an evil and corrupting influence, who must be defeated if Christabel is to triumph; in Blakean terms, on the other hand, she embodies the ambiguity of human energy, as capable of good as she is of evil and enacting that state of experience which his heroine must encounter and deal with if she is to win her way into what Blake called "organized innocence."[9] Between these two possibilities the poem falls into incompleteness, becoming in the process another great Romantic fragment.

Even *The Ancient Mariner,* at first sight a completed poem, suffers from such fragmentation. The universe in which the narrative is set turns out to be morally ambiguous, attempts to interpret it coming up against the contradictions by which an unthinking action is punished by consequences out of all proportion to it and controlling powers (unlike Einstein's God) are discovered at one point playing dice. Here again a visionary harmony is figured at one point in the dawn-vision when the spirits of the dead mariners dart back and forth to a central sun which is source of both light and musical harmony; but that optimistic interpretation is not established sufficiently authoritatively to assume moral control of the poem.

On this pattern artistic works that make it their business to interpret human affairs as a whole will fall into fragmentation of some kind; under this sign the Romantic poetic fragment will end up as such not in accordance with the artist's intentions but in spite of them. At the same time the other, more conscious version of poetic fragmentation which has already been mentioned is one that can in its implications for human beings be looked at in a more optimistic light. Here the deliberate presentation of experience in fragmentary form opens a space for the work of the creative imagination.

Two fragmentary poems of Wordsworth's to which Marjorie Levinson draws attention, "A Night-piece" and "Airey-Force Valley," display something of this power. Each presents an uncomposed scene in which, by some unexpected movement or disclosure, the work of nature itself performs the desired composing act, so that what might have been disturbing simply deepens its best effects. This is not the full work that can be performed by the fragmentary, however, since the poet remains too powerfully in control. Something much closer to its inaugurating capability is recorded in the experiences described by Wordsworth in *The Prelude,* as we shall see. An enthusiasm for such acceptance of the fragmentary is evinced in Keats's critique of Coleridge that he "would let go by a fine isolated verisimilitude caught from the Penetralium of mystery, from being incapable of remaining content with half knowledge" (*KL* 1:194–95). Although Keats's own greatest fragments, such as the two *Hyperion* poems, result from the clash of contradictions like those which prevent the completion of Coleridge's poems, some of the great odes show him ready to chance the suggestive or the ambiguous, to end a poem with a question rather than a statement and so leave opportunities for the reader's imagination to work on.

Typically, the Romantic poet worked toward a dialectical resolution of contraries in a final synthesis, only to find the fragmentary nature of the contraries obstinately surviving. Writers who came after them, undeterred by such omens, aimed at a potential wholeness which would harmonize the warring powers. For a late example one might turn to Margaret Schlegel's injunctions to her husband Henry Wilcox in Forster's *Howards End:*

> Only connect the prose and the passion, and both will be exalted, and human love will be seen at its height. Live in fragments no longer. Only connect, and the beast and the monk, robbed of the isolation that is life to either, will die.[10]

In subsequent years Forster himself experienced increasing doubts about the possibilities of such reconciliation. Now when he applied the formula to himself it was with less apparent hope of synthesis: "My defence at any Last Judgment," he wrote, "would be 'I was trying to connect up and use all the fragments I was born with.'"[11]

The realization by some English writers that one might need to accept fragmentation as a condition of human existence had long been anticipated in Germany. The fact that the societies which made up that country at the turn of the century were still largely free from the mercantile and industrial pressures that were already initiating processes of change in British culture did not entail immunity from consciousness of the changes themselves. On the contrary, the greater strength of university life in Germany led to a positive appetite for British writings and ideas, many of which were being produced in response to such pressures. Received in a form that was abstracted from their cultural context, their impact was all the purer. Hence these writings encouraged more theoretical modes of thinking. In one sense the history of Romanticism as it is commonly understood can indeed be identified with the history of German Romantic criticism. It was, for instance, through the influential lectures of August Wilhelm Schlegel that the idea of a Romantic movement became vivid to the consciousness of his contemporaries in Germany, and so, in turn, to English writers of the next generation. Yet, as has already been asserted, to put the matter in this way is to risk false assumptions. There are indeed areas in which critics such as Schiller were able to offer a program of what a true poetry conceived in their terms might be. But for the most part the interplay was more subtle and mutually interpenetrative: critics were responding to currents which they sensed to be at work in their time—and hoping in the process to speed the flow.

There are thus important differences between the rise of the idea of Romanticism in Germany and in England. In Germany one can actually see basic ideas unfolding and being developed in an orderly fashion as A. W. Schlegel gave his lectures at Jena, where the distinction between Romantic and classic was implicit rather than explicit; at Berlin, where contrasts such as that between classical purity of genre and Romantic mingling, plastic and picturesque art were discussed; and at Vienna, where various antitheses, as between the mechanical and the organic, or between the finite world of classical literature and the infinite universe of Romantic, were fully drawn out and systematized.[12] In England, by contrast, where current cultural trends were providing much of the material for the rise of a defined Romanticism, the process was gradual, heuristic, even haphazard. It is not uncommon to find an idea that is being developed systematically in Germany emerging in England as if by chance. This is so in the case of the organic: while Schlegel was elaborating on the difference between the mechanical and the organic in art and producing statements such as "No work of genius can want its appropriate form," the general interest in nature and the beginnings of biological research in England were encouraging Wordsworth and Coleridge to explore the idea of a "one Life" in the whole of nature. A few years later Keats was to write "if Poetry comes not as naturally as the Leaves to a tree it had better not come at all" (*KL* 1:238). In such explorations organic simile prepared the way for recognition of poetic creation as itself an organic process.

Schlegel's allegiance to an organic view is explicit both in his own work and in his statements about the sources of art. Referring to the "artistic or natural products which bear the name or form of poems," he asks,

> What are they, compared with the unformed and unconscious poetry which stirs in the plant and shines in the light, smiles in a child, gleams in the flower of youth, and glows in the loving bosom of women? This, however, is the primeval poetry without which there would be no poetry of words. Indeed there is not and never has been for us humans any other object or source of activity and joy but that one poem of the godhead the earth, of which we, too, are part and flower.[13]

The positive, visionary element that inhabits Schlegel's work—a vision grounded in the sense of a correspondence between the artistic creation and organic growth—had its English antecedents. Its appeal can be associated, for example, with the excitement aroused in Germany by Edward Young's *Conjectures on Original Composition,* including its assertion that "an *Original* may be said to be of a *vegetable* nature; it rises spontaneously from the vital root of Genius; it *grows,* it is not *made: Imitations* are often a sort of *Manufacture* wrought up by those *Mechanics, Art* and *Labour,* out of pre-existent materials not their own."[14]

Schlegel, however, was intent on pressing further the implications of the imagery. His visionary descriptions show him concentrating upon particular elements of the organic: most notably its power to develop an innate form that could not have been constructed as the sum of its parts, and to produce such forms in abundance. The focus being upon the vegetable creation, little is said about the behavior of animal energies—in spite of the fact that these also are a part of the organic. In that field English writers were more responsive.[15]

Schlegel was also an active champion of the aspiration to unity, as he showed in 1798, when he explained what he meant by Romantic poetry:

> Romantic poetry is a progressive, universal poetry. Its aim isn't merely to reunite all the separate species of poetry and put poetry in touch with philosophy and rhetoric. It tries to and should mix and fuse poetry and prose, inspiration and criticism, the poetry of art and the poetry of nature; and make poetry lively and sociable, and life and society poetical.[16]

The description continues at some length, continuing to list pairs of qualities that Romantic poetry tries to reconcile. At the same time it was an essential part of Schlegel's belief that the unity being described in such detail could never actually be achieved. To quote his account again,

> The Romantic kind of poetry is still in the state of becoming; that, in fact, is its real essence: that it should forever be becoming and never be perfected. It can be exhausted by no theory and only a divinatory criticism would dare try to characterize its ideal.

Schlegel was likewise one of the first to perceive the importance of the fragment as arguably the most characteristic form of the new age. In 1798, when he and his brother published their own "Fragments" in the *Athenaeum,* one of his own contributions actually dwelt on the appositeness of the form:

> Many of the works of the ancients have become fragments; many of the works of the moderns are fragments in their arising.[17]

For him the matter was crucial. He discussed the opinion that fragments were "the real form of universal philosophy." He also contended paradoxically for the necessary completeness of the fragment: "A fragment, like a miniature work of art, has to be 'entirely isolated from the surrounding world' and be complete in itself like a porcupine."[18]

More than a century before the pronouncements in *Howards End* by his namesake Margaret Schlegel (the resemblance of whose name may not have been coincidental so far as Forster was concerned[19]) his art, as well as his criticism, was dwelling on the fragmentariness of human experience. In his novel *Lucinde* the plot refuses to achieve the coherence that its narrator (and perhaps originally its maker as well) seems to be proposing for it. Instead, it is presented to the reader as a series of fragments. At the center is the story of a young man, Julius, whose past relationships with women have taught him a great deal about love. He has also found true love; but once only, and then the fact that the woman was loved by his best friend ruled out any hope that it could be realized. That possibility lost, his love for Lucinde gives him everything else that he could desire; accordingly it is described and enacted in fragmentary scenes and sketches, presenting the many facets of their relationship. Love is presented as a marvelous organic phenomenon, not a single one, moreover, but one to be accepted in all its delights, as a teeming landscape, alive with organisms which are always in a process of becoming, might be celebrated. There are also, and particularly among the fragments not included in the published version, hints of deeper contradictions, notably in the sense of death that enters at times. Not only can such love never achieve a final form, but it carries within itself possible elements of its own contradiction—particularly in the consciousness of the inevitability of death which must always subsist in human consciousness.

The differences between English and German Romanticism emerge most evidently in their respective treatments of the urge to unify. The traditional tendency to see this as a central theme found strong support in the writings of its main English practitioners, where the aspiration to unity remained wholehearted. Coleridge quoted with approval Jeremy Taylor's comment: "He to whom all things are one, who draweth all things to one, and seeth all things in one, may enjoy true peace and rest of spirit."[20]

Wordsworth's writings about his own poetic aims were cast in a similar spirit, looking forward to a future reconciling realization of harmony. The conclusion of *The Prelude* proposes famously a future for the denizens of the world in which they will learn truth, but in which what is to be understood will be the nature of the mind itself, becoming in the realization of its own divine nature more beautiful than the nature it contemplates (*W Prel* XIII. 445–52); in the prospectus for *The Recluse,* similarly, he presents himself as singing, "long before the blissful hour arrives," the "spousal verse" of a "great consummation"—which will turn out to be nothing other than the recognition that "the discerning intellect of Man" when "wedded to this goodly universe / In love and holy passion" will find the great visions of paradise, as presented in mythology, "A simple produce of the common day" (*WPW* 5:4–5). Despite the future tense, what is to be gained will be a recognition of what is already here but not, as yet, appreciated. Beyond the note of lyrical assurance, nevertheless, an uncertainty is detectable as Wordsworth calls on the approval of "lofty Minds" for his support. He was not sure how far he could claim general validity for his apocalypses of the everyday. His decision not to publish *The Prelude,* partly motivated by a desire to preserve its copyright for his children,[21] witnesses to his lack of assurance; had he thought it would have an immediate effect on his society, how could he have refrained from making it available immediately? The combination of assurance with signs of an undermining lack of confidence is in a different mode from that of German Romantic writing, where the accounts of what the ideal will be like and the counterpoising reminders that the ideal can never actually be achieved are set against each other with equal strength.

The double acknowledgment that Romanticism fosters within itself an impulse to unity which can never in fact be realized may indeed constitute its ultimate paradox, at least in its own time—a paradox intensified when the ideas of unity thus fostered have proved powerful enough for their thwarting to be greeted as invalidating the whole concept. Such a response is, however, inappropriate. What is needed is rather a revised view of Romanticism which no longer expects it to be readily graspable as a defined entity but sees in it—as do the contributors to the present volume—a site of questioning. We need to look behind the positive achievements of the age in which it grew up, similarly, to discover the tensions and fissures that coexisted with its positive achievements, all the more so since it is these that have survived most powerfully into our own time. As writers of the twentieth century, lacking the optimism of their predecessors, have come to see less and less unity in their culture, the fragmentary, the sign of a dislocatory force subsisting below the surface of all human aims and aspirations, has achieved more momentous status.

The kind of thinking generated by that perception reaches its full development with a writer such as Michel Serres, who thinks of knowledge in terms of "islands" or "archipelagoes":

> We are drifting towards the dark depth of the universe. . . . Knowledge is only at most the reversal of this drift. . . . To be or to know will henceforth mean: here are islands, rare or wealthy, fortuitous or necessary. . . . The only possible, i.e. vital, philosophy consists in repudiating the universal.[22]

Awareness of the contradictions that lurk in Western culture has led to a study of language and other such phenomena in terms not only of fractures and displacements but of a more radical discontinuity, regarded by some twentieth-century writers as inherent in all literature. In one of the most influential texts of the century Saussure proclaims that his main theories of language boil down to a single statement: "in language there are only differences." Derrida, picking up the further implications of this, and discerning within such linguistic variations the necessary operation of an endless deferral, has produced his own version of the concept, marked by the now familiar term *différance.*

A similar recognition informs the dualities of consciousness that are registered throughout Romantic writing. The more ready acceptance of such relationships as an essential feature of artistic endeavor was responsible for the widespread German interest in irony—a matter much less discussed in the English criticism of the time. British readers whose ideas of irony are founded on a reading of Swift have found it strange that the term should have been so intimately applied to Romanticism. Within British criticism irony refers primarily to a mode of writing that might be characterized briefly as presupposing the existence of two audiences, one naive and the other knowing. A significant element in the primary pleasure derived from reading such work comes from an assurance that one belongs to the second, more perceptive group, coupled with a confidence that other readers exist who will be taking the text literally. If this involves fragmentation, it is of a somewhat crude kind. When German writers used the term "Romantic irony," on the other hand, they were thinking less of an effect in writing than of the particular attitude a writer might adopt. Their chief model was not Swift, but Socrates and his famous use of an irony which, among other things, expressed a surface modesty while demonstrating for readers prepared to explore the depths of what he was saying an indisputable wisdom. To write so as to convey such modes of double consciousness became for the Germans a model procedure; it followed that in doing so they were not seeking a particular effect. The sympathy of the audience was being invoked more directly, as they were invited to participate in the feelings that were being presented and to share the tensions that were being generated. The difference between the German view of irony and that of the British is appreciated better once this use of irony as stance rather than method is recognized.

Even when scholars use the term in connection with English literature they are far from agreeing how it should be applied. In his short study *Irony*, D. C. Muecke includes Byron as his only English Romantic writer among forty world ironists,[23] a valuation which Kathleen Wheeler, by contrast, criticizes as "a sign that the concept of irony is not completely understood."[24] In her view it is Coleridge who should be regarded as the great protagonist of Romantic irony in England. Somewhere between the two positions, Anne Mellor criticizes Muecke for shifting the emotional emphasis of Schlegel's concept from celebration to desperation, while still accepting his view that Byron's mature works are "probably the most masterful artistic examples of romantic irony in English."[25] Although she finds room for discussions of Keats and Coleridge, consideration of the latter's work is largely restricted to his poems of the supernatural.

Each of the positions mentioned is in fact sustainable, depending largely on one's point of focus. If English Romantic irony is viewed against the perspective of Pope and Swift, Byron readily assumes a central position; if on the other hand one attends to the metaphysical preoccupations of ironists—as in Germany—Coleridge is likely to emerge as its chief British exponent. Both traditions may be associated with the skepticism of Hume, but whereas English ironists such as Byron reflected primarily the modes of satire he employed, the Germans were more alert to its logical implications—to the way in which his work could lead to a questioning of all metaphysical assertions.

So comprehensive was the German reception of these implications that the ironic attitudes that were approved there can be aligned with the more recent methods of deconstruction. These, as set forth by Paul de Man, are based on the acceptability of allegorical modes by comparison with those of symbolism, which are taken to involve "ontological bad faith."[26] De Man's detractors would argue that his own method leaves no room for faith of any kind, good or bad. And although Derrida has defended his own position against charges of nihilism, maintaining that he deconstructs only in order to reconstruct, it is less clear how the second process is to be carried out. If one is cultivating an organic view of art, certainly, it is natural to believe that the logical end of deconstructive process will be death.

Schlegel's methods of resisting such a conclusion become evident in those theoretical discussions of his which indicate most clearly his own positive practice. When he praises paradox, the ability to hold two opposed ideas in the mind at the same time, as "the *sine qua non,* the soul, source and principle" of irony,[27] he is moving beyond a simple organic position to one in which all contrarieties are to be found reconciled, as in his list of the qualities that are contained in "Socratic irony":

> In this sort of irony, everything should be playful and serious, guilelessly open and deeply hidden. It originates in the union of savoir faire and scientific spirit, in the conjunction of a perfectly instinctive and a perfectly conscious philosophy. It contains and arouses a feeling of indissoluble antagonism between the absolute and the relative, between the impossibility and the necessity of complete communication.[28]

While the sophisticated inclusiveness of this view can be applauded, however, it is easier to admire its aptness in describing particular works of art than to perceive how it might be applied universally to acts of artistic creation. Indeed, since it includes factors such as "instinct," conceived of as being in contradiction to consciousness, it follows that it contains within itself, literally, a necessary region of incomprehensibility.

To explore the implications of this self-limitation would take us well beyond the confines of the present discussion. It is perhaps sufficient to notice that a strain of thinking which was later to be branded as a cloak for reactionary views was in its origins rooted in the benevolent thinking of Spinoza.[29] One immediate effect of such modes of thinking was to focus attention on the Romantic fragment as an ironic mode. In Anne Mellor's exposition Schlegel's views on the subject are centered in the conception of a twofold role for the artist: "He must create or represent, like God, a finite, ordered world to which he can enthusiastically commit himself; and *at the same time* he must acknowledge his own limitations as a finite human being and the inevitably resultant limitations of his merely fictional creations." This hovering between self-creation and self-abnegation, marking a Romantic art which is also Romantic irony, pitches the artist between commitment to a program and a lack of such commitment. To quote Schlegel's own formulation, "It is equally fatal for the mind to have a system and to have none. It will simply have to decide to combine the two."[30]

Schlegel's version of Romanticism was particularly apposite to a German civilization which was fostering emotional enthusiasms and extravagances. The existence of a strong cult of feeling called out, almost as a natural reaction, a readiness to look at human experience from a more cynical point of view. A preceding work which could be held up as exemplary—and which he actually cited—was *Don Quixote.*

Within Schlegel's larger vision of the world, in which the whole universe is one of living creations, growing and decaying by turns—sometimes presenting sharp contrasts, sometimes mutually reinforcing one another—such contradictions could be seen to exist as part of a rough unity; but in everyday life they could not always be held together in the mind with such ease. There was, first and foremost, the problem of morality, exhibited in its most obvious form when Schlegel published *Lucinde.* The scandal provoked by this self-confessed work of Romantic irony, though no doubt predictable at the time, still provided a good example of the manner in which a straightforward Romantic ironist could discover that the moral imperatives and facts of experience which he hoped to reconcile were not so readily accommodated together in the minds of his contemporaries. A generation later, Byron's *Don Juan,* regarded by Anne Mellor as the greatest exemplar of Romantic irony,[31] fared better. Byron, also, had scandalized his contemporaries by his behavior, but his poem escaped full censure by reason of its comic presentation. The reader who looked at it with a sharp eye might have noted, nevertheless, examples of relativity in morality, such as the episode involving cannibalism, which showed how far the ironic mode was being extended.

More striking than the contemporary reaction to *Lucinde* among the bourgeoisie was Kierkegaard's attack on the same novel some years later in *The Concept of Irony.* The core of his accusation was that in it "the flesh negates the spirit." Within the terms of Schlegel's irony, he thought, the ego discovers its own freedom and constitutive authority but in so doing arrives not "at a still higher aspect of mind" but instead "at sensuality, and consequently at its opposite."[32] The work of irony within the economy of human life for which Kierkegaard was arguing must be of a different kind, performing a subordinate function by which it "limits, renders finite, defines, and thereby yields truth, actuality, and content; it chastens and punishes and thereby imparts stability, character and consistency."[33]

The kind of reservation Kierkegaard entered here would have been shared by some of Schlegel's English contemporaries, who did not embrace the conception of Romantic irony with the same wholeheartedness. While Coleridge did not go as far as Kierkegaard, his works show him moving through some of the same territory. His early poem "The Eolian Harp," in which an all-embracing delight in organic life is followed by a moralizing recoil, expressed in a surprisingly direct and unsophisticated manner, shows the awareness of the difficulty of reconciling the natural with the moral which was noted earlier as characteristic of his thought. While Coleridge's poetic strategy in this poem can be, and often has been, attacked on simple literary critical grounds, its importance for an understanding of his thought as a whole should not be underestimated. As Thomas McFarland pointed out in *Coleridge and the Pantheist Tradition,* his whole career as a thinker involved a recurring recognition of the dangers inherent in a simple "organic" reading of the human condition and a resistance to its pantheistic implications in favor of a more orthodox moral position.

For Coleridge the imaginative appeal of the natural world was nonetheless compelling, with the result that he was frequently the victim rather than the master of nature's ironies. He could not understand why he suffered so persistently from nightmares:

> Such punishments, I said, were due
> To natures deepliest stained with sin . . .
> But wherefore, wherefore fall on me? (*CPW* 1:390–91)

His stance as a Romantic ironist was complicated by the fact that the contradictions that disturbed him went to the very center of his existence. When one comes across irony in his work, therefore, it is not always easy to know how far he is in control.

As Romantic writers encountered such contradictions, they faced not only an increasing sense of fragmentation but an undermining of their sense of unity. Friedrich Schlegel's conversion to the Roman Catholic Church may mark a response to the need for stability corresponding to Coleridge's crippling sense of self-division. In Coleridge's case, the same kind of misgiving was responsible for subtle effects. In his poem "The Picture" a brief scene (which he later used to describe his failure to complete "Kubla Khan") expresses well his complex attitude to the process of fragmentation. Unknown to his beloved, a lover is contemplating her reflection in the pool by which she has been sketching, which she then destroys by throwing in some flowers she has gathered:

> Then all the charm
> Is broken—all that phantom-world so fair
> Vanishes, and a thousand circlets spread,
> And each misshape the other. Stay awhile,
> Poor youth! who scarcely dares lift up thine eyes—
> The stream will soon renew its smoothness, soon the
> Visions will return! And lo, he stays,
> And soon the fragments dim of lovely forms
> Come trembling back, unite, and now once more
> The pool becomes a mirror.[34]

Now, however, there is a crucial difference: the young woman has gone, and so there is no longer an image to be reflected. Yet once the narrator sees that she has left behind her the picture she was producing he realizes that he has an excuse for following her—and will indeed be justified in doing so, since the following can also be a guiding. The apparently insoluble natural situation is superseded by a pretext of responsibility, a true "resolution."

Although "The Picture" was based upon a German poem by Gessner (*CPW* 1:369–74), the drift of the original had been different: there the lover, who has been wandering in wilderness places and reflecting that he was thus exorcising the power of love, had only to see the footprint of a woman to abandon his resolve and set off in pursuit. The indulgent implication was that the firmest of resolutions will immediately be undermined by love. The irony, simple and active, made an immediate point within its knowing compass but was by the same token less subtle than the interplay between passive and active irony in Coleridge's poem, where the moral stance of the narrator, though open to cynical reflections on the reader's part, is presented seriously.

A more intricate example of such ironic play may be found in Coleridge's own reaction to the reception of *The Ancient Mariner.* In the visionary structure of this poem's universe, all creative processes in the universe, from the divine to the human, are envisaged as a fountainous process in which energies from the central being constantly go forth into the world in active music and energy (imaged by song and serpent), and in turn soar back (as echoes and winged creatures). There is a partial glimpse of the process in the Mariner's dawn vision. But if the universe *is* so constituted, its inhabitants are by the same token ironized, since they have no means of knowing it from their everyday sense experience. This ironization is, at some level, the subject matter of the poem. In any case, however, none of his readers (with the possible exception of Wordsworth) perceived such layers of significance, so that the poet found himself ironized in his turn. On reflection Coleridge himself must have seen the predictability of this reception. Presented in a narrative without interpretation, the visionary elements remained ironized in a more banal sense, subject to whatever pattern of interpretation any particular reader might impose.

There is, as it happens, a further twist to the matter. In *Biographia Literaria,* he related an anecdote concerning a person who had asked to be introduced to him but had also expressed hesitation since he had written a severe epigram under the title of "To the Author of *The Ancient Mariner*" (*CBL* 1:28n). To Coleridge's surprise, he says, it turned out to be one that he himself had published in the *Morning Post:*

> Your poem must *Eternal* be,
>   *Eternal!* it can't fail,
> For 'tis *incomprehensible,*
>   And without head or tail! (*CPW* 2:959)

A harmless enough anecdote, it might seem, apart from the fact that, as later researchers discovered, when he published the poem in the *Morning Post* it was not entitled "To the Author of *The Ancient Mariner*" but had a different title containing a pun that linked it with a recent poem by the Poet Laureate, Henry James Pye, who had recently published a "Carmen Seculare" to celebrate the end of the century: Coleridge's original title read "To Mr Pye, on his *Carmen Seculare* (a title which has . . . been . . . translated, 'A Poem *an age long*')." At this point the ironies proliferate.

First, there is the passive irony of a Coleridge who makes a bid for the reader's favor by showing himself to be capable of inventing, as well as taking a joke against himself when in fact nothing of the kind had apparently happened. Secondly, he is at least demonstrating that capability now by printing the poem at all. Thirdly, the poem was not basically his own invention, since further research has revealed that it was based on an epigram of Lessing's. Yet again (and fourthly), Lessing's poem was not a particularly good one, the pun on "eternal" there involving the heavy joke that such a poem was eternal because there would never cease to be bunglers to make up poems of such a kind.

The final depth of irony involved in this affair only becomes apparent when one investigates the central riddle. To be incomprehensible may be a mark of impenetrability, but it is also the traditional term for referring to the sublimity of eternity; a being without head or tail may seem shapeless, similarly, until one recalls that the serpent with its tail in its mouth has no obvious head or tail and is, again, one of the great symbols of eternity. Coleridge has, in other words, transformed Lessing's leaden wit into an ingenious double riddle. Taken at its face value as a comment on *The Ancient Mariner,* it would in fact display accurately the reactions of many of its first readers, as can be seen from the contemporary reviews, where it was described variously as containing stanzas many of which were "laboriously beautiful" but which were, taken in connection, "absurd or unintelligible," as displaying "the extravagance of a mad german poet" and as "the strangest story of a cock and a bull that we ever saw on paper."[35] On the other hand, he has produced a poem the connections of which become clear once it is seen that its serpent imagery, reflecting the eternal, beautiful energies in the universe, displays for those who have eyes to see the workings of the "one Life." And this is equally true of the energies in the poem itself. To the fully imaginative eye they may interweave as beautifully as the serpents, producing in the whole a poem that rounds itself into a perfectly circular narrative "with its tail in its mouth,"[36] as the Mariner returns, a changed man. Coleridge's irony thus rebounds back and forth across the gulf between himself and his readers, comprehending or uncomprehending, suggesting that his poem is, after all, either as incomprehensible as its first readers found it or a work of poetic energies so powerful as to contain the guarantee of their own, incomprehensible eternity.

This is Romantic irony indeed; within the labyrinths of this multilayered little episode one tracks a Coleridge who is at once the controller and the victim of ironies. He is revealed as a manipulator of the facts, seeking to present himself ingratiatingly and apparently falsely as someone who can initiate a joke against himself, but at another level not manipulatory at all, since the verse in question makes little sense unless we suppose him to have written it with *The Ancient Mariner* in mind, even if publicly he applied it, at a lower level of irony, to Mr. Pye's poem. The more esoteric dimension to the poem reveals him as a figure keeping desperate faith with his own imagination, believing that in some sense it holds a key to human existence.

The most prominent treatment of the fragmentary in recent times has been that of Thomas McFarland in *Romanticism and the Forms of Ruin.* McFarland sees the prominence of the fragment as a form in Romantic literature as the sign of a deeper quality, an inherent tendency toward fragmentation, which he terms the "diasparactive." Though it is present, he maintains, in all human experience, he finds it most markedly observed and expressed during the Romantic period. He has no difficulty in finding a wealth of illustration for what he is saying; particularly since his treatment of the fragmentary in terms of "incompleteness, fragmentation, and ruin"[37] allows him to contemplate both willed and involuntary fragmentations under the same sign.

Yet as soon as one has accepted his case, the need for further discriminations presses. McFarland's emphasis on ruin suggests an orientation toward the version of the diasparactive that was most common in the eighteenth century, with its tendency to concentrate on physical decline through time. It is true that from one point of view Romantic creative endeavor can be seen as a mode of instant ruination, all its efforts at unification, despite the hopes that accompany them, immediately collapsing into fragmentary relicts, yet this is only a part of the story. The willingness to write fragments as such was not necessarily conceived under such a melancholy foreboding; it could spring from an impulse like Keats's to remain content with half truths, particularly when those half truths, isolated, resonated with further imaginative possibilities.

Examination of English and German Romanticism suggests that while they were always subtly different from one another, their differences could be mutually enriching. German Romanticism, for all the various ideas that fell under its sway, remained permanently ambitious for large systematization—even if, as with Schlegel, that aspiration was nurtured alongside a recognition that no ultimate system existed. English Romanticism was characterized rather by a heuristic progress, constantly checking its more speculative ideas against a sobering awareness of the ironies of circumstance.

For some years during the Napoleonic Wars, the divergent progress of the two versions of Romanticism was assisted by the poor communications between England and Germany. The one figure able to cross the barrier was Coleridge, who had stayed in Germany long enough in 1798–99 to gain a sense of current developments. Among other things, his visit convinced him of the importance of Spinoza, whom he was reading shortly after his return. In the autumn of 1799 he contemplated the possibility of writing a poem on him; if he were to do so, he wrote in a notebook, it would begin thus: "I would make a pilgrimage to the burning sands of Arabia . . . to find the Man who could explain to me [how] there can be *oneness,* there being infinite Perceptions—yet there must be a *one*ness, not an intense Union but an Absolute Unity."[38] The question which he had articulated so emphatically continued to haunt him. A year or two later he elaborated it further:

> Eternal universal mystery! It seems as if it were impossible; yet it *is*—& it is every where!—It is indeed a contradiction *in Terms:* and only in Terms!—It is the co presence of Feeling and Life, limitless by their very essence, with Form, by its very essence limited—determinate—definite. (*CN* 1:1561)

One reason for the fascination of this particular opposition was that it exemplified others that were beginning to oppress him—as with that between personality and infinity cited earlier. He was recognizing increasingly that human thinking at its extremity involved a need to reconcile powers that were, considered strictly, incompatible. The problem of the one and the many provided a telling example, nevertheless, suggesting that in some way the close, intricate ability to collect and evaluate disparate data from the world of sense perception must be complemented by a power in the mind that could bring them into a unity.

A suspicion that fragmentariness might in the end be inseparable from human achievement lurks throughout Romanticism; yet there is also a constant aspiration toward wholeness, usually envisaged as a reconciliation between nature and supernature. In the course of its working out, two concepts play a particularly strong part: that of the organic and that of the symbol. The organic turns to the life of nature as offering physical forms more subtle than those constructed by the operation of a mechanical ordering and attempts artistic expression with the desire of making a work of art that will have something of the same quality. While cultivation of the symbol is often the result of a similar desire to make art conform to nature in its highest form, its fascination for many has more to do with its metaphysical promise. As McFarland has pointed out, it is the fate of that which is located as symbolic to change immediately for other observers into the allegorical mode. Yet that does not invalidate the quest. Coleridge once remarked that the true symbol is not allegorical but tautegorical—its ultimate demonstration, in other words, being not of difference but of identity. The imagery of divine light provides a supreme example: by nonbelievers it is immediately perceived as allegory, but to those who accept it in faith the two elements that are being set together are mutually reinforcing: spiritual illumination not only acts in the same way as spiritual light, but displays in its operation important things about its nature.

At first sight a number of Coleridge's minor poetic fragments can be seen as Romantic fragments in the "fashionable" mode described earlier, resonating with imaginative possibilities: in his notebooks lines can be found describing a simple sight in nature which seems to suggest the nature of life in an unusually significant fashion:

> The swallows interweaving there mid the paired
> Sea-mews, at distance wildly-wailing.—(*CN* 1:213)

Later fragments are more evidently attempts to locate a valid symbol for the divine in nature:

> Bright clouds of reverence, sufferably bright
> That intercept the dazzle not the Light
> That veil the finite form, the boundless power reveal
> Itself an earthly sun, of pure intensest White.[39]

A fragment such as this might be described as an attempt to locate the one Life and illuminate it by the one Light, yet it still involves something of the endeavor in the earlier fragments, where sense experience was being explored more open-mindedly in an attempt to locate more precisely the nature of the "one Life" itself. There is implicit in all such attempts an assumption that the empirical, if explored sincerely, honestly, and with insight will lead to metaphysical revelation of some kind.

Coleridge's intimately related preoccupation with the one and the many, which Wordsworth shared to some degree, combined a recognition of the fragmentary nature of human experience with a belief that a wholeness of truth was waiting to be found, if only the seeker were sufficiently diligent. Not every writer of the period or after shared this complex aspiration, or even understood it—hence the note of tolerant derision commonly to be heard in reactions to his writing. His own ability to sympathize with such hostile reactions, coupled with a stubborn insistence that his vision was worthwhile, resulted in a constant play of irony between himself and his reading audience and a layered effect in his own writing.

If few were willing to join Coleridge in his quixotic ambition to comprehend the whole of knowledge, the larger problems of fragmentation bore in on all his contemporaries, as the essays in this volume have shown. The first ones have explored the fragmentations in the culture. The desire to find a *lingua communis,* as A. C. Goodson points out, sprang from a growing recognition of the elusiveness of exactitude in language, a recognition that even shooting straight might involve a kind of deviancy. This quest was pursued by writers who themselves belonged to a select class: the ideals of Wordsworth and Coleridge in the Preface to *Lyrical Ballads* gave way in the later thought of both to a belief in the need for a highly educated class to lead the remainder of their fellows in society to a proper understanding. The discussions between Shelley and Peacock are representative of the dialogues that were still taking place in the next generation. Recognition of this sociological refinement gives point to Anne Mellor's contention that the criticism by women writers at this time, evincing a lack of experimentation and a preference for strong sense, registered the women's reservations concerning the preoccupations of some of their male colleagues and the fragmentation created by gender.

As in the case of Shelley, one of the more subtle fragmentations in the culture was provided by the gap between writers' ideals and their actual behavior: Martin Aske has brought out the manner in which writers such as Hazlitt, who like Coleridge, placed their faith in the imagination and in the affections of the human heart, could behave in ways which were far from the disinterested benevolence that might have been expected. A period in which love was most often proclaimed as the human ideal also saw some of the most rancorous behavior ever known in literary circles. No one was more fraught with self-contradiction than Hazlitt himself, his cherished idea of a buried republicanism in society, waiting to be expressed by artists, being countered by a sturdy individualism which prompted him to take his walks alone and keep alive his belief in the mission of Napoleon. In a more pronouncedly individual and direct fashion John Clare, conscious of his lowly position in society, could yet identify himself readily with the noble Lord Byron through the republicanism of the text. And as Nigel Leask demonstrates, the associated belief in a republic of the human heart could lead to strange conclusions: De Quincey found it natural to extend his view of aestheticism beyond the decorous bounds suggested by the work of his well-bred contemporaries, and look rather to the omnipresent fascination of murder as a pointer to what a truly universal aesthetic might be like. While De Quincey's point is made in a tone which must be at one level ironic, it seems, such is the force of the accompanying logic, hardly to be so.

The fate of such attempts to resolve the fragmentation in the culture returns us to a basic question—whether the true Romantic fragmentation does not lie rather in the relationship between human beings and the world of their perception. That further question is germane to the second part of this volume, beginning with Drummond Bone's account of a European Romanticism that suspends the reader between the contemporary universalizing trend and an equally powerful concentration on the validity of individual experience. Such considerations of consciousness necessarily involve intricate negotiations between inner and outer—which are equally characteristic of Romanticism. As Susan Wolfson shows in her discussion of poetic form, the Romantic creative process at its most typical is poised between the formal and the informal, the tensions involved being best expressed as a dichotomy between incompatibles.

Taking up the question of a universal aesthetic, and considering it at a European level, Tilottama Rajan examines it less as a cultural problem than as one of the structures of human consciousness, drawing out the various discriminations which are entailed by the work of Hegel, for whom the goal of identity and the norm of art as the organic integration of form and content, creating a gap which has on its other side the thinking of Nietzsche, is complicit with "the ideal of mimesis as the making present of representation."

This is not the only model for Romantic criticism, however, nor is it the only possible form of mimesis. On the contrary, Frederick Burwick's account of the theme of *idem et alter* claims that that is the characteristic Romantic form of the mode. In the discriminations between identity and alterity we find a different area for exploration, involving what are perhaps the most subtle fissures of all, and calling for a remarkably agile play of mind.

Finally Lucy Newlyn has concentrated on the play of mind itself as crucial to the question, showing how Romantic sublimity locates itself ultimately in the very indeterminacy which might have seemed to threaten its existence. In the ability to remain content with that which resists definition (to make the circle complete) the Romantic preoccupation with irony reveals its ultimate value.

Yet cultivation of the indeterminate, however assuaging, failed to satisfy the full yearning of the Romantic consciousness as expressed in its own time, involving as it did the quest for an unmediated absolute; nor could it fully satisfy the search for true love, which was equally typical of the Romantic mode of interpreting the world. The desire for absolute utterance and a finally authentic mode of action remained. In theology the deepest theological sympathies of Romantic thinkers lay with the idea of a God who was not only love but could be conceived of as "purest Act."[40] In human terms there was a similarly powerful attraction to an attitude such as that of the Byron who wrote

Could I embody and unbosom now
That which is most within me,—could I wreak
My thoughts upon expression, and thus throw
Soul—heart—mind—passions—feelings—strong or weak—
All that I would have sought, and all I seek
Bear, know, feel—and yet breathe—into *one* word
And that one word were Lightning, I would speak;
But as it is, I live and die unheard,
With a most voiceless thought, sheathing it like a sword.[41]

In Western Romantic literature this feeling for the value of the pure act was most likely to be associated first with political action. Yet it was as frequently compromised by experiencing such action in practice: the French Revolution was the first of a series of disillusioning encounters with the political world—which would also go on to include the support of liberal-minded writers for the Spanish insurrection of 1831. At a more imaginative level such action could be sought where Byron himself had eventually pursued it—in the East. The episode in chapter 27 of Scott's *Talisman* when Richard's exploits with his sword are out-topped by Saladin's ability to cut a cushion in half with his scimitar reverberates with emblematic significance.

The nature of the respect for the East shown in that episode encourages us to return to the opening phrase of Coleridge's note on the difficulty in conceiving how the one could also be many: "I would make a pilgrimage to the deserts of Arabia . . ." Why should Arabia have been for him the place where the riddle of the One and the Many might be solved?

The allusion is one that he shared with Wordsworth, who from time to time reverted to Arabia as the most potent source of romance known to the eighteenth-century world. References in Shakespeare and Milton[42] show that it had long had that status, but for children of that time, brought up in a world dominated by law, the discovery of the *Arabian Nights Entertainments* could be liberating in a more absolute manner. Coleridge as a small child had found his imagination totally possessed—so much so that his father destroyed the book (*CL* 1:347). The experience could be deeply satisfying or terrifying, according to the nature of a particular possessing. For Wordsworth as a schoolboy they were embodiments of romance which then turned into an actual emblem of unfulfilled desire: when he and a schoolfellow, who had been entranced by a small collection of the stories, learned that the full edition ran to no less than four volumes, they put aside money in the hope of being able to buy the complete collection—a dream of imaginative possession never to be satisfied (*W Prel* [1805] V. 482–500). Later the work of Sir William Jones brought to the attention of English readers the traditions of Arabian poetry, especially its roses and nightingales.

There was more to Arabia than the *Arabian Nights* and poetry, also. It was known as home to the Bedouin tribes, whose independent and wandering life must have appealed deeply to a young man such as Wordsworth. His desire to fortify his own philosophy by discovering isolated figures who had achieved wisdom far from the sources of conventional learning had been answered in the Lake District by his encounters with shepherds and wandering solitaries; but the Bedouin tradition, with its suggestions of a civilization that might combine rigorous thinking with adeptness in the skills of horsemanship was even more appealing. The knowledge that mathematics had flourished early in that part of the world gave rise to a welcome sense of a desert wisdom embodying the very contradictions he could trace in his own society, the intellectual discipline of mathematics existing side by side with a feeling for the refreshing power of romance. When he wished to express the effect of a Highland girl singing in solitude, the image of the nightingale of Arabian poetry came readily to his mind:

No Nightingale did ever chaunt
More welcome notes to weary bands
Of travellers in some shady haunt,
Among Arabian sands . . .[43]

And in his great dream of the stone and the shell his sense of the ultimate contraries that beset the human mind was mediated by the Arab horseman who carried under his arm both the stone of Euclidean mathematics and the shell which one could lift to one's ear to hear all the many voices of romance—whether attractive or menacing.

Just as Wordsworth found in the mountains and lakes of his own country a means of mediating the abysses that haunted eighteenth-century thinkers—and those of his own age—so he was to find in the deserts of Arabia an approachable resort of the otherness that he traced in the minds of his own contemporaries. Torn between the depression that beset him when he contemplated a universe dominated by mathematics and the fearful possibilities, opened up by the French Revolution, of a world where passion was given unrestricted freedom, the image of the Bedouin who might be not only a skillful horseman but a subtle mathematician and mouthpiece of a prophetic voice offered a kind of ultimate reassurance, enabling him to hold together in the mind near-incompatibles.

Much has been written in recent criticism about the impact of "Orientalism" on Western culture,[44] and particular attention has been given to the ways in which Western writers seized on images and lore relating to the East in the interests of an imaginative appropriation that was far from innocent, amounting rather to a cultural imperialism. It should not be forgotten, however, that from the Renaissance onward the East provided for some imaginative writers this different resource, no less distorting, perhaps, but more guileless—the suggestion not only of a delight in sensuousness, which might be refracting memories of a paradisal state that had been more decisively lost in Western culture, but in its most primitive forms of a desert simplicity that could cradle a unified culture, reconciling mathematics and artistic harmony, one which still might have a solution to offer for Western intellects, increasingly bewildered by the contradictions and fissures opening up in their own more "advanced" societies.

But was this more than a dream? Was there any way in which one might bridge the gulf between an Oriental divinity whose dream of a world brings it into being and the world of nature which was opening up itself to contemporary scientific investigation? Was there a true and valid "Word" in the Christian sense? Coleridge's intellectual career was dominated by the belief that there was; but his alternative presentation of himself simply as "inquiring spirit"—a stance which in all its ramifications produced the range of speculation and investigation that renders his achievement as a whole so impressive—bears witness to his recognition that if the truth of the Word existed, after all, only in fragmentation, the only authentic act available to human beings in the society that had emerged after the French Revolution was coming to be that of questioning.

Notes

Introduction

1. The difficulties and dangers involved in trying to isolate a concept of that name are well set out in the last chapter of Marilyn Butler's *Romantics, Rebels, and Revolutionaries* (Oxford: Oxford University Press, 1982), 178–87, and taken up again in Drummond Bone's chapter below.

2. A. O. Lovejoy, "On the Discrimination of Romanticisms," *PMLA* 39 (1924): 229–53; reprinted in his *Essays in the History of Ideas* (New York: Braziller, 1948), 228–53.

3. René Wellek, *A History of Modern Criticism, 1750–1950,* vol. 2, *The Romantic Age* (London: Jonathan Cape, 1955), 3.

4. René Wellek, "The Concept of 'Romanticism' in Literary History," *Comparative Literature* 1 (1949):147.

A. C. Goodson
Romantic Theory and the Critique of Language

1. A detailed reckoning of Romantic responses to Bacon is incorporated in Charles Whitney's sensitive and original study *Francis Bacon and Modernity* (New Haven: Yale University Press, 1986).

2. The suppression of rhetoric in the period is characterized by Brian Vickers, *In Defence of Rhetoric* (Oxford: Clarendon Press, 1988), 201f., with special reference to Kant. His discussion continues on other grounds some of the emphases of Herder's late attack on Kant, especially in "Eine Metakritik zur Kritik der reinen Vernunft" (1799). See Johann Gottfried Herder, *Sprachphilosophische Schriften* (Hamburg: Felix Meiner, 1960; rpt. 1975), 183–227. Herder's attention to the linguistic formation of ideas is distinctive, and would associate him with Leibnitz's critique of Locke on language. For recent commentary, see Rita Widmaier, "Die Idee des Zeichens bei Locke und Leibnitz in ihren Untersuchungen ueber den menschlichen Verstand," in Klaus D. Dutz and Peter Schmitter, eds., *Geschichte und Geschichtsschreibung der Semiotik* (Muenster: MAkS Publikationen, 1986), 133–49. Extended associations between English and German accounts of language in the period are recognized by Coleridge, for whom they are of real importance. In this context see his rehearsal of Leibnitz's critique of Locke in *CPL* 383–84.

3. For a recent narrative account, under the rubric "The End of Rhetoric: A Historical Sketch," see John Bender and David E. Wellbery, "Rhetoricality: On the Modernist Return of Rhetoric," in *The Ends of Rhetoric: History, Theory, Practice,* ed. Bender and Wellbery (Stanford: Stanford University Press, 1990), 5–22. The critique of language is figured here as a rationalist disruption of classical rhetoric, culminating in "the Romantic elimination of rhetoric as the basis of poetic theory" (11). What replaces it has usually been considered to be aesthetics. I shall be arguing for an expanded idea of Romantic value based on a broad reconstruction of linguistic value within the precritical tradition of reflection on language that I describe. "Critique of language" is not meant to prefigure or bear on the critical philosophy of Kant and his inheritors: "critique" is not "Critik" in this setting.

4. Cited from an influential early edition of *The Advancement of Learning* (*Of the Advancement of Learning or the Partitions of Sciences,* Oxford, 1640; reprint, Alburgh: Archival Facsimiles Limited, 1987), 251–52. This passage originates in *Novum Organum* LIX.

5. "In translating this passage into Latin Bacon found himself engaged upon the clearance of his own meaning. Where he had originally seemed to suggest that the defining of our words precludes confusion of judgement he now inserted 'attamen haec omnia non sufficiunt' and his analogy of the Tartar bowmen reads more cogently here than in the original English: '. . . retro in intellectum (unde profecta sint) retorqueant.'" Geoffrey Hill, *The Enemy's Country: Words, Contexture, and Other Circumstances of Language* (Oxford: Oxford University Press, 1991), 23.

6. For discussion of the paradox of Bacon's situation in established tradition, especially in *The Advancement of Learning,* see Whitney, *Francis Bacon and Modernity,* 55–75.

7. Saul A. Kripke, *Wittgenstein on Rules and Private Language* (Cambridge, Mass.: Harvard University Press, 1982), 62.

8. Texts cited by page number are from Draft A. See John Locke, *Drafts for the "Essay Concerning Human Understanding," and Other Philosophical Writings,* ed. Peter H. Nidditch and G. A. J. Rogers, vol. 1 (Oxford: Clarendon Press, 1990).

9. For discussion see Neal Wood, *The Politics of Locke's Philosophy* (Berkeley: University of California Press, 1983), 119–20.

10. For summary discussion see John B. Thompson, "Universal Pragmatics," in *Habermas: Critical Debates,* ed. Thompson and Held (Cambridge, Mass.: MIT Press, 1982), 116–33. Locke provides grist for Habermas's study of 1962, *The Structural Transformation of the Public Sphere: An Inquiry into a Category of Bourgeois Society,* trans. Thomas Burger with assistance of Frederick Lawrence (Cambridge, Mass.: MIT Press, 1989). The significance of the language question for the later Habermas resumes the empiricists' conviction of the inadequacy of ordinary linguistic practices, though the emphasis falls on ideas of language which represent the modern situation uncritically.

11. Eugéne Jolas, "The Revolution of Language and James Joyce," *transition* 11 (February 1928):109.

12. For exposition of the language question in Cambridge English, see A. C. Goodson, *Verbal Imagination: Coleridge and the Language of Modern Criticism* (New York: Oxford University Press, 1988), 3–80.

13. See Christopher Norris, *Paul de Man: Deconstruction and the Critique of Aesthetic Ideology* (London: Methuen, 1988).

14. Accounts of the rise of the man of letters in the period have entirely missed the significance of the critique of language for the role. See the treatment of the subject in, for example, Marilyn Butler, *Romantics, Rebels, and Reactionaries: English Literature and Its Background, 1760–1830* (Oxford: Oxford University Press, 1981).

15. Northrop Frye, *Fearful Symmetry* (Princeton: Princeton University Press, 1947; rpt. 1970), 3–29.

16. Robert Essick, *William Blake and the Language of Adam* (Oxford: Clarendon Press, 1989).

17. *BK* 783. References in the text refer to this edition.

18. See *Advancement of Learning,* part 2, p. 47, of first edition.

19. Angus Fletcher, *Colors of the Mind: Conjectures on Thinking in Literature* (Cambridge, Mass.: Harvard University Press, 1991), 93–95.

20. As Whitney illustrates (141), he pursued this to the point of deliberately inverting Baconian precepts, in "There is No Natural Religion" and "All Religions are One." Yet in reading Bacon via the empiricism to which his work gave rise, Blake neglected visionary qualities that Whitney is concerned to recuperate: "While Blake condemns Bacon's goal of restoring Adam's worldly dominion, he himself, reflecting in part the Judeo-Christian ideal of dominion in a different way, gives the Promethean consciousness embodied in 'true Man' or 'Poetic Genius' an even greater, though more ascetic, dominion over the natural frame: 'where man is not, nature is barren.' This ideal of ascetic dominion has sometimes meant (though not to Blake) sacrificing the link between literature and action, in effect acquiescing to the forces that marginalize literature's role in society and make it *merely* visionary, intellectual, or academic" (142–43). As a critique of the language of allegory, including Blake's own (despite the disclaimer), this responds effectively in behalf of Bacon's understanding.

21. Olivia Smith, *The Politics of Language, 1791–1819* (Oxford: Clarendon Press, 1984), 36ff.

22. See James Engell, "'That Eye, Which Sees All Things': Burke as Poet and Prophet," forthcoming. For the rhetorical background, see John E. Faulkner, "Edmund Burke's Early Conception and Poetry and Rhetoric," in *Studies in Burke and His Time* 12 (1971): 1747–63.

23. See James Chandler, *Wordsworth's Second Nature* (Chicago: University of Chicago Press, 1984).

24. For discussion see A. C. Goodson, "Burke's Orpheus and Coleridge's Contrary Understanding," *The Wordsworth Circle* 21, no. 1 (1991): 52–58.

25. Mark Parker, "The Institutionalization of a Burkean-Coleridgean Literary Culture," *Studies in English Literature* 31 (1991): 693–711.

26. Francis Jeffrey, *Edinburgh Review* 21 (October 1807): 217.

27. See Marilyn Butler, *Peacock Displayed: A Satirist in His Context* (London: Routledge & Kegan Paul), 272ff.

28. *A Defence of Poetry,* in *Peacock's Four Ages of Poetry; Shelley's Defence of Poetry; Browning's Essay on Shelley,* ed. H. F. B. Brett-Smith (Oxford: Basil Blackwell, 1945), 23.

29. "A Mathematical Problem," *CPW* 1:21–24.

30. See Paul de Man, "Shelley Disfigured," in *The Rhetoric of Romanticism* (New York: Columbia University Press, 1984), 93–123; and Jacques Derrida, "Living On," in *Deconstruction and Criticism,* ed. Harold Bloom (New York: Seabury Press, 1979).

31. For related discussion, concluding that "beneath Shelley's idealistic affirmation lies a depth of skepticism, which throws all affirmation into abeyance" (59), see John A. Hodgson, *Coleridge, Shelley, and Transcendental Inquiry: Rhetoric, Argument, Metapsychology* (Lincoln: University of Nebraska Press, 1989), 51 f.

32. The text glossed here is taken from "Brot und Wein" (1800):

> So ist der Mensch; wenn da ist das Gut, und es sorget mit Gaben
> Selber ein Gott für ihn, kennet und sieht er es nicht.
> Tragen muss er, zuvor; nun aber nennt er sein Liebstes,
> Nun, nun müssen dafür Worte, wie Blumen, entstehn.

33. Don Bialostosky, *Wordsworth, Dialogics, and the Practice of Criticism* (Cambridge: Cambridge University Press, 1992), 43. Bialostosky takes off from the argument of Paul Sheats, *The Making of Wordsworth's Poetry, 1785–1798* (Cambridge, Mass.: Harvard University Press, 1973).

34. Stephen Gill, *William Wordsworth: A Life* (Oxford: Clarendon Press, 1989).

35. See especially Paul Magnuson's careful study, *Coleridge and Wordsworth: A Lyrical Dialogue* (Princeton: Princeton University Press, 1988).

36. For background see James McKusick, *Coleridge's Philosophy of Language* (New Haven: Yale University Press, 1986), with some qualifications as detailed in Goodson, *Verbal Imagination,* 7–8, 89–119, and in *Studies in Romanticism* 28, no. 1 (1989): 178–81. See also Essick *(William Blake and the Language of Adam),* who recognizes the empirical dominant at work in Coleridge's idea of signification while tracing "the concept of the motivated sign through [his] scattered comments on language" (90) in McKusick's wake; and Hodgson *(Coleridge, Shelley, and Transcendental Inquiry),* who proceeds from Coleridge's foundational distinction of symbol and allegory to the "deeply revisionary theory of rhetoric" involved in his later work (10), making him a tropologist *avant la lettre.*

37. Thus *CPL* 71: "The aera in which Hesiod and Homer are generally supposed to have flourished; that is, about the year BC 907. In the great poems of this aera we find a language already formed, beyond all example adapted to social intercourse, to description, narration, and the expression of the passions. It possesses pre-eminently the perfections which our Milton demands of the language of poetry. It is simple, sensuous, and empassioned . . . It is the language of poetry, not of speculation; an exponent of senses and sensations, not of reflection, abstraction, generalization, or the mind's notice of its own acts." Such an idiom would approach Blake's language of Adam, with its transparence to pristine creation. The example of Milton links Coleridge's with Blake's understanding.

Elsewhere Coleridge argues that "the best part of human language, properly so called, is derived from reflection on the acts of the mind itself," against Wordsworth's insistence on the value of rustic language. The two contexts are associated at least rhetorically, yet the one appears to endorse the superiority of a rationally rarified language which the other would exclude from poetry. The apparent dissonance is interesting, reproducing as it does a sense of the progress of language resembling Peacock's while looking back with admiration on the great verse of the childhood of the race. Schiller's distinction between naive and sentimental poetry is at work here, as the editors' note intimates. Such a distinction would save poetry for enlightened understanding, against Peacock's insistence on the vitiating effects on imagination of a rationalized language. See *CBL* 2:54. Subsequent citations by page are to this edition.

38. *CN* 1:1623. This note of 1803 becomes the point of entry for a later essay in *The Friend* in defense of the purpose of his critique, which is affirmative, not negative. See *C Friend* 1:108.

39. Cited from the 1802 edition printed by W. J. B. Owen, *Wordsworth's Literary Criticism* (London: Routledge and Kegan Paul, 1974), 69.

40. [James Montgomery], *Eclectic Review* 4 (January 1808): 38. Rpt. *The Romantics Reviewed,* pt. A, vol. 1, ed. Donald H. Reiman (New York: Garland, 1972), 335.

41. For critical discussion of eloquence in this setting, see Charles Altieri, "Wordsworth's Poetics of Eloquence: A Challenge to Contemporary Theory," *Romantic Revolutions: Criticism and Theory,* ed. Kenneth R. Johnston, Gilbert Chaitin, Karen Hansen, and Herbert Marks (Bloomington: Indiana University Press, 1990), 371–407. This important essay includes the central recognition, belated among the Wordsworthians, that "Coleridge was essentially right in his criticism of those poems in *Lyrical Ballads* written in the spirit of the Preface's doctrines of the common life. In retrospect one might say that although Wordsworth was there trying to locate within a mimetic version of poetry the appropriate grounds for a 'more permanent, and far more philosophical language' for nourishing 'the essential passions of the heart' than he found in his predecessors (Zall, 41), in fact the strength of the theory and his talents as a poet lay elsewhere—in his capacity to cross that social milieu with modes of expressive eloquence best located in first person expression" (378).

42. See *CN* 3:4058 and 3268. The latter vividly lays out the problem: "Important Hint suggested itself to me, 10th Feb. 1808. The powers of conscious intellect increase by the accession of an organon or new word—try this in that abominable word, Idea/ how have I been struggling to get rid of it, & to find some exact word for each exact meaning—but no!—look into Bacon, Hooker, Milton, and the best Writers before Locke—& then *report.*—"

43. See Whitney, *Francis Bacon and Modernity,* 141, for discussion of Coleridge's difficulties in turning openly on Bacon: "Coleridge's admiration supplies a precedent for literary misconstructions of Bacon."

Anne K. Mellor
A Criticism of Their Own

1. For Anna Barbauld's comment on *The Rime of the Ancient Mariner,* see Coleridge's reminiscence, dated 31 May 1830, in *CTT* 1:27 and note 6. For an analysis of the unresolved contradictions in Coleridge's poem, see my *English Romantic Irony* (Cambridge, Mass.: Harvard University Press, 1980), 137–64.

2. René Wellek, *A History of Modern Criticism: 1750–1950* (New Haven: Yale University Press, 1955), 2:2–3. Beyond a single citation of Clara Reeve, Wellek does not consider the contributions of women to literary criticism in the Romantic period.

3. See *Abrams ML.*

4. On the popularity of Romantic women writers, see Ann H. Jones, *Ideas and Innovations: Best Sellers of Jane Austen's Age* (New York: AMS Press, 1986). For a complete discussion of the feminine Romantic ideology, see my *Romanticism and Gender* (New York: Routledge, Chapman & Hall, 1993); on the ideological cross-dressing performed by such male Romantic writers as Keats and Scott, see especially part 3. On Scott's feminine Romanticism, see Ina Ferris, *The Achievement of Literary Authority: Gender, History, and the Waverley Novels* (Ithaca: Cornell University Press, 1991).

5. Henry F. Chorley, *Memorials of Mrs. Hemans,* 2 vols. (New York and London, 1836), 1:243; 2:161 and 147; and Anna Seward, *Letters of Anna Seward: Written between the Years 1784 and 1807,* 6 vols. (Edinburgh: A. Constable, 1811), 6:359–60; 5:61.

6. Dorothy Wordsworth's collected poems are printed as appendix 1 of Susan Levin, *Dorothy Wordsworth and Romanticism* (New Brunswick: Rutgers University Press, 1987), 175–237, 207–8.

7. On the distinction between an ethic of care and an ethic of justice, see Carol Gilligan, *In a Different Voice: Psychological Theory and Women's Voice* (Cambridge, Mass.: Harvard University Press, 1982).

8. On the impact of lending libraries on women as readers and writers, and on the popularity of women writers in the Romantic era, see my *Romanticism and Gender,* chapter 1 and conclusion. Byron, for instance, greatly admired Joanna Baillie, claiming that she "is our only dramatist since Otway & Southern—I don't except [John] Home" and has somehow "borrowed" the "*testicles*" required to write tragedy (*BLJ* 3:109; 5:203).

9. Anna Laetitia Barbauld, "On the Origin and Progress of Novel-Writing," *The British Novelists; with An Essay, and Prefaces, Biographical and Critical* (London: Rivington, 1810), 50–51. Further citations from this essay will be given in the text.

10. For a superb study of the aesthetic politics of Wollstonecraft's literary reviews, see Mitzi Myers, "Sensibility and the 'Walk of Reason': Mary Wollstonecraft's Literary Reviews as Cultural Critique," in *Sensibility in Transformation: Creative Resistance to Sentiment from the Augustans to the Romantics,* ed. Syndy McMillen Conger (Rutherford: Fairleigh Dickinson University Press, 1989), 120–44.

11. Mary Hays, *Letters and Essays, Moral and Miscellaneous* (London, 1793), 90.

12. The locus classicus of this argument is Samuel Johnson's fourth *Rambler* (31 March 1750), reprinted in *The British Essayists,* ed. Alexander Chalmers (London: J. Johnson, 1802), 19.

13. Elizabeth Inchbald, *Remarks for The British Theatre (1806–1809),* facsimile reproductions with an introduction by Cecilia Macheski (Delmar, N.Y.: Scholars' Facsimiles and Reprints, 1990). Since this facsimile does not provide consecutive pagination, I will cite Inchbald's comments by author and play in the text.

14. Katherine M. Rogers, "Britain's First Woman Drama Critic: Elizabeth Inchbald," in *Curtain Calls: British and American Women and the Theater, 1660–1820,* ed. Mary Anne Schofield and Cecilia Macheski (Athens: Ohio University Press, 1991), 280. In addition to providing an excellent overview of Inchbald's critical principles, this essay reads Inchbald's prefaces as embedded autobiography.

15. Mary Wollstonecraft, *Analytical Review,* May 1792, p. 74.

16. Ibid., April 1796, p. 511.

17. Mary Wollstonecraft, review of *An Excursion to Brighthelmstone,* by Henry Wigstead and Thomas Rowlandson, in the *Analytical Review,* December 1790, p. 462.

18. Mary Wollstonecraft, "On Poetry and Our Relish for the Beauties of Nature," in *Posthumous Works of the Author of a Vindication of the Rights of Woman,* ed. William Godwin (London, 1798), 4:169, 171.

19. Mary Wollstonecraft, *Analytical Review,* December 1790, p. 433.

20. Mary Wollstonecraft, "On Poetry and Our Relish for the Beauties of Nature," 164, 175.

21. Catherine E. Moore, "'Ladies . . . Taking the Pen in Hand': Mrs. Barbauld's Criticism of Eighteenth-Century Women Novelists," in *Fetter'd or Free? British Women Novelists, 1670–1815,* ed. Mary Anne Schofield and Cecilia Macheski (Athens: Ohio University Press, 1986), 386.

22. Anna Laetitia Barbauld, *The Correspondence of Samuel Richardson . . . [with] Observations on his Writings by Anna Laetitia Barbauld* (London, 1804; reprint, New York: AMS Press, 1966), 1:xxiii–xxviii.

23. Katherine M. Rogers, "Britain's First Woman Drama Critic: Elizabeth Inchbald," 279.

24. Anna Seward, *Letters,* 1:244.

25. Clara Reeve, *The Progress of Romance and the History of Charoba, Queen of Aegypt* (London: Colchester edition, 1785), ed. Esther M. McGill (New York: Facsimile Text Society, 1930), 1:25. All further citations from this edition will be given in the text.

26. Joanna Baillie, Introductory Discourse to *A Series of Plays: in which it is attempted to Delineate the Stronger Passions of the Mind, each Passion being the Subject of a Tragedy and a Comedy,* in *Joanna Baillie: The Dramatic and Poetical Works* (1851; reprint, New York and Hildesheim: Georg Olms Verlag, 1976), 5, 3. All further citations from this edition will be given in the text. For a concise summary of Baillie's theory of dramatic art, see Marlon B. Ross, *The Contours of Masculine Desire: Romanticism and the Rise of Women's Poetry* (New York: Oxford University Press, 1989), 285–89.

27. Mary E. Hawkesworth, "Knowers, Knowing, Known: Feminist Theory and Claims of Truth," *Signs* 14 (1989): 550.

28. Anna Seward, *The Poetical Works of Anna Seward; with Extracts from her Literary Correspondence,* ed. Walter Scott, 3 vols. (Edinburgh, 1810), xiii.

29. On the existence and function of a social, as opposed to a public or a private, sphere in nineteenth-century Britain, a sphere controlled by women, see Denise Riley, *"Am I that Name?": Feminism and the Category of "Women" in History* (Minneapolis: University of Minnesota Press, 1988), ch. 3.

30. Terry Eagleton, *The Rape of Clarissa: Writing, Sexuality, and Class Struggle in Samuel Richardson* (Oxford: Basil Blackwell, 1982), 13; cf. 1–17, 95–101.

31. On the Victorian backlash against women novelists, see Gaye Tuchman, with Nina Fortin, *Edging Women Out: Victorian Novelists, Publishers, and Social Change* (New Haven: Yale University Press, 1989).

Martin Aske
Critical Disfigurings

1. *The Autobiography of Leigh Hunt,* ed. J. E. Morpurgo (London: Cresset Press, 1949), 214ff. The phrase "convulsions of criticism and contention" is Byron's, from a letter to Lady Melbourne (*BLJ* 4:53 [11 February 1814]).

2. *Autobiography of Leigh Hunt,* 215.

3. Leigh Hunt, *The Feast of the Poets* (London: James Cawthorn, 1814), 7.

4. William Gifford, *The Baviad, and Maeviad,* 8th ed. (London: John Murray, 1811), xv, 60n.

5. *Autobiography of Leigh Hunt,* 215, 216.

6. Ibid., 216. The couplet is from the *Baviad,* lines 27–28. Gifford's cruelly ironic allusion is to "'Light o'love'; that goes without a burden," from *Much Ado about Nothing,* III.iv.41.

7. *Autobiography of Leigh Hunt,* 217, 218.

8. Ibid., 218–19. The auction of the Duke of Roxburgh's library took place on 18 May 1812.

9. Charles Dickens, *David Copperfield,* ed. Nina Burgis (Oxford: Clarendon Press, 1981), 201 (ch. 16).

10. *On the Genealogy of Morals* (1887), in *Basic Writings of Nietzsche,* trans. Walter Kaufmann (New York: Modern Library, 1968), 472.

11. For a brilliant analysis of the "reactive" element in Nietzschean *ressentiment,* see Gilles Deleuze, *Nietzsche and Philosophy,* trans. Hugh Tomlinson (London: Athlone Press, 1983), 111–16. (I am grateful to John Hughes for drawing Deleuze's book to my attention.) The concept of *ressentiment* might offer a new way of understanding the disquiet provoked in both Hazlitt and Hunt by what they took to be an excess of "feeling" in Wordsworth's poetry. In a long note in *The Feast of the Poets* (87–109), Hunt criticizes Wordsworth for writing on subjects that encourage "morbid abstractions" and "eremetical vagueness of sensation" (97). He goes on to advise any young poet of the necessity of achieving a balanced relation between "study" and "society"; experiencing "a mere intimacy with what is called the 'world'" will breed in the alienated poet "a resentful melancholy" (123, 124). Hazlitt, of course, was famously critical of the "intense intellectual egotism" he found in *The Excursion,* and he suggests that the Wanderer's "philippic" against the "contractedness and egotism of philosophical pursuits" (the Solitary's "meditative spleen" [IV. 477]) could be applied to Wordsworth himself (*HW* 19:15). In the *Lectures on the English Poets* Hazlitt compares Wordsworth to Burns: "Mr. Wordsworth's poetry is the poetry of mere sentiment and passive contemplation: Burns's is a very highly sublimated essence of animal existence" (*HW* 5:131). To deny that Burns is "a sickly sentimentalist" (*HW* 5:128) is to imply that Wordsworth *is.* "Mere sentiment" threatens to turn into

the sickness of *ressentiment.* This was certainly Hazlitt's verdict on Crabbe: "a sickly, a querulous, a fastidious poet," for whom "the world is one vast infirmary" (*HW* 19:54, 53).

12. The term *public sphere* I have borrowed from Jürgen Habermas, *The Structural Transformation of the Public Sphere,* trans. Thomas Burger with the assistance of Frederick Lawrence (Oxford: Polity Press, 1992). See also Terry Eagleton, *The Function of Criticism: From the Spectator to Post-Structuralism* (London: Verso, 1984); and Peter Uwe Hohendahl, *The Institution of Criticism* (Ithaca: Cornell University Press, 1982).

13. Marilyn Butler, "Repossessing the Past: The Case for an Open Literary History," in *Rethinking Historicism: Critical Readings in Romantic History,* ed. Marjorie Levinson et al. (Oxford: Basil Blackwell, 1989), 72.

14. Kelvin Everest, *English Romantic Poetry: An Introduction to the Historical Context and the Literary Scene* (Philadelphia: Open University Press, 1990), 70.

15. The term *psychic economy* I borrow from Roger Chartier (*The Cultural Origins of the French Revolution,* trans. Lydia G. Cochrane [Durham: Duke University Press, 1991], 6), who in turn ascribes it to Norbert Elias, *The Civilizing Process: Sociogenetic and Psychogenetic Investigations,* trans. Edmund Jephcott (Oxford: Basil Blackwell, 1978).

16. Quoted in W. Jackson Bate, *The Burden of the Past and the English Poet* (New York: Norton Library, 1972), 87. See Johann Peter Eckermann, *Gespräche mit Goethe in den letzten Jahren seines Lebens, Dritte Auflage* (Leipzig: Brockhaus, 1868), pt. 3, p. 27.

17. *The Letters of Percy Bysshe Shelley,* ed. Frederick L. Jones, 2 vols. (Oxford: Clarendon Press, 1964), 2:263 (16 February 1821).

18. *The Letters of Charles and Mary Lamb,* ed. Edwin W. Marrs Jr., 3 vols. (Ithaca: Cornell University Press, 1975–78), 3:130 (7 January 1815). The "freezing" effect of Gifford's "jealous leer malign" is felt by Hazlitt as well: defending his account of *Coriolanus* in *Characters of Shakespear's Plays,* he accuses Gifford of leaving "the proud flesh about the heart to harden and ossify into one impenetrable mass of selfishness and hypocrisy" (*HW* 9:38). The "sickly" and "querulous" Crabbe (see above, note 11) "gives you the petrifaction of a sigh, and carves a tear, to the life, in stone" (*HW* 11:97). "Petrifaction" is a state associated not only with Dante's envious souls in Canto XIII of the *Purgatorio*—they are "shades with mantles / Not from the color of the stone diverse" (*The Divine Comedy of Dante Alighieri,* trans. Henry Wadsworth Longfellow, 3 vols. (London: George Routledge and Sons, 1867), 2:79 [ll. 47–48])—but also with Blake's Urizen, whose followers are represented as "Petrifying all the Human Imagination into rock & sand' (*BK* 281). Deleuze describes the man of *ressentiment* as "a being full of pain: the sclerosis or hardening of his consciousness, the rapidity with which every excitation sets and freezes within him, the weight of the traces that invade him are so many cruel sufferings" (*Nietzsche and Philosophy,* 116).

19. David Punter, in *William Blake: Selected Poetry and Prose,* ed. Punter (London: Routledge, 1988), 223.

20. The phrase "rancour of malevolence" is taken from the address "To the Reader" in Richard Lawrence's *Elgin Marbles, from the Parthenon at Athens* (London: Thomas Davison, 1818). Regretting in the "public mind" a growth of

"contemptuous indifference towards the productions of modern times," the author asks that artists "propitiate the gentler feelings of the mind by mild suggestion and temperate representation, not to disgust and alienate by the impertinence of dictation or the rancour of malevolence" (2, 3).

21. Patrick Parrinder, *Authors and Authority: English and American Criticism 1750–1990* (London: Macmillan, 1991), 64. See *CTT* 2:358.

22. Parrinder, *Authors and Authority,* 77. I am very grateful to Peter Kitson for directing me to recent criticism on *Biographia Literaria,* most of which, interestingly enough, remains silent on Coleridge's explicit fascination with the processes of envy in chapters 2 and 3. See, for example, the essays collected in *Coleridge's "Biographia Literaria": Text and Meaning,* ed. Frederick Burwick (Columbus: Ohio State University Press, 1989). Catherine Miles Wallace is surely wrong to interpret Coleridge's concern with envy as nothing more than some kind of scorn for the "frivolous game of politics and personalities" (*The Design of "Biographia Literaria"* [London: George Allen & Unwin, 1983], 23). It is precisely because he knows that it is *not* "frivolous" that Coleridge devotes so much analysis to the "complex feeling" that informs this "game."

23. Byron, *English Bards and Scotch Reviewers* (1809), l. 92. Writing to Byron on the death of Keats, Shelley claimed that he, unlike the "poor fellow" who succumbed to "Envy and calumny and hate and pain" ("Adonais," preface and l. 353), remained "morbidly indifferent to . . . praise or blame." It was on account of such "happy indifference" that "I can delight in the productions of those who can [write anything worth calling a poem]; nor has ill-success yet turned me into an unfeeling, and malignant critic; that second degree in the descending scale of the Academy of Disappointed Authors" (*Letters* 2:289–90 [4 May 1821]). In a draft of the preface to "Adonais," Shelley describes reviewers as "a most stupid and malignant race. As a bankrupt thief turns thief-taker in despair, so an unsuccessful author turns critic" (*Poetical Works,* ed. Thomas Hutchinson, a new edition corrected by G. M. Matthews [London: Oxford University Press, 1970], 444).

24. See Nietzsche, *Basic Writings,* 561ff.

25. Ibid., 553–54.

26. Behind the idea of the old poets' "evenness and sweetness of temper" lies Winckelmann's celebrated description of ancient Greek art in terms of *edle Einfalt* and *stille Grösse*—"noble simplicity" and "calm grandeur"—which is then rehearsed in Schiller's great essay *Über naive und sentimentalische Dichtung* (1795) as well as in August Wilhelm von Schlegel's *Vorlesungen über dramatische Kunst und Literatur* (1809–11). (Winckelmann's *Gedanken über die Nachahmung der griechischen Werke in der Malerei und Bildhauerkunst* [1755] was translated by Henry Fuseli in 1765 as *Reflections on the Painting and Sculpture of the Greeks.)* It also provides the model, of course, for Nietzsche's conception of "Greek nobility"—just as Schiller's comparison of the "naive" or "objective" art of the Greeks and the "sentimental" or "subjective" art of the "moderns" helps establish the context in which Nietzsche can elaborate his theory of modern *ressentiment.* (As I suggested in note 11 above, the etymological link between the "sentimental" and *ressentiment* acquires a particular significance in the Romantic discourse of "feeling.")

27. Eagleton, *The Function of Criticism,* 34.

28. *A Philosophical and Critical History of the Fine Arts, Painting, Sculpture, and Architecture,* 2 vols. (London: T. Cadell, 1793–95), 2:453.

29. *Library of the Fine Arts* 2 (1831):33.

30. In the *Mémoires d'un Touriste* (1838), Stendhal identifies the peculiarly modern emotions as "envy, jealousy, and impotent hatred" (quoted in René Girard, *Deceit, Desire, and the Novel: Self and Other in Literary Structure,* trans. Yvonne Freccero [Baltimore: Johns Hopkins University Press, 1976], 14).

31. William Godwin asked whether there was "anything that can look with a more malignant aspect upon the general welfare than an institution tending to give permanence to certain systems and opinions" (*Enquiry Concerning Political Justice and Its Influence on Modern Morals and Happiness* [1793], ed. Isaac Kramnick [Harmondsworth, Middlesex: Penguin, 1985], 568).

32. *Literary Gazette* 119 (1 May 1819):283.

33. *Annals of the Fine Arts* 3 (1818):110–11.

34. Everest, *English Romantic Poetry,* 73.

35. Nigel Leask, *The Politics of Imagination in Coleridge's Critical Thought* (London: Macmillan, 1988), 2–4. Robert Maniquis also concludes that "the *Biographia* participates in the ideological contradictions of which it is a representative. It is an embodiment of the conflict it describes between text and book, mass audience and intelligentsia, the divine Romantic artist and the growing numbers of citizens that would populate what Walter Benjamin would call . . . the age of mechanical reproduction" ("Poetry and Barrel-Organs: The Text in the Book of the *Biographia Literaria,*" in Burwick, ed., *Coleridge's "Biographia Literaria": Text and Meaning,* 267).

36. Jon Klancher, *The Making of English Reading Audiences, 1790–1832* (Madison: University of Wisconsin Press, 1987), 5.

37. *European Magazine,* n. s., 1 (1825–26):409, 411.

38. Herschel Baker, *William Hazlitt* (Cambridge, Mass.: Harvard University Press, 1962), 452.

39. *HW* 12:99. Another instance of appearing to want to displace the threat of envy occurs in the late essay "On Personal Identity," where he maintains that our "envying the possessions of others" is habitually tempered by our "self-love," which ensures that there would be "some trait or feature of character in the object of our admiration to which we cannot reconcile ourselves—some favourite quality or darling foible of our own, with which we can by no means resolve to part." It is exactly this kind of sophisticated argument that earns Northcote's censure in "On Envy." Significantly enough, Hazlitt's example of "displaced" envy comes from the world of art:

> "In passing through a fine collection of pictures, who has not envied the privilege of visiting it every day, and wished to be the owner? But the rising sigh is soon checked . . . when we come to ask ourselves not merely whether the owner has any taste at all for these splendid works, and does not look upon them as so much expensive furniture, like his chairs and tables—but whether he has the same precise (and only true) taste that we have—whether he may not be so blind as to prefer a Vandyke to a Titian, a Ruysdael to a

Claude;—nay, whether he may not have other pursuits and avocations that draw off his attention from the sole objects of our idolatry, and which seem to us mere impertinences and waste of time? In that case, we at once lose all patience, and exclaim indignantly, "Give us back our taste and keep your pictures!" It is not we should envy them the possession of the treasure, but they who should envy us the true and exclusive enjoyment of it." (*HW* 17:266, 267)

40. Klancher, *The Making of English Reading Audiences,* 7.

41. Max Scheler, *Ressentiment* (1915), trans. William W. Holdheim, ed. Lewis A. Coser (1961), second printing (New York: Schocken Books, 1976), 67–68.

42. The specifically *economic* origin of this scene of envious "diversion" is emphasized by John Landseer in the preface to his catalog of pictures in the National Gallery: "[It is] this hasty changing of the scenes, in consequence of the mercenary root of estimation, and even of existence, to which everything in our Mammon-island is doomed . . . [It is] this haste, where pecuniary and mental profit stand opposed to each other, that has given such a careless, flippant, superficial, temporary, touch-and-go, air and character, to the printed notices—sometimes with temerarious and unblushing stolidity or effrontery called 'Critical Dissertations' on works of Art . . . which abound in the periodical publications, and which have reduced and degraded the art or science of picture-criticism to a state so discreditably low, at the very time when sound and accurate criticism is most especially wanted" (*A Descriptive, Explanatory, and Critical, Catalogue of Fifty of the Earliest Pictures contained in the National Gallery of Great Britain* [London: Richard Glynn, 1834], xii).

43. Pierre Bourdieu, *Distinction: A Social Critique of the Judgement of Taste,* trans. Richard Nice (London: Routledge & Kegan Paul, 1986), 56.

44. *Library of the Fine Arts* 2 (1831):33.

45. In his marginalia to the *Discourses* Blake denounces Reynolds for his *ressentiment:* "His Praise of Rafael is like the Hysteric Smile of Revenge. His Softness & Candour, the hidden trap & the poisoned feast. He praises Michel Angelo for Qualities which Michel Angelo abhorr'd, & He blames Rafael for the only Qualities which Rafael Valued" (*BK* 452).

46. Bourdieu, *Distinction,* 56. One contemporary figure who apparently could never be accused of *ressentiment* was George Dyer—a man who, according to Southey, was "all benevolence" (Joseph Cottle, *Reminiscences of Samuel Taylor Coleridge and Robert Southey* [New York: Wiley & Putnam, 1847], 155). In a letter to Wordsworth, Lamb doubted whether Dyer had "the most distant guess of the possibility of one poem being better than another. The Gods by denying him the very faculty itself of discrimination have effectually cut off every seed of envy in his bosom" (*Works* 5:547 [26 April 1819]). The causal logic of Lamb's remark could be reversed: by withholding from Dyer a capacity for envy, the gods have denied him the faculty of discrimination. "All benevolence," he is innocent of the "jealous leer malign" that is forever threatening to distort the critic's gaze. Another exception to the rule, according to Charles and Mary Cowden Clarke, was George James De Wilde—editor of the *Northampton Mercury* and friend of John Clare—who is remembered not as possessing the "venomous eye of *ressentiment*" (Nietzsche, *Basic Writings,* 476) but rather a "bland, benign countenance,

beaming with a look of universal good-will, as though it expressed affectionate fraternity of feeling toward all human kind" (*Recollections of Writers* [Fontwell, Sussex: Centaur Press, 1969], 108).

47. Thomas Love Peacock, "An Essay on Fashionable Literature" (1818), reprinted in *Romantic Critical Essays,* ed. David Bromwich (Cambridge: Cambridge University Press, 1987), 195.

48. *Edinburgh Magazine,* n. s., 1 (1825–26): 410.

49. *Dictionary of the English Language* (1755), reprint (London: Times Books, 1979).

50. In the chapter on the French Revolution in his *Life of Napoleon,* Hazlitt is in no doubt that England's hostility to revolutionary France, manifesting itself in the repressive policies of the Pitt and Liverpool administrations, was simply the most blatant expression of the kind of political *ressentiment* found in Gifford and the *Quarterly:*

> What then was the crime which drew down on France the vengeance not only of the despots of the Continent, but the last enmity and implacable hatred of a free nation and of a constitutional king? She had dared to aspire to the blessings of the English Constitution. Was there treason, was there danger in this? Yes; for if they made a step in advance from slavery to freedom, it was thought that we might be tempted to keep the start which we had always maintained in the race of freedom, and become *too free!* To this illiberal, mean, and envious policy we were not merely to sacrifice the peace and happiness of the world, but were to abjure and reverse and load with opprobrium every sentiment and maxim on which our own freedom and pre-eminence rested . . . It was judged best to wait, to watch, and to improve opportunity; to regard "with jealous leer malign" the first attempts of liberty, to irritate by coldness and mistrust, to goad a people at all times too prone to excitement into frenzy, in order that they might be led back manacled to their prison-house, and to rouse the national prejudices of John Bull against the French, as if this were the old vulgar quarrel, instead of being the great cause of mankind. (*HW* 13:49–50)

51. Nietzsche, *Basic Writings,* 556 ff.

52. Ibid., 474.

53. This is not the only occasion when Hazlitt's imagery comes uncannily close to Nietzsche's language of *ressentiment.* Elsewhere he describes the "Ascetics of old" as "actuated by a morose and envious disposition"—in order to characterize, significantly enough, "the new school of reform" (*HW* 12:179). Thus the Utilitarians are perceived as no better than reactionary Tories such as Gifford: "The sour pedagogues of the *Westminster* school. . . . [H]ate and envy and would put an end to whatever gives others pleasure" (*HW* 20:256). Like Nietzsche's tarantulas, who preach equality out of "soured self-conceit" and "repressed envy" (*Thus Spoke Zarathustra* [1883–85], trans. R. J. Hollingdale [1961], reprint [Harmondsworth, Middlesex: Penguin Books, 1972], 123), the reformers are but "ferrets and inspectors of a *Police-Philosophy*. . . . Without air or light, they grope their way under-ground . . . and soured and disappointed, they wreak their spite and mortification on all around them" (*HW* 12:181, 182).

54. Nietzsche, *Basic Writings,* 484.

55. René Girard, *A Theater of Envy: William Shakespeare* (New York: Oxford University Press, 1991), 4.

56. *Letters of Charles and Mary Lamb,* ed. Marrs, 1:111 (13 June 1797).

57. Extolling Rousseau as the "founder of Jacobinism," Hazlitt represents him as the Nietzschean ascetic priest, the supreme exponent of the politics of *ressentiment:*

> The only quality which he possessed in an eminent degree, which alone raised him above ordinary men, and which gave to his writings and opinions an influence greater, perhaps, than has been exerted by any individual in modern times, was extreme sensibility, or an acute and even morbid feeling of all that related to his own impressions, to the objects and events of his life . . . His interest in his own thoughts and feelings was always wound up to the highest pitch; and hence the enthusiasm which he excited in others. He owed the power which he exercised over the opinions of all Europe, by which he created numberless disciples, and overturned established systems, to the tyranny which his feelings, in the first instance, exercised over himself. (*HW* 4:88,89)

In this version of personal politics, the "true revolutionary leaven" finds its energy in affronted "self-love," in "personal insult" rather than "political injury" (*HW* 4:379n). Noticing how "egotism," in Hazlitt's portrayal of Rousseau, becomes "universal in its benevolent effects," Seamus Deane has written that "Hazlitt is delving for something other than the conventional calculus of selfishness and altruism" (*The French Revolution and Enlightenment in England, 1789–1832* [Cambridge, Mass.: Harvard University Press, 1988], 133). I would venture to say that Deane's "something other" is, exactly, envy—"the deformed and distorted offspring of egotism" (*HW* 20:312) which may nevertheless have "benevolent effects."

58. James Northcote, *The Life of Sir Joshua Reynolds* (1814), 2d ed., 2 vols. (London: Henry Colburn, 1818), 1:268.

59. Martin Archer Shee, *Elements of Art* (London: William Miller, 1809), 145. On Shee, see John Barrell, *The Political Theory of Painting from Reynolds to Hazlitt* (New Haven: Yale University Press, 1986), 50–52.

60. Shelley, *Letters* 1:504 (8 September 1816).

61. On the "unavoidably autoreferential structure" of *ressentiment,* see Fredric Jameson, *The Political Unconscious: Narrative as a Socially Symbolic Act* (1981), university paperback edition (London: Methuen, 1983), 202.

62. On Hazlitt's deeply divided response to Burke, see John Whale, "Hazlitt on Burke: The Ambivalent Position of a Radical Essayist," *Studies in Romanticism* 25 (1986): 465–81. See also Mary Jacobus, "The Art of Managing Books: Romantic Prose and the Writing of the Past," in *Romanticism and Language,* ed. Arden Reed (London: Methuen, 1984), 228–31.

63. "Envious commands" is the phrase used by Satan in *Paradise Lost* (IV. 524) to describe God's prohibition to Adam and Eve.

Philip W. Martin
Authorial Identity and the Critical Act

1. Jerome Christensen, *Lord Byron's Strength: Romantic Writing and Commercial Society* (Baltimore: Johns Hopkins University Press, 1994), 19.

2. Peter J. Manning, "The Nameless Broken Dandy and the Structure of Authorship," in Peter J. Manning, *Reading Romantics: Texts and Contexts* (Oxford: Oxford University Press, 1990).

3. Andrew Bennett, *Keats, Narrative, and Audience: The Posthumous Life of Writing* (Cambridge: Cambridge University Press, 1994), 35.

4. For an explanation of Greenblatt's term, see Stephen Greenblatt, *Renaissance Self-fashioning: From More to Shakespeare* (Chicago: University of Chicago Press, 1980), 1–9.

5. Jon P. Klancher, *The Making of English Reading Audiences* (Madison: University of Wisconsin Press, 1987).

6. I am indebted to John Beer, the editor of this volume, for this idea of a fellow-citizenry of writers.

7. *The Later Poems of John Clare,* ed. Eric Robinson and David Powell, 2 vols. (Oxford: Clarendon Press, 1984), 1:98. *Don Juan,* ll. 263–64. All subsequent quotations from Clare's poetry are taken from the first volume of this edition.

8. *Beppo,* ll. 409–10, in *Byron,* ed. Jerome J. McGann (Oxford: Oxford University Press, 1986), 329. All subsequent quotations from Byron's poetry are taken from this edition, cited in the text. For a most interesting discussion of *Beppo,* see Manning, "The Nameless Broken Dandy."

9. Marilyn Butler, *Romantics, Rebels, and Reactionaries: English Literature and Its Background, 1760–1830* (Oxford: Oxford University Press, 1981), 118.

10. Bennett, *Keats, Narrative, and Audience,* 188, n. 19.

11. Greenblatt, *Renaissance Self-fashioning,* 3.

12. For a summary of radical unrest at this period, see Edward Royle and James Walvin, *English Radicals and Reformers, 1760–1848* (Brighton: Harvester Press, 1982), 93–107.

13. *The Romantics Reviewed,* ed. Donald H. Reiman, 3 parts, 9 vols. (New York: Garland, 1972), pt. B, vol. 4, pp. 1730–31. *Monthly Review,* 2d ser., 68 (May 1812).

14. Ibid. pt. B, vol. 2, p. 880. *Edinburgh Review* 27 (December 1816).

15. Ibid. pt. B, vol. 2, p. 485. *Edinburgh Monthly Review* 2 (October 1819).

16. See J. W. and Anne Tibble, *John Clare: A Life,* rev. ed. (London: Michael Joseph, 1972), 84–114, and *Clare: The Critical Heritage,* ed. Mark Storey (London: Routledge & Kegan Paul, 1973), 1–10.

17. J. W. and Anne Tibble, *John Clare,* 84.

18. Ibid. 52–59.

19. "I now followd gardening for a while in the Farmers Gardens about the village and workd in the fields when I had no other employment to go to Poetry was a troublesomely pleasant companion annoying & cheering me at my toils I could not stop my thoughts & often faild to keep them till night so when I fancyd I had hit upon a good image or natural description I used to steal into a corner of the garden & clap it down but the appearance of my employers often put my fancys to flight & made me loose the thought and the muse together." John Clare, "The Autobiography, 1793–1824," in *The Prose of John Clare,* ed. J. W. and Anne Tibble (London: Routledge & Kegan Paul, 1951), 32.

20. *The Letters of John Clare,* ed. Mark Storey (Oxford: Clarendon Press, 1985), 215.

21. Storey, *Critical Heritage,* 29.
22. Ibid., 30.
23. Ibid., 32.
24. For details see J. W. and Anne Tibble, *John Clare,* 102.
25. Storey, *Critical Heritage,* 57, 59.
26. Ibid., 61.
27. Ibid., 62.
28. For the famous passage on cant, see Byron's "Letter to **** ****** [John Murray], Esqre, on the Rev W. L. Bowles's Strictures on the Life and Writings of Pope," in *The Works of Lord Byron: Letters and Journals,* ed. Rowland E. Prothero, 6 vols. (London: John Murray, 1904), 5:542. It is quite possible that Clare would have been familiar with this later on, particularly because of his connection with Gilchrist, but of course Clare's letter predates Byron's.
29. Storey, *Critical Heritage,* 38, 40, 50.
30. Clare, *Prose,* 258.
31. For details, see J. W. and Anne Tibble, *John Clare,* 360.
32. Clare writes interestingly of this incident in the autobiographical writings, where he notes what he believes to be Byron's popularity among the "common people." See *Prose,* 99.
33. See "I am," in *Later Poems,* 1:396.
34. J. W. and Anne Tibble, *John Clare,* 373.
35. Elie Halévy, *A History of the English People in the Nineteenth Century,* 6 vols. (London: Ernest Benn, 1951), 4:7.
36. Klancher, *Making of Audiences,* 3.
37. Greenblatt, *Renaissance Self-fashioning,* 3.

Nigel Leask
Toward a Universal Aesthetic

1. To be more precise, the old *OED* attributed the first use of the adverbial form *aesthetically* to De Quincey (in the "On Murder" essay, which it misdated 1839). When the error of dating the first "Murder" essay was corrected, De Quincey's 1827 usage appeared to be inaugural, according to the old *OED*'s dating of early instances of the term. But the 1987 supplement corrected and predated the appearance of the word in "On Murder" by discovering Coleridge's earlier 1821 usage. The term *aesthetic* ultimately derives from Alexander Baumgarten's *Aesthetica* (1750–58). According to the *OED* the first English appearance of the word occurred in Dr. Willich's *Elements of the Critical Philosophy* (1798), but as with all usages before Coleridge's in 1821, this was in the limited context of a discussion of Kant's philosophy, where the term *aesthetic* had a broader application than the philosophy of taste.
2. That is to say, in relation to the science that treats of the conditions of sensuous perception.
3. *Blackwood's Edinburgh Magazine* 56, no. 10 (October 1821):254.
4. Jon Klancher, *The Making of English Reading Audiences, 1790–1832* (Madison: University of Wisconsin Press, 1987), 7.
5. For the "profit of disinterestedness," see Pierre Bourdieu, *The Field of*

Cultural Production: Essays on Art and Literature, ed. and trans. Randal Johnson (Cambridge: Polity Press, 1993), 75.

6. *Blackwood's,* 254.

7. See my *Politics of Imagination in Coleridge's Critical Thought* (London: Macmillan, 1988), 210–19, and Ben Knights's *The Idea of the Clerisy in the Nineteenth Century* (Cambridge: Cambridge University Press, 1978).

8. Klancher, *Audiences,* 55.

9. Grevel Lindop, *The Opium Eater: A Life of Thomas De Quincey* (Oxford: Oxford University Press, 1981), 245–46.

10. Jonathan Bate, "The Literature of Power: Coleridge and De Quincey," in *Coleridge's Visionary Languages: Essays in Honour of J. B. Beer,* ed. Tim Fulford and Morton Paley (Cambridge: D. S. Brewer, 1993), 138. See also my *British Romantic Writers and the East: Anxieties of Empire* (Cambridge: Cambridge University Press, 1992), 170–95, for a related reading of De Quincey's *Confessions* as a "response" to the *Biographia.*

11. De Quincey, in "On Murder," mentions Coleridge's witty "ideal of an inkstand" in his "celebrated correspondence with Mr Blackwood," a reference to the 1821 article (*DQW* 13:15).

12. John Whale, "'In a Stranger's Ear': De Quincey's Polite Magazine Context," in *De Quincey Bicentenary Studies,* ed. Robert Lance Snyder (Norman: University of Oklahoma Press, 1985), 48.

13. Klancher, *Audiences,* 5.

14. Joel Black, *The Aesthetics of Murder: A Study in Romantic Literature and Contemporary Culture* (Baltimore: Johns Hopkins University Press, 1991), 65.

15. It is significant in this light that De Quincey was greatly influenced by the German visionary writer Jean Paul Richter. See Frederick Burwick, "The Dream Visions of Jean Paul and De Quincey," *Comparative Literature* 20 (1968):1–26.

16. See Kant's account of taste as a kind of *sensus communis* in *The Critique of Judgement,* trans. James Creed Meredith (Oxford: Clarendon Press, 1952), 150–54. Kant takes pains to distinguish two meanings for "Common" (in "Common Sense"), one as "vulgar," the other as "public" (151), stressing that "the aesthetic, rather than the intellectual, judgement can bear the name of a public sense" (153). De Quincey's "Murder" essays seek to problematize Kant's distinction between "vulgar" and "public," dissatisfied with Coleridge's definition of a community of taste.

17. G. S. Gadamer, *Truth and Method,* trans. G. Barden and J. Cummings (London: Sheed & Ward, 1975), 26. See also Terry Eagleton's remarks on Kantian aesthetics in *The Ideology of the Aesthetic* (Oxford: Basil Blackwell, 1990): "Kant's turn to the subject is hardly a turn to the *body,* whose needs and desires fall outside the disinterestedness of aesthetic taste. The body cannot be figured or represented within the frame of Kantian aesthetics; and Kant ends up accordingly with a formalistic ethics, an abstract theory of political rights, and a 'subjective' but non-sensuous aesthetics" (21). This casts additional light on my discussion of De Quincey's "embodiment" of the philosopher in "The Last Days of Immanuel Kant."

18. Black, *The Aesthetics of Murder,* 14.

19. Allon White, "Hysteria and the End of Carnival," in *The Violence of Representation: Literature and the History of Violence,* ed. Nancy Armstrong and Leonard Tennenhouse (London: Routledge, 1989), 163.

20. For a background to this see Joseph Donohue, *Theatre in the Age of Kean* (Totowa, N.J.: Rowman & Littlefield, 1975).

21. See Josephine McDonagh, "Do or Die: Problems of Agency and Gender in the Aesthetics of Murder," *Genders* 5 (summer 1989):129–30.

22. White, "Hysteria and the End of Carnival," 165.

23. *Henry Crabb Robinson on Books and Their Writers,* ed. Edith Morley, 3 vols. (London: Dent & Sons, 1938), 2:740.

24. *Posthumous Works of Thomas De Quincey,* ed. Alexander Japp, 2 vols. (London: Heinemann, 1891), 2:51. Thanks to Daniel Roberts for this reference.

25. George Orwell, "The Decline of the English Murder," in *Collected Essays, Journalism, and Letters,* ed. Sonia Orwell and Ian Angus (London: Secker & Warburg, 1968), 4:124–27.

26. "Philosophy of Murder," *Tait's Edinburgh Magazine,* 18 (March 1851):172.

27. Whale, "'In a Stranger's Ear,'" 41.

28. William Hazlitt, "Modern Tragedy," in *Selected Writings,* ed. Jon Cook (Oxford: Oxford University Press, 1991), 109–10.

29. Ibid., 115.

30. George Steiner, "The Romantic Evasion of Tragedy," in *Tragedy: Developments in Criticism,* ed. R. P. Draper (London: Macmillan, 1980), 172, 174, 171.

31. William Hazlitt, "On Poetry in General," in *Selected Writings,* 319. Hazlitt is an important and largely unremarked influence on De Quincey, notably in relation to the latter's theory of the literature of knowledge and literature of power. This distinction, which De Quincey attributed to Wordsworth, is plausibly laid at Hazlitt's door by David Bromwich, who points out that Hazlitt first discussed the distinction in his essay "Why the Arts Are Not Progressive," but omitted the relevant passage in the better known *Round Table* version of his essay. See David Bromwich, *Hazlitt: The Mind of a Critic* (New York: Oxford University Press, 1983), 434. Bate ("Literature of Power," 148) plausibly suggests that "De Quincey failed to acknowledge Hazlitt's role in the conception of the literature of power because the latter linked artistic to political power and De Quincey wanted to avoid going down that road."

32. This is not to say that John Williams, De Quincey's Ratcliffe Highway murderer, doesn't have a distinguished lineage in English Romanticism, particularily in its more gothic moments. Matthew Lewis's *The Monk,* Godwin's *Caleb Williams* (a work De Quincey loathed, despite the fact that the novel's persecuted—and persecuting—hero shared a surname with his favorite murderer), Brockden Brown's *Wieland,* Wordsworth's *Borderers,* Coleridge's *Remorse,* Shelley's "Assassins" and *The Cenci,* Byron's *Lara* and *Cain,* Hogg's *Confessions of a Justified Sinner;* all offer themselves as a legitimate genealogy. Yet, following Steiner's point about Romantic tragedy, crime is often rationalized in these works, sometimes as a form of intellectual error (as in the case of Rivers in "The Borderers," whose misdeeds are strengthened by "the habit of picturing possible forms of society where his crimes would be no longer crimes" [*WPW* 1:346]), or as a result of social misconditioning. In both these categories, remorse places crime within a moral framework and works out a therapeutics of redemption for the criminal.

33. John Barrell, *The Infection of Thomas De Quincey: A Psychopathology of Imperialism* (New Haven: Yale University Press, 1991), 127.

34. Black, *The Aesthetics of Murder,* 46.

35. Michael Rossington, "'The voice which is contagion to the world': The Bacchic in Shelley," in *Beyond Romanticism: New Approaches to Texts and Contexts, 1780–1832,* ed. Stephen Copley and John Whale (London: Routledge, 1992), 113. For further discussion of Shelley and De Quincey's orientalism, see my *British Romantic Writers and the East,* chs. 2 and 3.

36. "On the Principles of Poetry" (*C Lects 1808–19* 1:52).

37. René Wellek, "De Quincey's Status in the History of Ideas," *Philological Quarterly* 23 (1944):260.

38. For De Quincey's narratives of "trauma" and "restoration," see Barrell, *Infection,* 22 and passim.

39. J. Hillis Miller, *The Disappearance of God: Five Nineteenth-Century Writers* (Cambridge, Mass.: Harvard University Press, 1975).

40. A. W. Schlegel, *A Course of Lectures on Dramatic Art and Literature* (1808–9), trans. J. Black, 2 vols. (London, 1840), 1:48.

41. Ibid., 1:68–70.

42. Ibid., 1:75.

43. Sigmund Freud, *Totem and Taboo,* in *Standard Edition of the Complete Psychological Works,* gen. ed. John Strachey, 23 vols. (London: Hogarth Press, 1953–56), 13:155–56. "In the remote reality it had actually been the members of the Chorus who caused the hero's suffering; now, however, they exhausted themselves with sympathy and regret and it was the Hero himself who was responsible for his own suffering" (156).

44. *Posthumous Works,* 1:9.

45. Ibid., 1:12.

46. The "Postscript" was first published in *Selections Grave and Gay,* an anthology of his past writings in which De Quincey evidently found himself at last free of the constraining magazine context and able to experiment with a new, and more ambitious, mode of address.

47. A. S. Plumtree, "The Artist as Murderer: De Quincey's Essay 'On Murder Considered as one of the Fine Arts,'" in Snyder, ed., *De Quincey Bicentenary Studies,* 155.

48. Black, *The Aesthetics of Murder,* 61–62.

49. Ibid., 62.

50. Ibid., 70.

51. Arthur Goldman, *The Mine and the Mint: Sources for the Writings of Thomas De Quincey* (Carbondale: Southern Illinois University Press, 1986), 140.

52. Ibid., 152.

53. "Philosophy of Murder," 175, 174.

54. Ibid., 173, 175.

55. McDonagh, "Do or Die," 131.

56. "Philosophy of Murder," 175; italics mine.

57. Randall McGowan, "Punishing Violence, Sentencing Crime," in Armstrong and Tennenhouse, eds., *The Violence of Representation,* 152.

58. Ibid., 167.

59. Quoted in Lindop, *Opium Eater,* 345.

Drummond Bone
The Question of a European Romanticism

1. Jerome J. McGann's recent *The New Oxford Book of Romantic Period Verse* (London: Oxford University Press, 1993) both introduces and avoids this issue. There are at least two words in question. The adjective *romantic* first occurs in 1650 (Baldensperger, "'Romantique,' ses analogues et ses équivalents: Tableau synoptique de 1650 à 1810," *Harvard Studies and Notes in Philology and Literature* 19 (1937): 13–105). The *OED* gives the first occurrence of the noun *romanticism* in 1803 (in the plural), and in the sense of an aesthetic in 1844. The usage of *Romantik* in the sense of *Romanticism* in Germany seems to date from around 1802, but the adjective remained much commoner in usage. (See Hans Eichner, "Germany/Romantisch—Romantik—Romantiker," in Eichner, ed., *"Romantic" and Its Cognates: The European History of a Word* [Manchester: Manchester University Press, 1972], 143; hereafter, Eichner, *Romantic.* George Whalley's chapter therein on English usage [157–262] is still authoritative and I have made considerable use of it here.) In France the adjective *romantique* seems to be taking on its broad aesthetic sense by 1804, when Senancour can in *Obermann* equate it with "la véritable sensibilité," but the noun arrives from German only in about 1816. It is of course the noun which raises the specter of a substance to the heterogeneous qualities. The debate on the Platonic or otherwise quality of the term goes back at least to A. O. Lovejoy's "On the Discrimination of Romanticisms," *PMLA* 39(1924): 229–53.

2. The terms *particular* and *individual* occur frequently in this chapter. Some have felt that my usage is imprecise; the trouble is indeed that in this discourse the usage is necessarily saturated in imprecision. What is seen by one person as an "individual" is for another a particularity, and anything but a singularity. From some points of view one cannot be an individual (person) without being a particularity. There is an inbuilt ambiguity that stems precisely from the kline-bottle inversions of individual and Universal with which the period was beset. Slippage from one term to another is likely to be freighted with metaphysical baggage.

3. Leaving aside the introduction of the term, what are now commonly called Romantic movements covered a wide timespan, varying not only from country to country but from art to art. If it is reasonable to speak of a full-fledged literary Romanticism in Britain and Germany by the mid- to late 1790s (the beginnings of what was to become *The Prelude,* the writing of "Kubla Khan"; the rise of the Jena group around Fichte and the Schlegels), one can also extend that back to 1789 in Britain (Blake's *Songs of Innocence*), or even to 1766 in Germany (Lessing's *Laocoön*). In France Napoleonic censorship effectively suppressed the first generation of Romanticism (though there are Chateaubriand, Constant, de Staël), and the main phase is often taken as running roughly from Lamartine's *Méditations poétiques* of 1819 to Hugo's *Hernani* of 1830. On the other hand, the influence on Baudelaire of Poe (and, through Poe, Coleridge and his German predecessors) means that Symbolism has at least as much to do with what is recognized as Romanticism in other countries as does French Romanticism proper, and this would push the date on to 1857 *(Les Fleurs du Mal).* In Italy we might fix a starting date at 1807, when Alfieri's collected tragedies began to

appear in print. But in the other arts the doubts multiply. In Germany, Caspar David Friedrich is recognized from his winning a prize from Goethe, no less, in 1805; but Böcklin is still painting in the mid-1860s (and lives into the twentieth century). In France, if it is sensible (and normal) to think of Géricault (*The Raft of the Medusa,* 1819) and Delacroix (*Dante and Virgil in Hell,* 1822) as Romantic, it is normal but somehow less intuitively obvious to put David or Ingres (despite his *Dream of Ossian,* 1809) in the same box. Here we are surely tempted to think of the tradition of the natural moment as the "really" Romantic line, in which case we might even start with Corot around 1840, and see Impressionism as the high point of Romanticism—which in turn seems very odd if we think of the term *Romantic* as artists themselves applied it by the time of the first Impressionist exhibition (1874). Monet, for example, attacked Turner's "Romanticism," though *we* may well see him as a precursor of Impressionism. Turner's "Romanticism" is itself often dated from his painting of the fire at the Parliament buildings, and is at its height in the later 1820s and 30s, but there are many works of the first decade of the century which are more quietly "romantic." In music we might highlight Beethoven's *Eroica* symphony as a useful marker (1804), but the apogee of musical Romanticism is surely around Berlioz (*Symphonie Fantastique,* 1830–31), Liszt (*Faust Symphony,* 1854), and Wagner (*Tristan und Isolde,* 1859), which leaves it very late. Throughout all this one is bedeviled by the question of whether one accepts the terminology of sometimes warring artistic factions, or whether one "imposes" the term *Romantic* where it seems appropriate on formal or contextual grounds. The former often seems arbitrary to the point of silliness, but the latter clearly presupposes a criterion of appropriateness.

4. Eichner, *Romantic,* 18.

5. *C Lects 1808–19* 1:480; B.M. Add. MS 34225, fols. 167–67^{V}, transcribed ibid., 1:492–93.

6. Ibid., 1:492n, citing A. W. Schlegel, *Vorlesungen über dramatische Kunst und Litteratur* (Heidelberg: Mohr & Winter, 1809–11), 1:15–29. Delivered in Vienna in 1808, these immensely influential lectures were translated into English in 1815. Coleridge possessed the Heidelberg edition. See also note 13 below for Friedrich Schlegel's equally broad approach to taxonomy, first published in 1814 but in general terms known long before.

7. Coleridge annotated a copy of the *Athenaeum,* though not this entry, in 1817. See Eichner, *Romantic,* 203; and *CM* 1:131–53.

8. *Athenaeum* (1800), "Ideen" 60, 47. In many ways the Ideas internalize the universalism of the Aphorisms of the previous two volumes of the *Athenaeum.*

9. B. M. MS Egerton 2800, fols. 19–20, transcribed in *C Lects 1808–19* 1:46; fol. 46, transcribed ibid., 1:437, 439.

10. *Abrams ML,* 21–26 and passim.

11. Aphorism 128 in *Athenaeum* (1798). See Hans Eichner, ed., *Kritische Friedrich Schlegel Ausgabe* (Zurich: Verlag Ferdinand Schoningh, Thomas-Verlag, 1967), 2:185.

12. *De la littérature considerée dans ses rapports avec les institutions sociales* (1800) developed the Schlegelian ancient/modern and north/south distinctions. Suppressed by Napoleon's censors, *De L'Allemagne* added the Romantic/Classic dimension and was first published in London in 1813. It was translated almost

immediately, and reviewed extensively. Byron first notes the Romantic-Classical distinction (as a current debate in Italy) in the dedication to *Childe Harold* canto 4 (1818).

13. Byron often linked the Schlegel brothers to de Staël after he met August Wilhelm at Coppet. Their common love of the grand generalization could irritate, as Byron bears testy witness to in his comment on Friedrich Schlegel's *Lectures on the History of Literature: Ancient and Modern* (1814, translated 1818): "[H]e always seems upon the verge of meaning; and lo, he goes down like a sunset, or melts like a rainbow . . . . [H]e speaks of things *all over the world* with a kind of authority that a philosopher would disdain." Journal entry for 29 January 1821. *BLJ* 8:38.

14. Novalis (Friedrich von Hardenburg), *Die Christenheit oder Europa* (1799).

15. J. G. Fichte, *Reden an die Deutsche Nation,* 1808, translated R. F. Jones and G. H. Turnbull (New York: Harper Torchbooks, 1968). For the connection between National Socialism and German Romanticism the most interesting source is Thomas Mann's novel *Doktor Faustus* (Stockholm: Bermann Fischer Verlag, 1947; trans. Helen Lowe-Porter, New York: Alfred A. Knopf, 1948). See also G. L. Mosse, *The Crisis of German Ideology* (London: Weidenfeld & Nicholson, 1966), particularly 13–30; and G. Mann, *The History of Germany since 1789,* trans. Marion Jackson (London: Chatto & Windus, 1968), esp. pt. 10, sec. 4.

16. A particularly striking example of the slippage from individual to Universal can be found in the passage on shepherds in *W Prel* (1805) VIII. 375–416, which starts from a man breakfasting with his dog, and ends with a vision of him as elevated like a mountain crucifix, a Christ on the cross.

17. J. G. Fichte, *Wissenschaftslehre* (1794), trans. P. Heath and J. Lachs (Des Moines: Meredith Corp., 1970). His *Ichphilosophie* does not deserve the parodies it received from writers as early as Goethe and Schiller, though perhaps the ease with which it could be misused was significant for its later history.

18. The perversion of love into narcissism was a besetting fear and desire, and images of narcissism projected into incest frequent. It could either be seen as a liberation from the world, an in-gathering of the resources of self, or as an escapist retreat from the human duty to reach out to the world. The image of the Ideal as a mere projection of self flits around incestual themes in Byron and Shelley, for example, whereas Wagner in the *Ring of the Nibelungs* uses incest as a gathering of the powers of the individual against the established social order.

19. By the time he came to write *Nietzsche contra Wagner* (1888) the philosopher had made up his mind. His doubts, however, are recorded as early as 1874 when he was working on his fourth meditation, intended as a eulogy of the composer.

20. F. Schlegel, *Über die Sprache und Weisheit der Indier* (1808); translated in E. J. Millington, ed., *The Aesthetic and Miscellaneous Works of Friedrich von Schlegel* (London: Bohn, 1849), 425–526.

21. P. B. Shelley, *A Defence of Poetry,* 1820. *SW* 8:112. Quoted from D. Reiman and S. Powers, eds., *Shelley's Poetry and Prose* (New York: Norton, 1977), 483.

22. F. Schlegel, *Über die Unverständlichkeit* (1800). Translated ("On Incomprehensibility") by P. Firchow (Minneapolis: University of Minnesota Press, 1971).

23. "Epipsychidion," line 33; "Ode on a Grecian Urn," lines 11–12.

24. "Adonais," stanza 52; "Mont Blanc," lines 25–26.

25. F. Schlegel, "On Incomprehensibility"; for example, J. Derrida, *Grammatology,* part 1, section 1, "The Signifier and Truth," trans. G. Spivak (Baltimore: Johns Hopkins University Press, 1974), 10–18.

26. Coleridge, "This Lime Tree Bower My Prison," as published in 1800. In the MSS of 1797 the poem ended not with Charles Lamb himself, but with the whole group who had gone on the walk without the poet, "My Sara and my friends." The point is the same, however—the movement outside the self is still domestically personalized. The progression of "Tintern Abbey" has something of the same quality.

27. *The Marriage of Heaven and Hell,* plate 14: *BK* 154, *BE* 38.

28. *Waverley,* close of chapter 16.

29. Scott, along with "Ossian," was of course for many *the* Romantic writer. Particularly in Europe both played a significant part in the rise of nationalism (in Bohemia, for example, the idea of Ossian forgeries was entirely self-consciously copied in the service of Czech nationalism). There is a profound irony in Scott's role in creating the idea of the American South (so distasteful—at least for a while—to Twain), given that it is precisely this kind of conservative revolution built on illusory nostalgia which is attacked in such novels as *Waverley.*

30. Schubert's last collection (1828) pushed his restless modulation to new limits, or rather to new levels of haziness, notably in the misty seascape of "Die Stadt."

31. "[In the marriage of poetry and music] the poet's thought becomes an instinctively enthralling moment of feeling, just as the music's emotional power therein acquires the faculty of definite and convincing utterance . . . . the vindicated necessity of an endless-reaching content, condensed from its farthest branchings into an utmost definite utterance of feeling." From *Opera and Drama,* 1850–51, as quoted in A. Goldman and E. Sprinchorn, eds., *Wagner on Music and Drama* (London: Gollancz, 1970), 209.

32. As Goldman and Sprinchorn note rather nervously in their introduction (ibid., 20), "This tendency to overstep the traditional limits of the various art media is unquestionably a reflection of the Romantic sense of reality. . . . Seen from this perspective, Wagner's synthetic artwork appears as the ultimate endeavor totally to encompass Romantic reality." The *Gesamtkunstwerk* may be seen indeed as a late development of Friedrich Schlegel's notion of *Mischgedicht,* "a work universal in both form and content. . . . utilizing all forms of literature" (see Eichner, *Romantic,* 111).

33. E. A. Poe, in *The Poetic Principle,* for example: "And thus, when by Poetry—or when by Music, the most entrancing of the Poetic moods. . . ."; or E. T. A. Hoffmann (on Beethoven's *Eroica*): "Music is the most Romantic of all the arts . . . the *sole* purely Romantic one."

34. See, for example, Hans Aarsleff, *The Study of Language in England, 1780–1860* (Princeton: Princeton University Press, 1967; new edition Minneapolis: University of Minnesota Press, 1983); T. Webb, *The Violet in the Crucible* (Oxford: Clarendon Press, 1976); Susan Bassnett, *Translation Studies* (London: Methuen, 1980).

Susan J. Wolfson
Romanticism and the Question of Poetic Form

1. See Geoffrey H. Hartman, "Beyond Formalism" (1966), reprinted in *Beyond Formalism: Literary Essays, 1958–1970* (New Haven: Yale University Press, 1970), 42–57; the quotation is from *The Fate of Reading and Other Essays* (Chicago: University of Chicago Press, 1975), vii.

2. René Wellek's "Concepts of Form and Structure in Twentieth-Century Criticism" (1958) offers a cogent overview of these definitions in a wider European scope and in their descent from the nineteenth century. Reprinted in *Concepts of Criticism,* ed. Stephen G. Nichols Jr. (New Haven: Yale University Press, 1963), 54–68. Wellek attends not only to a shared "recognition of the inseparability and reciprocity of form and content" (55), but also to the "very different [practical] consequences . . . drawn from this insight" (56).

3. R. S. Crane, *The Languages of Criticism and the Structure of Poetry* (Toronto: University of Toronto Press, 1953), 153. References hereafter appear parenthetically.

4. W. K. Wimsatt, "The Domain of Criticism" (1950), in *The Verbal Icon: Studies in the Meaning of Poetry* (Lexington: University of Kentucky Press, 1954), 231.

5. I quote Mukařovský from two essays collected in *The Word and Verbal Art,* trans. and ed. John Burbank and Peter Steiner (New Haven: Yale University Press, 1977): "On Poetic Language," 23 and 4; and "Two Studies of Poetic Designation" (1938/1941), 68. With a sense of the cultural relativism in the Russian Formalist distinction of ordinary and artful language, Mukařovský shares with other members of the Prague Circle an interest in how "a certain social context" determines what gets called "aesthetic" *(Aesthetic Function, Norm, and Value as Social Facts* [1936], trans. Mark E. Suino [Ann Arbor: University of Michigan Press, 1970], 3).

6. Hartman, *The Fate of Reading,* vii.

7. Wellek and Warren, *Theory of Literature,* rev. ed. (1942; New York: Harcourt Brace, 1956), 137; references hereafter appear parenthetically.

8. Charles Kingsley, "Alexander Smith and Alexander Pope," *Fraser's Magazine* 48 (October 1853): 460.

9. I quote Arnold from "The Function of Criticism at the Present Time" (1864; *APrW* 3:264) and Preface to *Poems of Wordsworth* (London: Macmillan, 1879), xiv–xv.

10. A. C. Bradley, "Poetry for Poetry's Sake" (1901), in *Oxford Lectures on Poetry* (London: Macmillan, 1920): 3–27. References hereafter appear parenthetically.

11. Bradley's term was soon taken up and given a mystical, ahistorical twist by Clive Bell's designation of visual art as an aesthetic of "pure form" (in both senses of *pure*), as opposed to works in which it is "the ideas of information suggested or conveyed by their forms that affect us" (*Art* [1914; London: Chatto & Windus, 1927], 17). Supercharging Bradley's notion into an intuitively and subjectively validated, but nonetheless "universal and essential" aesthetic of "Significant Form" (8, 11, 36), Bell in effect overruled Bradley's equation to elevate form as the dominant signifier, the identification of which (in a turn on Arnold) must be "the function of criticism" (9): even if there is a referential aspect (i.e., "a representa-

tive form"), its value, Bell contended, will be "as form, not as representation. The representational element . . . is irrelevant" (20, 25).

12. Wellek and Warren, *Theory of Literature,* 139; their quotation is from Lee's inaugural lecture in *The Place of English Literature in the Modern University* (London, 1913); cited in *Theory,* 293 n1. Ransom's remark is from *The New Criticism* (Norfolk: New Directions, 1941), 3.

13. This last quotation is from Brooks's "The Formalist Critic," *Kenyon Review* 13 (1951):72. Parenthetical references in this paragraph are to *The Well Wrought Urn: Studies in the Structure of Poetry* (1947; reprint, New York: Harcourt Brace Jovanovich, 1975); references hereafter appear parenthetically.

14. The sociopolitical disparagement of formalism is a legacy of Russian antiformalist polemics. As Tony Bennett points out in *Formalism and Marxism* (London: Methuen, 1979), "Formalists" was not a self-description (they called themselves "Specifiers"), but "a pejorative label applied by their opponents in the turbulent critical arena of post-revolutionary [Stalinist] Russia" (18).

15. For representative distortions, see Culler's charge that "the New Criticism," in "distinguishing what was external in favor of internal analysis," rejected historical explanation *(The Pursuit of Signs: Semiotics, Literature, Deconstruction* [Ithaca: Cornell University Press, 1981], 4), and Paul A. Bové's contention that both New Criticism and deconstruction are "radically anti-historicist" ("Variations on Authority: Some Deconstructive Transformations of the New Criticism," in *The Yale Critics: Deconstruction in America,* ed. Jonathan Arac, Wlad Godzich, and Wallace Martin [Minneapolis: University of Minnesota Press, 1983], 4).

16. One of Brooks's graduate students at Yale, my colleague Larry Danson, reports that in his seminars with Brooks the first half of the term was spent reading historical background, biography, and literary history, the second half reading the poetry. While the curriculum was not dialectical, it was also not exclusionary. As for the charge of mere technique: New Criticism was not really a technical formalism, at least in the Russian mode. As Wellek notes, it paid "little attention to what is traditionally called the form of a poem," focusing on the "psychological" organization of poetic structure, its orchestration of "tones, tensions, irony, and paradox" ("The New Criticism: Pro and Contra," *Critical Inquiry* 4 [1978]: 618). Although New Critics tended to describe this structure as "poetry's form," that they saw it reflecting "the structure of imagination itself" virtually conflated it with content, as Robert Con Davis and Ronald Schleifer remark in *Contemporary Literary Criticism: Literary and Cultural Studies,* 2d ed. (New York: Longman, 1989), 21.

17. Jerome McGann, "Keats and the Historical Method in Literary Criticism" (1979), in *The Beauty of Inflections: Literary Investigations in Historical Method and Theory* (Oxford: Clarendon, 1988), 22–23.

18. Karl Marx and Friedrich Engels, *Selected Works,* 2 vols. (London: Lawrence & Wishart, 1950), 1:328–29. I quote McGann in this sentence from *The Romantic Ideology: A Critical Investigation* (Chicago: University of Chicago Press, 1983), 3.

19. McGann, "Keats and the Historical Method," 12–14.

20. De Man, *Allegories of Reading: Figural Language in Rousseau, Nietzsche, Rilke, and Proust* (New Haven: Yale University Press, 1979), 249.

21. I refer to the famous essay by W. K. Wimsatt and Monroe Beardsley, "The Intentional Fallacy" (1956), in *The Verbal Icon,* 3.

22. De Man, "Form and Intent in the American New Criticism," in *Blindness and Insight: Essays in the Rhetoric of Contemporary Criticism,* rev. ed. (Minneapolis: University of Minnesota Press, 1983), 31 and 29.

23. I quote de Man from "Form and Intent" (32) and "The Dead-End of Formalist Criticism" (also from *Blindness and Insight* [230]). De Man's deconstruction, Tilottama Rajan remarks, was to read New Critical formalism "as a form of desire enmeshed in its own de-realization" and to emphasize "the radical difference between linguistic and organic structures" ("Displacing Post-Structuralism: Romantic Studies after Paul de Man," *Studies in Romanticism* 24 [1985]: 454). If de Man was thereby reading his own methodological desire as a subtext of New Criticism, a certain historical irony attends this affinity, for in a later turn, he voices their desires, with a touching tone of self-consciousness. In the preface to *The Rhetoric of Romanticism,* an anthology initiated by Columbia University Press (New York, 1984), he confesses "misgivings" over the "fragmentary aspect of the whole" collection—its failure, in effect, to be New-Critical enough as a critical artifact: "[The] apparent coherence *within* each essay is not matched by a corresponding coherence *between* them. . . . [T]hey do not evolve in a manner that easily allows for . . . historical totalization" (viii). De Man is aware that this result may be allied to "the historical study of romanticism itself" (ix).

24. The quotation is from "The Dead-End of Formalist Criticism," 232. In a later essay, de Man elaborates this application in sympathy with the aims of political critique, arguing that attention to "the linguistics of literariness is a powerful and indispensable tool in the unmasking of ideological aberrations, as well as . . . in accounting for their occurrence" ("The Resistance to Theory," *Yale French Studies* 63 [1982]: 11). In another late essay, "Aesthetic Formalization: Kleist's *Über das Marionettentheater" (The Rhetoric of Romanticism,* 263–90), he offers the sort of critique that interests historicist readers. For a sympathetic discussion of the political critique of aesthetic ideology in these essays, see Christopher Norris, *Paul de Man: Deconstruction and the Critique of Aesthetic Ideology* (New York: Routledge, 1988), 62–63, 116–24.

25. I quote Eagleton from "Ideology and Literary Form," in *Criticism and Ideology: A Study in Marxist Literary Theory* (1976; reprint, London: Verso, 1978), 129, 124–25.

26. I quote this last phrase from Eagleton's recent reflection on critical trends in his introduction to *The Ideology of the Aesthetic* (London: Basil Blackwell, 1990), where he is "glad to observe a certain unexpected convergence" between his analyses and de Man's later writing: "A valuable, resourceful politics is undoubtedly at work here, *pace* those left-wing critics for whom de Man is merely an unregenerate 'formalist'" (9–10).

27. Wimsatt and Beardsley, "The Intentional Fallacy," 6.

28. Fredric Jameson, *The Prison-House of Language: A Critical Account of Structuralism and Russian Formalism* (Princeton: Princeton University Press, 1972), 46.

29. The phrase is from "Dejection: An Ode," l. 86. The first legacy is clear in

Brooks's case for "the structure of a poem as an organism" (*The Well Wrought Urn,* 218) and in Elizabeth Nitchie's assertion, in 1957, that "surely form itself is good only if it is organically unified with content" ("Form in Romantic Poetry," in *The Major English Romantic Poets: A Symposium in Reappraisal,* ed. Clarence D. Thorpe, Carlos Baker, and Bennett Weaver [Carbondale: Southern Illinois University Press, 1957], 4). Crane emphasizes aesthetic agency in this project: in attempting to account for the way form operates in actual poetic composition (as opposed to theory), he complains that there is "nowhere present in [contemporary critical language] any means for dealing precisely and particularly with what *I shall call the forming principle or immediate shaping cause* of structure in individual poems" (140, my emphasis); as in Brooks, or Wellek and Warren, Coleridgean language appears, but in this case the debt is blatantly suppressed.

30. Brooks is quoted from "The Artistry of Keats," in Thorpe, Baker, and Weaver, eds., *The Major English Romantic Poets,* 251.

31. Jonathan Culler, "The Mirror Stage," in *High Romantic Argument: Essays for M. H. Abrams,* ed. Lawrence Lipking (Ithaca: Cornell University Press, 1981), 149. References hereafter appear parenthetically.

32. I have in mind as examples of the form-attentive Romantic studies of these decades W. J. Bate's *The Stylistic Development of Keats* (New York: MLA, 1945) and *John Keats* (Cambridge, Mass.: Harvard University Press, 1963), Stuart M. Sperry's *Keats the Poet* (Princeton: Princeton University Press, 1973), Earl R. Wasserman's *Shelley: A Critical Reading* (Baltimore: Johns Hopkins Press, 1971), Paul D. Sheats's *The Making of Wordsworth's Poetry, 1785–1798* (Cambridge, Mass.: Harvard University Press, 1973), David Ferry's *The Limits of Mortality: An Essay on Wordsworth's Major Poems* (Middletown, Conn.: Wesleyan University Press, 1959), Stephen Maxfield Parrish's *The Art of the "Lyrical Ballads"* (Cambridge, Mass.: Harvard University Press, 1973); and David Perkins's *The Quest for Permanence: The Symbolism of Wordsworth, Shelley, and Keats* (Cambridge, Mass: Harvard University Press, 1959).

33. Christopher Norris, *Deconstruction: Theory and Practice* (New York: Methuen, 1982), 116.

34. Northrop Frye, *Anatomy of Criticism: Four Essays* (1957; reprint, New York: Atheneum, 1970), 74, 352–53.

35. Hartman is quoted from *Criticism in the Wilderness: The Study of Literature Today* (New Haven: Yale University Press, 1980), 89–90, and *Wordsworth's Poetry, 1787–1814* (1964; reprint, New Haven: Yale University Press, 1975), xxi, xii, and 11.

36. Bloom is quoted, in order, from *The Anxiety of Influence: A Theory of Poetry* (New York: Oxford University Press, 1973), 11–12, and "The Breaking of Form," in *Deconstruction and Criticism* (New York: Seabury Press, 1979), 1. Hartman is quoted from *The Fate of Reading* (52); Lentricchia's remark is from *After the New Criticism* (Chicago: University of Chicago Press, 1980), 350.

37. De Man, "The Intentional Structure of the Romantic Image," in *The Rhetoric of Romanticism,* 6.

38. Hartman, *Easy Pieces* (New York: Columbia University Press, 1985), 190.

39. Eagleton, *Literary Theory: An Introduction* (Minneapolis: University of Minnesota Press, 1983), 19–20, 21.

40. Eagleton, "Ideology and Literary Form," in *Criticism and Ideology,* 103–4.

41. See, for instance, Jameson's description of Marx's dialectics of social process: "Here form is regarded not as the initial pattern or mold . . . but rather as . . . the final articulation of the deeper logic of the content itself" (*Marxism and Form: Twentieth-Century Dialectical Theories of Literature* [Princeton: Princeton University Press, 1971], 328–29)—an echo of the German and Coleridgean aesthetics of "organic" form realizing itself as it develops from within, in contrast to the *a priori* mechanic imposition from without.

42. Hartman, *The Fate of Reading,* 125.

43. In "Coleridge on Wordsworth and the Form of Poetry," Simpson argues that the organic aesthetic not only compensates for these material conditions; it tactically opposes mechanic form's display of "the signs of its own construction" and "the details of its own coming into being." Organic aesthetics are thus complicit with privilege-protecting political theories, such as Burke's, that represent "a contrived or constructed paradigm" as "innate," disguising "human agency as spontaneous evolution" (*Coleridge's Theory of Imagination Today,* ed. Christine Gallant [New York: AMS Press, 1989], 214–16).

44. The quotation in this sentence is from McGann, *The Romantic Ideology,* 134. Both he and Levinson cite Pierre Macherey's *A Theory of Literary Production (Pour une théorie de la production littéraire* [Paris, 1966]), trans. Geoffrey Wall (London: Routledge and Kegan Paul, 1978). With Etienne Balibar, Macherey elaborates this argument, training the question on the aesthetic structure of "realist" fiction ("On Literature as an Ideological Form: Some Marxist Propositions," trans. Ian McLeod, John Whitehead, and Ann Wordsworth, *Oxford Literary Review* 3 [1978]: 4–12). As Catherine Belsey paraphrases this argument, "the unconscious of the work is constructed in the moment of its entry into literary form. . . . [T]he text is a bearer of ideological meaning, but only in so far as literary form permits the production of meaning" (*Critical Practice* [London: Methuen, 1980], 134). McGann's representative and most influential critiques focus on book 1 of *The Excursion (Romantic Ideology)* and "To Autumn" (in *Beauty of Inflections*); Levinson's treat "Tintern Abbey," "Peele Castle," the "Immortality Ode," and "Michael" (*Wordsworth's Great Period Poems: Four Essays* [Cambridge: Cambridge University Press, 1986]).

45. McGann, ibid.; Levinson, ibid., 9–11, 4, 1, 10 (her italics).

46. I discuss my reservations about these tendencies more fully in "Questioning 'The Romantic Ideology,'" *Revue Internationale de Philosophie* 44 (1990): 429–47; compatible views are given by Peter J. Manning, "Placing Poor Susan: Wordsworth and the New Historicism" (1986), in *Reading Romantics: Texts and Contexts* (New York: Oxford University Press, 1990), 300–320, and David Simpson, *Wordsworth's Historical Imagination: The Poetry of Displacement* (London: Methuen, 1987), 14–15.

47. Donald Wesling, *The Chances of Rhyme: Device and Modernity* (Berkeley: University of California Press, 1980), 2.

48. Dryden, *Of Dramatick Poesie, An Essay* (1668), in *The Works of John Dryden,* 19 vols., ed. H. T. Swedenberg Jr. (Berkeley: University of California Press, 1961–79); vol. 17, ed. Samuel Holt Monk (1971), 79. Wordsworth is quoted

from the prefaces of 1800 (*WPrW* 1:126) and 1815 (*WPrW* 3:35). References to *Lyrical Ballads,* where not in *WPrW,* are to the edition of R. L. Brett and A. R. Jones, *"Lyrical Ballads": The text of the 1798 Edition with the Additional 1800 Poems and the Prefaces* (1968; reprint, London: Methuen, 1971).

49. German Romantic theory tends to be concerned less with techniques of poetic form than with the value of poetry as the expressive form for a metaphysics of perpetual flux, infinite possibility, and inclusiveness. The specific "form does not matter," argues Friedrich von Schlegel (*Athenäums-Fragment* #259), for genuine "romantic" poetry, "more than any other art form" aspires to, even embodies, "a state of becoming . . . never to be perfected" (#116); quotations follow *Critical Fragments from The Athenaeum 1798–1800,* trans. Peter Firchow, *Friedrich Schlegel's "Lucinde" and the "Fragments"* (Minneapolis: University of Minnesota Press, 1971). On this scale, the "artificial or natural products which bear the form and name of poems" contrast with "the unformed and unconscious poetry" to be tapped in the spiritual energies that inhabit and animate this flux (*"Dialogue on Poetry" and "Literary Aphorisms,"* trans. Ernst Behler and Roman Struc [University Park: Pennsylvania State University Press, 1968], 53–54).

This metaphysics, as we might expect, favors both an aesthetic of incompletion and the self-critical forms of "artistically arranged confusion," "chaotic form," and *"fantastische Form"* (Hans Eichner, *Friedrich Schlegel* [New York: Twayne, 1970], 64, 66–67). Yet none of these terms, Eichner argues, denotes "genuine confusion"; rather they describe "the semblance of chaos, tempered by an underlying order" (68–69). Alice A. Kuzniar (*Delayed Endings: Nonclosure in Novalis and Hölderlin* [Athens: University of Georgia Press, 1987]) proposes that the German Romantic "mistrust" of "the schematization offered by a philosophy of history, a teleology, or the myth of organicism . . . almost approaches a systemization in itself. Schlegel . . . writes of 'künstlich geordnete Verwirrung' [artistically staged disorder] and furthermore states that the highest order is that of chaos" (49). Walter Benjamin contends that the Romantic ideal of the absolute infinitude of art involves "the articulation of a medium understood to consist of a 'continuum of forms'" (Samuel Weber, "Criticism Underway: Walter Benjamin's *Romantic Concept of Criticism,*" in *Romantic Revolutions: Criticism and Theory,* ed. Kenneth R. Johnston, et al. [Bloomington: Indiana University Press, 1990], 312–13). Benjamin calls this an "irony of form," deriving from the fact that "all art is 'subordinated' to the 'objective lawfulness' of a certain formality; this irony thus 'attacks' the 'illusoriness' of the form of a work" but does not abandon form (Weber, 314, quoting Benjamin). For discussions of Schlegel's aesthetics, see chapter 3 of Eichner's study and, in relation to English Romanticism, Anne Mellor's *English Romantic Irony* (Cambridge, Mass.: Harvard University Press, 1980), 3–12.

50. William Hazlitt, "On the Living Poets" (Lecture 8 of *Lectures on the English Poets* [1818]); *HW* 5:161–62.

51. In addition to Blake's "London," I refer to *Jerusalem,* ch. 1, plate 10:20 (quotations follow *BE*).

52. Shelley, *A Defence of Poetry* (*SW* 7:137). References hereafter appear parenthetically.

53. Wesling, in fact, speaks of Romanticism's modernity as a "'laying bare,' in

the Russian Formalist sense as ironic exposure, of all the central Augustan devices" (*The Chances of Rhyme,* 10); Wellek and Warren comment briefly on this affinity (242).

54. The usual line on Russian Formalism—following Medvedev/Bakhtin (*The Formal Method in Literary Scholarship: A Critical Introduction to Sociological Poetics* [1928])—is that the movement is either apolitical or reactionary in sustaining an ideology of the aesthetic that refused reference to social reality. But Viktor Shklovsky (a leading voice of Russian Formalism) was willing to say, in Russia in 1921, that any writer willing to assault the familiar with a "violation of form" was an "extreme revolutionary" ("Sterne's *Tristram Shandy*" [1921], trans. Lee T. Lemon and Marion J. Reis, in *Russian Formalist Criticism: Four Essays* [Lincoln: University of Nebraska Press, 1965], 30–31); I agree with Tony Bennett that in "the actual conduct of their criticism," the Russian Formalists were not so "apolitical, ahistorical or asociological . . . as the stereotype would have us believe" (*Formalism and Marxism,* 29).

55. The references to Jeremiah 5:21 and Isaiah 6:10 are given by Bate and Engell (*CBL* 2:7, note 2).

56. See Cyrus Hamlin, "The Hermeneutics of Form: Reading the Romantic Ode," *boundary 2* 7, no. 3 (Spring 1979): 1–30, and J. Hillis Miller's discussion of the conflicting senses of the word *form* in classical poetics ("The Still Heart: Poetic Form in Wordsworth," *New Literary History* 2 [1971]: 295–310).

57. I take this description from Vernon Shetley, who observes "the New Formalist faith in the power of traditional poetic forms to give valid shape to subjectivity" (*After the Death of Poetry: Poetry and Audience in Contemporary America* [Durham: Duke University Press, 1993], 20).

58. Allen Tate, *Reason in Madness* (New York: G. P. Putnam's Sons, 1941), 110; Frost, "The Craft of Poetry" (1959), in *Interviews with Robert Frost,* ed. Edward Connery Lathem (New York: Holt, Rinehart & Winston, 1966), 203; Yeats, "A General Introduction to My Work," in *Essays and Introductions* (London: Macmillan, 1961), 522.

59. Coleridge, "On the Principles of Genial Criticism. Essay Third" (reprinted in *"Biographia Literaria," by S. T. Coleridge. With his Aesthetical Essays,* ed. John Shawcross, 2 vols. [1907; London: Oxford University Press, 1967], 238).

60. For a discussion of the various meanings and historical permutations conveyed by the words *formalist, form,* and *formalism,* see Raymond Williams's *Keywords: A Vocabulary of Culture and Society,* rev. ed. (New York: Oxford University Press, 1983), 138–40. Crane gives specific attention to the way notions of form have been mobilized in the first decade of postwar criticism by, among others, Brooks, Wellek and Warren, Leavis, and Bateson (*Languages of Criticism,* 92).

61. "Shelley's poetics everywhere resolves itself into the problems and consequences of integral form," remarks Wasserman (*Shelley: A Critical Reading,* 208); and he goes on to discuss Shelley's uncertain effort to negotiate the claim for poetic form as universal and eternal against its ties to historical conditions and values (208–10). William Keach's *Shelley's Style* (London: Methuen, 1984) provides a splendid account of the shifting attitudes to be traced, both in *A Defence* and in Shelley's poetic practice, toward the formal commitments and material

medium of poetry. I owe to him my reference to the first of Wordsworth's comments (from "Conversations and Reminiscences recorded by the Bishop of Lincoln [Christopher Wordsworth], in *The Prose Works of William Wordsworth,* ed. Grosart [1876], 3:458–67). The second comment is reported by E. J. Trelawny (*Recollections of the Last Days of Shelley and Byron* [Boston: Ticknor & Fields, 1858]) at the end of his first chapter (p. 14).

62. Antony Easthope, *Poetry as Discourse* (London: Methuen, 1983), 123 and 23. With a curious sense of this issue as "conventionally left unproblematized" (23), Easthope bluntly defines "English bourgeois poetic tradition . . . precisely as a regime of representation aiming to disavow enunciation so as to promote . . . the effect of an individual voice 'really' speaking by concealing the way it is produced as an effect" (46).

63. Quoted by Parrish, *The Art of the "Lyrical Ballads,"* 183.

64. "The Enquirer. No. VI. Is Verse Essential to Poetry?" (*Monthly Magazine* 2 [1796]:455). W. J. B. Owen and J. W. Smyser cite and quote briefly from this essay in their commentary on the Preface to *Lyrical Ballads* and identify the author as William Enfield (*WPrW* 1:173–74). Further references to this essay appear parenthetically.

65. According to Kenneth MacLean (*Agrarian Age: A Background for Wordsworth* [1950; reprint, Hamden, Conn.: Archon, 1970]), almost two and a half million acres were enclosed in the last four decades (14). For statistics as well as a discussion of the controversy, especially of the impact of enclosure on the unpropertied laborer, see pp. 12–26.

66. For a fuller discussion of how Romantic theory and practice contended with the problem of meter, see my "Romanticism and the Measures of Meter" (*Eighteenth Century Life* 16, n. s. 3 [1992]:221–46).

67. Quotation of Keats's poetry follows *John Keats,* ed. Elizabeth Cook (New York: Oxford University Press, 1990). Miriam Allott claims that the chief sense of "organic" by Keats's day was "organ-like" (*The Poems of Keats* [London: Longman, 1970], 293n), but Keats's sense would surely would have involved "organic form," a term used by Coleridge in his lectures on Shakespeare (1812–13), and "organic sensibility," the capacity that Wordsworth's Preface to *Lyrical Ballads* claimed in abundance for the poet (*WPrW* 1:126). Owen and Smyser (*WPrW* 1:170, note on line 132) remark that the latter means "belonging to or inherent in the organization of constitution of a living being," and Wordsworth equated it with the poet's "mechanically" enacted habits of mind. Even so, his use of *organic* for aesthetic production effectively reverses the older sense of *organic* as synonymous with *mechanic* as "done by means of instruments, mechanical" *(OED).* The oscillation of senses in Keats's phrase shows how, as Raymond Williams writes, "earlier and later senses . . . become actual alternatives in which problems of contemporary belief and affiliation are contested" (*Keywords,* 22); for an account of these developments and their implications for social discourse, see pp. 227–29.

68. In *Institutio Oratoria* (IX.i. 10–11), Quintilian reflects this ambivalence in describing the verbal "figure" as both a *forma sententia* (the form in which "thought is expressed") and a formal *schema* (a reforming of language from its ordinary or simple form); he joins these senses in designating figure as "a form of

expression to which a new aspect is given by art." Quotations follow the translation of H. E. Butler, 4 vols., Loeb Classical Library, 1921 (Cambridge, Mass.: Harvard University Press, 1966), 3:353. Wordsworth's library included Quintilian (Owen and Smyser cite the Rydal Mount Catalogue [*WPrW* 1:176, note on lines 328–30]).

69. See Milton's headnote on "The Verse" for the second edition of *Paradise Lost* (1674), in *Complete Poems and Major Prose,* ed. Merritt Y. Hughes (1962; reprint, New York: Macmillan, 1985), 4. Dryden's terms are from his dedicatory epistle to *The Rival Ladies* (1664; in *Works* [edition cited], 8:99) and *Essay of Dramatick Poesie* (1668; in *Works,* 17:66–67, 71–72).

70. Dryden, ibid. Byron is quoted in *Medwin's "Conversations of Lord Byron,"* ed. Ernest J. Lovell Jr. (Princeton: Princeton University Press, 1966), 236. While Dr. Johnson insisted that poetry could not just be verse to the eye but had to keep its distinction from prose "by the artifice of rhyme" ("Milton," in *Lives of the English Poets* [1783], ed. George Birbeck Hill, 3 vols. [Oxford: Clarendon Press, 1905], 1:192), Dryden suggested that even heroic couplets could be "rendered as near Prose" by using hemistiches, enjambments, and variety of cadence (*Essay,* in *Works,* 17:70). Thomas Sheridan's *Dictionary* thus insists on a "different manner" of recitation for verse and prose "to distinguish the one from the other" ("Of the Recitation of Poetic Numbers," in *A Complete Dictionary of the English Language, Both with regard to Sound and Meaning,* 3rd ed., 2 vols. [London: Charles Dilly, 1789], 1:lxxx); Kames agreed: for the ear to "distinguish verse from prose . . . there must be a musical pause at the end of every line; but . . . so slight as not to require a pause in the sense" (*Elements of Criticism by Henry Home, Lord Kames* [1762], ed. Abraham Mills [New York: Mason Bros., 1857], 289, 316). Blair's *Lectures* (1783) wavered: "On the Stage, where the appearance of speaking in verse should always be avoided, . . . the close of such lines as make no pause in the sense, should not be rendered perceptible to the ear. But on other occasions, this were improper: for what . . . end has the Poet composed in verse, if in reading his lines, we suppress his numbers; and degrade them, by our Pronunciation, into mere prose? We ought, therefore, certainly to read blank verse so as to make every line sensible to the ear" (ed. Harold F. Harding, 2 vols. [Carbondale: Southern Illinois University Press, 1965], 2:215). John Walker's opinion was a distinct minority: conceding that Sheridan's advice is approved by "Dr. Lowth, Mr. Garrick, and Dr. Johnson," he argues that to pause "where the sense does not require it" is artificial, for blank verse is often just "numerous or harmonious prose" ("Rules for Reading Verse," in *Elements of Elocution* [1781] 3d ed. [London: J. Johnson et al., 1806], 253n and 255); even Kames called Shakespeare's dramatic blank verse "a sort of measured prose" [317]).

For alerting me to some of these texts, I am indebted to David Perkins's resourceful essay "How the Romantics Recited Poetry," *Studies in English Literature* 31 (1991):655–71, esp. 663–64. Despite this history of self-consciousness about blank verse, Easthope reductively argues that pentameter suppresses "recognition of the work of metric *production*—and so of the poem as constructed artifice . . . in favour of a notion of the poem as spontaneously generated *product*"; it is "a mechanism by which the poem aims to deny its production" (*Poetry as Discourse,* 67).

71. Miller, "The Still Heart," 298–99; Miller views this deconstruction of form and substance as a shadowy legacy of Western metaphysics, registering with particular critical intensity on Romantic poetry, where the problem of form is not only thematized but is given to a figurative subversion of mimetic reference.

72. Easthope, *Poetry as Discourse,* 123; Eagleton, "Marxism and Aesthetic Ideology," in *Criticism and Ideology,* 187 and 180.

73. MS. V [3r]:67–80; *"The Prelude": 1798–1799,* by William Wordsworth, ed. Stephen Parrish (Ithaca: Cornell University Press, 1977).

74. The structure, in a way that Wordsworth's later sonnet writing would develop, avoids the standard pattern, here composed in units of 10½/3½; the only rhyme (a shadow of a summary couplet) is the faint harmony of "ministry" and "I" in the final two lines; and the cadence is not uniformly iambic or even pentameter. Wordsworth's sonnetlike verse paragraph reflects a habit of discerning such forms embedded in *Paradise Lost,* identifying some "fine fourteen lines," Henry Crabb Robinson reports, as "a perfect sonnet without rhyme" (*Henry Crabb Robinson on Books and Their Writers,* ed. Edith J. Morely, 3 vols. [London: J. M. Dent & Sons, 1938], 2:484). Donald H. Reiman offers the interesting suggestion that Wordsworth's eventual expansion of his autobiography to fourteen books was a conscious modeling of the poem as a "macro-sonnet" (*Romantic Texts and Contexts* [Columbia: University of Missouri Press, 1988], 227–29; *Intervals of Inspiration: The Skeptical Tradition and the Psychology of Romanticism* [Greenwood, Fla: Penkevill, 1988], 200–207). But if so, it is more likely that he was troping the blank-verse sonnets embedded in the epic than, as Reiman argues, the Italian form. Reiman's scheming of *The Prelude* into quatrains, octave, tercets, and sestet, is resourceful but, for me, unconvincing: not only are the divisions he demarcates overdetermined, but the obedience to the Italian form jars with Wordsworth's own resistance to the model: he disliked "the Italian mode" of "uniformly closing the sense with a full stop and of giving a turn to the thought in the terzines" and preferred Milton's way of "let[ting] the thought run over" (Robinson, ed. Morely 2:485). In the "better half" of Milton's sonnets, he observes, "the sense does not close with the rhyme at the eighth line, but overflows into the second portion of the metre"; it is the "pervading sense of intense Unity," rather than in its "architecture" of "parts," in which "the excellence of the Sonnet has always seemed to me mainly to consist" (*WL 1828–34* 2:604–5).

75. Karen Swann offers a shrewd analysis of the formalism of Wordsworthian subjectivity in the narratives rendered in Spenserian stanzas by the characters of *Adventures on Salisbury Plain.* The conspicuous formalism of the stanza, she argues, both "make[s] legible that which inhabits subjectivity as something foreign, archaic, and received" and, at the same time, and alternately, signifies a literary field "which the subject inhabits as figure or trope" ("Public Transport: Adventuring on Wordsworth's Salisbury Plain," *ELH* 55 [1988], 819).

76. In developing this essay, I have benefited from the generous attentions of Ronald Levao, John Beer, William Galperin, Peter Manning, William Keach, and Garrett Stewart.

Tilottama Rajan
Phenomenology and Romantic Theory

1. Although there were obviously other kinds of theory in the Romantic period, for the sake of convenience I shall use the term *Romantic theory* to designate only artistic and literary theory.

2. G. W. F. Hegel, *Aesthetics: Lectures on Fine Art,* trans. T. M. Knox, 2 vols. (Oxford: Clarendon Press, 1975), 1:77. References to this work (abbreviated as *HA*) will hereafter be provided in the text.

3. For further discussion of this point, see Tilottama Rajan, *The Supplement of Reading: Figures of Understanding in Romantic Theory and Practice* (Ithaca: Cornell University Press, 1990), 46, 91, 168–70, 280–81.

4. I refer in particular to Michel Foucault, "Nietzsche, Genealogy, History," in *Language, Counter-memory, Practice: Selected Essays and Interviews,* trans. Donald F. Bouchard and Sherry Simon (Ithaca: Cornell University Press, 1977), 139–64; Paul de Man, *Allegories of Reading: Figural Language in Rousseau, Nietzsche, Rilke, and Proust* (New Haven: Yale University Press, 1979); Jacques Derrida, *Spurs: Nietzsche's Styles,* trans. Barbara Harlow (Chicago: University of Chicago Press, 1979).

5. For instance Derrida, "The Pit and the Pyramid: Introduction to Hegel's Semiology," in *Margins of Philosophy,* trans. Alan Bass (Chicago: University of Chicago Press, 1982), 69–108; de Man, "Sign and Symbol in Hegel's *Aesthetics,*" *Critical Inquiry* 8 (1982): 761–75.

6. Alexandre Kojéve, *Introduction to the Reading of Hegel,* ed. Allan Bloom, trans. James H. Nichols (New York: Basic Books, 1969); Jean Hyppolite, *Genesis and Structure of Hegel's "Phenomenology of Spirit,"* trans. Samuel Cherniak and John Heckman (Evanston: Northwestern University Press, 1974).

7. Henry Sussman, *The Hegelian Aftermath: Readings in Hegel, Kierkegaard, Freud, Proust* (Baltimore: Johns Hopkins University Press, 1982); Sylviane Agacinski, *Aparte: Conceptions and Deaths of Søren Kierkegaard* (Gainesville: University Presses of Florida, 1988).

8. Jacques Derrida, *Positions,* trans. Alan Bass (Chicago: University of Chicago Press, 1981), 31.

9. Ibid., 28.

10. See Rajan, *Supplement of Reading,* 36–45, 81–98.

11. Slavoj Zizek, *The Sublime Object of Ideology* (London: Verso, 1989), 205–6.

12. This use of the concept of negativity is still present in the "phenomenological" reader-response theory of Wolfgang Iser. Iser is concerned with the role of the text as negativity in a process of self-understanding or "Bildung" displaced from Hegel's "world-historical spirit" to the individual reader.

13. David Wellbery, *Lessing's Laocoön: Semiotics and Aesthetics in the Age of Reason* (Cambridge: Cambridge University Press, 1984), 2–7, 44–47.

14. Friedrich von Schiller, *Naive and Sentimental Poetry,* in *Naive and Sentimental Poetry and On the Sublime,* trans. Julius A. Elias (New York: Frederick Ungar, 1966), 98.

15. Ibid., 125.

16. Stanley Corngold, "Nietzsche's Moods," *Studies in Romanticism* 29 (1990): 72.

17. Stanley Corngold, *The Fate of the Self: German Writers and French Theory* (New York: Columbia University Press, 1986), 210, 215.

18. German references are to "Uber naive und sentimentalische Dichtung," in *Schillers Werke in zwei Bänden,* vol. 2 (Munich: Knaur Klassiker, 1962), 656, 663, 669, 655, 651. Schiller also sometimes uses the word *Denkart* to characterize the naive and the sentimental (648, 651).

19. F. W. J. Schelling, *Philosophie der Kunst* (1802): see below, note 25. The naive, as the unity of sign and experience, is the equivalent of what Schelling calls the symbolic, while the sentimental would be the equivalent of the allegorical.

20. Wellbery, *Lessing's Laocoön,* 43–44.

21. Michael Podro, *The Critical Historians of Art* (New Haven: Yale University Press, 1982), xxiii, 104.

22. Wellbery, *Lessing's Laocoön,* 2.

23. It is important to remember that Hegel does not use the word *symbolic* in the same way as Goethe, Coleridge, Schelling, and more recently, de Man. The "symbolic" for Hegel is what Goethe calls the "allegorical," and Hegel does in fact use these two terms synonymously (*HA* 1:312).

24. D. A. Miller, *Narrative and Its Discontents: Problems of Closure in the Traditional Novel* (Princeton: Princeton University Press, 1981), ix–x.

25. Schelling's lectures were published only posthumously in 1859, but were delivered during 1802–3, and were certainly known to Hegel. All subsequent references will be to F. W. J. Schelling, *The Philosophy of Art,* ed. and trans. Douglas W. Stott (Minneapolis: University of Minnesota Press, 1989), which will be given in parentheses in the text as *ScP.*

26. While schematism dwells in the universal and can construct only in the abstract, and while allegory devalues the particular by reducing it to the sign of an Idea to which it can only point, the symbolic is "the synthesis of these two" (*ScP* 46). As the presence of the particular and the universal within each other, the symbolic marks the Idea's achievement of "historical significance" along with the informing of historical particulars with the universal significance that makes them "symbolic" rather than random (152).

27. Other forms are grouped around this point of balance as imperfect forms of the symbolic. Thus in his appropriation of Schiller's distinction between the naive and the sentimental, Schelling reduces the latter to an imperfect mode of the former, depriving it of any autonomous existence except as an imperfect form of the naive (*ScP* 91–92).

28. Philippe Lacoue-Labarthe and Jean-Luc Nancy, *The Literary Absolute: The Theory of Literature in German Romanticism,* trans. Philip Barnard and Cheryl Lester (Albany: SUNY Press, 1988).

29. "God" is sometimes Schelling's name for the absolute. See the "Translator's Introduction" by Douglas Stott in *The Philosophy of Art* (xxii).

30. Dominick LaCapra, *A Preface to Sartre* (Ithaca: Cornell University Press, 1978), 153–58.

31. Judith Butler, *Subjects of Desire: Hegelian Reflections in Twentieth-Century France* (New York: Columbia University Press, 1987), 186.

32. Hyppolite, *Genesis and Structure,* 166.

33. Søren Kierkegaard, *The Concept of Irony,* trans. Lee M. Capel (1965; reprint Bloomington: Indiana University Press, 1971), 242n.

34. See, for instance, *Positions,* 25.

35. Fredric Jameson, *The Political Unconscious: Narrative as a Socially Symbolic Act* (Ithaca: Cornell University Press, 1981), 41, 56.

36. I use this term in the same way as Jameson uses the term "Althusserian exegesis": neither Hegel nor Althusser actually provide exegeses of individual texts, and any account of Hegelian exegesis is therefore an extrapolation from his larger analysis of artistic modes.

37. Jameson, *The Political Unconscious,* 242.

Frederick Burwick
The Romantic Concept of Mimesis

1. Preface to the *Poems* 1815, in *WPrW* 3:26; the editors call attention to a similar emphasis on observation and description in the Preface to *Lyrical Ballads* (1800), 1:132; and the Essay, Supplementary to the Preface (1815), 3:73.

2. 18 January 1816; *WL 1812–29* 276.

3. Plotinus, *Enneads,* trans. A. H. Armstrong, Loeb Classical Library, 7 vols. (Cambridge, Mass.: Harvard University Press, 1967–84).

4. Oddone Longo, "The Theater of the *Polis,*" in *Nothing to Do with Dionysos? Athenian Drama in Its Social Context,* ed. John J. Winkler and Froma I. Zeitlin (Princeton: Princeton University Press, 1990), 12–19.

5. Göran Sörbom, *Mimesis and Art: Studies in the Irugun and Earlz Development of an Aesthetic Vocabulary* (Stockholm: Svenska Bokförlaget Bonniers, 1966), 146.

6. Eva Keuls, *Plato and Greek Painting,* Columbia Studies in the Classical Tradition, vol. 5 (Leiden: E. J. Brill, 1978), 24; Hermann Koller, *Die Mimesis in der Antike: Nachahmung, Darstellung, Ausdruck* (Bern: Francke, 1953), 7; Harald Feldmann, *Mimesis und Wirklichkeit* (Munich: Fink, 1988), 11–12; Ulrike Zimbrich, *Mimesis bei Platon* (Frankfurt: Peter Lang, 1984), 22.

7. Plato, *The Collected Dialogues,* ed. Edith Hamilton and Huntington Cairns (Princeton: Princeton University Press, 1961), 467–68.

8. Edith Watson Schipper, "Mimesis in the Arts in Plato's Laws," *Journal of Aesthetics and Art Criticism* 22, no. 2 (1963): 199–202.

9. Aristotle, *The Complete Works,* ed. Jonathan Barnes, 2 vols. (Princeton: Princeton University Press, 1984).

10. Thomas Lehnerer, *Die Kunsttheorie Friedrich Schleiermachers* (Stuttgart: Klett-Cotta, 1987), 169–77.

11. "Vorlesungen über die Ästhetik," ed. C. Lommatzsch, in *Friedrich Schleiermacher's Sämtliche Werke,* ed. L. Jonas, H. Schweizer et al., 31 vols. (Berlin, 1834–64), III Abt. Zur Philosophie, 7:25–86. Parenthetical references, by page number only, are from this edition. I have also consulted: Schleiermacher, *Ästhetik (1819/25): Über den Begriff der Kunst (1831/32),* ed. Thomas Lehnerer (Hamburg: Felix Meiner, 1984). Lehnerer, *Die Kunsttheorie Friedrich Schleiermachers,* 169–87, provides an excellent account of the dialectics of identity and difference.

12. Samuel Johnson, *Rasselas,* ch. 10: the business of the poet is to observe general nature, not to "number the streaks of the tulip." Preface to Shakespeare: "Nothing can please many and please long but just representations of general nature." *Works of Samuel Johnson,* 16 vols. (Cambridge. Mass.: Harvard Cooperative Society; New York: Bigelow, Smith & Co., 1912), 7:38; 11:328.

13. Schleiermacher, "Vorlesungen über die Ästhetik," 54: "Warum kann man also die Sache nicht umkehren und sagen, das Denken trägt noch die nationale Differenz in sich, wenngleich noch Identisches darüber liegt; und warum könnte man es nicht auch mit der Kunst umkehren und sagen, sie ist im allgemeinen identisch, aber sie differenziert sich in der Wirklichkeit? und wenn man es so umkehren kann, so ist der Gegensatz nicht festgehalten, sondern aufgehoben; die Differenz besteht, aber sie ist nichts, wonach man die Tätigkeit teilen kann."

14. Ibid., 60–61: "Fragen wir, warum sind die Bewegungen eines Zornigen z. B. nicht ebensogut ein Kunstwerk, wie wenn ein Zorniger auf der Bühne dargestellt wird, so ergibt sich, die Bewegungen des Zornigen halten kein Maß, und deswegen sind sie unschön; denn daß was gemessen sei, ist die ursprüngliche Forderung an das Kunstwerk. Allerdings gibt es etwas im Menschen, was wir durch Grazie bezeichnen, un wenn ein Mensch, der eine natürliche Grazie hat, wirklich zornig wird, so werden seine Bewegungen nie so unschön werden, als wie bei andern; aber tragen seine Bewegungen den Charakter des Vorherbewußten und Gemessenen, und machen sie so den Eindruck der Kunst, so werden wir sagen, er sei nicht mehr der Zornige, sondern das äußere Bild eines Zornigen sein in ihm erst innerlich geworden, und also eine Besinnung dazwischen getreten, die diese Bewegung hemmt, der Zornige an sich hat diese Hemmung nicht."

15. Lehnerer, *Die Kunsttheorie Friedrich Schleiermachers,* 214–29.

16. Georg Wilhelm Friedrich Hegel, "Vorrede," *Phänomenologie des Geistes,* in *Werke,* ed. Eva Moldenhauer and Karl Markus Michel, 20 vols. (Frankfurt: Suhrkamp, 1970), 3:36.

17. *Ginza: Der Schatz oder das Grosse Buch der Mandäer,* ed. and trans. M. Lidzbarski (Göttingen, 1925), 173.

18. Werner Beierwaltes, *Identität und Differenz* (Frankfurt: Vittorio Klostermann, 1980), 241–68.

19. Hegel, *Vorlesungen über die Ästhetik,* in *Werke,* 13:60: "Denn der Geist sucht im Sinnlichen des Kunstwerks weder die konkrete Materiatur, die empirische innere Vollständigkeit und Ausbreitung des Organismus, welche die Begierde verlangt, noch den allgemeinen, nur ideellen Gedanken, sondern er will sinnliche Gegenwart, die zwar sinnlich bleiben, aber ebensosehr von dem Gerüste seiner bloßen Materialität befreit werden soll. Deshalb ist das Sinnliche im Kunstwerk im Vergleich mit dem unmittelbaren Dasein der Naturdinge zum bloßen *Schein* erhoben, und das Kunstwerk steht in der *Mitte* zwischen der unmittelbaren Sinnlichkeit und dem ideelen Gedanken."

20. Ibid., 13:63: "Die Phantasie hat eine Weise zugleich instinktartiger Produktion, indem die wesentliche Bildlichkeit und Sinnlichkeit des Kunstwerks subjektiv im Künstler als Naturanlage und Naturtrieb vorhanden und als bewußtloses Wirken auch der Naturseite des Menschen angehören muß."

21. G. E. R. Lloyd, *Polarity and Analogy: Two Types of Argumentation in Early Greek Thought* (Cambridge: Cambridge University Press, 1966), 431–34.

22. Heidegger, *Platons Lehre von der Wahrheit,* 76: "Doch das Sein—was ist das Sein? Es ist Es selbst. Dies zu erfahren und zu sagen, muß das künftige Denken lernen. Das 'Sein'—das ist nicht Gott und nicht ein Weltgrund." Among the alterations from the fourth to the fifth edition of *Was ist Metaphysik?,* Heidegger's statement "daß das Sein *wohl* west ohne das Seiende" becomes "daß das Sein *nie* west ohne das Seienende." Beierwaltes, who cites both passages, presumes that the later version did suspend the postulate of "Sein als 'Es selbst,'" *Identität und Differenz,* 141.

23. Nicolaus Cusanus, *De Genesi,* 146, §4; "Diversum esse sibi ipsi idem," 146, §2; "Omnis enim diversitas in ipso est identitas," 142, §6; "Omnis identificatio reperitur in assimilatione. Vocat igitur idem non-idem in idem," 149, §8–9. See also the response to Proclus in Nicolaus Cusanus, *Directio speculantis seu De no aliud,* in *Opera omnia.* Issu et auctoriatate Academiae Litterarum Heidelbergensis ad codem fidem edita, 17 vols. (in 24) (1932– ; reprint and completion, Hamburg: Felix Meiner, 1959–88).

24. Marcus Fabius Quintilian, *Institutionis Oratoriae: Liber Decimus,* ed. W. Peterson (1891; reprint, Hildesheim: Georg Olms, 1967), 122–35.

25. Frederick Burwick, "Coleridge and the 'Heaven-Descended Know Thyself,'" in *Biographia Literaria: Text and Meaning,* ed. F. Burwick (Columbus: Ohio State University Press, 1988), 127–37.

26. I thank Thomas McFarland for sharing with me his extensive annotations and commentary to his forthcoming edition of the *Opus Maximum* for *The Collected Works of Samuel Taylor Coleridge.*

27. In addition to *Philonis Iudæi Opera,* ed. Thomas Mangey, 2 vols. (London: William Bowyer, 1742), which gave the Greek and Latin texts in parallel columns, Coleridge may have been familiar with earlier Latin versions. Because all but fragments of the Greek text of Philo's *Quaestionum et solutionum in Genesin* had been lost, it had been published only from Latin transcription. Early editions were *Philonis Judaei quaestiones centum et duae, et totidem responsiones morales super Genesin,* ed. August Justinian (1520); *Philonis Iudaei Alexandrini, libri antiquitatum,* ed. J. Sichardus (1527); *Philonis Judaei quaestionum et solutionum in Genesim liber* (1538).

28. Thomas McFarland, *Coleridge and the Pantheist Tradition* (Oxford: Clarendon Press, 1969), 240–41; see also 209, 226, 237, 360, 372–74.

29. Nicolaus Cusanus, *De Genesi,* 147; 149, 2; 150, 7; *De Coniecturis,* I, 9.39.2–3; I, 11.57.11–12; *Directio speculantis seu De non aliud,* 6; 14, 13–15; 19; 47, 9–10. See Beierwaltes, *Identität und Differenz,* 118–20; Beierwaltes, "Deus oppositio oppositorum," *Salzburger Jahrbuch für Philosophie* 8(1964): 175–88.

30. See Howard L. Goodhart and Erwin R. Goodenough, "A General Bibliography of Philo Judaeus," in *The Politics of Philo Judaeus* (New Haven: Yale University Press, 1938), 125–348; on editions in Greek, 187–97; in Latin, 198–201.

31. Thomas Billings, *The Platonism of Philo Judaeus* (Chicago: University of Chicago Press, 1919), 1–12, dates the first questioning of Philo as authority for Christian doctrine from Dionysius Petavius, *Opera de theologicis dogmatibus* (1644). Rather than accepting him within the Christian patrologia, following the *Historia ecclesiae* of Eusebius, scholars of the seventeenth century emphasized his

Platonism: Cudworth, *The True Intellectual System of the Universe* (1678); Fabricius, *De Platonismo Philonis Judaei* (1693).

32. Richard Kidder, "The Testimony of Philo the Jew concerning the Holy Trinity, and the λόγος considered," in *Demonstration of the Messias* (London, 1700); Stephen Nye, "An Account of the Opinions and Books of Philo Judaeus, more especially, concerning the Λόγος or Word," in *Doctrine of the Holy Trinity* (London, 1701), 58–98; Johannes Benedictus Carpzov, *De* λόγῳ *Philonois, non Iohanneo adversus Thomam. Mangey* (Helmstadt, 1749); Christopher Friedrich Loesner, *Observationes ad Novum Testamentum e Philone Alexandrino* (Leipzig, 1777); Jacob Bryant, *The Sentiments of Philo Judaeus concerning the* Λόγος, *or Word of God; together with large extracts from his writings, compared with the Scriptures, on many other particular and essential doctrines of the Christian religion* (Cambridge, 1797); Heinrich Christan Ballenstedt, *Philo und Johannes, oder fortgesetzte Anwendung des Philo zur Interpretation der Johanneischen Schriften, mit besonderer Hinsicht auf die Frage: Ob Johannes der Verfasser der ihm zugeschriebenen Bücher seyn könne?* (Göttingen, 1812).

33. Elinor S. Shaffer, *"Kubla Khan" and "The Fall of Jerusalem": The Mythological School in Biblical Criticism and Secular Literature, 1770–1880* (Cambridge: Cambridge University Press, 1975), 71.

34. "Essay on Faith," in *The Complete Works of Samuel Taylor Coleridge,* ed. W. G. T. Shedd, 7 vols. (New York: Harper, 1853–54), 5:563.

35. *On the Constitution of the Church and State,* ed. J. Colmer. CC 10:84–85.

36. On Philo's allegorical method, see Emile Bréhier, *Les idées philosophiques et religieuses de Philon d'Alexandrie,* 3d ed. (Paris: Librairie philosophique J. Vrin, 1950), 35–66; Max Heinze, *Die Lehre vom Logos* (Oldenburg, 1872), 204–98; Henry Austyn Wolfson, *Philo: Foundations of Religious Philosophy in Judaism, Christianity, and Islam* (Cambridge, Mass.: Harvard University Press, 1947), 1:115–38.

37. *Philonis Alexandrini Opera quae supersunt,* ed. Leopold Cohn and Paul Wedekind, 5 vols. (Berlin: de Gruyter, 1896–1906), 1:7, *De Opificio Mundi,* §22: τάξιν, ποιότητα, ἐμψυχίαν, ὁμοιότητα, ταυτότητα, τὸ εὐάρμοστον, τὸ σύμφωνον πᾶν ὅσον τῆς κρείττονος ἰδέας; 4:292, *De Decalogo,* §104: τὴν γοῦν ἐν ὁμοιῳ ταυτότητα. σῴζοντα δολιχεύει τὸν αἰῶνα μηδεμίαν ἐνδεχομενα τροπὴν καὶ μεταβολήν.

38. *Philonis Alexandrini Opera,* 5:252, De Specialibus Legibus. Liber IV (De Iustitia), §187.

39. *CBL* 2:16–17. In their note to Coleridge's statement on the "reconciliation of opposites," Engell and Bate cite Schelling's *Abhandlungen zur Erläuterung des Idealismus:* "der Begriff von Materie [geht] *ursprünglich* aus einer Synthesis entgegengesetzter Kräfte durch die Einbildungskraft [hervor]"; they add that "C's concept of the aesthetic as the balance of 'opposites' (especially of 'self-possession' and 'enthusiasm,' and of power and play with control) is indebted to German critical thinking generally after Kant and particularly to Schiller's *AE*" (= *Ästhetische Erziehung*).

40. Schelling, *Über das Verhältnis der bildende Künste zu der Natur* (Landshut: Universitätsbuchhandler Philipp Krull, 1807), in *Sämmtliche Werke,* ed. Karl Friedrich August Schelling, 14 vols. (Stuttgart: J. G. Cotta, 1856–61), 7:311.

41. Beierwaltes, *Identität und Differenz,* 93–95, 183–84, 230–32; Billings, *The Platonism of Philo,* 26–46; Bréhier, *Les idées philosophiques et religieuses de Philon,* 112–57; Wolfson, *Philo,* 1:360–412.

42. Kant, *Kritik der Urteilskraft,* §14, in *Werke,* ed. Wilhelm Weischedel, 6 vols. (Darmstadt: Wissenschaftliche Buchgesellschaft, 1975), 5:303–6; Jacques Derrida, *The Truth in Painting,* trans. Geoff Bennington and Ian McLeod (Chicago: University of Chicago Press, 1987), 63–64.

43. Lessing, *Laokoon: oder, über die Grenzen der Malerei und Dichtung,* in *Werke,* ed. Herbert Göpfert et al. (Munich: Carl Hanser, 1979), 6:50–51; the sculpturesque and picturesque become metaphors for the differences between the classical and the modern: Jean Paul, *Werke,* ed. Norbert Miller, 9 vols. (Munich: Carl Hanser, 1960–85), 5:71, 83, 87, 90, 221, 289–93; A. W. Schlegel, *Vorlesungen über dramatische Kunst und Literatur,* in *Kritische Schriften und Briefe,* ed. Edgar Lohner, 7 vols. (Stuttgart: Kohlhammer, 1965–74), 2:ii, 15–16; *C Lects 1808–19* 1:348–49, 368; 2:439; *DQW* 10:315, 350–59; 11:303; 13:118.

44. Lessing, *Laokoon,* in *Werke,* 6:56–57: "Man ahmet nach, um ähnlich zu werden; kann man aber ähnlich werden, wenn man über die Not verändert? Vielmehr, wenn man dieses tut, ist der Vorsatz klar, daß man nicht ähnlich werden wollen, daß man also nicht nachgeahmet habe."

45. Billings, *The Platonism of Philo Judaeus,* 26. Julius Elias, *Plato's Defence of Poetry* (Albany: State University of New York Press, 1984), studies Plato's reliance on myth, his advocacy of basic myths of eschatology, cosmology, love and the soul, the origins and ideals of the state, as well as his reliance on methodological myths in his theory of forms, memory, and consciousness.

46. De Quincey, who may well have adapted the example of the waxwork figures directly from Coleridge, repeats it in his account of the *idem in alio* in "Conversation and S. T. Coleridge," in *The Posthumous Works of Thomas De Quincey,* ed. Alexander H. Japp, 2 vols. (London: Heinemann, 1891), 2:96.

47. *W Prel* IV.247–614; VIII.711–41, discussed also by Lucy Newlyn in her chapter below.

Lucy Newlyn
"Questionable Shape"

Portions of this chapter appear in a different form in my book *"Paradise Lost" and the Romantic Reader* (Oxford: Oxford University Press, 1993).

1. *Paradise Lost* II. 666–72. All references are to Alastair Fowler's edition (London: Longmans, Green, 1968). References hereafter appear in the text.

2. Edmund Burke, *A Philosophical Enquiry into the Origin of Our Ideas of the Sublime and Beautiful,* ed. J. T. Boulton (1958; reprint, Oxford: Oxford University Press, 1990), 59; abbreviated hereafter as *Enquiry.*

3. See "The Sublime and the Avant-Garde," in *The Lyotard Reader,* ed. Andrew Benjamin (Oxford: Oxford University Press, 1989), 204.

4. Ibid.

5. Ibid; my emphasis.

6. Thomas Docherty, *On Modern Authority: The Theory and Condition of Writing, 1500 to the Present Day* (Brighton: Harvester, 1987), 132.

7. Augustine, *City of God,* trans. Henry Bettenson (Harmondsworth: Penguin, 1972), 519–20.

8. See ll. 1–4 of "A Valediction, Forbidding Mourning." Evidence for the persistence of the Augustinian argument is provided by Docherty, *On Modern Authority,* 131–64.

9. Ibid., 132.

10. The *Oxford English Dictionary* lists, among others, the following meanings: 1. "of a person: that may be interrogated, of whom questions may be asked;" 2. "of persons or acts: liable to be called to account *(obsolete)*"; 3. "of things, facts: that may be questioned or called into question;" 4. "of qualities, properties etc: about the existence or presence of which there may be question;" 5. "of doubtful nature, character or quality; dubious in respect of goodness, respectability, etc."

11. In his essay on the "unheimlich," Freud argues that each of us has been through an individual phase of development that corresponds to "the animistic stage in primitive men," and that we preserve "certain residues and traces of it which are still capable of manifesting themselves." The uncanny "fulfils the condition of touching those residues of mental activity within us and bringing them to expression." See Sigmund Freud, *Art and Literature,* in the Pelican Freud Library (Harmondsworth: Penguin, 1985), 14:363.

12. *The Republic,* trans., H. P. Lee (Harmondsworth: Penguin, 1955), 278–86.

13. See, for instance, Coleridge's "The Destiny of Nations," ll. 18–23: *CPW* 1:132.

14. "And I saw, and behold a white horse: and he that sat on him had a bow; and a crown was given unto him: and he went forth conquering, and to conquer."

15. The oedipal implications of this Shakespearian echo have been discussed by, among others, Jonathan Wordsworth, *William Wordsworth: The Borders of Vision* (Oxford: Oxford University Press, 1982), 63; David Ellis, *Wordsworth, Freud, and the Spots of Time* (Cambridge: Cambridge University Press, 1985), 17–34; and Jonathan Bate, *Shakespeare and the English Romantic Imagination* (Oxford: Oxford University Press, 1986), 116.

16. T. S. Eliot, *Little Gidding* (1942), II. 42, reprinted in *Collected Poems, 1909–1962* (1936; reprint, London: Faber & Faber, 1963).

17. Roland Barthes, "The Death of the Author," included in David Lodge, ed., *Modern Criticism and Theory: A Reader* (London: Longman, 1988), 172.

18. See Thomas Weiskel, *The Romantic Sublime: Studies in the Structure and Psychology of Transcendence* (Baltimore: Johns Hopkins University Press, 1976), 83–106.

19. The relevant meanings are recorded in the *Oxford English Dictionary* as follows: *finish* (noun), 2b: "The last coat of paint or plaster laid upon a surface"; and *finish* (verb), 4: "to perfect finally or in detail; to put the final and completing touches to." I thank Tim Fulford for clarifying this.

20. Immanuel Kant, *The Critique of Judgement,* trans., with analytical indexes, J. C. Meredith (1952; reprint, Oxford: Oxford University Press, 1978), 92.

21. *Milton,* ed. William Cowper, 4 vols. (Chichester, 1810), 2:453.

22. Bishop Lowth, *Lectures on the Sacred Poetry of the Hebrews,* 2 vols. (London, 1787), 1:169.

23. "Some degree of obscurity is the necessary attendant upon prophecy," Lowth claims; and "a part of the future" must inevitably be repressed or witheld from the reader (ibid., 200).

24. According to Jerome McGann, "the polemic of Romantic poetry . . . is that it will not be polemical; its doctrine, that it is non-doctrinal; and its ideology, that it transcends ideology"; see *The Romantic Ideology: A Critical Investigation* (Chicago: University of Chicago Press, 1983), 1.

25. "Lectures to the London Philosophical Society," lecture 7 (9 December 1811), in *C Lects 1808–19* 1:311.

26. Ibid., 201.

27. John Locke, *An Essay Concerning Human Understanding,* ed. P. H. Nidditch (Oxford: Oxford University Press, 1975), 136.

28. *C Lects 1808–19* 1:311.

29. Lowth, *Lectures* 1:353.

30. Ibid., 1:264–65.

31. There is a possibility that Shelley's use of "substance" and "shadow" metaphors may allude to Milton's Death.

32. This is a paradoxical development, given that it was an age which produced dictionaries, and was preoccupied by the idea of Adamic language. Nonetheless, see Tilottama Rajan, *The Supplement of Reading: Figures of Understanding in Romantic Theory and Practice* (Ithaca: Cornell University Press, 1990), 20–21.

33. For a reading of the spoof-letter which restores unity to *Biographia* by examining it in terms of "Romantic Irony," see K. M. Wheeler, *Sources, Processes and Methods in Coleridge's "Biographia Literaria"* (Cambridge: Cambridge University Press, 1980), 98–106; and for a skeptical dismissal of "ironic" approaches, see Paul Hamilton, *Coleridge's Poetics* (Oxford: Blackwell, 1983), 20.

34. Rajan, *Supplement of Reading,* 25.

35. Rajan is right to claim that the *Biographia* is "not just Coleridge's theory of imagination, but a theory of how to read that theory" (ibid., 104).

36. For general works connecting Coleridge with hermeneutics, see Elinor Shaffer, *"Kubla Khan" and "The Fall of Jerusalem": The Mythological School in Biblical Criticism and Secular Literature, 1770–1880* (Cambridge: Cambridge University Press, 1975); Jean-Pierre Mileur, *Vision and Revision: Coleridge's Art of Immanence* (Berkeley: University of California Press, 1982); and A. J. Harding, *Coleridge and the Inspired Word* (Montreal and Kingston: McGill-Queen's University Press, 1985). For more specialized work on the application of hermeneutic approaches to *Biographia Literaria,* see Wheeler, *Sources, Processes and Methods in Coleridge's "Biographia Literaria";* Jerome Christensen, *Coleridge's Blessed Machine of Language* (Ithaca: Cornell University Press, 1981); and Elinor Shaffer, "The Hermeneutic Community: Coleridge and Schleiermacher," in *The Coleridge Connection: Essays for Thomas McFarland,* ed. R. Gravil and M. Lefebure (Basingstoke: Macmillan, 1990).

37. From the fragment known as "In Storm and Tempest," ll. 15–20; text in J. Wordsworth, *The Music of Humanity* (London: Nelson, 1969), 172–73.

38. Kant, *Critique of Judgement,* 101. To take a Lowthian example, we cannot say *how* God is infinite.

39. Ibid., 108. For a full analysis of this Kantian phenomenon, see Neil Hertz, "The Notion of Blockage in the Literature of the Sublime," in *The End of the Line* (New York: Columbia University Press, 1985), 40–60.

40. As the editors of the Norton *Prelude* (New York: Norton, 1979) point out, the allusion is to *Aeneid* VI.454; and Milton uses a similar trope in *Paradise Lost* I. 783–84.

41. Mary Jacobus argues that the Cave of Yordas lines "had to be excised" from book 6 because they "too nakedly revealed the condition of *The Prelude* as the lifelessness of a written book." See *Romanticism, Writing, and Sexual Difference: Essays on "The Prelude"* (Oxford: Oxford University Press, 1989), 16.

42. Tzvetan Todorov argues, in "Reading as Construction," that "a text always contains within itself directions for its own consumption." See *The Reader in the Text: Essays on Audience and Interpretation,* ed. Susan R. Suleiman and Inge Crosman (Princeton: Princeton University Press, 1980), 77.

43. The problems Wordsworth faces, in attempting to secularize hermeneutic practice, are similar to those identified by Tilottama Rajan in Coleridge's "Conversation Poems." There is an uneasiness in "translating a traditional hermeneutic protected by its association with the Bible into a secular context whose psychological and social complexities are harder to ignore": see *Supplement of Reading,* 101.

44. Wordsworth refers to Burke's most celebrated example of "judicious obscurity." But this passage is also to be seen in the wider context of anti-Lockean epistemology. For the Enlightenment's association of "Wit" or "fancy" with insanity, see Wolfgang Iser, *Laurence Sterne: Tristram Shandy* (Cambridge: Cambridge University Press, 1988), 1–54; and Michel Foucault, *The Order of Things: An Archaeology of the Human Sciences* (1970; reprint, London: Routledge, 1989), 23–24, 49–51.

45. Umberto Eco, *The Role of the Reader: Explorations in the Semiotics of Texts* (Bloomington: Indiana University Press, 1979), 50. Eco has consistently attempted to restrain "unlimited semiosis" by the scientific analysis of codes. In a recent publication, he restates his intention to uncover "the dialectics between the rights of texts and the rights of their interpreters," and voices an anxiety that "in the course of the last decades, the rights of the interpreters have been overstressed." See *Interpretation and Over-interpretation,* ed. Stefan Collini (Cambridge: Cambridge University Press, 1992), 23. A similar anxiety may be implied in Wolfgang Iser's inconsistent approach to plurality of interpretation: as Susan Suleiman points out, his "theoretical description of the reading process allows for a great deal more latitude in individual realization than does his actual critical practice" (*Reader in the Text,* 24).

46. Tilottama Rajan traces the transitional status of the reader at a time when logocentric assumptions were beginning to be eroded. She claims that "in transforming the reader from recipient to supplement, the author renounces his authority over the reader." Yet, as she points out, hermeneutics plays a crucial historical role at this period, as "conserver of a continued though problematical logocentric impulse in Romanticism"; see *Supplement of Reading,* 2, 29.

47. Despite their evident differences, both Shakespeare and Milton have become "metaphorically sacred in the course of their reception." This gives their

texts a kind of invulnerable mystery—a mystery Eco associates with hermetic and gnostic traditions of secrecy (*Interpretation and Over-interpretation,* 23–66).

48. The difference between "heuristic" and "hermeneutic" reading practices is that the former renounces the closure of the sign: see Rajan, *Supplement of Reading,* 33.

49. I have analyzed the reception of Milton's indeterminacies at considerable length in *"Paradise Lost" and the Romantic Reader.*

50. According to Rajan, Coleridge asks us "to treat writers as sources of inspiration if not of revelation, and thus to credit them with an authority to which the reader must remain sympathetically subordinate" (*Supplement of Reading,* 102). This description applies equally well to Wordsworth, as my discussion of his narratorial method in *The Prelude* has shown.

51. In this respect, allusions to Milton may be more genuinely "critical" than formal essays about him. Harold Bloom bases his theory of the "anxiety of influence" on the belief that poetic rivalry caused Milton's successors to "misread" him in radically creative ways. He posits a system of "revisionary ratios," which can be read as both rhetorical tropes and defense mechanisms, marking the extent of the Romantics' divergence from their "strong precursor." See *The Anxiety of Influence: A Theory of Poetry* (Oxford: Oxford University Press, 1973) and *A Map of Misreading* (Oxford: Oxford University Press, 1975).

52. Charles Lamb, "On the Tragedies of Shakespeare, considered with reference to their fitness for stage representation," in *Lamb as Critic,* ed. Roy Park (London: Routledge & Kegan Paul, 1980), 86.

53. See Hugh Grady, *The Modernist Shakespeare: Critical Texts in a Material World* (Oxford: Oxford University Press, 1991), 36–37.

54. Charles Lamb, "Oxford in the Vacation," *London Magazine* 3 (October 1820): 367; in *The Romantics on Milton,* ed. Joseph A. Wittreich (Cleveland: Press of Case Western Reserve University, 1970), 298.

55. Thomas McFarland, in *Romanticism and the Forms of Ruin: Wordsworth, Coleridge, and Modalities of Fragmentation* (Princeton: Princeton University Press, 1981), concentrates on the "diasparactive" as an existential condition; while Marjorie Levinson, in *The Romantic Fragment Poem: A Critique of a Form* (Chapel Hill: University of North Carolina Press, 1986), argues for the "RFP" as a form which sustains its own generic coherence through observable reception mechanisms. Both are implicitly concerned with the ways in which Romantic writers evaluate the unfinished; but in neither case is there an attempt to define indeterminacy as an aesthetic criterion, nor to observe the uses to which it is put by Romantic writers as readers.

56. The *Cornell Wordsworth* series offers the most obvious recent example in the field of English Romantic studies.

57. I refer not just to indeterminate postmodernist texts, but to strategies of demystification (at their most extreme in the work of Jacques Derrida and Paul de Man) which have provoked intense hostility among those of a liberal humanist persuasion. M. H. Abrams, for instance, characterizes the text as it is seen by deconstructionists as "a sealed echo-chamber in which meanings are reduced to a ceaseless echolalia, a vertical and lateral reverberation from sign to sign of ghostly non-presence emanating from no voice, intended by no one, referring to nothing,

bombinating in a void." See "The Deconstructive Angel," *Critical Inquiry* 3 (1977): 431. I thank Christopher Butler for his comments on my chapter.

John Beer
Fragmentations and Ironies

1. For a justification of this assertion see Laurence Lipking, "The Genie in the Lamp," in *High Romantic Argument: Essays for M. H. Abrams*, ed. Geoffrey Hartman et al. (Ithaca: Cornell University Press, 1981), 136–38.

2. Richard Price, *A discourse on the Love of our Country, delivered on 4 November 1789 . . . to the Society for Commemorating the Revolution in Great Britain* (London, 1789); Edmund Burke, *Reflections on the Revolution in France* (London, 1790).

3. His son Charles Cowden Clarke writes of lending to his schoolfellow Keats Leigh Hunt's *Examiner,* which his father took in, adding that this "no doubt laid the foundation of his love of civil and religious liberty." See Walter Jackson Bate, *John Keats* (Cambridge, Mass.: Harvard University Press, 1963), 25. When Keats's guardian Abbey heard about it he said "if he had fifty children he would not send one of them to that school." Quoted in Aileen Ward, *John Keats: The Making of a Poet* (London: Secker & Warburg, 1963), 34. Hunt's father was a Unitarian minister; his own views are described by Ward as those of an "aesthetic Unitarian"; ibid., 82.

4. Marjorie Levinson, *The Romantic Fragment Poem* (Chapel Hill: University of North Carolina Press, 1986), 204.

5. Ibid., 213, 220.

6. Anne Janowitz, *England's Ruins: Poetic Purpose and the National Landscape* (Oxford: Blackwell, 1990).

7. R. Mayo, "The Contemporaneity of the *Lyrical Ballads,*" *PMLA* 69 (1954): 512–14.

8. The image may have been lodged in Coleridge's imagination by seeing the huge fragments in the Valley of Rocks near Linton. Coleridge may well have been visiting this site shortly before writing his poem: see my essay "Coleridge: Poems of the Supernatural," in *S. T. Coleridge,* ed. R. L. Brett (London: G. Bell & Sons, 1971), 53n–54n.

9. See his note in *The Four Zoas,* "Unorganiz'd Innocence: An Impossibility" (*BK* 380). For an interpretation of "Christabel" along these lines see my *Coleridge the Visionary* (London: Chatto & Windus, 1959), ch. 6.

10. E. M. Forster, *Howards End* (1910), ch. 23: Abinger edition, ed. O. Stallybrass (London: Edward Arnold, 1973), 183–84.

11. From a letter to Forest Reid of 1925, quoted in P. N. Furbank's introduction to his *Maurice* (London: Edward Arnold, 1971), viii.

12. See René Wellek, *A History of Modern Criticism, 1750–1950,* vol. 2, *The Romantic Age* (London: Jonathan Cape, 1955), 57–60.

13. A. W. Schlegel, *Dialogue on Poetry.* See Anne Mellor, *English Romantic Irony* (Cambridge, Mass: Harvard University Press, 1980), 7.

14. Edward Young, *Conjectures on Original Composition, in a Letter to the Author of Sir Charles Grandison* (London: Millar & Dodsley, 1759), 12.

15. See, for example, my articles "Coleridge and Wordsworth: The Vital and the Organic," in *Reading Coleridge,* ed. W. Crawford (Ithaca: Cornell University Press, 1979), and "Coleridge's Originality as a Critic of Shakespeare," *Studies in the Literary Imagination* 19 (1986).

16. *Athenaeum* Fragment 116, in *Friedrich Schlegel's "Lucinde" and the Fragments,* trans. P. Firchow (Minneapolis: University of Minnesota Press, 1971), 175–76.

17. "Viele Werke der Alten sind Fragmente geworden. Viele Werke der neuern sind es gleich bey der Entstehung." *Athenaeum* Fragment 24, trans. Firchow, p. 164; quoted in Levinson, *Fragment Poem,* 10, and McFarland, *Ruins,* 22. Levinson omits the word "many" in each case.

18. *Athenaeum* Fragments 259, 206, trans. Firchow, 199, 189: cited in Mellor, *English Romantic Irony,* 21.

19. See, for example, Uncle Ernst's critique of Pan-Germanism and the learned men of contemporary Germany: "They collect facts, and facts and empires of facts. But which of them will rekindle the light within?" (*Howards End,* ch. 4, Abinger ed. [London: Edward Arnold, 1973], 27). This might be compared with the quotation from Schlegel below, note 28.

20. Quoted by Coleridge in a notebook entry of 1800, *CN* 1:867, and reproduced at the end of chapter 12 in *Biographia Literaria: CBL* 1:294.

21. Letter to T. N. Talfourd, c. 10 April 1839: *WL 1835–39,* 680.

22. M. Serres, *La Distribution, Hermes IV* (Paris, 1977): quoted and translated by Denise Degrois, "Coleridge on Human Communication," in *Coleridge's Visionary Languages: Essays in Honour of J. B. Beer,* ed. T. Fulford and M. D. Paley (Cambridge: D. S. Brewer, 1993), 107.

23. D. C. Muecke, *Irony* (London: Methuen, 1970), 2–3. In addition to the studies cited here, reference should be made to Ernst Behler's excellent account "The Theory of Irony in German Romanticism," in *Romantic Irony,* ed. Frederick Garber (Budapest: Academiai Kiado, 1989), 43–81.

24. Kathleen Wheeler, *Sources, Processes and Methods in Coleridge's "Biographia Literaria"* (Cambridge: Cambridge University Press, 1980), 61.

25. Mellor, *English Romantic Irony,* 23–24.

26. "The Rhetoric of Temporality," in *Interpretation: Theory and Practice,* ed. Charles S. Singleton (Baltimore: Johns Hopkins Press, 1969), 194, quoted in Mellor, *English Romantic Irony,* 5.

27. Friedrich Schlegel, *Literary Notebooks,* 1797–1801, ed. Hans Eichner (London: Athlone Press, 1957), no. 1068: Mellor, *English Romantic Irony,* 21.

28. *Lyceum* Fragment 108, trans. Firchow, 156: Mellor, *English Romantic Irony,* 12.

29. See Thomas McFarland, *Coleridge and the Pantheist Tradition* (Oxford: Clarendon Press, 1969).

30. *Athenaeum* Fragment 53, trans. Firchow, 167: Mellor, *English Romantic Irony,* 16.

31. Mellor, *English Romantic Irony,* 5.

32. Søren Kierkegaard, *The Concept of Irony, with Constant Reference to Socrates,* trans. L. M. Capell (London: Collins, 1966), 305–16: cited Mellor, *English Romantic Irony,* 181.

33. *The Concept of Irony,* 339: Mellor, *English Romantic Irony,* 181.

34. *CPW* 1:296. A note by E. H. Coleridge acknowledges that the conception of the poem was "suggested" by Gessner's "Der feste Vorsatz," but it should be noted that parts of the opening lines are almost a literal translation from that poem. On the other hand, 45 lines of German have become 186 in Coleridge and the conception is so refined and expanded as to become a very different poem.

35. The phrases are, respectively, from reviews in the *Critical Review,* October 1798, the *Analytic Review,* December 1798, and the *Monthly Review,* June 1799, gathered in *Coleridge: The Critical Heritage,* ed. J. R. de J. Jackson (London: Routledge & Kegan Paul, 1970), 51–57.

36. For this phrase of Coleridge's see his letter to Joseph Cottle of March 1815: *CL* 4:545.

37. Thomas McFarland, *Romanticism and the Forms of Ruin* (Princeton: Princeton University Press, 1981), 4.

38. Notebook entry of 1799, *CN* 1:556, revised as below in 1803.

39. *CPW* 2:998; text from *CN* 2:2921. See also ibid., 2921n, tracing the starting point for the notebook entry to Fulke Greville's *Alaham.*

40. For Coleridge's interest in this concept, see *CAR* Excursus Note 6, p. 555.

41. *Child Harolde's Pilgrimage,* III. xcvii.

42. In Shakespeare the association is often with the Phoenix, the bird on "the sole Arabian tree" of "The Phoenix and the Turtle." See also *Antony and Cleopatra* III. ii. 12; both Shakespeare and Milton refer to exotic scents: see *Macbeth* V. i. 57 and *Paradise Lost* iv. 162–63—the latter picked up by Wordsworth in Ecclesiastical Sonnet II. xxxix: *WPW* 3:381.

43. "The Solitary Reaper," *WPW* 3:77.

44. Notably Edward Said, *Orientalism* (London: Routledge & Kegan Paul, 1978). See also Nigel Leask, *British Romantic Writers and the East: Anxieties of Empire* (Cambridge: Cambridge University Press, 1993).

Contributors

Martin Aske, who lectures at the Cheltenham and Gloucester College of Higher Education, is author of *Keats and Hellenism* and other studies. His *British Romantic Art Criticism: Sources and Documents* is forthcoming.

John Beer is Emeritus Professor of English Literature at the University of Cambridge and Fellow of Peterhouse. He has written *Coleridge the Visionary, The Achievement of E. M. Forster, Blake's Humanism, Blake's Visionary Universe, Wordsworth and the Human Heart, Wordsworth in Time, Coleridge's Variety* (ed.), *Coleridge's Poetic Intelligence,* and *Romantic Influences: Contemporary—Victorian—Modern;* he has also edited Coleridge's *Aids to Reflection (Collected Coleridge)* and his *Poems.*

Drummond Bone is Dean of the Faculty of Arts at the University of Glasgow. He was for ten years the academic editor of the *Byron Journal,* has contributed the section on Romantic poetry to *The Year's Work in English Studies,* and is currently co-editor of *Romanticism.* He has written on Byron, Shelley, Wordsworth, and various aspects of Romantic theory and is at present working on a study of the methodological problems in inter-art criticism.

Frederick Burwick is Professor of English and Comparative Literature at the University of California at Los Angeles. His publications include *Approaches to Organic Form, The Haunted Eye: Perception and the Grotesque in English and German Romanticism,* and *Illusion and the Drama,* along with other studies of English and German Romanticism; he recently edited the volume *Coleridge's "Biographia Literaria": Text and Meaning* and is contributing to the new complete edition of De Quincey's writings.

A. C. Goodson, Director of Comparative Literature at Michigan State University, is the author of *Verbal Imagination: Coleridge and the Language of Modern Criticism.*

Nigel Leask lectures in English at the University of Cambridge and is a Fellow of Queens' College. He is author of *The Politics of Imagination in Coleridge's Critical Thought, British Romantic Writers and the East: Anxieties of Empire,* and other studies.

Philip W. Martin, who lectures at the Cheltenham and Gloucester College of Higher Education, is author of *Byron: A Poet before His Public* and *Mad Women in Romantic Writing* and joint editor of *Reviewing Romanticism.*

Anne K. Mellor is Professor of English Literature at the University of California at Los Angeles and author of *English Romantic Irony, Romanticism and Gender,* and *Mary Shelley: Her Life, Her Fiction, Her Monsters.*

Lucy Newlyn is Official Fellow and Tutor in English at St. Edmund Hall, Oxford. Her publications include *Coleridge's Imagination: Essays in Memory of Pete Laver,* edited with Richard Gravil and Nicholas Roe, *Coleridge, Wordsworth, and the Language of Allusion,* and *"Paradise Lost" and the Romantic Reader.*

Tilottama Rajan is Professor of English at the University of Western Ontario. Her publications include *Dark Interpreter: The Discourse of Romanticism, The Supplement of Reading: Figures of Understanding in Romantic Theory and Practice,* and other studies.

Susan J. Wolfson, Professor of English at Princeton University, is author of *The Questioning Presence: Wordsworth, Keats, and the Interrogative Mode in Romantic Poetry* and numerous articles on Romanticism.

Index

Library of Congress Cataloging-in-Publication Data

Questioning romanticism / edited by John Beer.
p. cm.
ISBN 0-8018-5052-5 (cl.).—ISBN 0-8018-5053-3 (pbk.)
1. English literature—19th century—History and criticism—Theory, etc. 2. English literature—18th century—History and criticism—Theory, etc. 3. Criticism—Europe—History. 4. Romanticism. I. Beer, John B.
PR457.Q47 1995
820.9'145—dc20 94-49331